IRAQ

A project of the International Peace Academy

IRAQ

Preventing a New Generation of Conflict

edited by
Markus E. Bouillon
David M. Malone
Ben Rowswell

LYNNE
RIENNER
PUBLISHERS

BOULDER
LONDON

Published in the United States of America in 2007 by
Lynne Rienner Publishers, Inc.
1800 30th Street, Boulder, Colorado 80301
www.rienner.com

and in the United Kingdom by
Lynne Rienner Publishers, Inc.
3 Henrietta Street, Covent Garden, London WC2E 8LU

Library of Congress Cataloging-in-Publication Data
Iraq : preventing a new generation of conflict / edited by Markus E. Bouillon, David M. Malone, and Ben Rowswell.
      p. cm. — (A Project of the International Peace Academy)
Includes bibliographical references and index.
ISBN 978-1-58826-528-9 (hardcover : alk. paper)
ISBN 978-1-58826-504-3 (pbk. : alk. paper)
1. Peace-building—Iraq. 2. Nation-building—Iraq. 3. Iraq War, 2003—Peace.
I. Bouillon, Markus E., 1975– II. Malone, David, 1954– III. Rowswell, Ben. IV. International Peace Academy.
JZ5584.I72I73 2007
327.1'7209567—dc22

                                                       2007005438

British Cataloguing in Publication Data
A Cataloguing in Publication record for this book
is available from the British Library.

Printed and bound in the United States of America

The paper used in this publication meets the requirements
of the American National Standard for Permanence of
Paper for Printed Library Materials Z39.48-1992.

5 4 3 2 1

To the Iraqis,
who have paid the price of a generation of instability,
in hopes that another generation will not join them

Contents

Tables and Figures

Foreword

Terje Rød-Larsen,
President, International Peace Academy

THIS VOLUME, a remarkable collection of original essays, is published at a crucial time for Iraq, the Middle East, and the wider world. With Iraq on the brink of state failure and collapse, it is both a courageous effort and an important endeavor to edit a volume on *Iraq: Preventing a New Generation of Conflict*. As the editors write in their concluding chapter, the consequences of continued state fragility or failure in Iraq would be too grave for the international community to do nothing now but stand by and despair.

Instead, governments must work together to overcome the divisions that emerged in the run-up to the US invasion in 2003 and that remain as obstacles to concerted action on Iraq. The growing instability in the Middle East, and the ever greater convergence and interrelation of the once disparate conflicts in the region, have profound economic, political, and security impacts beyond the region, giving the rest of the world an inherent interest in working cooperatively toward the stabilization of Iraq. The key priority in this endeavor, as this volume makes clear, should be to build a grand political settlement. The international community faces tough challenges in supporting and steering this process, while leaving ownership of it in Iraqi hands. In the end, it is Iraqis themselves who need to prevent a new generation of conflict in their country.

Iraq: Preventing a New Generation of Conflict brings together a truly outstanding group of scholars and practitioners; it is a shining example of the bridge building between academic experts and policymakers for which the International Peace Academy always strives. Most of the authors have long been engaged in research on the ground in Iraq, or have worked in the country for prolonged periods of time, and their firsthand impressions directly shape their analysis and policy advice. The book is also truly multidisciplinary in its approach, looking at the historical, cultural, economic, and social dimensions of the Iraqi challenge and taking into account the political dynamics at the domestic, regional, and international levels. The chapters address diplomatic considerations and offer both comparative insights and concrete policy proposals. They also provide strong arguments, for both Iraqis and those beyond Iraq, in favor of maintaining the Iraqi state and against abandoning it to disintegration and state failure.

I warmly commend David M. Malone for initiating this project. He and his coeditors—Ben Rowswell and Markus E. Bouillon—have done a marvelous job in bringing the project to fruition and in making it one of the IPA's most timely book projects.

I can now only hope that this volume will make a modest contribution to addressing the challenges that Iraq, its people, and the surrounding region face. State building is a major task, as I have learned over more than ten years of direct involvement in the Middle East peace process and in Lebanon. It is a challenge that confronts many of the peoples in the Middle East, and one that in every single case is of deep interest to the international community. If we fail Iraqis, Palestinians, and Lebanese, we only fail ourselves. It is for this reason that I recommend this book and hope that its analysis and policy recommendations will be closely studied by all relevant players.

I would also like to express my deepest thanks and gratitude to the Human Security Program of Canada's Department of Foreign Affairs and International Trade, which has underpinned this volume and made its early publication possible. The work we do at the IPA would not be possible without the generous support of donors—governmental, nongovernmental, and private. Whereas this publication is financed by Canada, our Middle East work in general has been made possible by the generous support of the government of Norway. I would like to thank both, as well as all our other donors and supporters.

Acknowledgments

THIS BOOK GREW from our concern that the conflict in Iraq could continue for decades if the international debate remains mired in the divisions triggered by the 2003 invasion by the United States and its allies. We sought to develop new terms that would ground the debate in the reality of contemporary Iraq as understood in the light of historical trends that date back well before 2003.

We began by bringing Iraqis and experts on Iraq from the fields of diplomacy and academia to a conference in Ottawa on May 11 and 12, 2006, organized by Canada's Department of Foreign Affairs and International Trade. That initiative culminates in this volume, which we hope offers a comprehensive analysis of state fragility as the underlying cause of Iraq's ongoing instability, as well as options for Iraqis and the international community to consider in their efforts to alleviate the violence.

We should record, at the outset, that the views expressed in the volume are those of the contributors and of the editors alone. They do not reflect those of the government of Canada nor of the International Peace Academy (which by definition is home to a multitude of views and opinions).

At the conference, we were grateful to benefit from the remarks delivered by Lakhdar Brahimi, the UN Secretary-General's first Special Envoy for Iraq. Mr. Brahimi brought a wealth of wisdom acquired through years of working with Iraqis to address the causes of instability in their country, as well as comparative experience in the management of conflicts in many other countries.

Central to our discussions were the contributions of Iraqis themselves. In particular we would like to thank Bakhtiar Amin, Ghassan Atiyyah, Asos Hardi, Najmaldin Karim, Laith Kubba, Fareed Yasseen, and Iraq's ambassador to Canada, Howar Ziad. Their contributions and reactions had a considerable influence on the analyses and insights generated by this project. Salman Ahmad, Elizabeth Cousens, Ambassador Hussein Hassouna of the

Arab League, Robert Olson, and John Packer also added invaluable perspectives. Our deliberations at the conference were ably guided by the chairing skills of Canadian diplomats Mark Bailey, Tim Martin, and Michael Small.

Many others shaped our thoughts and contributed to this project along the way. Among those to whom we are deeply grateful are Rick Barton, Gareth Bayley, Edward Chaplin, Nawal Hamidi, Rosemary Hollis, Farouk Kaspaules, Jehangir Khan, Gordon Peake, Steven Siqueira, Charles Tripp, Karen Von Hippel, Sami Zubaida, and Canada's ambassador to Iraq in 2005–2006, John Holmes.

Our project would not have come to fruition without the support and efforts of further institutions and individuals. First, we would like to express our deep gratitude to Canada's Department of Foreign Affairs and International Trade, which employs two of the coeditors (David M. Malone and Ben Rowswell) and which organized the Ottawa conference. DFAIT also funded production of this volume through a contribution to the International Peace Academy from its Human Security Program. The commitment of DFAIT to independent policy research demonstrates a commitment to excellence in developing foreign policy. In much the same way, the IPA provides a stimulating and intellectually enriching environment, for which any researcher could only be grateful.

Our colleagues at both DFAIT and the IPA deserve our thanks for their support, hard work, and patience with us when we were preoccupied with this particular project. Special gratitude is due to Pierre-David Jean, Anna Pollock, Meera Shah, and Nur Laiq for their dedicated research and organizational assistance—without them, this volume would not have seen the light of day. Benoît Girouard, Maciej Hawrylak, Apeksha Kumar, John Orr, Karen Sleiman, Audrey Schreyer, and Charles Vanderloo all provided essential organizational support.

We would also like to thank Lynne Rienner for her support and early commitment to publish this volume when our project was still very much in the stage of conceptual development. Adam Lupel deserves our thanks for his editorial work and assistance.

Finally, this volume is the result of a truly collaborative effort by the three of us, and it has blossomed thanks to the warm and fruitful partnership that we have established. We hope that the book will make a modest contribution to the effort to define Iraq's future and to achieve what we have ambitiously set as the aim of our project: preventing a new generation of conflict.

—*Markus E. Bouillon, David M. Malone, and Ben Rowswell*

IRAQ

1

Looking Back:
State Fragility and a
Generation of Conflict

Ben Rowswell, Markus E. Bouillon, and David M. Malone

HAVING ENDURED a generation of devastating conflict under Saddam Hussein and in the chaos following his overthrow in 2003, Iraq may now be gearing up for another generation of violence. The potential consequences for Iraq, the region, and the world are incalculable. What drives this conflict? Where do the sources of this ongoing instability lie? What options do Iraqis have to bring stability to their country? What levers does the international community have to help them? These are the questions this volume seeks to address.

■ Instability in Iraq: A Tale of Collective Failure

When on February 22, 2006, a suicide bomber struck the ancient shrine at Samarra in the province of Salah al-Din, the world held its breath in apprehension at what lay ahead. In the following days, Shia Arab militants, outraged by the attack on a symbol sacred to their sect, struck out on a campaign of retribution that destroyed dozens of Sunni mosques. Within five days, more than three hundred people had been killed in Baghdad alone. There were reports of incidents eerily reminiscent of the 1975 massacre of Palestinians that launched the Lebanese civil war, as militants were reported to have stopped a bus and shot dead a number of Sunni Arabs.[1]

Civil war has erupted at long last, some said, ominously referring to this period of strife and bloodshed as "Iraq's 9/11."[2] Others pointed out that the bomb attack on the sacred Shia shrine and subsequent reprisals against Sunni mosques and killings of Sunni Arabs were only "the latest and bloodiest indication" that Iraq was "teetering on the threshold of wholesale disaster."[3] Many saw in the attack confirmation of their argument that the legacy of the military takeover of the country by the United States and its allies would be a war lasting for years and leaving all worse off than when it started.

In the aftermath of the bombing, the situation in Iraq deteriorated noticeably. Sectarian strife saw ever-higher numbers of victims of suicide bombings and retaliatory acts. Scores of Iraqis were found shot in trenches, their bodies often blindfolded and showing signs of torture. A United Nations (UN) report released toward the end of the year affirmed that more than 34,000 Iraqi civilians had been "violently killed" in 2006 alone, with an average of 94 losing their lives every day; more than 36,000 Iraqis had been wounded. The report of the United Nations Assistance Mission for Iraq (UNAMI) also singled out the sectarian violence, especially in Baghdad, "as a major cause for an ever-growing trend in displacement and migration of all Iraqis, as well as the targeting of various professional groups, including educators, medical professionals, journalists, judges and lawyers, religious and political leaders."[4] According to the United Nations High Commissioner for Refugees (UNHCR), by the end of 2006 at least 2.3 million Iraqis had fled the growing violence and 1.8 million had sought refuge abroad.[5]

As Iraqi casualties mounted, so did the numbers of coalition troops killed and injured. October and December 2006 became the months with the highest casualty tolls suffered by the United States and its allies since 2004. By January 2007, a Brookings Institution report opened with the words, "by any definition Iraq is already in a state of civil war," and probed how to contain the spillover under the title "things fall apart."[6] A month earlier, the bipartisan Iraq Study Group, led by former secretary of state James A. Baker III and former congressman Lee H. Hamilton, had concluded:

> The situation in Iraq is grave and deteriorating. . . . Violence is increasing in scope and lethality. It is fed by a Sunni Arab insurgency, Shiite militias and death squads, al Qaeda, and widespread criminality. Sectarian conflict is the principal challenge to stability. . . . If the situation continues to deteriorate, the consequences could be severe. A slide toward chaos could trigger the collapse of Iraq's government and a humanitarian catastrophe.[7]

A United States National Intelligence Estimate, published in January 2007 and reported widely, betrayed no greater optimism with its key judgment:

> Iraqi society's growing polarization, the persistent weakness of the security forces and the state in general, and all sides' ready recourse to violence are collectively driving an increase in communal and insurgent violence and political extremism. Unless efforts to reverse these conditions show measurable progress during the term of this Estimate, the coming twelve to eighteen months, we assess that the overall security situation will continue to deteriorate at rates comparable to the latter part of 2006.[8]

Iraq's troubles, however, began neither in 2006 nor in 2003. The calamity in Samarra and the subsequent intensification of sectarian violence became part of what had already been a long series of misfortunes to befall

Iraq over the past generation—if not since its creation. Stability was never assured in a land that had been a cradle of ancient civilization and an influential capital during the golden age of the Islamic empire. Ever since its creation by the British in the years following World War I, Iraq has been astonishingly fertile soil for conflict at the domestic and regional levels.

In consequence, instability in Iraq has persistently presented a threat to international peace and security. Indeed, since Saddam Hussein's invasion of revolutionary Iran in 1980, Iraq has featured without interruption on the agenda of the United Nations Security Council.[9] In the period of a single generation, Iraq has lived through internal strife, two wars with its neighbors, a humiliating defeat by an international coalition under a UN mandate, the mass murder of Kurdish and Shia Arab populations, one of the most stringent and devastating sanctions regimes in recent history, another defeat and military occupation by a US-led international coalition (without a UN mandate), and an insurgency and worsening sectarian strife, which have made the car bomb a feature of daily life in Baghdad.[10]

Just as Iraqis have not found a way out of the chronic instability that has plagued their nation, so have outsiders faced tribulations in Iraq. Neighboring countries have been damaged by their conflicts with Iraq. Iran remained locked in a deadly embrace with its western neighbor for most of the 1980s. Kuwait became the victim of Iraqi aggression in August 1990. The other states of the Arabian Gulf have been affected by the climate of insecurity, founding the Gulf Cooperation Council in 1981 not least in reaction against the turmoil of the Iran-Iraq War.[11]

Others have equally been affected and remained so in recent years since the overthrow of the Saddam Hussein regime. The United States managed to force a change in Iraq's government but created for its coalition allies and itself a quagmire that has cost thousands of its soldiers' lives and hundreds of billions of dollars, and a rift with many of its closest allies in the North Atlantic Treaty Organization (NATO) and elsewhere. For friends of the United States, this has been painful, as mostly they prefer to act in unity with Washington. One largely hidden cost has been the collapse of assumptions of US military invincibility, which had shielded its allies to a degree for so long, and which probably had for some years acted as a deterrent on some "rogue" actors. North Korea's nuclear test of October 2006 has been interpreted by many to be related to this development and to the growing belief that the possession of nuclear weapons can actually deter US military threats.

While many had warned that "British and American military forces will find occupying Iraq more difficult than conquering it" prior to the invasion and in its immediate aftermath,[12] by 2006, harsher terminology was in widespread use. "The mood has certainly changed," A. G. Hopkins wrote in January 2006. The "harrowing experience of Iraq" had aged all positive and optimistic views related to the US-led invasion beyond its years; "the soaring rhetoric of imperial altruism had given way to more sober, if also grimmer calculations."[13] Some in the United States put it even more bluntly, arguing that with the inability to turn Iraq into a success story, "the United States has sunk to a new low in its standing in the world."[14] By early January 2007, political positioning in anticipation of the presidential race in 2008 and new congressional politics following the November 2006 mid-term electoral victory for the Democrats had sent the United States into a major debate over how to handle Iraq, with increasing numbers of senators and congressmen favoring an early withdrawal.

The United States was not the only country affected by the situation in Iraq. The Arab world witnessed with dismay the occupation by foreign military forces of one of their own on a massive scale reminiscent of the European occupations during the mandate period in the Middle East. It also confronted broader questions, many of which were linked with the situation in Iraq: growing tensions between Sunni and Shia Muslims and with the neighboring Islamic Republic of Iran over its nuclear program and aggressive pursuit of Shia interests; questions over how to cope with increased outside pressure to reform and democratize, while maintaining stability and preventing the continued rise to prominence and power of Islamist forces, some of whom advocate a radical agenda. By 2006, the Arab world was faced with a situation more complex, more fragile, and more dangerous than it had been for a long time, and many of its problems in one way or another were connected with Iraq.

The international community at large has also met failure in Iraq. Western states were more divided by the 2003 conflict than they had been since World War II. By early 2007, they still did not seem to have fully recovered from the fallout of their disunity, which had serious consequences for all of the European Union, its Common Security and Foreign Policy, and the transatlantic alliance.

The United Nations, which had succeeded in depriving Saddam's regime of weapons of mass destruction, saw its own credibility undermined as unresolved debates among member states and UN staff paralyzed its ability to act in Iraq with clarity and effectiveness. By the end of 2005, the UN's "continued relevancy to the hardest security challenges" was at best uncertain.[15] Indeed, broader questions were raised as to the continued existence and relevance of a multilateral, interdependent world order, as some saw in the 2002–2003 crisis at the UN preceding the Iraq war "evidence of a transformative disintegration of an existing UN-centered world order," which was replaced by "a Hobbesian race for security."[16]

The organization's involvement in Iraq has become a source of institutional trauma. The effects of the bombing of UN headquarters in Baghdad on August 19, 2003, continue to reverberate. Iraq caused lasting political damage to the organization as well through sharp divisions in the Security Council, a stalled reform effort, and allegations over corruption and mismanagement of the oil-for-food program. After Kofi Annan's *annus horribilis* in 2004, it seemed that in spite of his international leadership on normative issues such as human rights, the responsibility to protect, and the rule of law, the challenges he met relating to this one country could well threaten to overshadow an otherwise highly successful tenure as Secretary-General. And as a new Secretary-General took the helm of the organization, it remained unclear just how deep Ban Ki-Moon and the United Nations might be drawn into the difficulties of Iraq.

Iraq, in short, has been a story of collective challenge, of collective disappointment, and of collective failure. Thus far, all major actors have emerged losers from a generation of instability in Iraq. In order to address and rectify the continued instability in Iraq, and to prevent the damage a second generation of conflict would cause, it is now vital to reflect on the sources of that instability.

■ Domestic Sources of Instability

Iraq's continued instability and its prolonged embroilment in conflict and war has been seen as a sign that the country may simply be unviable. As Kamran Karadaghi pointed out, Iraq has long been torn by sectarian and ethnic divisions, with the domination of the minority Sunni group being a constant feature of the state since the Ottoman period, fomenting tensions in Iraq's diverse society.[17] Against this background of sectarian and ethnic tension, Leslie Gelb argued in November 2003 that the "inherent enmity" between Sunni and Shia Arabs and between Arabs and Kurds could be resolved only if each community gained its own sovereign state.[18] Others joined Gelb with strong advocacy of communal separatism. In a more nuanced argument for separatism, Liam Anderson and Gareth Stansfield have written:

> The history of modern Iraq indicates that trust among society's major groupings has mostly been in pitifully short supply. In the absence of any developed sense of national identity, a basic consensus over the legitimacy of the Iraqi state, and a reservoir of mutual trust and understanding to draw upon, it is difficult indeed to locate the foundation on which a liberal democratic Iraqi state can be constructed.[19]

By contrast, other students of Iraq and of the Middle East have been less convinced of the merits of partition. As they point out, despite the improvised manner in which Western governments assembled often largely artificial Middle Eastern states in the early twentieth century, the Iraqi state did succeed in generating a sense of national identity in subsequent decades.

Indeed the fierce rivalries that fueled domestic political violence since Iraq's creation were propelled less by regional actors seeking to wrest power away from Baghdad and more by competition to control central state institutions. Rival ethnic or sectarian identities have not been responsible for "inevitable" violence and bloodshed. Rather, violence became a tool in the ruthless competition between rival political groups to control the single entity of the Iraqi state. Such competition and rivalry has historically been the principal source of instability in Iraq ever since independence in 1932, as Charles Tripp has argued.[20]

The chronic inability of the Iraqi polity to channel competition in peaceful, legitimate ways did not produce a failed state, but it has kept the Iraqi state notoriously unstable. As Hanna Batatu pointed out, "recurring conflicts during years of English rule and in the monarchic period reflected an underlying structural discordance."[21] Indeed, Toby Dodge argues that it was "Britain's failed attempt, during the 1920s and 1930s, to build a liberal state in Iraq [that] forms the historical backdrop against which the removal of Saddam Hussein in 2003 and its aftermath should be understood."[22] Thus, violence and instability resulted from the original failure to successfully build a state and have continued to be the pattern until and throughout the ouster of the Saddam Hussein regime and the widespread violence that gripped Iraq since its fall.

Against this background, it would be hard to overestimate the monumental nature of the task confronting those seeking to stabilize and build peace in Iraq. In his 2003 study, Dodge identified "four interlinked structural problems," which had been dominant in Iraqi politics from the creation of the state until the removal of Saddam Hussein, and which "fuelled the state's domestic illegitimacy, its tendency to embark on military adventurism beyond its own borders, and even the Baathist regime's drive to acquire weapons of mass destruction":

> first, the deployment of extreme levels of organized violence by the state to dominate and shape society; second, the use of state resources—jobs, development aid, and patronage—to buy the loyalty of sections of society; third, the use of oil revenue by the state to increase its autonomy from society; and finally, the exacerbation and re-creation by the state of communal and ethnic divisions as a strategy of rule.[23]

By this reading, the Iraqi state has been itself a central factor behind the country's instability, exacerbating internal divisions and thus accelerating fragmentation and intensifying state fragility. Decades of discrimination and ethnic favoritism sustained by the regime politicized the difference between Iraq's communities, and, Isam al-Khafaji argues, was largely absorbed and intuited by the communities themselves.[24] The regime's constant purges and reliance on a vast security network tied closely to Hussein's clan displayed its weak legitimacy and aggravated the constant perception of instability. Security forces were strictly accountable to the president, precisely "to encourage competition and to ensure that no one service will become strong enough to threaten Saddam."[25] Loyalty was also bought through an oil-fueled political economy of patronage, driven by personal relationships and crony capitalism.[26]

Saddam Hussein

Certain individuals matter greatly in the history of nations, for good or ill (sometimes both). Napoleon Bonaparte springs to mind. Delusions of grandeur (reminiscent of those of the Shah of Iran, which contributed to his downfall in 1979) were embedded in the personality cult that Saddam Hussein encouraged from the time of his own accession to ultimate power in 1979—but his pursuit of absolute control for himself and primacy for Iraq was deadly earnest and purposeful. His early and aggressive interest in a nuclear weapons program, thrust into the spotlight by the Israeli bombing on June 7, 1981, of Iraq's nuclear reactor at Osiraq, has now been fully documented.

Saddam Hussein was born near Tikrit in 1937, in the heart of the Sunni-dominated center of Iraq, in conditions of poverty. Accounts of his early life are not authoritative. His father disappeared early on, replaced by a brutal stepfather. A more overt influence in his life was an uncle, a former military officer, cashiered after a coup attempt. By 1956, Saddam Hussein was himself participating in an unsuccessful coup against the monarchy. Having joined the fledgling Iraqi Baath Party (an offshoot of the original Syrian Baath movement) a year later, he participated in 1959 in an assassination attempt on strongman Abdul Karim Qassem, fleeing first to Syria, then to Egypt, when the operation failed. In 1964, he plotted again, against President Aref, leading to a crackdown on the party and two years in prison.[27]

His involvement in the Baath Party is replete with intrigue. When the party split in 1963, Michel Aflaq, the Baath's leading ideologue and cofounder, sponsored him for a position in the party's "regional command." He was further helped by the prominent position within Baath circles of his cousin, General Ahmed Hassan al-Bakr, who, in 1965, became the party's secretary-general. From then until 1979, when Saddam Hussein would supplant al-Bakr as president of Iraq, he figured in official Baath iconography as the latter's loyal deputy. In fact, soon after the successful Baath takeover of 1968, he started operating as the regime's strongman, managing the state security apparatus and the party machinery so as to place elements loyal to him in key positions. Vicious outbursts of violence were to mark his career, such as the 1969 public hanging of fourteen alleged participants in a Zionist spy ring, eleven of them Jewish.

Most murderous of all was the purge that followed his appointment as president in July 1979, when up to five hundred individuals he judged to be disloyal or treacherous were eliminated. From that point on, the cult of his personality in Iraq was unconstrained.[28] Soon Saddam Hussein saw himself not just as the leader of Iraq, but also of the Arab world (the Baath styled itself a pan-Arab movement even though it never took hold beyond Syria and Iraq). If anything, his leadership pretensions were boosted by Israel's attack on the Osiraq nuclear facility.

Early appraisals of Saddam Hussein within the Arab world (and beyond, sad to say) tended toward the hagiographic. Not atypical is the claim that, against the backdrop of the Iran-Iraq War, Saddam Hussein displayed "exceptional ability to direct a war."[29] Apologists from within the Arab world were not the only ones pointing to Saddam Hussein's genius and Iraq's potential. Due in large part to hostility toward revolutionary Iran, Iraq and its ambassador, Nizar Hamdoun, were the toasts of much of Washington during the 1980s, and a number of US scholars and security experts burned their reputations in the heat of their enthusiasm. Not all were taken in. Samir al-Khalil noted:

> Saddam Hussein exercised a very special kind of power. He had become an institution unto himself, one virtually without checks. His leadership was related to sentiments of the broad mass of Iraqis in a complicated and yet resilient way as proven by the later course of the war once the initial self-confidence had ebbed away. He presided over a regime that had gradually, but nonetheless inexorably, changed all the parameters affecting societal and state-organized violence. Eventually, expansion of the means of violence—army, police, security apparatuses, networks of informers, party militia, party and state bureaucracies—underwent the classic inversion: from being a means to an end, the elimination of opponents and exercise of raw power, they became horrific ends in themselves, spilling mindlessly across borders that had once contained them.[30]

The Fragility of the Iraqi State

Saddam's rule undermined the institutions that ensure the long-term viability of the state. Recent academic literature on the nature of failed and fragile states offers insights into the nature of the state Saddam Hussein had bequeathed and offers clues to the more comprehensive failure triggered by the 2003 coalition military action.[31]

Robert Rotberg, for example, has argued that if the purpose of a state is to provide its citizens with political goods such as security, education, health services, economic opportunity, environmental surveillance, a legal framework and judiciary to guarantee rule of law, and basic infrastructure, then state fragility can be assessed by the inability to fulfill these obligations.[32] Security, according to Rotberg, is the key indicator, with failed states typically enduring widespread violence against the existing regime, conflict between communities within the state, an inability to control their territory and borders, the growth of criminal violence, and a tendency by the authorities to "prey on their own constituents." Failed states are also characterized by weak institutions, the absence of the rule of law, a highly politicized military, and a deteriorating or destroyed infrastructure.[33]

Furthermore, Rotberg has argued, socioeconomic indicators can help to identify failed states. Failed states are thus marked by unequal access to economic opportunity, which remains largely limited to the ruling oligarchy. Living standards deteriorate, as financial rewards increasingly are distributed only to favored families, clans, or small groups. Corruption is endemic, gross domestic product is in decline, and infrastructure wastes away. On the political side, norms of governance are subverted, legislatures and bureaucracies are coerced, the rule of law is subverted, civil society is blocked, and attempts are made to control the security and defense forces, while patronage of a favored group, clan, class, or kin prevails. As fragility edges toward failure, the state delivers fewer and fewer economic and political goods, thus losing further legitimacy with its population.[34]

Rotberg's definition of state fragility complements Nazih Ayubi's concept of the "fierce" Arab state, which is equally instructive in the case of Iraq. According to Ayubi, the Arab state is

> not a natural growth of its own socio-economic history or its own cultural and intellectual tradition. It is a "fierce" state that has frequently to resort to raw coercion in order to preserve itself, but it is not a "strong" state because (a) it lacks—to varying degrees of course—the "infrastructural power" that enables states to penetrate society effectively through mechanisms such as taxation for example; and (b) it lacks ideological hegemony (in the Gramscian sense) that would enable it to forge a "historic" social bloc that accepts the legitimacy of the ruling stratum.[35]

It is the second characteristic of the "fierce" but not strong state that is particularly applicable to Iraq and underlines the intrinsic instability of Iraq throughout its history. Ayubi reflected Christine Buci-Glucksmann's work on this subject in arguing that states seeking to maintain their social cohesion through violence and coercion fail to achieve the stability offered by ideological consensus. Thus, though their coercive powers may make them appear strong, such authoritarian states are inherently weak and fragile.[36]

Indeed, Robert Rotberg has identified Iraq as belonging within a special category of fragile states: a seemingly strong, always autocratic state, which rigidly controls dissent and is thus itself secure, but provides few political goods. The fragility of such states, Rotberg has further suggested, is compounded by the fact that because they are held together entirely by repression and not by performance, an end to or an easing of repression could create destabilizing battles for succession, resulting anarchy, and the rapid rise of non-state actors. In nation-states made secure by punishment and secret intelligence networks, legitimacy is likely to vanish whenever the curtain of control lifts.[37]

During the rule of Saddam Hussein, exclusivity, communal mistrust, patronage, and the exemplary use of violence constituted the main elements of governance and were woven into a system of dependence on and conformity with the will of a small number of men at the center of the state in the name of social discipline and national destiny.[38] The security and intelligence networks, with their close links to the president, were the lead instrument of state control and domestic repression, well known for their disregard of human rights and systematic use of torture and summary executions.[39] The parochial nature of the regime and the widespread use of patronage to create a system of control and dependence were well entrenched even before Hussein officially took power in 1979 and were reinforced under his rule.[40]

The military defeat of 1991 and the subsequent imposition of sanctions only served to strengthen the system of patronage, which served as a "protective shield" for the regime and ensured its survival.[41] The main beneficiaries of this system were predominately but not exclusively Sunni Arabs in Iraq, especially those who shared origins with Hussein in the regions north and west of Baghdad.[42] They enjoyed privileged access to the hoarded resources of the Iraqi state, as well as to various oil and commodity smuggling enterprises set up by Hussein to insulate himself and those close to him from the effects of sanctions.[43] The rise of Saddam's Tikriti clansmen, the heavy reliance on local connections, and the need to strongman the state underlined Saddam's tenuous hold on power and the illegitimacy of the state, despite the populist rhetoric of Baath ideology.[44]

The National Assembly established in 1980 was little more than a façade meant to create the impression of popular supervision of government, in actuality powerless and controlled by the security services. National institutions such as the Baath Party, trade unions, peasant organizations, the General Federation of Iraqi Women, and the National Assembly were in fact "webs of patron-client networks, sustained by violence used against those who challenged the system, dispensing the ruler's patronage along lines which gave the lie to the official myth of a distinctive, unifying identity."[45] As such, state and quasi-state institutions became tools of both intimidation and cooptation in what became known as the "republic of fear."[46]

Yet the Iraqi state never went entirely unchallenged, and, to reflect Ayubi's terminology, it never successfully established hegemonic control. The government repeatedly faced armed insurgencies, using the same system of tribe and family affiliation to collectively punish dissidents and their families.[47] In March 1980, attempts to overthrow Saddam Hussein by Shia groups such as the Islamic Task Organization and Al-Dawa resulted in mass arrests and executions, provided with the semblance of legality by a retroactive decree making membership in Al-Dawa punishable by death.[48] The Kurdish north was equally used by Saddam as a "field of opportunity for demonstrating his power and ruthlessness."[49] In response to information that the Barzani clan had helped Iranian forces during the Iran-Iraq War, Iraqi security forces rounded up an estimated eight thousand men and boys in 1987 and killed them. In response to ongoing violence, villages and agriculture were destroyed, and chemical weapons were deployed to inspire terror as much as to achieve any military purpose. By the time the war ended in 1988, the Kurdish opposition had been quelled, with the government executing those it had captured and continuing to enforce loyalty through terror.[50]

In the wake of the military defeat of 1991, a widespread rebellion reignited among the Kurds of the north. With the assistance of the no-fly zones imposed by Western military forces, a Kurdish autonomous area was created, representing a clear loss of the Iraqi state's ability to control its territory. Revolts also broke out in 1991 in Shia cities such as Basra and Karbala. These revolts were brutally suppressed by the Republican Guard, however, and the south brought back under the heel of Baghdad. Shia communities were subjected to prolonged persecution during the 1990s, as the regime attempted to break up opposition.[51] Writing in 1978, Hanna Batatu underlined that the Baath regime

> reposes ultimately upon a narrow social foundation. . . . In view of the distrust or disapproval with which it was initially met by the other political forces, its sense of vulnerability, at least in the beginning, was stronger than that experienced by the regime which it supplanted. This and the desire to cow its enemies or win popularity account for the calculated harshness with which it stamped out "conspiracies" and "espionage rings."[52]

In this sense, whether Saddam Hussein's Iraq could best be understood as "fierce" or "failed," in Ayubi's and Rotberg's terms, respectively, it certainly was fragile.

■ External Sources of Instability

Iraq's instability has not been the product of domestic factors alone. Iraq's location in a hub of geo-political and global economic interest has made it particularly vulnerable to outside influence.

International involvement, while often justified as support for stabilization, has often also had the effect of exacerbating instability in Iraq and of ultimately undermining the interests not only of Iraqis but of the intervening powers as well. Looking back on the initial British attempt to create Iraq in the 1920s and 1930s, Dodge offered the following warning to US policymakers in 2003:

> The British did not mean to undermine the nascent Iraqi state. But, hobbled by an ideologically distorted view of Iraqi society and facing financial and political limits, they did. The United States in Iraq today must understand that it is both living with the consequences of that failure and is in danger of repeating it.[53]

There are other examples of external intervention exacerbating instability in Iraq. Facing the bloodiest conflict the world had seen since World War II, external actors not only failed to end the 1980–1988 Iran-Iraq War for its first seven years but may have contributed to prolonging it. Once the war had been launched with the Iraqi invasion into Iran in September 1980, Iran's objective was not limited only to repelling the attack. Indeed, it became Iran's intent to impose military defeat on Iraq and to overthrow its secular government in the hope that a Shia regime similar to its own would take power and spread the Islamic revolution launched by Ayatollah Ruhollah Khomeini. Alarmed by this prospect, Western powers and the Soviet Union tacitly supported Iraq, supplying it with arms and funding, thus also exacerbating the war. The parallel and subsequent domestic repression and "retaliation" pursued by Saddam Hussein sowed the seeds of further instability, as outside actors turned a blind eye to the widespread persecution of Shia Iraqis and the murder of hundreds of thousands of Kurds in a bid to keep the pressure on Iran (although Western governments were shocked into protest over Baghdad's use of chemical weapons against Iran and against Kurdish communities).[54]

The late 1980s represented a dramatic break from the pattern in international involvement in Iraq with an exceptional commonality of purpose arising among outside actors. An unprecedented period of Security Council unity began with Secretary-General Javier Perez de Cuellar's efforts to end the Iran-Iraq War, encouraged by the five permanent members (P5) of the Security Council.[55] After that unity helped secure a cease-fire, Iraq soon redirected its military machine toward another neighbor in its August 1990 invasion of Kuwait. The unity of the international community held as President George H. W. Bush drew together an international coalition to fight the invasion and won a Security Council mandate for the liberation of Kuwait. However, the external intervention failed to address the major source of instability posed by the Iraqi state itself, ultimately shying away from a march on Baghdad once Kuwait had been freed.

The P5 unity of the late 1980s and early 1990s broke down, however, in the long period of UN involvement that followed the 1991 Gulf War. The Security Council set up an extensive sanctions regime to force Iraq to disarm itself of the weapons of mass destruction that coalition forces had discovered in the wake of the Iraqi retreat from Kuwait and southern Iraq. However, it did not have the capacity to enforce this unprecedented regime itself and tacitly approved unilateral enforcement measures by states such as the United States and the United Kingdom, which did have the means but failed to produce a strategy explicitly agreed upon in the Security Council. Periodic aerial bombardments of a noncompliant Iraq soon became a regular counterpoint to a major humanitarian initiative launched in 1996 to alleviate the effect of the sanctions the bombardments were meant to enforce. Torn between the imperatives of disarmament and humanitarian objectives, the P5 mostly turned a blind eye to the systematic violation of sanctions by Iraq's neighbors and by the Iraqi regime's manipulation of the oil-for-food program to fill its own coffers and thus remain in power.[56]

The cross-purposes at which the international community operated became most apparent after 1997, as Security Council members began to disagree openly about the fundamental goals being pursued. The United States publicly oriented its Iraq policies toward regime change from 1997 on, and the United Kingdom also came to endorse regime change. This flatly contradicted the logic of a sanctions regime, which was an instrument of behavioral, not regime, change. With no end in sight to the sanctions, and a promise that the United States and the United Kingdom would continue to seek to overthrow his regime, Saddam Hussein lost any incentive he might have had to comply with the international mandate.

In 2003, by pressing on with a military solution in the absence of international support, US and UK actions—and the opposition thereto of France, Germany, and Russia—shattered any remaining pretense of coherence by the international community in its approach to the problems of Iraq. The coalition occupation of the country proceeded without a coherent plan or a critical mass of international (particularly regional) support, aggravating a new civil conflict generated by an insurgent movement that arose to oppose the presence of foreign forces on Iraqi soil.

The UN might still have been useful to Iraqis by taking on a role similar to that played by Lakhdar Brahimi (first at the Bonn Conference of 2001 and later on the ground in Kabul) in Afghanistan by brokering a return to a politics of greater normalcy while operating formally at one remove from the major powers intervening militarily in the country. However, the bombing of UN headquarters in Baghdad in August 2003, costing the lives of Secretary-General Special Representative Sergio Vieira de Mello and twenty-one others, induced a de facto UN retreat from meaningful engagement with Iraq, briefly interrupted by a mission carried out by Brahimi at the request of the United Nations and the United States in early 2004 to help form an Iraqi government. The absence of other significant international actors overtly engaged in the Iraqi political equation has left coalition leadership singularly exposed.[57]

◼ Preventing a Further Generation of Conflict

Domestic sources of instability in Iraq have thus been exacerbated by international involvement. Some argue that since international engagement vis-à-vis Iraq has exacerbated instability, the answer lies in ending external intervention altogether. Such arguments miss what is at stake in Iraq. If a single generation of instability in Iraq has produced three wars, genocide, social and economic degradation, and the modern use of weapons of mass destruction, the prospects for another generation can seem nothing but grim.

Given these high stakes, the international community will, for better or for worse, remain called upon to stay involved in Iraq and shoulder the responsibility of helping Iraqis to lay the foundations for a more successful state. Against the backdrop of this challenge, this volume brings together contributions from distinguished scholars of Iraqi history and politics and noted practitioners and experts in various relevant fields to explore how another generation of violence can be prevented in Iraq.

This book aims to explore the Iraqi conflict in the terms of state fragility. It intends to provide a convincing analysis of drivers of violence and to offer recommendations and options for Iraqis and the international community to consider in their quest to alleviate the conflict. The contributions were first developed for a conference organized by Canada's Department of Foreign Affairs and International Trade in Ottawa on May 11 and 12, 2006.

The proceedings of the conference were deeply influenced by a keynote address delivered by Lakhdar Brahimi, the UN Secretary-General's first Special Envoy for Iraq. Brahimi drew on his experience in consulting with all representatives of Iraq's fragmented political class in the early months of 2004 as the UN sought to assist in the establishment of a viable Iraqi interim government to reclaim sovereign authority from the Coalition Provisional Authority. Because it is primarily relations between Iraqis that perpetuate the violence in that country, any solution must start with them. Any outside powers that wish to influence the course of the conflict must do so with humility, seeking primarily to help Iraqis find their own solutions and bolstering their efforts with the broadest possible base of partnership and international legitimacy. Brahimi's insights have informed this introduction and our conclusions as well.

In the present volume, Part 1, "Iraq in Turmoil," begins by outlining three dimensions of the crisis in Iraq. Toby Dodge examines the nature of the security challenges facing Iraq today, making a forceful argument that they are best understood as consequences of state failure. Phebe Marr explores Iraq's identity crisis through dozens of interviews she held with leaders of all major communities in 2005. Jon Pedersen interprets data on the socioeconomic conditions that face Iraqis today, based on the comprehensive Living Conditions Survey that Norway's Fafo Institute helped conduct for the Iraqi Central Organization for Statistics and Information Technology in 2004. Abdel Salam Sidahmed complements the discussion of Iraq's identity crisis by examining the evolution of Islamism, Iraqi nationalism, and sectarianism over the past generation.

Of the many drivers of today's conflict in Iraq, we then highlight three of particular concern. Roel Meijer delves into the complex politics of the Sunni Arab community, home terrain for many of the insurgency movements that have dominated the Iraqi landscape for the past four years, but also ripe for political engagement, as he demonstrates. Juan Cole studies the disturbing phenomena of Shia militia groups through the exemplar of the Badr Organization (formerly the Badr Corps), affiliated with the increasingly powerful Supreme Council for the Islamic Revolution in Iraq. Finally, Joost Hiltermann explores a fault line that threatens to open a new front in the Iraqi conflict if not managed carefully, one that pits the Kurdish community against its rivals for control of the nerve-center city of Kirkuk.

Amid the gloom that envelops any consideration of Iraq's current predicament, Part 2 maps out thematic areas in which solutions might be found. We were fortunate to have the primary international adviser to the Iraqi constitutional process contribute to our research initiative. Nicholas "Fink" Haysom led the Constitutional Unit of the United Nations Assistance Mission for Iraq starting in the spring of 2005. His experiences of working with the constitutional committee of the Iraqi National Assembly led him to conclude that it is indeed possible for Iraqis to coalesce around a broad political framework that could lead the country out of violence. He outlines his call for an inclusive and enduring "social contract" in Chapter 9.

The subsequent two chapters focus more specifically on the constitutional process. David Cameron advised the constitutional committee in his capacity as member of the International Forum of Federations. He shares his impressions of the long process that lies ahead in developing a federal system that exists in only skeletal format following the adoption of the 2005 constitution. John McGarry captures a debate that dominated much of the Ottawa conference on the merits of the highly decentralized federation outlined in the constitution. In his chapter, he argues that the liberal consociationalism that informed the development of the text provides the most realistic basis for unity among Iraq's very different communities. Brendan O'Leary adds to this perspective in the next chapter, providing a flavor of the often robust advocacy that characterizes the debate.

James Dobbins opens the discussion of the role of outside actors in Iraq's conflict by arguing that the United States is running out of options in stabilizing the country and must turn to the international community, particularly to Iraq's neighbors in the region, for help. Jon Alterman sheds light on the perspectives that Iraq's Arab neighbors bring to the conflict, while examining how their respective bilateral relations with the United States may affect their willingness to engage further in Iraq.

Turning to the broader international level, Nora Bensahel explores the various contributions that external forces make to Iraq's security, concluding that there are few alternatives to the United States. Pierre Gassmann, who led the Baghdad office of the International Committee for the Red Cross in 2003 and 2004, argues that all parties to the conflict should take greater care to ensure the protection of civilian life and suggests that external forces in particular would gain greater legitimacy if their mandate were explicitly reorganized around the "responsibility to protect." Michael Bell takes the discussion from security to donor assistance in order to evaluate the state of the international effort in this area.

International actors are only likely to engage further in Iraq under different arrangements than those in place since 2003. Bruce Jones surveys others conflicts to suggest models for improving the coordination of international involvement in Iraq should the United States relinquish the dominant role it has played while seeking a more effective mechanism than the coalition it assembled in 2003.

If the primary source of conflict is state fragility, then state building is the logical response. We therefore conclude the volume with a synthesis of the various recommendations brought forward in this book. These emphasize the central role Iraqis themselves must play at the domestic level in leading their country out of violence, but also examine efforts at the regional and international levels that could lend much-needed support to this effort.

Not all contributors to this volume agree with the premise that state fragility lies at the heart of Iraq's persistent instability. All do agree, however, that the stakes of the conflict are tremendous. Twenty-five years of instability have caused untold damage to Iraq as well as to international peace and stability. In a period of despair for Iraq's prospects, this book is an attempt to identify where hope may lie for a more stable future should the international community find the unity of purpose necessary to help Iraq escape another generation of conflict.

▪ Notes

1. See Robert F. Worth, "Blast Destroys Shrine in Iraq, Setting Off Sectarian Fury," *New York Times,* 22 February 2006; Ellen Knickmeyer and K. I. Ibrahim, "Bombing Shatters Mosque in Iraq: Attack on Shiite Shrine Sets Off Protests, Violence," *Washington Post*, 23 February 2006; and "Iraq Erupts into Fresh Violence," *Al-Jazeera Online*, 1 March 2006.

2. "Iraq in Civil War, Says Former PM," *BBC News Online*, 19 March 2006.

3. International Crisis Group (ICG), "The Next Iraqi War? Sectarianism and Civil Conflict," *Middle East Report* 52 (27 February 2006).

4. UN Assistance Mission for Iraq (UNAMI), *Human Rights Report 1 November–31 December 2006* (Baghdad: UNAMI, December 2006).

5. United Nations High Commissioner for Refugees (UNHCR), *UNHCR Briefing Notes: Iraqi Displacement*, www.unhcr.org/news/NEWS/454b1f8f2.html.

6. Daniel L. Byman and Kenneth M. Pollack, *Things Fall Apart: Containing the Spillover from an Iraqi Civil War*, Saban Center Analysis (Saban Center for Middle East Policy at the Brookings Institution) no. 11 (January 2007).

7. James A. Baker III and Lee H. Hamilton, Co-Chairs, with Lawrence S. Eagleburger, Vernon E. Jordan Jr., Edwin Meese III, Sandra Day O'Connor, Leon E. Panetta, William J. Perry, Charles S. Robb, and Alan K. Simpson, *The Iraq Study Group Report* (New York: Vintage, 2006), xiii–xiv.

8. *Prospects for Iraq's Stability: A Challenging Road Ahead*, United States National Intelligence Estimate (NIE), published by the National Intelligence Council, January 2007.

9. Phebe Marr, *The Modern History of Iraq*, 2d ed. (Boulder, CO: Westview, 2004).

10. The literature on Iraq and its embroilment in conflict is vast, but on the Security Council's interplay in and around Iraq, our account is informed largely by David M. Malone, *The International Struggle over Iraq* (New York: Oxford University Press, 2006).

11. See Charles Tripp, "Regional Organizations in the Arab Middle East," in *Regionalism in World Politics: Regional Organizations and International Order*, ed. Louise Fawcett and Andrew Hurrell (Oxford: Oxford University Press, 1995).

12. Daniel L. Byman, "Building the New Iraq: The Role of Intervening Forces," *Survival* 45, no. 2 (summer 2003): 57. See also Graham Day and Christopher Freeman, "Policekeeping Is the Key: Rebuilding the Internal Security Architecture of Postwar Iraq," *International Affairs* 79, no. 2 (2003): 335.

13. A. G. Hopkins, "The 'Victory' Strategy: Grand Bargain or Grand Illusion?" *Current History* 105, no. 687 (January 2006): 14.

14. Lieutenant-General William Odom (ret.), "Withdraw Now," *Current History* 105, no. 687 (January 2006): 3.

15. See Malone, *International Struggle over Iraq*, 265–266.

16. James Cockayne with Cyrus Samii, *The Iraq Crisis and World Order: Structural and Normative Changes*, International Peace Academy (IPA) Conference Report, 16–18 August 2004, Bangkok.

17. Kamran Karadaghi, "Minimizing Ethnic Tensions in a Post-Saddam Iraq," in *How to Build a New Iraq After Saddam* (Washington, DC: Washington Institute for Near East Policy, 2002).

18. Leslie Gelb, "The Three-State Solution," *New York Times*, 25 November 2003. Gelb has now revisited this view and in May 2006 argued instead for a large degree of autonomy for each of the three major communities in Iraq. See Leslie Gelb and Joseph R. Biden Jr., "Unity Through Autonomy in Iraq," *New York Times*, 1 May 2006.

19. Liam Anderson and Gareth Stansfield, *The Future of Iraq: Dictatorship, Democracy, or Division*, rev. ed. (New York: Palgrave MacMillan, 2005), 10.

20. Charles Tripp, *History of Iraq*, 2nd ed. (London: Cambridge University Press, 2002). See also Efraim Karsh and Inari Rautsi, *Saddam Hussein: A Political Biography* (London: Futura, 1991), 3.

21. Hanna Batatu, *The Old Social Classes and the Revolutionary Movements of*

Iraq: A Study of Iraq's Old Landed and Commercial Classes and of Its Communists, Baathists, and Free Officers (Princeton: Princeton University Press, 1978), 1113.

22. Toby Dodge, *Inventing Iraq: The Failure of Nation Building and a History Denied* (New York: Columbia University Press, 2003), xii.

23. Ibid., 169.

24. Isam al-Khafaji, "State Terror and the Degradation of Politics in Iraq," *Middle East Report* (May–June 1992): 19.

25. Ibrahim al-Marashi, "Iraq's Security and Intelligence Network: A Guide and Analysis," *Middle East Review of International Affairs* 6, no. 3 (September 2002): 1.

26. Faleh A. Jabar, *Formative Forces in the Development of the Modern Iraqi State* (Washington, DC: United States Institute of Peace, 15 April 2004).

27. On this episode, see Karsh and Rautsi, *Saddam Hussein*, 27–28.

28. The cult-related bureaucracy in Iraq was extensive. On this, see Simon Henderson, *Instant Empire: Saddam Hussein's Ambition for Iraq* (San Francisco, CA: Mercury House, 1991), 78–79.

29. Fuad Matar, *Saddam Hussein: The Man, the Cause, and the Future* (London: Third World Centre, 1981), 15.

30. Samir al-Khalil (Kanan Makiya), *Republic of Fear: The Politics of Modern Iraq* (London: Hutchinson Radius, 1989), 271.

31. Good examples, with direct reference to the Middle East, albeit espousing very different perspectives, are Joel S. Migdal, *Strong Societies and Weak States: State-Society Relations and State Capabilities in the Third World* (Princeton: Princeton University Press, 1988); Roger Owen, *State, Power, and Politics in the Making of the Modern Middle East* (London: Routledge, 1992); and Nazih Ayubi, *Over-Stating the Arab State: Politics and Society in the Middle East* (London: I. B. Tauris, 1995).

32. Robert I. Rotberg, "The New Nature of Nation-State Failure," *Washington Quarterly* 25, no. 3 (summer 2002): 85–96. See also Robert I. Rotberg, "Failed States in a World of Terror," *Foreign Affairs* 81, no. 4 (July–August 2002): 127–140, and the introduction to Robert I. Rotberg, ed., *State Failure and State Weakness in a Time of Terror* (Washington, DC: Brookings Institution Press, January 2003).

33. See Rotberg, "New Nature," 85–88.

34. See Rotberg, "Failed States."

35. Ayubi, *Over-Stating*, 3.

36. Ibid., 7. See also Christine Buci-Glucksmann, *Gramsci and the State* (London: Lawrence and Wishart, 1980).

37. Rotberg, *State Failure*, 5.

38. Tripp, *History of Iraq*, 194. See also al-Khafaji, "State Terror."

39. See al-Marashi, "Iraq's Security and Intelligence Network."

40. Tripp, *History of Iraq*, 205–208 and 214–219. See also Batatu, *Old Social Classes*.

41. Batatu in 1978 described the patronage system around Hussein's rule of the Baath Party and Iraq itself as an attempt "to build the Baath and its auxiliaries into protective shields for the government." Batatu, *Old Social Classes*, 1132.

42. Batatu points out that the center of power in the Baath Party structure, the Revolutionary Command Council, was dominated by Sunnis and in particular Tikriti Sunnis following Hussein's rise to power; see ibid., 1085–1086.

43. Tripp, *History of Iraq*, 264–265.

44. Batatu, *Old Social Classes*, 1079, 1085.

45. Tripp, *History of Iraq*, 226–227. See also ibid., 1096.

46. Al-Khalil, *Republic of Fear*. See also Karsh and Rautsi, *Saddam Hussein*.

47. Al-Khafaji, "State Terror," 18.

48. See Hanna Batatu, "Shi'ite Organizations in Iraq: Ad-Da'wa al-Islamiya and al-Mujahidin," in *Shi'ism and Social Protest*, ed. Juan R. Cole and Nikki Keddie (New Haven: Yale University Press, 1986), 196.

49. Tripp, *History of Iraq*, 244–245.

50. Ibid.

51. Ibid., 270–271. See also Karsh and Rautsi, *Saddam Hussein*, 274–281.

52. Batatu, *Old Social Classes*, 1093.

53. Dodge, *Inventing Iraq*, xii.

54. Samantha Power, *A Problem from Hell: America and the Age of Genocide* (New York: HarperCollins, 2002).

55. Cameron R. Hume, *The United Nations, Iran, and Iraq: How Peacemaking Changed* (Bloomington: Indiana University Press, 1994).

56. These paragraphs draw again primarily on Malone, *International Struggle over Iraq*.

57. In late 2004, the coalition countries successfully engineered an international conference on Iraq in Sharm el-Shaikh, but Arab actors, particularly the Arab League, failed to take the bait. The Arab League's passivity on this issue—indeed its recent miserable track record more broadly—is much to be deplored.

PART 1

Iraq in Turmoil

2

State Collapse and the
Rise of Identity Politics

Toby Dodge

EVER SINCE US TROOPS arrived in Baghdad on April 9, 2003, Iraqi society has been dominated by a profound security vacuum. The opportunities provided by the collapse of the state and the disbanding of the Iraqi army were seized upon by a myriad of groups deploying violence for their own ends. Organized crime continues to be the dominant source of insecurity in the everyday lives of ordinary Iraqis.[1] For coalition and Iraqi security forces, the diffuse groups fighting the insurgency in the name of Iraqi nationalism, increasingly fused with a militant Islamism, have caused the highest loss of life. But the destruction of the al-Askariya Mosque in Samarra on February 22, 2006, and its violent aftermath, may prove to be a watershed moment because it brought to the fore the specter of sectarian violence, a communalist civil war.

It is sectarian violence that now has the greatest potential to destabilize post-Saddam Iraq beyond the point of no return, derailing attempts at state building and driving US forces from the country. This dynamic was heralded in August 2003 by the massive explosion outside the Imam Ali Mosque in Najaf (one of the holiest shrines of Shia Islam) that killed over one hundred people, including Ayatollah Mohammad Baqir al-Hakim, the leader of the Supreme Council for the Islamic Revolution in Iraq (SCIRI). In February 2004, the tactic was extended to the area controlled by the Kurdish Regional Government (KRG), when two suicide bombers killed 101 people, including the deputy prime minister of the KRG, Sami Abdul-Rahman, at the offices of the main Kurdish parties, the Kurdistan Democratic Party (KDP) and the Patriotic Union of Kurdistan (PUK) in Erbil. Attacks in March 2004 targeted the large crowds that had gathered to commemorate the Shia festival of Ashura in Baghdad and Karbala, in a clear attempt to trigger a civil war between Iraq's different communities. This assumption was strengthened by the discovery in Baghdad of a letter allegedly written by the senior jihadi figure, the Jordanian Abu Musab al-

23

Zarqawi. The letter asserted that the only way to "prolong the duration of the fight between the infidels and us" was by "dragging them into a sectarian war, this will awaken the sleepy Sunnis who are fearful of destruction and death at the hands of the Shi'a."[2]

Estimates of those civilians killed in the immediate aftermath of February's destruction of the al-Askariya Mosque vary from 220 to 550.[3] US military sources judge that Baghdad's homicide rate tripled from eleven to thirty-three deaths a day.[4] Of even greater concern is the displacement of the population triggered by intimidation and the threat of sectarian violence. The Iraqi government has estimated this to be as high as sixty-five thousand people, with the majority coming from in and around Baghdad.[5] The influential "Correlates of War" project has developed an operational definition of civil war that has become dominant in the social-science literature: "sustained military combat, primarily internal, resulting in at least 1,000 battle-deaths per year, pitting central government forces against an insurgent force capable of effective resistance, determined by the latter's ability to inflict upon government forces at least 5 percent of the fatalities that the insurgents suffer."[6]

There are no definitive statistics for civilian casualties but rough-and-ready estimates range from 350 to 600 a month to former prime minister Ayad Allawi's claim of fifty a day.[7] Figures released by the Iraqi government at the beginning of 2007 estimated that 13,896 Iraqis, civilians, police officers, and soldiers died during 2006. The United Nations in Baghdad, which also collates casualty figures, has put a much higher number on the death toll for 2006. In mid-January 2007, it calculated that 34,452 civilians had been killed in 2006.[8] A team from Johns Hopkins Bloomberg School of Public Health writing in *The Lancet* estimated that as of July 2006, 654,965 more Iraqis had been killed than if the invasion had not taken place.[9]

Against this statistical background, Iraq is clearly in the midst of an increasingly bloody civil war. Arguments to the contrary are primarily driven not by facts on the ground but by the political ramifications in both Baghdad and Washington of admitting the obvious.

■ Seeking to Understand Violence in Iraq

The dominant approach used to explain Iraq's descent into civil war and to draft policy proposals to end the violence is simply to impose a primordial template onto the political and societal complexities of the situation. This argument starts with an a priori assertion of a deeply divided society. David Phillips, for example, claims: "Iraqis lack a sense of national identity. They are deeply divided along ethnic and sectarian lines."[10] Leslie Gelb and Peter Galbraith have become the chief promoters of this approach. For them Iraq has "three distinct and sectarian communities," Sunni, Shia, and Kurd.[11]

These communities, it is claimed, are largely geographically homogeneous and mutually hostile. They have been locked in an artificial, Sunni-dominated state for eighty-five years. This analysis leads its promoters to view the post-Saddam civil war as tragic but largely unavoidable. This approach asserts that Iraqi politics has always been and will continue to be animated by deeply held communal antipathies; the civil war is simply an outcome of this. From this perspective, there can be only one policy option: the situation will be stabilized by dividing the country into three smaller, ethnically purer and more manageable units. There is a possibility that this could be done through a form of drastic decentralization, as proposed by US senator Joseph R. Biden and Leslie Gelb. But the primordialization of Iraq has led Gelb and others to argue consistently for its complete division into separate states.[12]

From an academic, as well as a policy point of view, the primordial approach, although increasingly influential, is far from satisfactory. Those studying the social and political evolution of Iraq as a whole and over a broad sweep of its modern history since 1920 (as opposed to a specific focus on the Kurdish region during the 1990s), have long stressed that to describe it as divided into three mutually hostile communities is a static caricature that does great damage to a complex, historically grounded, reality.[13]

Comprehensive and comparative academic explanations of the role that ethnic and religious identities play in political mobilization stress their fluid, historically discontinuous, and contingent roles.[14] The political utility of communal identity is defined by and reacts to the changing nature of society and crucially how a state seeks to interact with and control its population. With this in mind, it is clear that Iraqis, like people everywhere, have several different aspects to their individual and collective societal identities: familial, professional, and geographic, as well as ethnic and religious. These are clearly not static but change over time and react to the politics of any given historical moment. A political situation and its history will determine which social identity will be most important to the individuals involved. Clearly on certain occasions, ethnic or religiously based identities may come to dominate political mobilization. But an accurate assessment of a given situation needs to explain why communalist affiliation, as opposed to other identities, becomes the dominant vehicle for political mobilization.

Crucial to the success of political mobilization is the institutional capacity of those groups and organizations seeking to mobilize support and the ideological resources at their disposal. At base, one has to explain how individuals perceive their position within their immediate social groupings and beyond that the role they and these collectives have in the wider society, in this case Iraq. To continue to select one aspect of an individual's identity above all others, in this case ethnic and religious identity, or to insist that this identity will be deployed adversarially, leading to violence or civil war, is overly deterministic, if not racist. An analytical judgment of how Iraq's population will mobilize over the coming months and years will certainly focus on its religious and ethnic divisions. But it must do this in historical perspective, seeking to identify the sources of political identity and trends that either run counter to religion and ethnicity or support them. An accurate conflict assessment focused on contemporary Iraq needs to look at three aspects of the present violence: It should first judge the institutional capacity of the state and then compare this to the capabilities of different organizations seeking to mobilize the population and deploy violence for political advantage. Finally, it needs to be aware of the political discourses available to individuals and subnational and national groups to understand their present situation and to shape their future.

To explain the evolution of violence in Iraq today, the collapse of the state in April 2003 is of equal if not greater significance to the supposedly transhistorical existence of communal antipathies. The collapse of a state's institutional capacity means the loss of national authority but also of the central focus for identity formation. In the aftermath of state failure, authoritative institutions, societal and political, quickly lose their capacity and legitimacy.[15] The geographic boundaries, within which national politics and economics are enacted, simultaneously expand and contract. On one level, because the state has lost its administrative and coercive capacity, the country's borders become increasingly meaningless, and decisionmaking power leaks out to neighboring capitals, as regional and international actors are drawn into the conflict. More damagingly, however, power devolves into what is left of society, away from the state capital and down to a lower level, where organizational capacity begins to be reasserted. Politics becomes both international and also highly local.[16] In the aftermath of state collapse, public goods, services, economic subsistence, and ultimately physical survival are to be found through ad hoc and informal channels: "When state authority crumbles, individuals not only lose their protection normally supplied by public offices, but are also freed from institutional restraints. In response, they often seek safety, profit, or both. Their motives become more complex than when they could depend on the state."[17] Once state capacity is removed, civil society's ability positively to influence events quickly disappears.[18] People will look to whatever grouping, militia, or identity offers them the best chance of survival in times of profound uncertainty.[19] The result is certainly a fracturing of the polity. But path dependencies built up before the collapse of the state help structure what emerges, which local, substate, and ethnic identities provide the immediate basis for political organization.[20] For communalistic identities to triumph as an organizing principle in this fluid and unpredictable situation, there needs to be a certain type of subnational elite. These entrepreneurs, ethnic or otherwise, have to supply what the wider community desperately needs, a degree of stability and certainty. They can then legitimize their role in terms of communalistic identity and the competition for scarce resources.[21] However, once this process has been set in motion, when ethnic entrepreneurs, in the face of state failure, have mobilized a significant section of the population on the basis of communalistic identity, the process quickly solidifies.[22] Previously "fuzzy" or secondary identity traits become politicized and "enumerated."[23] The struggle to survive, to gain a degree of predictability for yourself and your family, then becomes obtainable primarily through the increasingly militant deployment of ethnic or sectarian identity. There is nothing inevitable about the unfolding of this process; the primary causal factor in its evolution is the collapse of the state and the subsequent security vacuum, not the communalistic conflict that emerges in its wake.

■ Complexity Beyond Sectarianism: Societal Atomization, Nationalism, and Islamism

The whole process of stabilizing Iraq, of building administrative, coercive, and political capacity in the aftermath of regime change, has been greatly complicated by the legacy of thirty-five years of Baathist rule. The Baathist regime, built by Hassan al-Bakr beginning in 1968 and consolidated under Saddam after 1979, created a powerful set of state institutions through the 1970s and 1980s. These deliberately reshaped Iraqi society, breaking organized resistance to Baathist rule and effectively atomizing the population. During the 1980s and 1990s, however, both the Iraqi state and its relations with society were transformed. The eight-year war with Iran, the 1990–1991 Gulf War, and finally the imposition of sanctions, changed the Iraqi state, and with it Saddam's strategy of rule. From their application in 1990 until 1997, when UN-supervised oil revenues arrived, sanctions proved to be extremely efficient. They restricted the government's access to large-scale funding, which meant that economic policy was largely reactive, dominated by the short-term goal of staying in power. From 1991 until 2003, the effects of the sanctions regime combined with government policy in southern and central Iraq led to hyperinflation, widespread poverty, and malnutrition. The historically generous state welfare provision that had been central to the regime's governing strategy disappeared, and the government was forced to cut back on the resources it could devote to the armed forces and the police. The large and well-educated middle class that formed the bedrock of Iraqi society became impoverished and Iraq's once complex and all-pervasive bureaucracy was hollowed out. Bribery became commonplace, as civil servants' official wages rapidly devalued. State employees, teachers, and medical staff had to manage as best they could, extracting resources from the impoverished people who depended upon their services. Many professionals left public service, took their chances in the private sector, or fled into exile. Put simply, there was no functioning civil society in southern and central Iraq before regime change in 2003.[24] The Baathist regime's attack on the organizing capacity of society meant that personal ties to family and extended family, town, city, or neighborhood, as well as to province and religion, were the only ones to survive.[25]

In the aftermath of regime change, as meaningful research in southern and central Iraq became possible, a complex picture of the Iraqi polity has emerged. Opinion polling in a country that has recently emerged from dictatorship and is racked with profound uncertainty and violence is bound to be an inexact science. Results from several polls from 2003 to 2005 have been somewhat contradictory, but offer an indication of developments in public opinion.[26] During the 1990s, as sanctions devastated Iraqi society, there was a retreat into the certainties of religion. This trend was encouraged by the regime's *al-hamla al-imaniyya*, or faith campaign, which relaxed the rules governing religious observance and channeled state resources into mosque building.[27] This has left its mark on Iraqi society, particularly in the south and center. In an April 2004 poll, 67 percent identified religion as the most important expression of their identity.[28] Counter to some orientalist descriptions of contemporary Iraq, only 1 percent of those questioned gave their tribe as the most important expression of identity. Interestingly, across the country as a whole, only 12 percent cited their ethnicity, with the figure rising to 66 percent in the area controlled by the Kurdish Regional Government. The dominance of Islam as a marker of identity runs in tandem with strong support across Iraqi society for democracy, but not necessarily on a European or US model. Of three thousand Iraqis polled in May 2004, three-quarters said that they "want to live in a moderate Islamic democracy, rather than a secular liberal one."[29]

More surprisingly, Iraqi nationalism and even remnants of Baathist ideology appear to have resonance within the population, with the majority supporting a strong interventionist state. The Iraqi Center for Research and Strategic Studies found that 64.7 percent favored "a politically centralized, unitary state as opposed to a federation," with 67 percent saying that they wanted both fiscal and administrative centralization. The Oxford Research International polls of February, March, and June 2004 and November 2005 found broadly similar views. In February and November, the question "Which structure should Iraq have in the future?" was answered by 79 percent of respondents; 70 percent agreed with the statement "one unified Iraq with a central government in Baghdad." Although the figures differed according to the geographic location of those questioned, only 12 percent of those in areas controlled by the Kurdish Regional Government, and 3.8 percent of all those surveyed in 2004, called for Iraq to be broken up into separate states, with the figure rising to 20 percent—and 9 percent overall—in November 2005.

What these figures clearly indicate is that Iraqi public opinion is far more complicated than the caricature of three clearly delineated and mutually hostile communities divided by religion and ethnicity. The polling data indicate a popular sense of national identity and a widespread wish for a strong unitary state centered on Baghdad. Obviously this commitment to a new Iraqi state varies across different sections of society and in different areas of the country. Pundits have been correct in stressing a widely held suspicion about renewed, Baghdad-based, state capacity among those in areas controlled by the KRG. However, opinion across the country is clearly fluid, as are political identities and the basis for political mobilization. Having long been the target of state oppression, the Kurdish populations in the north of Iraq will need to be convinced that new state structures will not be used to oppress them, but these fears about the uses of the state are neither transhistorical nor insurmountable. Against this background of both historically grounded suspicion but also ahistorical primordial understandings of Iraq it is essential that care should be taken as the nascent state institutions set about interacting with the population. If done incorrectly or on the basis of widely held misperceptions about Iraqi society, the state could continue to exacerbate sectarian and religious tensions. If, however, the state encourages a civic nationalism based on equal citizenship for all in a legal, rational, democratic state, then Iraqi politics could stabilize and the state could evolve into a legitimate and sustainable organization.

■ The Organizations Driving Conflict in Iraq

The main driving force behind violence in Iraq is the absence of state institutions. The Iraqi state on the eve of the invasion was on the verge of collapse. It had survived three wars in twenty years and thirteen years of harsh international sanctions. The combination of war, sanctions fatigue, and rampant criminality led to a complete state breakdown. The three weeks of looting that greeted the arrival of US troops in Baghdad was estimated to have cost $12 billion, with seventeen of the Iraqi government's twenty-three ministry buildings destroyed.[30] In the aftermath of regime change, the Iraqi state ceased to exist in any meaningful form and has yet to be reconstituted.

The resultant security vacuum has given birth to or empowered three distinct sets of groups deploying violence and ultimately driving Iraq toward civil war. The first are the "industrial strength" criminal gangs who are still the most potent source of violence and instability. These groups were born in the mid-1990s when Saddam Hussein's regime was at its weakest. Encouraged by the regime's decision to empty the jails before the invasion, criminal gangs were quick to reconstitute in the aftermath of regime change. Although there is clear overlap between simple criminality and politically motivated violence, especially where kidnapping is con-

cerned, the continuing crime wave is the most glaring example of state inca-
pacity. The persistent reports that crime is as big a problem for the citizens
of Basra as Baghdad indicate that the state's inability to impose and guarantee order is a general problem across large swathes of southern and central
Iraq. The high levels of criminal activity across the majority of Iraqi territory indicate that violence is driven primarily by state weakness, not the
antipathy of competing groups within Iraqi society. Crime is obviously
instrumentally driven and primarily noncommunal and the key factor dele-
gitimizing the state. Going well beyond the government's ability to increase
electrical output or stimulate the job market, the continued ability of criminal gangs to operate is indicative of a failed state.

The second set of groups that have capitalized on the inability of occupation forces and the Iraqi government to impose order are the plethora of
independent militias, estimated to hold between 60,000 and 102,000 fighters in their ranks.[31] These militias have overtly organized and legitimized
themselves by reference to sectarian ideology. Although they may not enjoy
widespread popular support, their existence is testament to the inability of
the Iraqi government to guarantee the personal safety of Iraqis on the basis
of equal citizenship, not sectarian identity. The militias themselves can be
divided into three broad groups, depending on their organizational coherence and relation to national politics. The first group is made up of the two
Kurdish militias of the KDP and PUK. These two separate forces number, in
total, between 50,000 and 75,000 fighters. On the one hand, the Kurdish
militias are the most organized, institutionalized, and comparatively disciplined in the country. With a long history of fighting against the central government in Baghdad, the KDP and PUK quickly set about imposing order
on their respective fighting forces once the United Nations had given their
enclave protection in the aftermath of the 1991 Kurdish uprising. However,
their fractured political loyalties were highlighted by the damaging civil
war that broke out between the two parties in the 1990s over control of the
profits from oil smuggling. This had a highly detrimental effect on the governing structures of Iraqi Kurdistan. The two militias remain separate and
represent little more than the political and personal ambitions of their two
leaders.

Another distinct set of militias are those that were organized in exile
and brought back to Iraq in the wake of Saddam's fall. The most powerful
of these is the Badr Corps, the military arm of SCIRI. The Badr Corps,
along with SCIRI itself, was set up as a foreign policy vehicle for the
Iranian government. Indeed, the Badr Corps was trained and officered by
the Iranian Revolutionary Guard, at least until their return to Iraq. It is the
integration of Badr Corps into the security forces, especially the police and
paramilitary units associated with the Ministry of Interior, which has done
so much to delegitimize the state-controlled forces of law and order. The

use of the police and National Guard units for electioneering in January 2005 by both the Shia list in the south and Allawi's coalition in and around Baghdad gave an indication of the blatant politicization of the nascent security services so early on in the life of the new state.[32] Along with SCIRI, the majority of the formerly exiled parties likewise set up militias to provide security for their leaders and to exert coercive influence beyond the newly created democratic structures of government.

The third group of militias includes those that have been set up at local village or town levels across southern and central Iraq. These are a direct response to the lawlessness that followed regime change. They vary in size, organization, and discipline, from a few thugs with guns to militias capable of running whole towns. In combination with the insurgency itself, the militia fighters are a key factor in the civil war. Although they were formed as an instrumental response to the security vacuum they have attempted to legitimize themselves by the deployment of hybrid ideologies—sectarian and religious but also nationalistic.

The most powerful and well-organized indigenous militia in southern and central Iraq is Muqtada al-Sadr's Mahdi Army. Capitalizing on a large charitable network set up before regime change by his late father, Sadr has used radical anti-US rhetoric to rally disaffected Iraqis to his organization. As the occupation failed to deliver significant improvements to people's lives, Sadr's popularity increased. During the first weeks of April and again in August 2004 Sadr, faced with an arrest warrant for murder, launched a rebellion across the south of the country. The resulting revolts in the key towns of Basra, Amara, Kut, Nassiriya, Najaf, Kufa, and Karbala, as well as Baghdad, showed that Sadr's organization had been preparing for just such a confrontation from regime change onward.[33] More worryingly, the geographic spread of the uprisings indicated that smaller militias were using Sadr's confrontation to assert autonomy against the nascent state.

Sadr cannot simply be written off as a rabble-rouser deploying sectarianism to mobilize cannon fodder. The constituency that Sadr aspires to represent, the economically disadvantaged and politically alienated, has, if anything, increased since the revolts of 2004. Sadr successfully utilized nationalist and radical Islamic trends amongst sections of the Shia population. His use of radical anti-US rhetoric has extended his support into the lower ranks of the religious establishment, where he has found significant backing from young clerics, attracted by his youth, his lack of a religious education (younger clerics face long and arduous training), and the promise of a shortcut to moral and political influence.[34] Finally, within Najaf, Sadr has capitalized on tensions between the large number of returning exiles and those who feel threatened by their arrival.[35]

Finally, other organizations fueling the spiral of increasing violence are those of the insurgency. Those organizations fighting the occupation and the new Iraqi government are frequently described as "the Sunni insurgency."[36] But this blanket term runs the risk of giving too much organizational and ideological coherence to those who are fighting. It is important to remember that several key individuals on the Bush administration's "most wanted" list of insurgent leaders are actually Shia.[37]

In the aftermath of regime change, the insurgency was born in a reactive and highly localized fashion as the US military's inability to control Iraq became apparent. This process saw the creation of a number of small, autonomous fighting groups built around dyadic ties of trust, cemented by family, locality, or friendship. Since the summer of 2003, it has been estimated that between fifty and seventy-four such groups have been fighting to rid the country of US forces.[38] With between twenty thousand and fifty thousand fighters in their ranks, it is this force that has to date proved to be the most destructive.[39] Over the past three years, they have been able to innovate both in the technology they deploy and the tactics they use.[40] US troops initially formed the main target, especially where they were at their most vulnerable, along supply lines and during troop transportation. But as US troops were redeployed to decrease their vulnerability and political visibility, the insurgents increased their targeting of Iraqis who were serving with fledgling state institutions. In addition, international institutions, specifically foreign embassies, the United Nations, and the Red Cross, have been targeted, signaling the high costs of any attempt to multilateralize postwar state building. Finally, a growing radical Sunni jihadist section of the insurgency has sought to encourage civil war by murdering high-profile Shia and Kurdish political figures and deploying suicide bombers in mass casualty attacks on specific sections of the community.

The year 2005 saw a degree of organizational consolidation around four or five main groups. These include Al-Jaysh al-Islami fi'l-'Iraq (the Islamic Army in Iraq), Jaysh Ansar al-Sunna (the Partisans of the Sunna Army), Jaysh al-Mujahidin (the Mujahidin's Army), Jaysh Muhammad (Muhammad's Army), Harakat al-Muqawama al-Islamiya fi'l-'Iraq (the Islamic Resistance Movement in Iraq), and Al-Jabha al-Islamiyya li'l-Muqawama al-'Iraqiya (the Islamic Front of the Iraqi Resistance).[41] In terms of numbers, the role played by Arabs from neighboring countries, and behind them the organizing capacity of Al-Qaida in Mesopotamia (Tandhim al-Qa'ida fi Bilad al-Rafidayn), appears to be comparatively low, estimated by the US Army to be around 10 percent of the total. But they have played a disproportionately large role in the insurgency's increased ideological coherence, fusing the powerful appeal to Iraqi nationalism with an austere and extreme Sunni Salafism. It is Al-Qaida in Mesopotamia that has claimed responsibility or has been blamed for most of the violence that increased sectarian tensions in the country. However, the organizations behind the sectarian attacks are much more likely to be a hybrid, with elements of the old regime acting in alliance with indigenous Islamic radicals and a small number of foreign fighters. This has allowed midranking members of the old regime to deploy their training and weapons stockpiles. They have sought to ally themselves with a new brand of Islamic nationalism, seeking to mobilize Sunni fears of Shia and Kurdish domination and a widespread resentment at foreign occupation.

Over the last year, widespread political violence has increasingly been justified in sectarian terms and this instability has certainly been a major causal factor behind the growth of communalistic identity. However, explanations of this phenomenon that focus solely on the deeply divided nature of Iraqi society run the risk of mistaking effect for cause. It is the criminality and violence that dominated post-regime-change Iraq that has driven the rise in sectarian identity politics: Faced with state collapse and profound insecurity, the population in southern and central Iraq has been placed at the mercy of those groups that could quickly build coercive capacity. Organized initially on a street, neighborhood, and town level, the resultant informal militias have been ad hoc coalitions thrown together by those with weapons and military training. The result has been an implicit deal between populations and those with coercive capacity in their neighborhoods: recognition for protection, which has then been partially legitimized through the guise of sectarian identity politics. At a regional and national level, this process was somewhat different. Muqtada al-Sadr gained an organizational and ideological head start because of the mantle he inherited from his late father, Ayatollah Muhammad Sadiq al-Sadr. Initially Sadr's political message was less sectarian, merging a militant Iraqi nationalism with a commitment to Islamic radicalism. The personnel of the SCIRI, Badr, and Al-Dawa groups were primarily exiles who returned to a post-Saddam Iraq. They found it difficult to mobilize a population suspicious of those who had spent many years outside the country and had come back under the auspices of the US military. For them, a specifically sectarian ideology was deployed to break this suspicion and rally a significant section of the population to vote for them in the two elections of 2005. Against this background, the primary cause of Iraq's civil war is not the deeply divided nature of the population, but the political dynamics of a foreign occupation trying to reconstitute a state in the midst of profound violence.

■ State Building as the Only Solution

The Gelb and Galbraith thesis of simply dividing Iraq into three ethnically purer states misses the main cause of the violence: the lack of institutional and coercive state capacity across the whole of central and southern Iraq. The radical decentralization of political power runs the distinct danger of devolving the violent struggle for supremacy. This could localize the conflict between SCIRI and Sadr's Mahdi Army or reignite the conflict between the KDP and PUK. Those arguing for decentralization would be hard pressed to explain how their policy recommendations would reduce the violence that erupted in Basra in April and May 2006, forcing the new prime minister, Nuri al-Maliki, to declare martial law. The city has a very small Sunni population. The militias that were responsible for the deaths of 174 Iraqis in April and May 2006 were made up of Iraqi Shias. They were not fighting over religion or even ideology, but money.[42] Basra is the center of Iraq's oil exports and the conflict was primarily concerned with the division of the spoils.[43] What Iraq desperately needs is one coherent and functioning state, not three. Its governing institutions, bureaucratic, military, and political, must be rebuilt from the ground up across the territorial extent of the country.

Crucial to the state's ability to perform these tasks is the veracity of its claim to "binding authority" over its citizenship and ultimately "over all actions taking place in the area of its jurisdiction."[44] Its capacity is ultimately grounded in the extent to which its "administrative staff successfully upholds the claim to the monopoly of the legitimate use of physical force in the enforcement of its order."[45] The degree to which a state has reached this ideal-typical level can be judged by the ability of its institutions to impose and guarantee the rule of law, to penetrate society, mobilize the population, and extract resources.[46]

Iraq is a very long way from this standard. The speed with which the United States rebuilt the Iraqi army and police force means most of its personnel are ill-trained and ill-equipped. If the Iraqi military is still very much a work in progress, then the police force poses an even graver cause for concern. As with the new army, police training has been extremely hurried. There is clear evidence in Basra and Baghdad that the loyalty of the police is not to the state but to various local militias. Across Iraq, but particularly in the south of the country, there is strong evidence to suggest that the political militias have targeted the police force, infiltrating their members into its ranks and placing their own senior commanders in regional management positions. Against this background, the recruitment, training, and management of the security services will have to be revisited for state building to stand any chance of gaining momentum. International assistance should focus on increasing the capacity of security-force management, both to impose law and order and to resist the massive pressures to use the police and army as tools of the political parties.

Ultimately, however, the sustainability of state capacity is anchored in the extent to which its actions are judged to be legitimate in the eyes of its citizens.[47] This is not primarily an issue of ethnic identity; the evolution of state power is intimately linked to the ability of state institutions to penetrate society in a regularized fashion and become central to the population's ongoing and daily "strategies of survival."[48] Both Joel Migdal and Michael Mann argue that the success of this process, the positive relevance of the state to the everyday lives of its citizens, is the key to society tolerating state institutions and ultimately to the growth of state legitimacy.[49] The record of the three Iraqi governments that have held power since the handover of sovereignty in June 2004 is very poor. One of the key reasons for this is that constitutionally real political power is vested in the political parties, not in the office of prime minister or president. Electoral success is rewarded by dividing up the spoils of government—cabinet portfolios and the jobs and resources they bring with them. The result has been highly variable governance, with some ministers managing their institutions fairly efficiently. A sizable minority, if not majority, of others, however, set about carving out fiefdoms for personal or factional benefit. Large swathes of the government have disengaged from the pressing need to build state capacity and extend this across the geographical extent of the country. To make inroads in such a situation both international diplomacy and donor assistance need to be highly coordinated. The United Nations, the European Union, and the United States need to present Iraqi ministers with the same specific demands for good governance and reduction of the scope for corruption, patronage, and abuse in return for further aid and assistance.

The growth of stable state institutions, with a meaningful presence in people's lives, forms the framework within which the longer-term goal of successful state building, the reconstruction of an Iraqi nation, can be achieved. The successful creation of state capacity would reestablish a framework within which a civic identity based on a shared vision of the future could be built.[50] Civil society could then become the vehicle for building a national, collective sense of identity that can rival or even replace substate, centrifugal political mobilization. A collective appreciation of administrative capacity and a loyalty toward the state would bind individuals together and to the government.[51] Indeed, successful sustainable state building "entails much more than merely forming a state, which may be achieved, say, by granting independence to a previous colony. It entails in addition forming a community where none previously existed, or shoring up one that was not firmly or properly constructed."[52] It is this process of imposing order—building institutionalized administrative capacity and developing a civic identity—that could slow Iraq's slide deeper into civil war.

However, if this process continues to fail and international policy coordination cannot improve the quantity and quality of state building, then public goods, services, economic subsistence, and ultimately physical survival will be obtained through ad hoc and informal channels.[53] In Iraq, this process has fueled the rapid growth in sectarian identity. People have sought out whatever local group, militia, and identity that can provide a modicum of predictability and security in times of profound uncertainty. The result is a fracturing of the polity, with local, substate, and ethnic identities providing the immediate basis for political organization.[54] If this process continues, then the fracturing of the polity will likewise continue. Given the collapse of the state and the legacy of Saddam's totalitarianism it is extremely unlikely that this process will end in the dominance of one faction or militia over all others. Instead, this war of all against all will solidify not in state building but warlordism. Militias will carve out small islands of domination from a sea of violence. Groups may triumph on a local scale, receiving help from neighboring states or their own institutional capacity. However, the Iraqi civil war, if left unchecked by the international community, will result in numerous unstable statelets or fiefdoms. This would be highly destabilizing for the region and the international community beyond.

■ Notes

1. In 2004, the US military estimated that 80 percent of all violence in Iraq is "criminal in nature." There is no reason to think this situation has radically changed. See Eric Schmitt and Thom Shanker, "Estimates by US See More Rebels with Funds," *Guardian*, 23 October 2004.

2. For discussion of the text, see Dexter Filkins, "Memo Urges al-Qa'ida to Wage War in Iraq," *International Herald Tribune*, 10 February 2004; and Justin Huggler, "Is This Man the Mastermind of the Massacres?" *Independent on Sunday*, 7 March 2004.

3. See Michael E. O'Hanlon and Nina Kamp, *Iraq Index* (Washington, DC: Brookings Institution, April 27, 2006).

4. Jeffrey Gettleman, "Iraqis Bound, Blindfolded, and Dead," *New York Times,* 2 April 2006.

5. See Andrew North, "Iraq Unrest Forces 65,000 to Flee," 14 April 2006, newsvote.bbc.co.uk/mpsppd/pagetools/print/news.bbc.co.uk/1/hi/world/middle_east/.

6. See Errol A. Henderson and J. David Singer, "Civil War in the Post-Colonial World, 1946–92," *Journal of Peace Research* 37, no. 3 (May 2000); and Juan Cole, "Civil War? What Civil War? Desperate to Convince Voters We're Winning, Bush Is Denying That Iraq Is Having a Civil War. But the Facts Contradict Him," *Salon,* March 23, 2006, www.salon.com/opinion/feature/2006/03/23/civil_war/print.html.

7. See Larry Diamond, "What Civil War Looks Like. Slide Rules," *New Republic*, March 13, 2006, 11; and Juan Cole, "Civil War?"

8. See Damien Cave and John O'Neil, "UN Puts '06 Iraq Toll of Civilians at 34,000," *International Herald Tribune*, 17 January 2007; and Associated Press, "Iraq Sets Toll of Civilians at 12,000 for 2006," *New York Times*, 3 January 2007.

9. See Gilbert Burnham, Riyadh Lafta, Shannon Doocy, and Les Roberts, "Mortality After the 2003 Invasion of Iraq: A Cross-Sectional Cluster Sample Survey," *Lancet On-line*, 11 October 2006, DOI: 10.1016/S0140-6736(06)69491-9, www.thelancet.com. They place this figure within a margin of error that estimates the lowest casualty figure at 392,979 and the highest at 942,636.

10. David L. Phillips, *Losing Iraq: Inside the Post-War Reconstruction Fiasco* (Boulder, CO: Westview, 2005), 337.

11. For a short account of this argument, see Leslie H. Gelb, "Divide Iraq into

Primordial argument

Three States," *International Herald Tribune*, 26 November 2004. Peter W. Galbraith develops it at greater length in "How to Get Out of Iraq," *New York Review of Books*, 13 May 2004. Both Gelb and Galbraith have professional experience in the Balkans and may be influenced by their understanding of the violent breakup of Yugoslavia in the mid-1990s.

12. See Joseph Biden and Leslie Gelb, "Unity Through Autonomy in Iraq," *New York Times*, 1 May 2006; and Gelb, "Divide Iraq into Three States."

13. See for example, Reidar Visser, "Centralism and Unitary State Logic in Iraq from Midhat Pasha to Jawad al-Maliki: A Continuous Trend?" April 22, 2006, historiae.org; and Toby Dodge, *Iraq's Future: The Aftermath of Regime Change* (London: Routledge, 2005), especially Chapter 3.

14. For an excellent summary of the literature on this subject, see Nelson Kasfir, "Explaining Ethnic Political Participation," in *The State and Development in the Third World*, ed. Atol Kholi (Princeton, NJ: Princeton Univ. Press, 1986). Also see David D. Laitin, *The Russian-Speaking Populations in the Near Abroad* (Ithaca, NY: Cornell Univ. Press, 1998), 13–21 and 325–329; and Joseph Rothchild, *Ethnopoltics: A Conceptual Framework* (New York: Columbia Univ. Press, 1981).

15. See I. William Zartman, "Posing the Problem of State Collapse," in *Collapsed States: The Disintegration and Restoration of Legitimate Authority*, ed. I. William Zartman (Boulder, CO: Lynne Rienner, 1995), 6.

16. Ibid., 5.

17. Nelson Kasfir, "Domestic Anarchy, Security Dilemmas, and Violent Predation," in *When States Fail: Causes and Consequences*, ed. Robert I. Rotberg (Princeton, NJ: Princeton Univ. Press, 2004), 55.

18. Daniel N. Posner, "Civil Society and the Reconstruction of Failed States," in *When States Fail: Causes and Consequences*, ed. Robert I. Rotberg (Princeton, NJ: Princeton Univ. Press, 2004), 237, 240.

19. Andrea Kathryn Talentino, "The Two Faces of Nation-Building: Developing Function and Identity," *Cambridge Review of International Affairs* 17, no. 3 (October 2004): 569.

20. See Laitin, *Russian-Speaking Populations*, 16.

21. See Rothchild, *Ethnopolitics*, 29.

22. See Andreas Wimmer, "Democracy and Ethno-religious Conflict in Iraq," *Survival* 45, no. 4 (winter 2003–2004): 120.

23. On this distinction, see Sudipta Kaviraj, "On the Construction of Colonial Power, Structure, Discourse, Hegemony," in *Contesting Colonial Hegemony: State and Society in Africa and India*, ed. Dagmar Engles and Shula Marks (London: British Academic Press, 1994), 21–32.

24. Faleh A. Jabar, "Sheikhs and Ideologues: Deconstruction and Reconstruction of Tribes Under Patrimonial Totalitarianism in Iraq, 1968–1998," in *Tribes and Power: Nationalism and Ethnicity in the Middle East*, ed. Faleh A. Jabar and Hosham Dawod (London: Saqi, 2003), 89.

25. International Crisis Group (ICG), *Governing Iraq* (Baghdad,Washington, DC, Brussels: ICG, August 2003), 1; and Faleh A. Jabar, "Post-conflict Iraq: A Race for Stability, Reconstruction, and Legitimacy," *United States Institute of Peace Special Report* 120 (May 2004): 10.

26. On the difficulties of opinion polling in Iraq, see Brendan O'Neill, "Another Dodgy Dossier," *Guardian*, 25 March 2004. On the misuse of opinion polls, see James Zogby, "Bend It Like Cheney," *Guardian*, 29 October 2003.

27. See Ahmed S. Hashim, "The Sunni Insurgency," *Middle East Institute Perspective* (August 15, 2003): 10, www.mideasti.org/articles/doc89.html.

28. The poll was commissioned by *USA Today* and CNN. It questioned 3,444

people across Iraq between March 22 and April 2, 2004. The confessional breakdown was: Shia—73 percent, Sunni—76 percent, and Kurd—33 percent.

29. See www.bridgesconsortium.org.

30. See George Packer, *Assassin's Gate: America in Iraq* (New York: Farrar, Straus and Giroux, 2005), 139, and Phillips, *Losing Iraq*, 135.

31. See L. Paul Bremer III with Malcolm McConnell, *My Year in Iraq: The Struggle to Build a Future of Hope* (New York: Simon & Schuster, 2006), 274; and Larry Diamond, *Squandered Victory: The American Occupation and the Bungled Effort to Bring Democracy to Iraq* (New York: Times Books, 2005), 222.

32. For examples, see "Iraqi Police Drawn into Poll Contest as Gloves Come Off," *Financial Times*, 19 January 2005.

33. This is based on interviews carried out in Baghdad in the aftermath of the fall of the regime.

34. See International Crisis Group, *Shi'ism: Varied Social Settings, Rival Centre of Power, and Conflicting Visions* (Baghdad, Washington, DC, and Brussels: ICG, 2003), 8; and Faleh A. Jabar, *The Shi'ite Movement in Iraq* (London: Saqi, 2003), 26.

35. International Crisis Group, *Iraq's Shiites Under Occupation* (Baghdad and Brussels: ICG, 2003), 18.

36. See, for example, Packer, *Assassin's Gate*, 132.

37. As late as 2005, several of the coalition's "most wanted" insurgent leaders were Shia. Its February 10, 2005, list of twenty-nine most wanted, for example, included Rashid Ta'n Kadhim (a former senior Baath Party member) and Mahmud al-Hasani (a former member of Najaf's religious circles). International Crisis Group, *In Their Own Words: Reading the Iraqi Insurgency* (Baghdad, Washington, DC, and Brussels: ICG, 15 February 2006), 5 (fn. 28).

38. The International Crisis Group, from studying Web traffic, estimates fifty groups, whereas the figure of seventy-four comes from coalition intelligence sources.

39. See the interview given by General Muhammad Abdullah Shahwani, Iraq's intelligence chief, to *Asharq al Awsat*, 4 January 2005, and Eric Schmitt and Thom Shanker, "US Says Resistance in Iraq Up to 20,000," *Guardian*, 23 October 2004.

40. See Dodge, *Iraq's Future*, Chapter 2.

41. See International Crisis Group, *In Their Own Words*.

42. See Sabrina Tavernise and Qais Mizher, "Iraq's Premier Seeks to Control a City in Chaos," *Washington Post*, 31 May 2006; and Tom Lasseter, "Iranian-backed Militia Groups Take Control of Much of Southern Iraq," Knight Ridder Newspapers, 26 May 2006.

43. See Mariam Karouny, "Shi'ite Faction Menaces Iraq's Basra Oil Exports," Reuters, 26 May 2006.

44. See Max Weber, *Economy and Society*, vol. 1 (Berkeley: Univ. of California Press, 1978), 56.

45. Ibid., 54.

46. See Joel S. Migdal, *Strong Societies and Weak States: State-Society Relations and State Capabilities in the Third World* (Princeton, NJ: Princeton Univ. Press, 1988).

47. See Talentino, "Two Faces of Nation-Building," 571.

48. See Migdal, *Strong Societies and Weak States*.

49. See Michael Mann, "The Autonomous Power of the State: Its Origins, Mechanisms, and Results," in *States, War, and Capitalism: Studies in Political Sociology*, ed. Michael Mann (Oxford: Blackwell, 1988).

50. Talentino, "Two Faces of Nation-Building," 558.

51. Jens Meierhenrich, "Forming States After Failure," in *When States Fail: Causes and Consequences*, ed. Robert I. Rotberg (Princeton, NJ: Princeton Univ. Press, 2004), 154–162.

52. Amitai Etzioni, "A Self-Restrained Approach to Nation-Building by Foreign Powers," *International Affairs* 80, no. 1 (2004): 3.

53. Robert I. Rotberg, "The Failure and Collapse of Nation-States: Breakdown, Prevention and Repair," in Rotberg (ed.), *When States Fail,* 9.

54. Talentino, "Two Faces of Nation-Building," 569.

3

Iraq's Identity Crisis

Phebe Marr

IRAQ IS ON THE EDGE of a profound transition, struggling to make its way across the divide to a new order and stability. It will be a difficult passage. Much of the state structure has been destroyed since 2003, and is still under siege. Even if the insurgency is gradually reduced in lethality, it is likely to continue for some years, acting as a drain on Iraq's economy and the polity. The insurgency is now intertwined with ethnic and sectarian strife, which, if not contained, will be an added burden on the future. Reducing the insurgency and stabilizing the polity will require continuous effort and resources from the United States, the international community, and the region, but these efforts will come to naught unless they are based on a realistic assessment of the situation and a reasonable strategy for addressing it.

Moreover, while international assistance is needed, the solution to Iraq's problems lies mainly with Iraqis. The international community and regional actors can help (or hinder) but only Iraqis can take the actions that will end the insurgency, stem the tide of ethnic and sectarian bloodletting, and find the formula for coexistence. Hence, this chapter will focus on the newly emerging political leaders in Iraq, their various aims and outlook, and what this may portend for the future.

Iraq is currently undergoing two revolutions. The first revolution, well under way, is a fundamental change in domestic political leadership and the direction it is taking the country.[1] This upheaval has involved the uprooting (not just the removal) of the former leadership cadre of the Baath Party, the entire military and security structure that supported it, and the marginalization of the Arab Sunni and nationalist-oriented population favored by the Saddam regime. This upheaval has removed the previous governing elite, and created space for new—and often unknown—faces. Politics is now dominated not only by different political parties but by leaders of different ethnic and sectarian backgrounds. The political center, consisting of those with a strong Iraqi identity, has lost ground in successive elections.

41

The second revolution—still in an incipient stage—is a potentially radical change in the state itself. Indeed, the continued existence of the Iraqi state may be at stake. The direction of this revolution can be most clearly seen in the new constitution, an instrument with an extraordinary degree of decentralization (in contrast to the formerly highly centralized totalitarian model) and a federal (some would say confederal) system that expresses a desire, at least among some key groups (Kurds, possibly some Shia political parties), for a high degree of autonomy or separatism.[2] At the same time, identities among communities living in diverse regions have sharpened.

■ Communal Identity Politics

The most significant political trend in Iraq has been the shift from a relatively unified country with a nationalist orientation (under the Baathists) to an emerging political dynamic based on ethnic and sectarian identity. An overall Iraqi identity, which should form the basis for the newly constructed state, is not absent, but it is weak and rapidly diminishing. Kurdish self-rule—developed over the last fifteen years—has been recognized, but sectarian strife is relatively new. Where some sectarian identity existed before, it has now become the chief organizing factor in social and political life, with distrust, animosity, fear, and hostility between Arab Sunni and Shia communities rising to an alarming degree and resulting in some rearrangements of demography, especially in areas of mixed populations. Whether this trend takes firm root or gradually subsides will be an important factor in shaping the new Iraq.

The clearest indication of the nature of the new divisions in Iraq and its sharpening of communal identities was the series of elections held in 2005; two for representatives of the National Assembly and the third a referendum on the newly drafted constitution.[3] The first of these elections, in January 2005, produced two main winners. The first was the United Iraqi Alliance (UIA), an umbrella group of Shia candidates including several religio-political parties (the Supreme Council for the Islamic Revolution in Iraq [SCIRI], the Dawa, the Sadrist trend, Fadila, and a number of independents), which won a slight majority of seats. The second was a Kurdish list consisting of the two main Kurdish parties (the KDP and the PUK) and a smattering of others. The main losers were the more secular parties of the center, notably the Iraqi List, led by Ayad Allawi, a former Baathist opponent of Saddam. In this election, the Sunni population was virtually absent, either because Sunnis refused to vote or because they were intimidated.

The main task of the resulting assembly was to draft a constitution. Given the election results, the resulting document reflected a bargain between the two winning tickets—the Shia coalition and the Kurds. Drawn up under pressure of time, the document had numerous gaps and inconsistencies and on balance gave considerable weight to the aims and desires of the two main Kurdish parties and the UIA. Hence, the final document emphasized federalism and gave considerable powers to regions that could be formed under the constitution, leaving a weak central government. The constitution was then submitted to a referendum in October 2005. This time Arab Sunnis voted in large numbers, but almost entirely against the constitution; Kurdish and Shia areas voted in favor. The process further illustrated how Iraqi voters had become polarized around ethnic and sectarian identity.

Finally, the third election in December 2005 brought to power a permanent government installed in May and June of 2006. Essentially there were four main winners in this election. The same political alliances ran again with little change in their makeup. The Shia parties were grouped under the UIA; the Kurds united under the Kurdish Alliance, except for the Kurdish Islamic Union (KIU), which ran independently and won some seats. The centrists on the Iraqi List included moderate nationalists, communists, liberals, and secularists, both Sunni and Shia. The difference this time was that Sunnis ran. Their main vehicle was the Tawafuq (the Iraqi Consensus Front), which included the religiously oriented Iraqi Islamic Party (IIP) and other more secular Iraqi groups. Again, Iraqis overwhelmingly voted along ethnic and sectarian lines. The UIA won a plurality of the seats, the Kurdish Alliance came in second, and the Tawafuq came in third. The more secular centrists got even less of the vote this time, at 9 percent. A mainly Sunni secular list, the Hiwar (Dialogue), under an ex-Baathist, Salih al-Mutlaq, came in a weak fifth.

The subsequent national unity government that was formed included all of these groups except the Hiwar, in a complex formula designed to represent not only the winning parties but ethnic and sectarian communities as well. As Iraq's first permanent government, this cabinet is more inclusive of various sectors of Iraq's population and gives them a greater stake in the future, but it is so carefully balanced that no one group or its views can dominate, making future decisions difficult. Where does that leave Iraq and the political process?

Differing Visions of Iraq

These voting patterns, and the statements of political leaders, show that a common vision for Iraq has almost—but not quite—disappeared (polling of the population at large indicates a greater identification with Iraq than does the vote or discussions with leaders of parties, but if such identity exists on the ground, it is not politically organized and has not been able to significantly affect the political process).[4] Leaders with more moderate, centrist views have not been able to garner votes; rather, those who have won have done so mainly by playing to ethnic and sectarian identity to mobilize and organize a base.

But communal identity is not the only factor operating among political leaders; there are other dimensions to political dynamics, including, of course, an intense personal desire for power and its spoils. One is the divide between "insiders" and "outsiders."[5] The dominant leaders of almost all of the winning parties and groups have been outsiders—individuals who have long been in opposition to Saddam's regime and who have lived and operated outside of Iraq, often for decades. (Some have been in the West, others in Iran, still others in various Arab countries. This would include the Kurdish leaders as well who have operated in the north free of Saddam's control.) Insiders for the most part are only slowly making their way to the top. Muqtada al-Sadr and his followers are an exception and Sadr is not yet in a leadership position. Among these outsiders, it is opposition to the old order that has colored their views and visions for Iraq. The elite group that remained in Iraq was usually part of the Baath apparatus and shared its benefits and much of its outlook. It now finds itself out of power and resentful. Much of this group is Arab Sunni, as well as passive or active supporters of resistance to the new order. Some of these Sunnis are now part of the parliament and government but others are reluctant to participate. Ways will have to be found to integrate them into the new political order to achieve stability. This inclusion will necessitate winning over Shia and Kurdish coalitions whose suspicions of former leaders—and their possible return—are intense. These factors make de-Baathification a key issue.

Second is the militia factor.[6] As violence has increased, militias have played an ever greater role in the political equation. Political parties with strong militias have come to dominate the scene. They can provide order in territory they control, get out the vote on election day, and supply services, especially security, to their followers. This is clearest in the case of the Kurds, whose *peshmerga* now constitute the force that enables the KDP and the PUK to collectively control the Kurdish Regional Government (KRG). SCIRI derives strength in Baghdad and some provinces in the south from the Badr Brigade, said to number some thirty-five thousand. Many have been incorporated into the Ministry of Interior security forces, where they have been accused of sectarian attacks on Sunnis. Sadrists also have a militia of at least ten thousand—the Mahdi Army—with strength in Sadr City and some areas of the south. Fadila and its militia control much of Basra and the port facilities. Sunni parties and secularists have no militias, but there are questions about the ties of elected Sunni parties to the Sunni resistance movement, backed in part by former Iraqi army officers and by foreign resistance fighters. These provide the Sunni community with a measure of force as well.

The role of the insurgency is another factor. Ethnic and sectarian identity has now become intertwined with the insurgency and the reaction to it. Nested almost entirely in the ousted Sunni community, the insurgency—particularly the "resistance" of Arab Sunni communities and ex-Baathist leaders—reflects a collection of resentments, anxieties, and increasingly fears of gradual annihilation. Loss of jobs, income, and status by former army officers, civil servants, and others, has led to active support for or acquiescence in acts of violence against both US forces and the newly elected government considered responsible for their changing circumstances. Meanwhile, those who have spent years in opposition to that regime and the people in it view this resistance as a vicious and existential threat. The overlap of these fears and anxieties has spilled over into sectarian violence in mixed areas, like the city of Baghdad, where Sunni-Shia killing—and population displacement on a sectarian basis—is taking place for the first time in Iraq's modern history.

Both the insurgency and the accompanying sectarian violence are increasing the propensity for a breakdown of the state or, at the least, its reemergence in a new form. What direction Iraq will take depends largely on the new leadership emerging in Baghdad. In these circumstances, understanding the differing perspectives of the main actors in the political drama is critical. What do the new leaders want? What do they think about Iraq's most pressing political issues? How do they want to shape the future of Iraq?

The conclusions expressed here are based on an ongoing study of over 160 of Iraq's political leaders since 2003 (essentially those occupying the main positions in the central government). In addition to examining their backgrounds and factors that have shaped their outlook, the author has interviewed over sixty heads of parties, government ministers, and influential intellectuals. These interviews have been designed to probe five key issues driving Iraq's politics: (1) Where does the leadership's primary identity lie—with Iraq or with some other competing ethnic or sectarian community? (2) What does the leadership see as the most appropriate political structure for Iraq? What elements (federalism, elections, rule of law) are paramount? (3) What is the role of religion and the clergy in the state? (4) What is the attitude of the leadership toward the West and toward Iraq's various neighbors? and (5) What is the role and importance of economic development? In analyzing the results, the study puts emphasis on areas where overall patterns emerged, or do not emerge, where the differing priorities of the various groups lie, and where convergence is most likely.[7]

■ The Kurdish Alliance

Among the Kurdish leaders, the clearest pattern emerges. There is near unanimity among leaders (and much of the populace) in defining Kurdish identity as paramount. This is particularly true of a younger generation of leaders raised on textbooks that have taught Kurdish rather than Iraqi history and who know little or no Arabic. Among the older, more pragmatic generation of leaders, the sense of Kurdish identity is tempered by a realization that Kurds will be living in Iraq for the foreseeable future. But this identification with Iraq will be conditioned by the nature of the political system that emerges in Baghdad and how secure Kurds feel within it. If a stable, inclusive government with some commitment to human rights emerges in Baghdad, Kurds can be incorporated into Iraq up to a degree; if not, the desire for separatism will grow.

Not surprisingly, on the issue of Iraq's political structure, the concept of federalism dominates. The Kurdish definition of federalism is closer to confederation—a state structure agreed on by two equal groups (Arabs and Kurds)—than to federalism as it is usually defined. A peaceful, more secure Iraq and more democratic practices in Baghdad could change that equation, but for the most part, that is a distant vision. Kurdish leadership is currently focused on consolidating Kurdish rule in the three provinces it controls under the Kurdish Regional Government and extending that control to cities and towns—even provinces—considered to have a Kurdish majority. That includes the city of Kirkuk. Meanwhile, in the constitutional process and on the ground, Kurdish leadership is strengthening its independence from Baghdad, even while cooperating at the center.

Within the Kurdish region, however, there is considerable complexity and diversity of views. Minority ethnic and sectarian groups (mainly Turkmen, Christians, and Arabs) have mixed feelings about a state dominated by the two Kurdish parties. Competing political parties (especially Islamic parties) are uneasy over their monopoly of power. A younger generation of Kurds is dissatisfied with the absence of real democracy in the north, the iron grip of the two parties on their respective regions, and the limits on employment and economic opportunity in the current situation.

The current Kurdish leadership is the most secular component in the leadership spectrum and believes in a separation of mosque and state. Most of the current leaders view with dismay the intrusion of increasingly conservative religious norms emanating from the more extreme Islamic movements and from Iran, but they will guard against this by maintaining as much independence from Baghdad as possible. Islamic political groups in the north (such as the KIU) are relatively moderate; while committed to Islam and the *sharia*, they do not want to see clerics in power and believe the *sharia* should be one, but not the only, source of law.

The current Kurdish leadership is also the most pro-US, pro-Western political contingent in the country. Kurdish leaders of all kinds are open in their desire for a continued US presence in Iraq, but this is not without limits: Kurds would expect US support for inclusion of Kirkuk in their region through a legitimate vote, continuation of the *peshmerga* as Kurdistan's domestic and border security force, and a Kurdish role in Iraq's foreign policy apparatus.

The Kurds are skeptical of their neighbors, including Iran, with whom they have had considerable dealings. Attitudes toward Turkey, a traditional adversary, have shifted, with some hope that the European Union can modify Turkey's traditional hostility to Kurdish self-rule. Economic ties with Turkey have increased and Kurds are using this as a hedge against mishaps in Baghdad. Relations with the Arab world are seen as troubling because of Arab reluctance to accept the newly emerging order in Iraq, especially Kurdish aspirations and fear of a spillover of the insurgency from Arab Sunni areas.

■ The United Iraqi Alliance

The Shia alliance is diverse, and virtually all of its leading members are new to national politics. As a result, there is less unanimity in views than among the Kurdish leadership. Among the extreme elements in these parties, there are significant divisions. Indeed, it is not clear that the UIA can remain united as the voice of the Shia majority.

Among virtually all alliance leaders the primary identity is Iraqi, but their sense of nationalism and their support for the state, from which they suffered under Saddam Hussein, are weak. This also varies among the different parties. A strong Shia identity has emerged, not only from competition in elections but from the polarizing effects of an insurgency that has focused on killing Shia, especially those in government. But for the most part, until recently, a Shia identity has not been strong enough to pull them toward separatism.[8] Rather, as the majority within the Iraqi population, they have aspired to be the dominant voice in a unified state. Some (but by no means all) have been concerned over Kurdish separatism as a negative development, which should be curtailed. The strongest support for a unified Iraqi state among the UIA comes from the Sadrists, who are also insiders who have not left Iraq and have not had much foreign exposure. Second comes the Dawa, which has, since its inception in the late 1950s, been associated with an Iraqi national identity. However, SCIRI's leader, Abdul Aziz al-Hakim, has proposed creating a nine-province region in the south of Iraq, reaching from Baghdad to Basra, which would replicate the KRG. Not all within SCIRI favor this solution, but whatever the reasons behind the proposal, it clearly indicates that for many of SCIRI's leaders, a Shia identity has sharpened. It is significant in this context that SCIRI's top leadership has spent decades in Iran under a Shia religious theocracy, which has deepened Shia, rather than Iraqi, ties.[9]

The UIA leadership (and the Shia community as a whole) also has several competing orientations. Arabism and tribal ties have both played a role in shaping Shia identity, and, until recently, both have been strong (Shia participation in the Iran-Iraq War owed a great deal to both sentiments). However, that war and its antecedents produced the exile of tens of thousands of Iraqi Shia to Iran, where many have lived for decades, strengthening Shia ties to that country.[10] Such ties are seen as a liability by most other Iraqis; hence, they are often downplayed by the leadership. Sorting out these shifting and nebulous identities and finding a "center" for the Shia will be critical in the coming decade and it will play a considerable role in negotiations over the future of the Iraqi state.

On the question of Iraq's new political structure, the UIA does not yet have a cohesive view, but some strands of thought continually surface. Most important is the view that Shia form a clear majority within the Iraqi state (55–60 percent) and hence should dominate the government. UIA leaders strongly favor the electoral process, which has given them the lion's share of power. (This presumes that votes can continue to be mobilized along communal lines, rather than some other platform.) The UIA also favors a parliamentary system with power reposing in a prime minister, who would be a Shia, and the cabinet he selects. What this will mean in terms of policy or the political and economic direction Iraq should take has not been spelled out yet.

These views pose a conundrum for the Shia as the dominant group in power. Most Shia leaders—as opponents of the former Baath regime—do not want to revive a strong central government, or its military arm, but they find themselves in the midst of a virulent and brutal insurgency, directed largely against themselves and the government they dominate. Will a weak central government without adequate national forces be able to control Iraq's borders, fight insurgents, and provide the law and order most of Iraq's citizens want? A reemployment of some of Iraq's former army would allay Sunni fears and help solve the security problem, but such a solution also rouses intense fears by the new and as yet fragile Shia alliance that its hold on power could be short-lived. Hence, de-Baathification is one of the most contentious issues facing the new Shia leadership.

With respect to the role of religion, the Shia leaders are much clearer. They tend to emphasize Iraq's Islamic identity. How this would be defined and whether they could make common cause on this issue with Sunni Islamists is not yet clear, but it is possible. One key issue here is the role of *sharia* law in shaping policy and as a basis for law in the state. Both religious Shia and Sunnis espouse more *sharia* law in governance than was previously the case.

More divisive is the role that clergy should play in the polity. UIA leaders run a gamut on this question. Some say that religious leaders should play a role in times of crisis (such as the present) but otherwise stay out of the political arena. Others may harbor desires for a clerical role closer to the

Iranian model, although they would avoid calling it *wilayat al-faqih*, given widespread opposition to this proposition outside the Shia community and even within it. But most of the UIA leadership claims that religious leadership (the *hawza*) has a rightful role to play in leading "society," and they favor Ayatollah Sistani's quietist political role behind the scenes. This position runs counter to Sunni religious views and is even more opposed by secularists.

On the issue of relations with the West—and especially the occupation—the UIA leadership has thus far shown considerable pragmatism. None are pleased with occupation, or the way in which it has been carried out, nor do they want a permanent presence, but they do recognize the need for help in maintaining power until they are able to stand on their own feet. Sadrists have been an exception: removal of occupation has been a key plank in their platform, and their militia has fought twice in 2004 to end the occupation. However, Sadr has now been brought into the political system to some extent and has some stake in its continuance, which may moderate his behavior.

With respect to Iraq's neighbors, the Alliance has evinced hostility and suspicion toward many of Iraq's Arab Sunni neighbors—primarily Syria and Jordan to the West, and Saudi Arabia to the south. These countries are seen as sources of funds and recruits for the Sunni-based insurgency. There is much more ambiguity toward Iran and varying degrees of affiliation. The closest ties are those of SCIRI, which is a creation of Iran (in 1982), and the Badr Organization (formerly the Badr Brigade), trained and officered by Iran. The Iranian connections and orientation of the various Shia components of the UIA, and its leadership as a whole, is one of the most contentious issues in Iraq today. The ties—and the balance Iraq must maintain between Iran and the United States—may also become increasingly difficult to manage as US-Iranian relations become more contentious over nuclear and other issues, which could make Iraq a battleground.

■ Arab Sunni Leadership

The political leadership of the Arab Sunni community runs a gamut from those willing to participate in the new political order to complete rejectionists, still fighting the occupation and the newly elected government (foreign fighters and jihadists loyal to non-Iraqi organizations such as Al-Qaida are not considered here). Iraqi insurgents, whether Islamist, ex-Baathist, or simply nationalist, need to be brought into the system if violence is to be reduced. This process has begun, with the election of Tawafuq and Hiwar members to the Council of Representatives, and the inclusion of Tawafuq adherents in the cabinet in 2006. However, the extent to which these groups represent those still fighting, much less the larger Arab Sunni community, is not clear, though they are now the ones who will negotiate for that community within the new order.

In terms of identity, the Arab Sunnis are the most nationalist community in the spectrum. Leaders of the Tawafuq and Hiwar parties favor a united Iraq and may find it difficult to accommodate a large measure of Kurdish separatism. They are opposed to a separate Shia region in the south, which they feel will divide Iraq. While they have a strong identification with the Iraqi state, many also have a strong secondary Arab identity and look to Sunnis in neighboring Arab states for support. Although many reject a sectarian identity, under pressure of events (the insurgency, a new Shia-led government, the reduction of Arab Sunnis to minority status, and retaliatory attacks on Sunnis by Shia militias), Sunni identity has become stronger.

Arab Sunni parties, as well as a number of nationalist Shia, want a strong central government and are opposed to the degree of decentralization laid out in the constitution, although some are willing to consider administrative decentralization and the Kurds as a special case. Instead of elections, they emphasize the rule of law, the return of order, and a government based on competence. As many in this group constitute the former professional and technocratic class, this would benefit them. Not surprisingly, they oppose the de-Baathification program.

On the issue of religion and the state, the Arab Sunni leaders vary. Some, particularly in the IIP, and of course the Muslim Scholars' Association (AMS), which is not in power, favor more of a role for the *sharia* in the state and may well agree with some Shia on this. Yet in general, Sunni religious groups and parties do not favor clerical control of the political system. In particular, they fear the role exercised by the Shia *marja'iyya*. Many of the new Arab Sunni leaders are secular, especially the ex-Baathists and professionals, and are opposed to any role for *sharia* law in the state.

In the end, the key issue for the Arab Sunnis and nationalists who are just reentering the political process is the occupation and Western political domination in Iraq, which they reject, although their need for protection from Shia death squads has softened their position slightly. Ultimate withdrawal of foreign forces from Iraq and independence from foreign control is what these otherwise disparate groups want. The same is true of the foreign orientation of the Arab Sunnis. They clearly look to a variety of Arab Sunni countries—the religiously oriented to Saudi Arabia and the Gulf; the secularists to Syria and Jordan—for support in terms of moral, financial, and, for those still fighting, military assistance. Above all, they share with their fellow Arab neighbors an intense suspicion of Iran and the ties of the new Shia parties to the Iranian regime. Indeed, many see the old frontier with Iran disappearing.

▪ Centrists

What about the centrists, the putative "moderate middle," most of whom ran on the Iraqi List but ended up getting less than 10 percent of the vote in December 2005? As their name implies, they have a clear sense of Iraqi identity and make a point of rejecting sectarianism. Although these centrists would accept federalism and a reasonable degree of autonomy for the Kurds, they stop well short of any dismemberment of Iraq. On the issue of government structure, they come closest to the old Baathist formula of a centralized (but more benevolent) state. On the issue of religion, this group is secular and wants a clear separation of religion and politics, as well as freedom to reject Islamic strictures, such as dress codes. On foreign policy, the secular centrists (most of them educated in the West) are relatively tolerant of the occupation as long as necessary. Like their counterparts in the Arab Sunni community, they tend to be suspicious of Iran and Iranian influence in Iraq and are more favorably disposed toward other Arab countries, but this would stop well short of tolerating any support for rebels.

While the views of the centrist leaders on the Iraqi List are probably the most compatible with overall US and Western goals in Iraq, the problem is that they have too little support to play much of a role in the political dynamics of the future because of their increasingly poor showing in elections. They now have a few seats in the cabinet but their role, at best, will be modest.

Surprisingly, none of the leaders in power have yet put much emphasis on economics. Economic development does not appear to be of paramount concern among the Shia, the new Arab Sunni tickets, or even the centrists. The Kurds are an exception because they have security and are interested in building the sinews of a self-reliant entity. While all of these parties give lip service to the necessity of economic development and jobs, few put it at the top of their list of priorities. Nor do they appear to have given much thought to the direction the economy should take. This may well be because other issues—politics (getting and maintaining power), crafting a constitution (the nature of the state), and identity and religion—have crowded out concern for economics or because many feel economics equates to oil. At local levels, however, in provincial and municipal councils and on the "street," leaders—and the populace—appear to put much more emphasis on economics and the need to get the economy moving.[11] This indicates a disconnection between political leadership at the national level and their constituents, which will need to be adjusted if stability is to be achieved. It also demonstrates the primacy of politics in the new Iraq, one outcome of a focus on elections, a redistribution of power, and establishing a new constitutional order.

■ Conclusion

What, if any, convergences can be found in these positions? The problem for the new Iraqi leadership is that crosscutting issues and values between and among Iraq's new political leaders are not strong. The new Iraqi leadership will have to work hard to find a new vision around which most Iraqis can willingly coalesce and cooperate. Yet the concept of a single Iraqi state that finds room for the expression of Iraq's diversity, without definitively dividing the country into separate territorial units, still appears to have the best chance of success and to be the least costly. Most Iraqis do not want a breakup or a breakdown of the state or the disorder that will go with it. Although a new vision could be centered on a more democratic culture and institutions, this will take time to develop. In the meantime, Iraqis need to step back from the politics of "identity," which is driving much of the process and producing much of the violence. Instead, leaders should be encouraged to concentrate on interests and goals, where all communities could gain by cooperating. Economic development, for example, not currently a focus of most leaders, needs to be raised to a higher priority. Oil legislation, which encourages a shared development of Iraq's main resources, as well as the equitable distribution of its revenues, is a prime example of how such mutual interests could be encouraged.

Secularism is a crosscutting issue but it can also be divisive and is further weakening at present. Many middle-class Iraqis, whether Shia, Kurd, or Sunni, want room for secularism and some separation of mosque and state. But secularism runs counter to the dominant trend in the winning Shia coalition, the UIA, and goes against growing Islamist sentiment among the Sunnis, especially those in the IIP. While the boundaries between religious and secular space will continue to be a subject of debate, and undoubtedly shift over time, the problem lies less with political leaders, who are generally willing to compromise, than with the "street," where militias and more radical Islamist elements enforce their own standards. What is needed are stronger human rights standards and stronger enforcement of the law at local levels.

On the issue of the new state structure, there is little cohesion as yet. Although a constitution is in place, at least one major group, the Arab Sunnis, want it substantially modified or have rejected it. The constitutional document that has been ratified leaves many issues to be resolved, most importantly that of federalism and the powers of the central government. Some leaders among Arab Sunnis, centrists, and much of the professional class want a stronger central government. However, decentralization is a fact of life in current Iraq, torn by strife, and is desired by several powerful groups in power (the Kurdish Alliance and SCIRI). The relatively successful model of the KRG has exercised a pull on other regions, such as Basra, to emulate the model. The question is whether establishing new regions can be accomplished without splitting Iraq along ethnic and even sectarian lines, given the strong trend in favor of communal identity. This could be avoided if decentralization could be organized along different lines, which recognized regional and local differences and strengthened local government. At all levels, governance needs to be restored.

This raises the inevitable question of the capacity of the central government. If a stronger, more effective government is needed, how is it to be achieved under the current unstable conditions? Thus far, the emphasis has been placed on bringing disparate groups into power with a view toward giving them a stake in the future, and thus reducing violence, especially that of the insurgency. But the slow process of building a consensus may come at the cost of cohesion and decisiveness. The time spent on accommodating different groups will make decisions and agreement on direction difficult and may delay delivery of services and economic development. But in the end, the most important contributor toward stability will be to limit the insurgency, putting a floor under the slide toward ethnic and sectarian identity and violence. This is a race against time. The negotiations that must ensue to allow new political leaders to agree on compromises will take time and require patience. If they are successful, they will produce a greater degree of cohesion among the new stakeholders, a sense of direction. But in the meantime, lack of government and the accompanying instability is resulting in Iraq "breaking down"—not into cohesive territorial units based on ethnic and sectarian identities but into fiefdoms controlled by militias, political parties, and shadowy local figures.

There are few good options in Iraq. The main task of the United States and the international community must be to encourage the process of compromise and the construction of a new consensus based on interests, not identity. In the end, however, reconciling differences is essentially a task for the Iraqis. It will be difficult and time-consuming and they will need help—and patience—from outside. Security and economic development are the missing links. A gradual return of these two elements will ease, if not solve, the identity problem. The international effort must go into restoring effective government in Iraq faster than the insurgency—and now ethnic and sectarian violence—can tear it down. Otherwise, Iraq will become a truly failed state.

It is unlikely that the trends outlined here can be soon reversed although prospects over a decade or more may be better. The costs of the Iraqi venture have already been high, but the costs of failure are sufficiently dire to focus minds on preventing them and encouraging the long-term effort that will be required.

■ **Notes**

1. Finding new leaders was always going to be one of the most difficult tasks, given Saddam's tight control of the state. See Phebe Marr, "Iraq 'the Day After,'" *Naval War College Review* 61, no. 1 (winter 2003): 13–29.

2. For an English translation of the latest draft of the constitution, see

www.usip.org/ruleoflaw/projects/unami_iraq_constitution.pdf. For analysis of the constitution, see Jonathan Morrow, "Iraq's Constitutional Process II: An Opportunity Lost," *USIP Special Report* 155 (November 2005); Jonathan Morrow, "Weak Viability: The Iraqi Federal State and the Constitutional Amendment Process," *USIP Special Report* 186 (July 2006); and Nathan Brown, "The Final Draft of the Iraqi Constitution: Analysis and Commentary," *Carnegie Endowment for International Peace*, 16 September 2005, www.carnegieendowment.org/files/FinalDraftSept16.pdf.

3. See Adeed Dawisha and Larry Diamond, "Iraq's Year of Voting Dangerously," *Journal of Democracy* 17, no. 2 (2006): 89–103.

4. In an April 20, 2005, poll by the International Republican Institute, over 50 percent of Arab Iraqis identified most strongly with their country, while only 20 percent and 12 percent most strongly identified with their religion and ethnic group, respectively. In the same poll, only 28 percent of the Kurdish respondents identified most strongly with their country, while 37 percent most strongly identified with their ethnic group. However, in an October 2004 poll by the State Department Office of Research, over 50 percent of Kurds identified as either equally Iraqi and Kurdish or primarily Iraqi and then Kurdish.

5. Reidar Visser, "The Maliki Government—What It Could Mean to Southern Iraq," 23 May 2006, www.historiae.org/Maliki-Government.

6. For a detailed, in-depth report on Iraq's militias, see Dexter Filkins, "Armed Groups Propel Iraq Toward Chaos," *New York Times,* 23 May 2006.

7. Much of the following is drawn from Phebe Marr, "Who Are Iraq's New Leaders? What Do They Want?" *USIP Special Report* 160 (March 2006).

8. A very good article by Reidar Visser, "Centralism and Unitary State Logic in Iraq from Midhat Pasha to Jawad al-Maliki: A Continuous Trend?" available at www.historiae.org/maliki.asp, documents the long history, strength, and persistence of Iraqi identity among Iraqi Shia.

9. For instance, Abdul Aziz al-Hakim, Bayan Jabr, Humam Hammoudi, Adil Abdul Mahdi, and Hadi al-Amiri have all spent at least a decade in Iran.

10. Estimates of the number of Iraqis returning from Iran range between 250,000 and 500,000, and the Badr Brigade, which was organized and trained in Iran, numbers between 30,000 and 40,000.

11. Polling data from the International Republican Institute and the State Department Office of Research indicate that Iraqis consistently rate the economy as either the number one issue or second only to security. For an archive of IRI opinion polling in Iraq, see the Brookings Institution's *Iraq Index* at www.brookings.edu/iraqindex.

4

Three Wars Later . . . Iraqi Living Conditions

Jon Pedersen

IT IS TEMPTING to ascribe the socioeconomic situation of present-day Iraq solely to the sanctions period, invasion, subsequent occupation, and insurgency. Nevertheless, these events are just recent chapters in Iraq's turbulent modern history, which has taken a particularly brutal turn since 1980. Moreover, the response of the regime to the turbulence, and also the response of the international community, has been to create a state that relied on buying political support and quelling unrest through direct transfers and subsidies paying for the basic livelihood of the population. Such a state is inherently unstable, because it rests on its ability to continue paying for the loyalty of the population.

This chapter sets out by considering Iraq's destitution caused by its recent history, particularly in the fields of infrastructure, health, and education. It then discusses the overall distribution of living conditions, in light of the mitigation policies that successive governments of Iraq, as well as the international community, have pursued. The main body of data drawn upon is the 2004 Iraq Living Conditions Survey.[1] The interpretation of the data leads to the conclusion that conflicts and mitigation efforts in Iraq have resulted in a social and economic organization that allocates resources and welfare in quite different ways than occurs within a nonconflict society. To create a viable economy and social structure major restructuring is needed, a restructuring that is likely to generate new conflicts.

It is clear that the economic and social effects of occupations are far from uniform. In particular, the occupant's management of the economy of the occupied country varies considerably. Thus, the German occupation of France during World War II served as a way for the Germans to exploit the resources of France.[2] The resource extraction and the war itself had several effects. Among the more obvious ones were that some sectors of the economy were hit hard, such as the tourism sector. Moreover, an underground economy and racketeering also developed, partly in order to keep resources away from the Germans. However, in general, the economic infrastructure was not destroyed, because the Germans needed it. In contrast, in Shanghai, during the Japanese occupation, the Japanese did not initially pursue a systematic economic policy.[3] Economic life was seriously disturbed, in part because productive equipment could not be moved, but foreign concessions continued to operate, and in fact economic exchange proceeded with nonoccupied China. Then, in 1943, a badly managed command economy was introduced with the purpose of supporting the Japanese war effort, and the economy promptly collapsed. Yet another contrast is with the Japanese occupation of Malaya, where deliberate, and successful, attempts were made to have a consistent economic policy geared toward serving the Japanese empire.[4]

In a review of US peacebuilding efforts, a RAND Corporation team illustrates the diversity and variability of occupation situations and postconflict reconstruction that US forces have been involved in.[5] Common denominators are few, and the lessons learned fairly general. Thus, the level of effort in time and resources is deemed important, as are unity of command and broad participation; a large stabilizing force is better than a small one; accountability for past injustices is considered important, as is the constructive involvement of neighboring states. The RAND study focuses on the organization of occupation and political process. In contrast, the argument in this chapter rests on a consideration of the social and economic organization left by the conflict.

▪ Decades of Decline, Destitution, and Subsidies

From 1980 to 1988, the Iran-Iraq War inflicted enormous human and material costs. Three years later, subsequent to the Iraqi invasion of Kuwait, the Gulf War erupted and nearly destroyed Iraq's electricity-generating capacity. The knock-on effects for water treatment plants and telecommunications were severe. UN sanctions followed. By the time of the US-led invasion of March 2003, Iraq had been under a sanctions regime for more than a decade, with predictably severe consequences for the import of goods to service the country's war-damaged and failing economy and infrastructure. In addition, the Hussein government waged a war against the Kurds in the three northern governorates. While keeping a tight rein on the other governorates, it crushed the uprising in the south after the Gulf War.

The UN oil-for-food program, and later the public distribution system, supplied food rations to more than 90 percent of the Iraqi population. In November 2003, the monthly value of the food rations was about US$23, corresponding to about forty-six hours of work at the average wage in Iraq.[6] In addition, the Saddam Hussein government instituted a far-reaching subsidy program, including fuels, electricity, utilities, and agricultural inputs.

For example, regular gasoline had, in 2005 (and also in the years before), a price of about 1 US cent (20 Iraqi dinars) per liter. The various subsidies currently make up about 56 to 67 percent of gross domestic product (GDP).[7]

The shocks to which Iraq and its people have been exposed have had dramatic consequences for virtually every aspect of life in Iraq. In 1990, between the end of the war with Iran and the beginning of the Gulf War, Iraq had the second highest development score among its neighbors in the Middle East, behind only the United Arab Emirates (Table 4.1). Since then, its score has declined—in sharp contrast to every other Middle Eastern country, whose scores have all improved. In 2000, Iraq was in the second-worst position, developmentally speaking, scoring just above Yemen—a sobering development for the country that had the fastest increase in literacy in the world between 1970 and 1985.[8]

A similar trend is evident in the indicators associated with the Millennium Development Goals (MDG). In a review of achievements toward realizing the MDG, the UN Development Programme found that Iraq had regressed on most indicators—again in contrast to most other countries.[9] Iraq is probably the only middle-income country in recent history to have experienced a decline in GDP for twenty-five years.

Table 4.1   Human Development Index Ranking of Countries in the Middle East, 1975–2002

Country	1975	1980	1985	1990	1995	2000	2002
Egypt	0.438	0.487	0.539	0.577	0.608	—	0.653
Iraq	—	—	—	0.759[a]	0.617[b]	0.567[c]	—
Jordan	—	0.639	0.663	0.682	0.707	0.741	0.750
Kuwait	0.761	0.776	0.778	—	0.810	0.834	0.838
Lebanon	—	—	—	0.673	0.732	0.752	0.758
Oman	0.493	0.546	0.640	0.696	0.733	0.761	0.770
Palestine	—	—	—	—	—	—	0.726
Qatar	—	—	—	—	—	—	0.833
Saudi Arabia	0.602	0.656	0.671	0.707	0.741	0.764	0.768
Syrian Arab Republic	0.534	0.576	0.611	0.635	0.663	0.683	0.710
United Arab Emirates	0.744	0.777	0.785	0.805	0.803	—	0.824
Yemen	—	—	—	0.392	0.435	0.469	0.482
Turkey	0.590	0.614	0.651	0.683	0.713	—	0.751
Iran	0.565	0.569	0.610	0.649	0.693	0.723	0.732

Sources: All except Iraq: UNDP, *Human Development Report 2004* (New York: UNDP, 2004).
  a. UNDP, *Human Development Report 1990* (New York: UNDP, 1990) .
  b. UNDP, *Human Development Report 1995* (New York: UNDP, 1995).
  c. UNDP, *Human Development Report 2001* (New York: UNDP, 2001). Figure for 1999.
More recent calculation of the HDI is not available for Iraq.

The impression given by the macro-level comparisons above is reflected in the responses of Iraqi households as evidenced by the Iraq Living Conditions Survey carried out in April and May 2004. People were struggling economically: in response to a survey question asking whether the respondent household could raise about US$70 (100,000 Iraqi dinars) should a vital need arise, as many as 28 percent of households said no. Furthermore, household economic problems had been long-standing: asked when their economic difficulties started, 49 percent replied before the UN sanctions started, 42 percent said after the sanctions started, and 6 percent indicated that it was after the last war. Regional variations, in terms of both the percentage of households reporting difficulties and the difficulties' origins, reflected the overall narrative of the past two and a half decades (Figure 4.1). For example, the northern governorates of Suleimaniyeh and Erbil, long-standing targets of the Hussein regime, had a high percentage of households unable to raise US$70, and most of the difficulties started before the sanctions.

■ Infrastructure

The cumulative devastation of infrastructure in Iraq was nearly complete at the end of the 2003 invasion. While houses were indeed connected to electricity lines, piped water, and in many cases, to sewage systems, the infrastructure did not work. Electricity is a particularly telling example. Up to 97 percent of households were connected to the electricity network in 2004, but only 15 percent actually had a stable electricity supply from the network.

The effect of insufficient electricity supply is illustrative of a more general point, namely how adaptations to crisis themselves are costly. Because generating capacity was below demand and the distribution system was run down, 8 percent of households invested in generators. An additional 23 percent of households invested in generators together with their neighbors. Thus, meager funds were used to buy equipment that would be superfluous the day supply is regularized. Furthermore, although the running costs of generators are not currently excessive due to artificially low prices for fuel—in 2004 Iraqis paid about half a US cent for a liter of diesel—any reform in the subsidy system would strongly impact the ability of households to use their generators. In any event, the private solution to widespread power shortages is an archetypal example of how failure in overall governance creates costs for citizens.

Sanitation is another area where Iraq suffers. In urban areas, 53 percent of households were not connected to a sewage system, and among those that were, 43 percent experienced frequent problems with the functioning of the

Figure 4.1 Inability to Raise 100,000 Iraqi Dinars and Period When Difficulties Started

Percentage Unable to Raise 100,000 Dinars

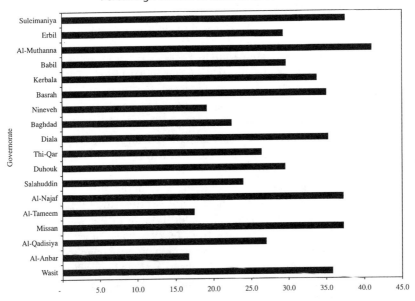

Period When Difficulties Started

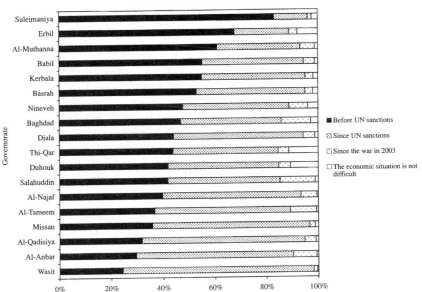

system, while 11 percent of those connected always had problems. The reasons for improper functioning or lack of connection are both lack of maintenance and bombing. During the fieldwork of the Iraq Living Conditions Survey in 2004, interviewers were asked to record, for each household, if sewage was visible outside the respective dwelling. In urban areas, interviewers indicated that sewage was present outside 40 percent of households surveyed.

Only 54 percent of the population had safe and stable drinking water in 2004; 29 percent had safe but unstable water and 17 percent had unsafe drinking water. The regional variations were large: in Basra governorate, only 11 percent of households had safe and stable water. As was the case with electricity, lack of safe and stable water incurs costs in terms of securing an alternative supply. Such costs include fetching water from a more distant water source, waiting for a tanker truck to come, or health costs in using a substandard water supply.

A particular adaptation to low water pressure in the piped water is the practice of mounting pumps on the household intake for water. Unfortunately, such pumps create an underpressure in the water mains, thereby increasing inflow of sewage from leaky sewage pipes. Inflow of sewage into water mains is a common problem in cities in many parts of the world, but the combination of a lack of upkeep, war, and household adaptation gives the problem a particular twist. Significantly, while the frequency of diarrhea among children usually is negatively correlated with the presence of piped water in the household, the inverse is the case in Iraq: parents of children living in households with water piped to the dwelling reported somewhat more diarrhea than the parents of other children.

■ Human Resources

Despite the devastation in infrastructure, the greatest toll of the war years on Iraq may be in human resources, that is, in the health and education of its population. Iraq has a young population, of which approximately 39 percent are fifteen years of age and younger. As in other populations with such a structure, Iraq's youthfulness is primarily caused by a high fertility rate, rather than the early deaths of adults. A corollary of the high fertility rate has been a high growth rate, which has generally been around 3 percent per year for the last fifty years. Thus, the population has more than quadrupled in size since 1950. Fertility is currently decreasing, from a total fertility rate of approximately six children per woman in 1990 to around four now. Thus, regardless of the fact that Iraq has witnessed a socioeconomic development rather different from that of surrounding countries, the fertility decline has been broadly similar.

Infant mortality is a good measure of the health of children. The measure also serves as a proxy for the overall health of the population. Infant mortality declined until 1991, but after 1991 the Iraq Living Conditions Survey and previous surveys diverge in their findings. While previous surveys found that infant mortality jumped to an extremely high level (about 100 deaths per 1,000), the Iraq Living Conditions Survey found that there had been a steady increase over the last fifteen years. Regardless of the exact pattern and eventual extent of the change in infant mortality, it is beyond dispute that there has been an increase. Again, this is atypical of the Middle East in general, where rates have generally been declining quite rapidly, or have remained roughly stable, as in the West Bank and Gaza Strip.

A corollary to the increasing infant mortality rate is the health status of children. An important finding of the Iraq Living Conditions Survey is that acute malnutrition is significant in Iraq. A national level of 7.5 percent, similar to that of Burundi, is unacceptable.[10] In some of the southern governorates, such as Al-Muthanna, the level is even more elevated. Sadly, malnutrition in Iraq is nothing new, as evidenced by the figures on stunting (chronic malnutrition): 23 percent of children aged six months to five years have suffered malnutrition. Another survey, carried out by the World Food Programme, finds a lower level of acute malnutrition at 4.4 percent.[11] Again, regardless of the exact level, all the evidence points to the fact that there is significant malnutrition in Iraq.

Diarrhea is also widespread among children, with 9 percent of children suffering from it during the two weeks preceding the interview. Considering the scale of this problem, it is extremely worrying that the treatment of diarrhea is inadequate: only 37 percent of children with diarrhea received oral rehydration therapy—the treatment of choice—while as many as 68 percent received antibiotics, a treatment that is only indicated in a few cases and is generally ineffective and potentially harmful. These results are reason for concern on their own. In addition, they point to a health system that has not managed to implement recommended treatment procedures in a widespread and systematic way.

Reproductive health is an area in which the statistics look quite good from one perspective, yet much worse from another. For example, birth attendance by a doctor, nurse, or midwife is high (96 percent of births). However, a midwife in Iraq is not necessarily trained to the standard that one would expect from a "skilled birth attendant," and, when one considers that in rural areas nearly half of the births take place at home—and half of these again in places that an ambulance cannot reach—the picture appears even bleaker. Thus, what looks like a surprisingly good situation on the surface looks somewhat less rosy when examined more thoroughly. Another important finding is that, as is common in the Middle East, women receive health checks during pregnancy, but nearly 60 percent do not receive care after delivery of their child.

Furthermore, the number of health centers now stands at half the 1990 level (of approximately 1,800). From the data, it is difficult to evaluate whether Iraqis are sick more frequently than people of other countries. Instead, the data are more likely to indicate overall patterns of health in the population, such as that—unsurprisingly—the prevalence of disease increases with age. However, in contrast to what is often found, health problems are not strongly dependent on income or social status.

The education system has also been hit hard by the developments in the last thirty years. The overall picture is that Iraq has been unable to improve its in-country stock of educational skills during the last three decades. The percentage of people that have never attended school is constant, at about 10 percent, for people within the age group fifteen to thirty-five. The total percentage of those who either never attended or have incomplete primary education is also constant, comprising roughly 30 percent of that age group. Looking at education beyond the secondary level, the highest percentage of this level of attainment is found among those aged thirty-five to forty-four years. These figures are partly due to decreases (or lack of increase) in enrollment, and partly to emigration of educated people.

The situation of women over time in Iraq follows the arc described above—initial progress, then stagnation or reversal. During the 1970s and early 1980s, the Baath Party emphasized the emancipation of women. This emphasis led to the introduction of a number of progressive laws, a concerted effort to eradicate illiteracy (also among women), and increased female enrollment in school. However, in recent years, the positive trends have flattened out and, in some cases, reversed. Particularly telling is the fact that literacy rates for women aged fifteen to twenty-four years are about the same as those aged twenty-five to thirty-four. Scant comfort is derived from the fact that for men, the situation is even worse: men aged fifteen to twenty-four have a lower literacy rate than their twenty-five-to-thirty-four-year-old counterparts. Men in all age groups have a higher literacy rate than women in the same age categories.

■ The Distribution of Living Conditions

The findings discussed above each contribute to a larger picture of conditions in Iraq. Seen together, they also underline a major premise of the study of living conditions, namely that the living conditions of an individual and household are multifaceted and interdependent. Thus, no single measure can easily summarize all aspects of how households or individuals live.

When a household (or individual) is well off on one indicator but poorly off on another, it becomes difficult to decide which criteria to use in determining how households fare comparatively. For example, better-than-average access to public services, housing, and infrastructure may very well be combined with low income, even though low-income households are more likely than high-income households to have poor housing conditions. When living conditions factors combine in such a way, it becomes necessary to weigh the different aspects against each other to find an overall measure. That weighing is necessarily arbitrary: for example, is crowding a worse problem than humidity within the house? In light of this dilemma, a valuable alternative exercise is to examine how various aspects of living conditions go together.

There are three different ways that living conditions may logically be ordered. First, they may be clustered: good things or bad things go together. A typical example of positive "heaping" is a highly educated person who is also employed, earning a high salary, living in a good neighborhood, and sending his or her children to a good school. Contrast this with the not uncommon plight of rural women in Iraq, who give birth to children at home, with no qualified assistance, and in a location without access to an ambulance—a classic case of negative heaping. Second, living conditions factors may be compensatory. In such a case, a household that is badly off on one indicator may make up for it by scoring well on another. A relevant example here is that although many Iraqis have little income, they are compensated by the food distribution system and the extremely high subsidies on power and water. Thus, generally speaking, we do not see very large socioeconomic differences when it comes to access to basic infrastructure. Third, the factors that constitute living conditions may simply be randomly organized. In such cases, one cannot predict from knowledge of one factor what the levels for others will be.

One way to depict how living conditions are ordered is through multivariate techniques. Figure 4.2 is a spatial representation of the first dimension of a so-called categorical principal components analysis of a set of variables describing the quality of life at the household level.[12] The result is relatively easy to interpret: on the map, darker areas have worse conditions than lighter ones. This indicates that, overall, conditions are best in the Baghdad area and in Suleimaniyeh and worst in parts of Niniveh. Otherwise, good and bad areas are patchily distributed.

A second aspect of the distribution of the living conditions in Iraq is that, apart from the geographical patchiness and inequalities, heaping of living conditions is not very pronounced. Thus, for example, while having a connection to the sewage system is to some degree associated with income, the association is not very strong. The same is the case for a number of other indicators, such as malnutrition, treatment of diarrhea, literacy, and others (Table 4.2).

The lack of heaping—that is, the geographic patchiness and the weak

Figure 4.2 Spatial Representation of Quality of Life at the Household Level

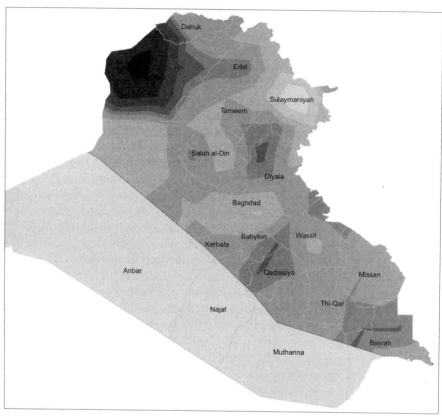

Darker areas mean worse conditions. Because few people live in the west of Iraq, estimates for that part of the country are not shown.

association between income and other aspects of living conditions—does not imply that Iraq is without differentiation. Far from it, income inequality is similar to that of other Arab countries. The 2004 Iraq Living Conditions Survey found a Gini coefficient of 0.35 for 2003 and 0.42 for the two-week period prior to the interview in 2004.[13] Despite the differences, households have not been able to retain advantages. Thus, the 2004 survey indicates that there is surprisingly little correlation between the income of a household in 2002 and that of 2003 to that of the two weeks prior to interview in 2004.

While the lack of heaping may be seen as a benefit, the observations just made also indicate a more dysfunctional side, namely that income is not easily or systematically converted to welfare in a tangible sense.

Table 4.2   Association Between Total Income Per Capita in 2003 and Selected Indicators (percentage within income quintiles)

	Income Quintile					
Indicator	Lowest	Low	Middle	High	Highest	Total
Gender of household head	89	89	89	90	87	89
Children with both parents alive	95	96	96	97	97	96
Connection to sewage system	31	35	35	38	42	37
Safe and stable drinking water	54	58	61	63	68	61
Acute malnutrition (age 6–59 months)	7	9	7	8	7	8
Treatment of diarrhea with oral rehydration salt	35	36	39	40	45	37
Literacy (population, age 15+)	47	51	56	60	67	65
Net enrollment in primary school	74	79	81	82	82	79

■ **Bad but Improving?**

In late December 2004, the Central Organization for Statistics and Information Technology of Iraq (COSIT) and the Fafo Institute carried out an opinion poll in Iraq, to throw light on how the population perceived their current situation. The results of this poll, and many others, are somewhat surprising, in that 62 percent of Iraqis answered "much better" (22 percent) or "somewhat better" (40 percent) to the question, "Compared to the last three years, are things overall in your life much better now, somewhat better, about the same, somewhat worse, or much worse?" Thus, people consider that there has been an improvement. More interesting, perhaps, than the overall figures are the distributions of the answers by region in Iraq. While people in the north (the Kurdish areas) and in the south (the Shia-dominated areas) answer predominantly that their life has improved, the population in Baghdad and especially in the governorates surrounding Baghdad considers the improvement to have been smaller (Table 4.3). Nevertheless, even people living in areas usually considered to be the core of the insurgency believe their life has improved. An ABC News poll carried out in November 2005 indicated that 10 percent fewer people answered that life had improved, but with 52 percent still considering that their life had improved and 19 percent believing that it had remained the same, the evaluation is still surprisingly positive.

From the above findings, two conclusions might be drawn: First, there is little correlation between where people consider their living conditions to be improved and the overall level of those conditions as revealed by more objective indicators. Second, to a certain extent, there is an association between areas of current conflict and perceived improvement, but there is a relatively weak association between conflict and living conditions.

Table 4.3   Perception of Improvement in Life by Region (percentage)

Question: Compared to the last three years are things overall in your life much better now, somewhat better, about the same, somewhat worse, or much worse?

			Region		
Answer	South	Baghdad	Center	North	Total
Much better	36	14	6	32	22
Somewhat better	41	38	38	46	40
About the same	16	32	22	15	22
Somewhat worse	5	12	22	7	12
Much worse	1	3	12	0	4
Don't know/No answer	0	1	0	0	0
Total	100	100	100	100	100

A probable reason for this finding is that, at least up to the last year of insurgency, people experienced considerably more security while, at the same time, economic conditions did not worsen. For some groups, conditions improved considerably. Wages for public employees, for example, were raised substantially in the fall of 2003.[14]

In most societies, one of the most significant arenas of distribution of benefits and welfare is the labor market. The Iraqi labor market shows several peculiarities. The level of unemployment that the Iraq Living Conditions Survey found in Iraq is much lower than the general expectation or assumption. However, this good news must be considered alongside the fact that unemployment can be measured in several ways. Applying the same procedure used in Western countries to measure unemployment, the Iraqi unemployment rate was around 10.5 percent in 2004. In contrast, using a more relaxed definition of unemployment, by including those people who do not work and those that have given up seeking work because they are convinced they cannot find a job, the unemployment rate almost doubles, to 18 percent. Yet this is still lower than the rate reported by other sources for the period in question; for example, the Coalition Provisional Authority (CPA) itself reported a rate of about 30 percent.[15] Nevertheless, with the exception of military personnel—most of whom lost their jobs when the armed forces were disbanded by the CPA—there is little to indicate that the invasion itself caused a massive loss in jobs.

More Iraqis may be working than expected, but the wages they bring home are not large: the average wage is about US$0.50 per hour. The low wage rate, combined with the relatively low level of unemployment, is somewhat surprising, given the high level of aid. The argument that humanitarian aid removes the incentive for recipients to engage in productive work is an old one, and has, at least since the Indian Famine of the 1770s, been used cynically to avoid supporting people in need.[16] It is, however, not applicable here.

One of the major problems in the labor market is not unemployment, but insufficient wages. Still, there are considerable wage differentials, and regression analysis of these differentials reveals insights into how the Iraqi labor market works, which are of relevance for the present discussion. The model used is a so-called Heckman selection model.[17] This model considers the fact that when analyzing how wages are determined the population can be divided into two groups: those that actually work, and those that do not. If the choice of whether or not to work was completely random, an ordinary regression that links a number of variables to the wage paid would be enough. However, there is no reason to believe that the decision of whether or not to work is independent of the characteristics of the person. Thus, it may be that some people who are not working would have very low wages, and this would lead to a selection bias if they were just omitted from the analysis. For example, it is common that women in the Middle East only occupy relatively well-paid jobs, because those that would get lower-paid work are not willing to work. In order to avoid this bias, the Heckman model first predicts who is working, then uses the result of that prediction as one of the inputs in the wage-prediction equation.

The regression results (not shown in detail here) indicate that education increases wages in two ways. First, having a high level of education increases the probability of working; second, the higher the education, the higher the wages. This may seem an obvious result. However, the effect in Iraq is quite strong and signifies that considerable structure still remains even in a society that has been, and continues to be, riveted by conflict. Even in a situation such as Iraq's—or perhaps especially in this situation—having an education is an important resource for people.

The results also indicate, unsurprisingly, that women have a much lesser probability of working than men, but that once they work, being a woman surprisingly increases wages. The fact that women on average have higher wages than men is due to women working more often in the public sector—a sector that is wage-leading after the CPA instigated an increase in public-sector wages immediately after the occupation. Nevertheless, as the regression shows, a positive wage effect of being a woman is seen even when controlling for sector.

In a somewhat perverse way, the positive discrimination of women in the labor market may be seen as a sign of serious distortion of the labor market in Iraq. The norm in other Middle Eastern countries is for substantial negative wage discrimination against women. The Iraqi case means most likely that a return to normality will weaken the position of women in the labor market, thereby creating a substantial realignment of employment. It is also very probable that the results demonstrated for women indicate a wider mismatch of the allocation of human resources between present-day Iraq and a peaceful, normal nation in the Middle East. Such a mismatch may be between ethnic or religious groups, or reflect socioeconomic differences. It is difficult to demonstrate such a mismatch for other groups, but it is reasonable to suppose that they exist, given the fact that there seems to be a mismatch in terms of gender. Thus, the peculiar role of women in the Iraqi labor market may be taken as a proxy indicator for a labor market that functions in very specific ways.

War, sanctions, and occupation have impinged on the overall organization of the economy, most likely resulting in a rather different outlook from what a peacetime economy would look like. To some extent this has had positive side effects, such as a marked lack of systematic social differentiation (although it has to be said that this is in a context where nearly everyone is badly off) and the increased role of women in the labor market. Nevertheless, a labor market with distributional functions that are unlikely to be very similar to peacetime ones, and a distribution of living conditions that differs markedly from that of a normal society, are likely to create considerable friction in the future.

■ Conclusion: The Worst Is Yet to Come

The argument put forward here is that wars, unrest, repression, and sanctions, together with the creation of a primitive welfare state, have had huge consequences for the distribution of wealth and resources within the population, as well as for the stagnation in the development of human resources. While the resulting relative equity of distribution is a positive trait, the economy has also been twisted into a shape that is unsustainable, even in the short run. Thus, a radical structural adjustment of the economy is necessary. At the best of times, even in a peaceful society, such restructuring is painful and conflict-ridden, because it necessarily realigns and redistributes resources between groups. In Iraq, it will add new conflicts to existing ones.

Since the current distribution of resources and assets is only partly related to economic activity, and often, and rightly, is seen as a compensation for being put in hopeless predicaments by successive governments, the redistribution of resources will be necessarily difficult. Given the extent of subsidies in Iraq and the fact that criminal and political violence is endemic, restructuring is likely to be an even more painful process.

As should be clear from the discussion above, getting the infrastructure and the backbone of health and education services into working order is an enormous and necessary task, but perhaps more importantly, the weaknesses that have developed in human resources, particularly in health and education, must be addressed. It is tempting to continue to address these issues through the maintenance of blanket subsidies, because the immediate political cost is less.

Opinion polls carried out in Iraq indicate that subsequent to the US-led invasion, Iraqis considered that their lives had improved, compared to the period before. However, the number of Iraqis who consider that there has been improvement has been declining recently. That may indicate that the little room that existed for structural reforms may be growing smaller and smaller.

The Iraqi case appears to be close to the ideal-typical model of a society emerging from conflict—one having endured a combination of prolonged sanctions, occupation, internal violence, and buying off the population with rudimentary welfare and a large humanitarian effort. The contention is that this particular combination of factors makes transition into a peaceful society extremely difficult, because the economy and social organization of the society has diverged far from any normal society. Thus, the challenge is how to build the necessary human and physical infrastructure without further strengthening the imbalances existing in the Iraqi economy and social organization.

▨ Notes

1. The 2004 Iraq Living Conditions Survey was carried out by the Central Organization for Statistics and Information Technology of Iraq (COSIT) in cooperation with the Norwegian research institute Fafo. It was funded by the United Nations Development Programme (UNDP). Using a representative sample of twenty thousand households, the survey mapped a wide range of living conditions. The data presented here derive directly from the raw data files.

2. See H. R. Kedward, *Occupied France* (Oxford: Blackwell, 1985), and J. Sweets, *Choices in Vichy France: The French Under Nazi Occupation* (Oxford: Oxford Univ. Press, 1986).

3. C. Henriot and Wen-hsin Yeh, eds., *Shadow of the Rising Sun: Shanghai Under Japanese Occupation* (Cambridge: Cambridge Univ. Press, 2004).

4. See P. H. Kratoska, *The Japanese Occupation of Malaya: A Socio-Economic History* (Honolulu: Univ. of Hawaii Press, 1997).

5. See J. J. Dobbins et al., *America's Role in Nation-Building from Germany to Iraq* (Santa Monica: RAND, 2003).

6. See World Food Programme (WFP), *Baseline Food Security Analysis in Iraq* (Rome: World Food Programme, 2004), 66.

7. See World Bank, *Rebuilding Iraq: Economic Reform and Transition* (Washington, DC: World Bank, 2006), 50.

8. See UNDP, *Human Development Report 1990* (New York: UNDP, 1990), 22.

9. United Nations Development Programme, *The Millennium Development Goals in Arab Countries, Toward 2015: Achievements and Aspiration* (New York: UNDP, 2003).

10. See UNICEF, *The State of the World's Children 2004* (New York: UNICEF, 2004).

11. See WFP, *Baseline Food Security Analysis in Iraq.*

12. The principal component analysis used the following variables: "Education of household head," "Household has children that are not enrolled in school," "Household has illiterate members," "Household has acutely malnourished children," "Household has stunted children," "Household has obese women," "Household has members that have been forcibly resettled," "Household has members with war-related injuries," "Additive wealth index," "Household has underemployed members," "Household has unemployed members," "Income 2003 per capita—quintiles," "Is able to raise US$23 within a week," "An ambulance can get by road to the dwelling," "Condition of windows in dwelling," "Connection to sewage," "Functioning sewage," "Safe drinking water," and "Sewage observed in the streets outside household." The first component is used for the map, which employs inverse distance weighting in order to extrapolate values for locations between observations (survey clusters).

13. The Gini measure has the value 0.0 when all have the same income, and 1.0 when one has all and the others nothing. Due to the higher intrinsic variance of income when it is measured over a two-week period rather than for a year, it is not clear if the apparent increase in the Gini from 2003 to 2004 is real.

14. CPA, "Reform of Salaries and Employment Conditions of State Employees," Coalition Provisional Authority Order No. 30, September 8, 2003, www.cpa-iraq.org/regulations.

15. IrinNews.org (2004).

16. See Mike Davis, *Late Victorian Holocausts: El Niño Famines and the Making of the Third World* (London: Verso, 2000).

17. See J. Heckman, "The Common Structure of Statistical Models of Truncation, Sample Selection, and Limited Dependent Variables and a Simple Estimator for Such Models," *Annals of Economic and Social Measurement* 5 (1976): 475–492.

5

Islamism, Nationalism, and Sectarianism

Abdel Salam Sidahmed

NATION BUILDING in post-Saddam Iraq is facing tremendous challenges. Although the authoritarian regime of Saddam Hussein was ousted rather easily by the US-led invasion of Iraq in 2003, four years later the prospect of building a democratic, inclusive, consensual, and efficient political system appears a remote possibility. The problem has been compounded by the collapse or deliberate destruction of the state institutions following the fall of the previous regime and the subsequent occupation of Iraq by the US-led coalition.

Meanwhile, the political climate is characterized by a persistent insurgency punctuated by intercommunal violence, a political process dominated by sectarian and ethnic agendas, and the predominance of Islamism as the major form of discourse and political mobilization at various levels.

This chapter traces the rise and evolution of nationalist and Islamist ideologies in Iraq, notes the ideological transformation in the country as signified by the rising tide of Islamism, and outlines the dominant ideological discourses in post-Saddam Iraq. It also examines the roots of sectarianism, its manifestations and contributing factors in the post-Saddam era, takes a closer look at the competing Islamist visions in today's Iraq, and explores possible options regarding Iraq's political future.

■ Background

The rise of an Iraqi polity brought together various ethnic and sectarian communities in a difficult coexistence. As is well known, Iraq is composed of three major ethno-religious communities: the Shia Arabs, who constitute the majority, the Sunni Arabs, and the Sunni Kurds; in addition to other minorities composed of non-Muslim Arabs and other linguistic groups.[1] Under the British mandate and the monarchy, a political elite drawn from the Sunni Arabs, though a minority, first assumed control of the state, then

71

maintained that control through a combination of oppression and patronage.[2] Thenceforth, despite their size as the majority community in Iraq, the Shia were largely excluded from power and other positions of control and remained so for the best part of Iraqi history. The same fate befell the Kurds, whose demands for self-government and cultural autonomy were either ignored or actively suppressed.[3] The sectarian and ethnic composition of Iraq does not mean that its three major communities represent monolithic political communities, but the fact that the state has been dominated by a circle drawn from one minority group to the exclusion of the other two has definitely played a part in the troubled history of modern Iraq and shaped the response of its various communities.

Nonetheless, the Sunni-based political elite that controlled the state from the time of the monarchy onward often projected itself as ruling on behalf of all Iraqis. At the ideological level, Iraqi nationalism, whether advanced as an anticolonial discourse or as a catalyst for the unity of the multiethnic, multisectarian Iraq, became a feature of Iraqi politics particularly during the monarchical period. During the revolutionary and militarist eras in the 1950s and 1960s, both Arab and Iraqi nationalisms, as well as populism and socialism, became the main ideologies in circulation at both government and civil society levels. Beyond these discourses and window dressings, the structure of the state changed very little. Apart from the change in the political elite incurred by the transition from monarchy to republic, the state remained more or less the monopoly of a restricted circle of rulers who more often than not resorted to military force to access and sustain power.

One important feature of these ideologies is that they were all packaged within a secular and nationalist framework. The rise of the Baath Party to power in 1968 represented, at least in theory, a victory of Arab nationalism, a cornerstone of Baathist ideology. Pan-Arabism may be traced to King Faisal I, the founder of Iraqi monarchy (1932–1958); Iraq also occupied a special place in the history of pan-Arabism during the 1930s and 1940s. Iraq then emerged, alongside Syria, as a springboard of Baathist ideology. Despite these historical connections with pan-Arabism, Iraq's ethnic and sectarian composition was at odds with a pan-Arab project.[4] For historical, demographic, and ideological reasons, pan-Arabism became closely associated with the Sunni community. Hence, projected in the Iraqi context, pan-Arabism was bound to be perceived as the hegemony of the Sunni Arabs over the Shia and the Kurds.[5] Nonetheless, the Baath Party launched itself as the vanguard of Arab nationalism and maintained that discourse following its assumption of power in 1968. In practice, however, while Arab nationalism was primarily deployed to secure a leading role for Iraq in the Arab world, it was gradually wearing thin at the national level. During the 1980s, policy choices and pragmatic considerations of the Iraqi leadership, strained relations with the other Baathist regime in Syria, and more importantly the long-drawn conflict with Iran, all combined to enhance Iraqi nationalism (*al-wataniyyah*) rather than Arab nationalism (*al-qawmiyyah*).[6]

Under the hegemony of Saddam Hussein, who assumed direct control as president of Iraq from 1979 on, the state grew more authoritarian and oppressive, with the president eventually holding ultimate control and power over and above state institutions. By the same token, the Baath Party was transformed from a ruling organization with an ideology and vision into a tool of control of the state and society; in their turn, the party's institutions became subjugated to the whims and ambitions of Saddam Hussein.[7] Nevertheless, despite the growing hegemony of a personalized dictatorship that placed loyalty to Saddam Hussein above any other allegiance, there remained a semblance of a national character in the state institutions, particularly the army and civil service. The overall framework of politics and ideology—still in forms of Iraqi and Arab nationalism—remained secular.

Islamism rose in Iraq, as elsewhere, primarily as an opposition movement. Among the Shia, Hizb al-Dawa (the Call [to Islam] Party), or Al-Dawa, was established around 1957, first as a religious body with a social and cultural agenda and subsequently developing into a political party, signaling a departure from the agelong tradition of Shia quietism in Iraq.[8] During the 1970s and the 1980s, Al-Dawa engaged in violent confrontations with the Iraqi regime. The Supreme Council for the Islamic Revolution in Iraq (SCIRI) was established in 1982 among Iraqi exiles in Iran, first as a coordinating body for Shia-based opposition groups, but soon emerging as an organization in its own right.[9] Al-Dawa and SCIRI remained the main Islamist opposition organizations throughout the Saddam years, and while they maintained a clandestine presence inside Iraq, their leaderships, recruitment ground, and main activities shifted outside Iraq, among Iraqi exiles in the neighboring countries and elsewhere. Though the two organizations shared the same constituency and broad objectives of overthrowing Saddam's regime in favor of an Islamic order or state, they were characterized by important differences at the structural, political, and ideological levels. In political and ideological terms, though the two groups apparently subscribed to the intellectual legacy of Ayatollah Muhammad Baqir al-Sadr (executed in 1980), they seemed to have held divergent views with regard to the nature of an Islamic state, particularly the Khomeini doctrine of *wilayat al-faqih* (guardianship or rule of the jurist).[10] Unlike SCIRI, which clung to *wilayat al-faqih* throughout its opposition years, Al-Dawa was gradually moving away from that doctrine from the mid-1980s onward.[11] Furthermore, Al-Dawa, unlike SCIRI, appeared more attached to its Iraqi and Arab identity, and some of its leaders expressed readiness to consider establishing a Western-style parliamentary democracy in post-Saddam Iraq.[12]

Other significant groups among the Shia community included the loose movement that grew around the charismatic and populist cleric Ayatollah Muhammad Sadiq al-Sadr, father of the current Shia leader Muqtada al-Sadr.[13] Ayatollah al-Sadr's influence generated what came to be known as *al-tayar al-Sadri* (the Al-Sadr movement); it was transformed into a political movement under the leadership of Muqtada al-Sadr after the fall of Saddam's regime.

There were also Sunni-based Islamist groups, as in the cases of the Iraqi Islamic Party (founded in 1960) and the Kurdish Islamic Union; both were manifestations of the Muslim Brotherhood trend.[14] Their influence, however, remained very limited even within the Sunni community.

■ The Legacy of the Saddam Years

Years of systematic oppression and prohibition of independent political or organizational activity resulted in the gradual destruction of national and secular platforms, whether political parties, trades unions, or other civil society organizations. The once powerful Iraqi Communist Party was subjected to a massive campaign of oppression that drove all its leadership and most of its active rank and file into exile by the early 1980s. The same fate befell other opposition secular parties such as the National Democratic Party and others. Trade unions, professional syndicates, students, youth, and women's organizations were all brought under the tight control of the Baath Party and the ruthless security forces of the regime.

With the destruction of national civil and secular platforms, ethnic and religious structures emerged as the only viable alternatives of political mobilization. This was more evident in the cases of the disfranchised Shia and Kurdish communities who were poised to fall back on their religious and ethnic strongholds to garner protest or articulate their demands. At the same time, the Saddam regime had mounted a ruthless campaign of repression and discrimination against the Kurdish and Shia communities in tandem with the Iraq-Iran War. Historically, both communities were indeed disfranchised throughout successive Iraqi regimes, but the repression they were subjected to under the Saddam regime, particularly during the 1980s and early 1990s, was unprecedented.[15] The aim of the campaign, which primarily targeted the political or religious leaderships of both groups and the circles of activists around them, was not sectarian or ethnic cleansing but rather cultivation or imposition of loyalty to the regime among these communities (particularly among the Shia, given their status as the country's majority). Hence those who proved their loyalty were drawn into the web of the state-run patronage systems and rewarded with positions or material benefits.[16] Nonetheless, the overwhelming feeling among the majority of the Shia and Kurdish communities was one of collective grievances and immense hostility to the regime.

With various groups turning to primary loyalties such as religious and ethnic structures, hence placing more emphasis on particular identities, as well as on local and sectarian tendencies, the regime came to project itself as the only representative and custodian of national politics. Indeed, the regime emerged with a virtual monopoly over secular and national platforms with its nationwide structure of the Baath Party, a huge national army, and a nationwide bureaucracy at both the local and central levels. Such a de facto situation may have given some substance to the regime's ideological claim to be the embodiment of Iraqi nationalism.

The ideological garb of Saddam's regime started to change with the invasion of Kuwait in August 1990, which triggered the Gulf War and the imposition of economic sanctions by the United Nations. Both related developments contributed to enhancing the profile of religion, Islam, in public life. Following the invasion of Kuwait and in the runup to the war, Saddam and his aides started to employ more and more Islamic symbols and discourse, ranging from inscription of the phrase *Allah Akbar* (God is great) on the Iraqi flag to the deployment of the theme of jihad against the "crusaders," in the form of the US-led coalition troops. Saddam himself resorted to using Islamic imagery in his speeches with ample quotations from the Quran, referring to his war as jihad, and was often depicted praying while inspecting his troops.[17] Furthermore, Saddam linked withdrawal from Kuwait with Israel's withdrawal from the occupied Palestinian territories and called on Muslims to wage a jihad in order to liberate Jerusalem as well as the holy places of Mecca and Medina, which fell under "Western control" as a result of the Saudi monarchy's invitation of US troops.[18] Indeed, the Iraqi leadership had also used Islam as a legitimizing and mobilizing force during the war with Iran, but with the Gulf War, the Iraqi regime's Islamism signaled a far-reaching ideological shift.

At the regional level, the mood in the "Arab and Muslim street," as manifested in massive demonstrations across the Arab and Muslim world, was one of support for Iraq and Saddam Hussein as the one Arab leader who defied US hegemony and advocated the liberation of Palestine. The Gulf War's pro-Iraq protests appeared to have coalesced around the unpopularity of the Gulf monarchies, deep-rooted suspicion of Western intentions in the Muslim world, and a hope for escape from pressing economic, social, and political problems that became rampant in most Arab countries.[19] The main forces behind those protests were the Islamist opposition groups and the Arab nationalist tendency (broadly conceived). From this collaboration emerged a broad anti-US coalition built around an alliance between Arab nationalists and Islamist groups.

At the national Iraqi level, the regime resorted to usage of more and more Islamist overtones at the expense of secular and socialist doctrines, which were among the cornerstones of the now defunct Baathist ideology.[20]

Following the ousting of Iraq from Kuwait, and the cessation of hostilities in 1991, Iraq came fully under the tough regime of UN-imposed sanctions that was to last for over a decade. The impact of sanctions was the rapid deterioration of economic conditions and impoverishment of the mass of the Iraqi people. During this difficult era, there appeared a growing tendency toward religion among Iraqis in various walks of life owing to the collapse of their livelihood, mounting hardships, and growing insecurity due to rising crime. On its part, the regime maximized the dose of its Islamist discourse, signaling an almost complete ideological transformation. During the 1990s, the regime launched what was known as *al-hamla al-imaniyyah* (the faith campaign), which included building and expanding mosques, imposing restrictions on alcohol consumption, a clampdown on prostitution and theft, and so forth. The campaign was partially a response to growing crime and worsening economic conditions that threatened social unrest and partially an attempt to shore up the regime's legitimacy. The period therefore saw a growing role of religion as a result of both popular and official appeal to it as a refuge and a savior. It has also been observed that as a result of this campaign, the Sunni areas in particular witnessed a boom in the construction of mosques, which subsequently became a breeding ground for Salafist groups and ideology.[21]

Meanwhile, Iraqi nationalism continued to command some support and appeared even to have strengthened in the face of the Gulf War and US-led military campaign on Iraq, as well as in response to the regime of sanctions, which ended up collectively victimizing the whole of the Iraqi people, rather than the regime.

Post-Saddam Iraq: Islamism, Nationalism, and Sectarianism

During the post-Saddam era, the political frameworks and ideological discourses took a different shape and orientation. On the one hand, the antioccupation, anticoalition insurgency emerged with the avowed objective of ending the occupation and thwarting any attempt by the US-led coalition and its Iraqi allies to rebuild the country and its state. On the other hand, the US-led coalition launched a controlled political process aimed at gradually transferring power to Iraqi-led institutions through constitutional measures and elections. The discourse of the insurgency emphasized nationalism and Islamism; the coalition's political process was pursued under the banner of freedom and democracy. On closer examination, however, both competing agendas appear tainted with sectarianism. The political process set in motion by the United States became heavily sectarianized, whether in the allocation of positions and political spoils or in the formation of electoral blocs to contest general or local elections. Similarly, for all the insurgency's espousal of a "national liberation struggle," it remained a Sunni-based movement, and some of its factions have actively pursued a clear sectarian agenda. Sectarianism emerged as the predominant feature of post-Saddam politics.

Islamist Nationalism

There are four main insurgent groups in Iraq: Tandhim al-Qa'ida fi Bilad al-Rafidayn (Al-Qaida in Mesopotamia); Jaysh Ansar al-Sunna (Partisans of the Sunna Army); Al-Jaysh al-Islami fi'l-'Iraq (the Islamic Army in Iraq); and Al-Jabha al-Islamiyya lil-Muqawama al-'Iraqiya (the Islamic Front of the Iraqi Resistance). There are also smaller groups such as Jaysh Muhammad (Prophet Muhammad's Army) and Harakat al-Muqawama al-Islamiyya fi'l-'Iraq (the Islamic Resistance Movement in Iraq), among others. The widely held perception that there are two strands within the Iraqi insurgency, one nationalist and one Islamist, does not appear to be well sustained. Indeed, the two trends do exist but they do not necessarily exist in separate or conflicting structures. As the names of the four main groups indicate, there is a strong Islamist orientation in all of them, and in the case of Tandhim al-Qa'ida even a global jihadist tendency. All groups seemed to have gradually settled on a discourse that blends Islamism in a jihadist-Salafist form with Iraqi nationalism.[22]

In a sense, the various insurgency groups seemed to have inherited the discourse that dominated the ideology of the Iraqi establishment since the Gulf War, namely the blend of Islamism and Iraqi nationalism. Likewise, the insurgency's discourse represented a manifestation and a further development of the alliance struck between Islamists and Arab nationalists in the wake of the Gulf War, as well as the loose anti-US posture that became a feature of popular Arab politics since the early 1990s. Placed in a wider context, the Iraqi insurgency purports to be a response to the chain of "Western offensives" against the Arabic-Islamic world since 9/11, starting with the war on Afghanistan, through the global war on terrorism, and including the invasion of Iraq itself. Furthermore, the insurgency also dips into the well-entrenched collective grievances rampant in the region against the United States and its Western allies centering on the problem of Palestine and US support of the region's authoritarian and "corrupt" regimes. In such a situation, the presence of foreign fighters or "volunteer mujahidin" becomes a logical by-product of a global confrontation between the Western and Islamic worlds, even if such a confrontation may well be more allegorical than real.

Iraqi and Arab nationalism has been deployed by some insurgency groups to mobilize support for the resistance at the national and regional levels on ideological and/or patriotic grounds. Hence, although pioneer cells were probably established by smaller groups of disgruntled individuals with personal or local agendas, the expanding networks of insurgent groups drew on patriotic and nationalist sentiments to recruit supporters.[23] Yet Islamism remained more emotive and by far the most effective tool of mobilization, centering around a renewed emphasis on jihad. Beyond the objective of liberation and driving away the foreign enemy, the concept of jihad has a very strong religious connotation. Leaders of Islamist and insurgent groups have argued—quoting classical and contemporary jurists—that once one's land has been occupied by a foreign "infidel" enemy, the duty of jihad becomes an imperative on every individual Muslim (*fard 'ayn*), particularly those in the concerned territory.[24]

As such the various insurgency groups seemed to have gradually converged around an Islamist nationalist discourse with a strong Salafist outlook.[25] Salafism is the ideology that emphasizes monotheism (unity of God), belief in the message of Prophet Muhammad, and strict adherence to his tradition and that of the righteous companions who joined him, as well as a rejection of innovations, particularly in matters of religion.[26] Its dominance of the insurgents' landscape may be understood from several perspectives: (1) it is simple and straightforward, a factor that facilitates recruitment; (2) it is primarily apolitical and thereby suits a movement that has not elaborated a political program beyond the liberation of Iraq, and (3) it can easily be converted into a jihadist movement inasmuch as it sees the world as basically driven by a struggle between good and evil. This categorization does not necessarily mean that each and every member of an insurgent group is a converted Salafist. Some may have been primarily attracted by the jihadist tendency of the groups; others may have joined out of their nationalist sentiments or other personal considerations. For the leaderships, however, Salafism is a formidable legitimizing discourse because it is categorical, uncompromising, and easily preached to a Muslim audience.

Another group that blended nationalism and Islamism is the Sadr movement, led by the young Shia figure Muqtada al-Sadr. The Sadr movement may be classified as a "quasi-insurgent" group in the sense that it rejected the occupation from the outset, initially shunned the US-sponsored political process, and battled with the US forces through its militia the Mahdi Army (Jaysh al-Mahdi) during the spring and summer of 2004. Although Muqtada al-Sadr and his group eventually reconciled themselves to other Shia-based groupings and became party to the political process through taking part in the general elections of December 2005, they remained decidedly opposed to the US-led coalition and its policies. Al-Sadr's political discourse resembled more that of the Sunni-based groups with its emphasis on the unity of Iraq, antifederalism, and withdrawal of foreign troops from Iraq.

Sectarianism

The rise in sectarianism in post-Saddam Iraq has sometimes been attributed to a natural explosion of suppressed identities following the removal of Saddam's dictatorship. Proponents of this view may point to the Balkans' example after the collapse of communism. It is indeed true that postdictatorship societies normally witness an upsurge in political activism and a mushrooming of parties and various interest groups. In the case of Iraq, the legacy of Saddam's regime was less the suppression of sectarian, religious, and ethnic loyalties than the systematic destruction of national and secular structures and all forums of independent political, societal, and ideological activism. As such the Baathist regime remained the only manifestation of national institutions and politics. Hence, its destruction also meant the collapse of national politics; sects, ethnic groups, and clans emerged as the only viable alternatives for activism. Consequently, the only political groupings to succeed in mobilizing and commanding a sizable following in the post-Saddam era are those built around particular religious, often sectarian, or ethnic identities.[27]

The other factor to enhance sectarianism was the legacy of the Coalition Provisional Authority (CPA). The CPA appeared to have contributed to the sectarianization of Iraqi politics on at least two accounts: the allocation of posts to the Interim Governing Council (IGC) and the de-Baathification process. In the first instance, when the CPA established the IGC in July 2003, it adopted sectarian criteria to fill the council's seats with a "balanced" list of representatives of various sects and ethnic groups. The formula was to allocate a number of seats proportionate to the size of each community. One may argue that the CPA intention was to ensure adequate representation of all communities, and that in the absence of secular or national platforms, the only option was to fall back on ethnic and sectarian identities. However, once deployed, sectarian criteria soon became the determinant factor in deciding the allocation of important political and administrative positions; sectarianism became the dominant feature of the political process set in motion by the CPA. With de-Baathification on the other hand, the CPA, by a stroke of a pen, wiped out more or less the entire managerial class of the state institutions. Apart from the vacuum created by this measure, the rebuilding of these institutions soon fell victim to the sectarian outlook of the ministers and their political patrons, who were entrusted with the transitional process in 2004 to 2006.[28]

Once deployed in the Iraqi political process, sectarianism then took on a life of its own. Each community started to view the process primarily through a sectarian lens to demand adequate representation on these grounds and began to reorganize its ranks in a manner that would maximize its gains. Such was the logic that governed the two general elections in January and December 2005. The Shia-Kurdish partnership that dominated the transitional government, eager to redress decades of marginalization, discrimination, and disfranchisement, soon started to fill their respective ministries, armies, and security forces with their coethnics and coreligionists.[29] The response of the Sunni Arabs to these tendencies and developments has been one of fear and resentment. The group that dominated the country since the creation of the modern Iraqi state suddenly found itself excluded from power and may even find itself more marginalized within the current balance of power. Within such a framework, it is not surprising that the Sunni political and religious leadership and even the community at large seem to have thrown in their lot with the insurgency as the main leverage to gain a foothold in the unfolding political equation.

On another level, rather than pursuing a system of transitional justice and accountability for past violations, certain sectarian militias—particularly from Shia-based groups—started to target individuals and groups, such as associates of the former regime, with the aim of settling old scores.[30] The Sunni Arab community, on their part, started to complain that they were collectively targeted for the crimes committed by a regime of which they were themselves victims. Meanwhile certain groups, such as Abu Musab al-Zarqawi's Tandhim al-Qa'ida, deliberately adopted and pursued an agenda of stirring sectarian violence by targeting Shia groups, including civilians.[31] These disputes triggered intercommunal violence that became more frequent throughout 2005 and 2006 and that threatened to drag the whole country into a devastating civil war.

■ Contending Islamist Visions

It is rather ironic that nationalism appears associated more with the insurgency, the anticoalition groups in general, and the Sunni Arab community at large, while sectarianism appears more a feature of the political process set in motion by the US-led coalition. This is not to suggest that the insurgency is devoid of any sectarian base or agenda—because it does have one—but the issue is how the ideological polarization is being packaged. It is not surprising that given their consistent control of power throughout the history of modern Iraq, the political elite of the Sunni Arabs would be espousing a nationalist outlook. In the present situation, the Sunni Arabs would see their interests as identifiable more with a nationalist agenda concerned with preserving the unity and integrity of Iraq; otherwise they will be reduced to a landlocked minority with no access to any significant resources. For their part, the insurgency groups, which no doubt share the same outlook of their main constituency, would naturally be projecting a nationalist discourse since they had set for themselves the task of ridding Iraq of occupation. In any event, Iraqi nationalism has been conflict-driven as demonstrated by the contemporary history of Iraq since the start of the war with Iran.

On their part, the Shia and Kurdish groupings appear more inclined to court a particularistic agenda due to the decades of disfranchisement, marginalization, and oppression that the two communities suffered under successive regimes in Iraq. Their main concern is to redress this situation through sectarian or ethnic-based alliances that would ensure their control of the state and its institutions. As such, the Shia-Kurdish coalition is not really interested in a brand of belligerent nationalism that could only be reminiscent of the days when both communities were severely repressed.

What appears to be common between all groups, with the exception of the Kurds, is their subscription to Islamism. The main Shia-based bloc (the United Iraqi Alliance), the Sunni political bloc (the Iraqi Consensus Front) that contested the last elections, and the main insurgent groups all respectively subscribe to one form or another of an Islamist ideology. Unlike the secular parties and blocs, which failed to get any significant representation in the assembly, the two sectarian blocs won most of the votes in their respective constituencies. These results confirm the strength of religion as a force of mobilization and its ideological domination of post-Saddam Iraq. The domination of Islamist ideology may be traced to the legacy of the Saddam years, the erosion of secular platforms and ideologies, and the rising tide of Islamism in Iraq as well as the region at large.

For now, both the Sunni and Shia parliamentary blocs are bound to emphasize commonalities within their respective coalitions to secure adequate representation in the state structures, as opposed to advocating potentially divisive political programs. As pointed out above, for the Shia groups, the crucial objective is to redress years of disfranchisement and secure a representation in the state proportionate to their numerical size as the majority community in Iraq. For the Sunni community, their battle is to negotiate a political arrangement, preferably within a unified Iraq, that would accord them their proper place in Iraqi society and ensure them adequate access to power and resources. In religious terms, the two sectarian blocs may share several features with regard to the primacy of religion, a common stand on religious morality, and religious-based legislation. Yet their concepts of an Islamic state are of course different, given the divergent traditions and historical animosities between the Sunni and Shia communities. Likewise, their political programs and visions for a future Iraq are bound to be miles apart, if not diametrically opposed. That said, one should not regard the two sectarian blocs in monolithic terms. In societal terms, both the Sunni and Shia communities are respectively composed of multiple identities on account of location, social status, and a host of other differentiating factors. Furthermore, even when they share an Islamist platform, as is presently the case between the two sectarian blocs, there are likely to be internal differences on political or ideological grounds.

In ideological terms, the Shia-based groups may be influenced by divergent positions existing within clerical circles, ranging from quietist to activist, liberal to conservative. As noted above, there used to be ideological differences between the two main Shia groups, Al-Dawa and SCIRI, with regard to the concept of *wilayat al-faqih*. The situation may have evolved further given the Iranian practical experimentation with that very concept for nearly three decades and the emergence of pluralist politics in post-Saddam Iraq. What is yet to be explored, however, is the ideological impact, if any, of the reformist-conservative dispute in Iran on Iraqi Shia groups, in view of the regular intellectual exchanges between Najaf and Qum.[32] Important as these ideological considerations are, one would argue that at the moment they are bound to be put on a back burner.

At the present stage, political considerations take precedence in the minds of the Iraqi Shia groups. Hence, with regard to Iran, discussion normally revolves around an Iranian role in Iraq for the former's own strategic considerations, rather than questions pertaining to Shia political thought. As is the case with other matters, the various Shia groups are not necessarily in agreement with regard to Iran's political role and influence in Iraq. Here, for example, SCIRI and the Sadr movement appear to hold opposite views. The former naturally maintains closer ties with Iran, whereas the latter advocates closer ties between Iraq and the rest of the Arab world. On a more general note, although the Sadr movement is currently part of the Shia coalition, its political outlook appears to be closer to the Sunni groups than to some of its partners in the Shia bloc.

For their part, the Sunni Islamist bloc also emphasizes the political over the ideological, judging by the discourse of the Iraqi Islamic Party (IIP), the oldest group in the coalition. The IIP political program of 2005 set the main aims of the party as the liberation of Iraq, consolidating national unity, and building the Iraqi state on grounds of national unity and independence. References to Islam in the IIP program are mainly geared toward reform of society and injecting its values and principles in the state.[33]

Yet despite emphasis on political programs over substantive ideological considerations in the discourse of the two blocs, there is a clear ascendancy of Islamist ideology on the Iraqi political scene in the post-Saddam era. Islam has definitely emerged as the most effective source of mobilization within the various communities and groupings across the Iraqi sectarian spectrum.[34] As alluded to earlier, with the collapse, destruction, or weakening of secular political structures and ideologies, religious identity emerged as the most effective catalyst for political organization in post-Saddam Iraq. In such an atmosphere, mosques—both Sunni and Shia—have become the focal points of political mobilization and vehicles for "assembly, propagation, and recruitment."[35]

On the other hand, a closer look at the discourse of the various Islamist groups and electoral blocs indicates that Islamism appears to be more of a vehicle for mobilization than a vision to reconstruct the state and society on the basis of Islam. Should stability return, the various political forces would indeed be required to elaborate their visions and programs with regard to the country's administration and welfare. Stability, however, looks a rather remote prospect, and the pertinent question is whether Iraqi unity can be salvaged.

■ The Way Ahead

How should Iraqi authorities address the problematic political situation in Iraq in a manner that would restore stability and open avenues for the country's reconstruction and establishment of a viable political system? There is no obvious answer to such a question, but this section will look into three options or scenarios regarding the political future of Iraq:

1. *Reversed oppression.* This scenario imagines the maintenance of the current status quo, with power primarily resting in a Shia-Kurdish alliance, with a token representation from the Sunni community. The underlying logic is that this is a democratically elected government, reflecting the will and mandate of the Iraqi majority, and thereby is entitled to rule without necessarily going out of its way to accommodate the "Sunni skeptics." This option would obviously treat the insurgency as a security problem above all; hence efforts would focus on ways and means to achieve a military victory over it. This scenario would also consider revitalizing the ability of the state to render services, improve the economic situation, and accelerate the process of reconstruction of Iraq to eliminate the genesis of discontent among the population at large.

2. *Controlled dismembering of Iraq.* Some observers argue that US-led nation building has failed; that given the degree of violence that is ravaging the Iraqi society on a daily basis, and the apparent difficulties in reaching a political formula acceptable to all communities, the division of Iraq is inevitable.[36] This view maintains that it is better to recognize such a reality and move on to adopt a loose federation or a confederacy that would ensure autonomy of the respective three regions (the Kurdish north, the Sunni central-west, and the Shia south) and negotiate a reasonable formula for natural resources, particularly oil, and for the governance of the capital of Baghdad and other mixed cities such as Kirkuk.

3. *An inclusive, accommodating, democratic system.* Whereas it is imperative that the security situation should be brought under control, including by dealing with insurgent-driven or communal violence, clearly a security solution is not sufficient by itself. There should be a concerted effort to hold wide consultations among various communities regarding ways for reaching stability and a viable political system. Due attention

should also be paid to reaching an acceptable formula for power and resource sharing in Iraq. In this context, there are a number of issues that need extensive discussion and revision such as the form Iraqi federalism should take, the place of religion in public life, and the best formula for coexistence between Iraq's divergent ethnic and religious groups.

It is difficult to pass definitive judgment as to which of these three options will be followed; all depend on choices and actions of the main players on the Iraq scene as well as how the situation unfolds on the ground. Yet it is safe to argue that continuing with the status quo in Iraq would escalate the current problems of chronic insecurity and economic hardship and, more importantly, would fossilize the cleavages in Iraqi society. A "reversed oppression" option is undoubtedly a recipe for another generation of conflict. Breaking up Iraq, on the other hand, is not the answer: There are plenty of reasons why such an option would actually make things worse in Iraq and beyond. To start with, Iraq's main ethno-sectarian groups—Sunna, Shia, and Kurds—are not monolithic groups, a factor that would likely impact the homogeneity and durability of political structures created on the basis of these communities. Another problem is related to major metropolises such as Mosul, Kirkuk, Basra, and Baghdad, and how these political and economic centers are to be divided or ruled in a divided Iraq given their ethnic and sectarian mix. Last but not least, there is the thorny question of dividing the country's resources, particularly oil (which accounts for 90 percent of the country's earnings), and the impact that a breakup of Iraq would have on the central-western region, the resourceless, and landlocked home of the Sunni community.[37]

The third option represents a difficult and complex process, but it is indeed a necessity if there is a real will that Iraq should rise up from the ashes of wars and violence and the multiple sufferings of its people redeemed. The central objective for Iraq's policymakers should therefore be the restoration of national politics in a way that is consensus-based, accommodative, participatory, and equitable in terms of power and resource sharing for the various Iraqi communities and regions. Such a process would require painstaking and concerted efforts from all parties concerned: domestic Iraqi players, the Multi-National Force in Iraq (MNF-I), the UN, and regional powers concerned with Iraq.

If this option is to be pursued, there would still be the question of how it would transcend a current landscape dominated by sectarian politics, ethnic divisions, and the hegemony of an Islamist ideology. At this juncture, it may be useful to explore the respective roles of religion and nationalism in the current Iraqi setting. With regard to the role of religion, one may argue that Islam, being the religion of the majority of Iraqis across the sectarian and ethnic divide, could be a unifying force in the current situation, particularly as the major political groups subscribe to an Islamist ideology. To this factor, the heritage of Iraqi nationalism would provide a broader framework bringing together Muslim and non-Muslim communities on the basis of Iraqi national identity.

There are, however, serious obstacles in the face of a unity built around a pan-Islamic framework. In the Iraqi context, pan-Islamism is often understood and pursued as pan-Shiism, pan-Sunnism, or Sunni Salafism and when politicized it usually opens the door for further subdivisions on political and ideological grounds or other dynamics of identification. On the other hand, the history of modern Iraqi society has shown that the multiple identities of its various sectors and communities were built around their respective narratives and their actual or perceived grievances vis-à-vis the state or other communities. As such, an Islamist framework, far from being a force of unity would most likely sustain the current fragmentation of Iraqi society and enhance its sectarian politics. Moreover, experiences of Islamist regimes in the region have more often than not shown a tendency toward policies and legislation that discriminate among citizens on the basis of religious affiliation and human rights violations on the basis of *sharia*-based legislation.[38]

As for Iraqi nationalism, as a potential umbrella under which various Iraqi groups and communities may be brought together, there are also serious doubts over its capacity as a unifying dynamic. As pointed out above, Iraqi nationalism has primarily been conflict-driven, breeding on the various wars and on hostility toward international or regional powers (US and Western powers, Iran, Kuwait, and so forth). It was also associated with a narrow-based, authoritarian, and ruthlessly oppressive regime. Currently, Iraqi nationalism appears to be associated at least partially with the insurgency, which is by and large opposed to the political process and mostly hostile to the Shia-Kurdish coalition and the political groups associated with it. As in the case of Islam, rather than being a unifying force, nationalism appears rather as divisive as sectarianism and its related Islamist ideologies.

Islam and Iraqi identity will nevertheless remain crucial to any peacebuilding process for present-day and future Iraq. One option is to explore the possibility of advancing a vision of Islam devoid of sectarianism and an Iraqi identity based on national consensus rather than a narrative of domestic oppression and external antagonism. Such a vision needs time to evolve and may well require leadership of strong and charismatic personalities to effect the necessary molding together of Iraq's disparate communities and groupings in a cohesive national framework.

For now, the most realistic approach is first to recognize the respective limits of the various ideologies and discourses that currently dominate the Iraqi political scene, namely Islamism, sectarianism, and Islamist nationalism; and second, to attempt a restoration of Iraqi national politics on the basis of (1) a secular platform that is neutral but not hostile toward the various religious and sectarian affiliations, (2) the protection and promotion of human rights, and (3) the adoption of the concept of citizenship as the basis of all rights and entitlements.

■ Notes

1. Various sources estimate Iraqi Shia as ranging between 55 and 60 percent, Sunni Arabs between 15 and 20 percent, Sunni Kurds between 20 and 25 percent, and the rest around 4 to 5 percent. See, for example, Joyce Wiley, *The Islamic Movement of Iraqi Shi'as* (Boulder, CO: Lynne Rienner, 1992), 8–9.

2. Charles Tripp, *A History of Iraq* (Cambridge: Cambridge Univ. Press, 2002).

3. Ibid., 114ff.

4. Samir al-Khalil (aka Kanan Makiya), *Republic of Fear: The Inside Story of Saddam's Iraq* (New York: Pantheon Books, 1989), 149ff.

5. Ibid.

6. In 1982, the final report of the ninth congress of the Regional Command of the Baath Party downplayed Arab nationalism and socialism and stressed the primacy of Iraq, the significance of religion, and the importance of wealth creation and private enterprise. See Tripp, *History of Iraq*, 236.

7. Ibid., 223ff.

8. Wiley, *Islamic Movement*, 31ff.

9. Ibid., 60–62.

10. The Shia believe that a descendant of the Prophet Muhammad who went into hiding during the tenth century CE, hence known as the Mahdi, or Hidden Imam, would reappear toward the end of time and restore justice on earth. According to Ayatollah Khomeini, then, rather than waiting passively for the return of the Hidden Imam, the Shia should engage actively in the establishment of an Islamic order ruled by the *sharia* law under the guidance and leadership of the ulama (jurists). This doctrine came to be known as *wilayat al-faqih*. See Ayatollah Ruhollah Khomeini, *Islamic Government* (New York: Manor Books, 1979).

11. Amatzia Baram, "Two Roads to Revolutionary Shi'ite Fundamentalism in Iraq," in *Accounting for Fundamentalisms: The Dynamic Character of Movements*, vol. 4 of the Fundamentalism Project, ed. Martin Marty and R. Scott Appleby (Chicago: Univ. of Chicago Press, 1994), 531–588.

12. Ibid.

13. Aayatollah Muhammad Sadiq al-Sadr was assassinated by Saddam's agents in February 1999; see *Al-Hayat*, 2 February 1999.

14. It seemed that the Islamic Party emerged first as an amalgam of Hizb Al-Dawa and the Muslim Brotherhood, but apparently became confined to representing the latter tendency. See Wiley, *Islamic Movement*, 36; Tripp, *History of Iraq*, 160–161.

15. See Tripp, *History of Iraq*; Amnesty International Reports on Iraq 1980–1999.

16. At the time of the invasion of Kuwait in 1990, the Shia numbered 50 percent of the Baath Regional Command, 20 percent of the army generals, and headed 50 percent of the state-owned enterprises. See Jerry Long, *Saddam's War of Words: Politics, Religion, and the Iraqi Invasion of Kuwait* (Austin: Univ. of Texas Press, 2004), 63.

17. Ibid., 94–96.

18. James Piscatori, ed., *Islamic Fundamentalisms and the Gulf Crisis,* A Fundamentalism Project Report (Chicago: Univ. of Chicago Press, 1991), 3–11.

19. Ibid., 11–18; Long, *Saddam's War of Words*, 100ff.

20. See Long, *Saddam's War of Words*, 81ff.

21. I am indebted to Bakhtiar Amin, former Iraqi minister for human rights, for this observation.

22. International Crisis Group, "In Their Own Words: Reading the Iraqi Insurgency," *Middle East Report* 50 (February 2006).

23. Toby Dodge, *Iraq's Future: The Aftermath of Regime Change* (London: Routledge, 2005), 14–19.

24. See International Crisis Group, *Middle East Report* 50, 11–12.

25. Ibid., 10–11.

26. Mahmoud A. al-'Asqalani, *Al-Da'wa al-Salafiyya* [The Salafist Call] (Alexandria: Dar al-Iman, 2004).

27. Gareth Stansfield argued that "ironically, by removing the Baath Party, the United States effectively eliminated the one organization that could perhaps claim a national support base and had the means to project power"; see Gareth Stansfield, "The Transition to Democracy in Iraq: Historical Legacies, Resurgent Identities and Reactionary Tendencies," in *The Iraq War and Democratic Politics*, ed. Alex Danchev and John Macmillan (London: Routledge, 2005), 141.

28. International Crisis Group, "The Next Iraqi War? Sectarianism and Civil Conflict,"*Middle East Report* 52 (February 27, 2006), 8–11, 17.

29. Ibid., 19–21.

30. Ibid., 17–19.

31. Ibid., 14–17; see also Loretta Napoleoni, *Insurgent Iraq: Al-Zarqawi and the New Generation* (London: Constable & Robinson, 2005), 159ff.

32. Najaf and Qum are the two eminent Shia learning centers in Iraq and Iran, respectively.

33. See www.IraqiParty.com (Arabic), accessed 25 May 2006.

34. An exception to Islam as the primary source of mobilization may be seen within the Kurdish groups, which primarily rallied around a platform of Kurdish nationalism.

35. International Crisis Group, "The Next Iraqi War?" 22.

36. See, for example, Gareth Stansfield, "Breaking Up Iraq: A Radical Plan to Save the Country," *Prospect* (May 2006), 22–27.

37. See Anthony Cordesman, "Three Iraqs Would Be One Big Problem," *New York Times*, 9 May 2006.

38. Reference here is to Iran, Saudi Arabia, and Afghanistan under Taliban rule. *Sharia* is commonly translated as Islamic law, though it refers to both matters of worship as well as normal legal sanctions regulating interhuman or societal relations.

6

Sunni Factions and
the "Political Process"

Roel Meijer

THIS CHAPTER ANALYZES the relationship between two Sunni political forces with respect to the differing views and strategies in their approaches to what has been called the "political process." The "political process" is not a neutral term. It was coined by L. Paul Bremer III and implies the political cooperation of all Iraqi religious and ethnic groups in achieving some kind of compromise under US aegis to ensure the establishment of democracy.[1] For most Sunnis, this endeavor has taken on a singularly malignant form. During the past four years, they have become appalled by the growing influence of Iran, terrified of the increasing power of the Shia, who are much better organized than they are, and perplexed by their own rapid marginalization. They believe that as a community they have been the main victim of the US invasion. For although they had depended on the Baathist state to defend their interests, many Sunnis also suffered under Saddam Hussein's brutal dictatorship and feel deeply humiliated and dishonored by the collective punishment the United States has meted out to their community.[2] The dismantling of the army, the de-Baathification of the four highest ranks of the party, and the installation of the Interim Governing Council (IGC) in July 2003, based on proportional representation of the different communities—allegedly laying the foundations of sectarian politics—are all regarded as measures especially directed against them.[3] Consequently, Sunnis not only regard the US "liberation" universally as an occupation, but the concept of the political process has been largely discredited. In their struggle against "minoritarization," both Sunni political currents stand for the same basic goals: retaining (at least some of) the former power of the Sunni elite, upholding a united Iraq on the basis of common Arab and Islamic identity, and retaining a centralized state. They differ, however, in their strategies for achieving these goals.

The first of the two Sunni currents, the Iraqi Islamic Party (Al-Hizb al-Islami al-'Iraqi, or IIP), holds the view that participation in the political process, however it might be skewed to their disadvantage, is the only option. By taking part in political negotiations, splitting the broad Shia list of the United Iraqi Alliance (UIA), and bringing the moderate nationalist Shia parties over to their side, the IIP hopes to achieve greater power than is warranted on the basis of their new minority status. In the party's view, this is also the only way of integrating the insurgency into the political process. However, due to the neglect of the United States of the Sunni community, the IIP did not play a major political role within the governing bodies the United States established, which were dominated by Shia and Kurds. Only after the IIP joined the Iraqi Consensus Front (Jabha al-Tawafuq al-'Iraqi, or the Tawafuq) in October 2005, and won forty-four seats during the general elections of December 2005, did it gain more credibility, although its mandate is conditional and grudgingly consented, due to the deep mistrust by the Sunnis of the political process.

The second major Sunni political force is represented by the Association of Muslim Scholars (Hay'at Ulama al-Muslimin, or AMS).[4] In contrast to the IIP, this body believes that the goals of the Sunni community can only be reached by boycotting the political process, supporting the armed struggle, and winning the most pro-Arab radical Shia groups, such as the followers of Muqtada al-Sadr (at least in the summer of 2004), to join the armed "national" resistance against the US occupation as well as the pro-Iranian SCIRI (Supreme Council for the Islamic Revolution in Iraq). This current gained ascendancy during the boycott of the general elections of January 2005 but lost ground to those in favor of participating in the political process after the ballots. This by no means signifies that those in favor of the political process have won the day. A further escalation of the civil war can block the effectiveness of politics for years.

The importance of these two forces is measured by their capacity to represent the Sunni insurgency by either integrating it into the present political process (IIP) or by waiting until the armed struggle has strengthened the bargaining position of the Sunnis and then taking part in political negotiations (AMS). Both strategies suffer from severe liabilities. The problem with the strategy the AMS pursues is that although the insurgency is able to disrupt and destabilize the establishment of a new regime, it is generally assumed that it is incapable of obtaining a military victory over US and Iraqi (mainly Shia) auxiliary troops.[5] Moreover, although it has achieved greater unity since 2004, when the former Baathist, tribal, and Salafist groups became more unified on the basis of a mixed Salafi-Iraqi nationalist program, and now coordinates its actions, it has neither a common program nor a common leadership.[6] Some, like the al-Zarqawi current, Al-Qaida in Mesopotamia, which intends to create chaos and turn the insurgency into a civil war, argue that they should fight the United States and the Shia as infidels until the bitter end. Other, more nationalist-orientated insurgent groups, who are more interested in liberating the country from the occupation, have a more pragmatic view, directing their attacks against Shia security forces as collaborators working together with the United States. Their growing "politicization" is confirmed by their support of the referendum on the constitution in October 2005.[7] Further encouraging signs in favor of political participation were picked up at the end of 2005 when the insurgency formulated a common platform as a preliminary step toward negotiations.[8]

To engage the insurgency in negotiations and strengthen the Sunni participation in the political process has also been the US policy since the appointment of Zalmay Khalilzad as US ambassador to Iraq in the summer of 2005. The major problem for the IIP, supposedly the main beneficiary of this policy, is that the insurgency derides the existing political actors, sometimes even regarding them as collaborators with the United States because they are willing to take part in the maligned political process.[9] Ironically, the more the IIP leans on the United States the more it is viewed as their tool, and the more credibility it loses.

This chapter concentrates on the different strategies the Sunni political forces have developed and the political terminology they have used, as well as how these relate to the insurgency during the past four years. In addition, it will address the question whether US policy has been successful since its revision under Zalmay Khalilzad to include the Sunnis in the political process. The analysis covers the period between April 2003 and the presentation of the cabinet of Nuri al-Maliki on May 20, 2006.

■ Ascendancy of the AMS

The Association of Muslim Scholars was founded five days after the fall of the regime of Saddam Hussein in April 2003, with the goal of supporting and defending nationwide Sunni religious institutions such as mosques and madrasahs.[10] The AMS was established as a nationwide organization for Sunni religious scholars of all types, whether they were traditional ulama, modernists, Sufis, or Salafis. In theory, it is ethnically inclusive, addressing itself to Sunni Kurds and Turkmen, although in practice the AMS is primarily a network of Sunni Arab ulama, with a few Kurdish and Turkmen members. Its headquarters is the huge Umm al-Qura Mosque, formerly the Mother of All Battles Mosque (Umm al-Ma'raka), built by Saddam Hussein in Baghdad.

The leadership of the AMS is represented by its secretary-general, Harith al-Dhari, and its official spokesmen: his son Muthanna al-Dhari, Abd al-Salam al-Kubaysi, and Bashar al-Faydhi, as well as its foreign spokesman, Muhammad Ayyash al-Kubaysi, who also doubles as chief ideologue of the AMS. In line with its modern character, they are well versed in using the media to propagate the ideology of the AMS and its political program. This is done through a continuous stream of communiqués (*bayanat*), regular press conferences, and continuous updates on the AMS presented on its website,[11] as well as in its daily newspaper, *Al-Basa'ir*.[12] In addition, numerous interviews with its leadership in the regional Arab media, and especially the television station Al-Jazeera in Qatar, have the purpose of bringing the ideas of the AMS across. In fact, many commentators argue that its access to the media accounts for its growing power, as normal communications in Iraq have been problematic.

The message the AMS has disseminated since its founding has had the same uncompromising content: the US presence is not only illegal and to be considered an "occupation" but it is also aimed at harming the general interests of Iraq as a nation. The AMS is mostly an Islamo-nationalist movement that legitimates the struggle for liberation in nationalist and religious terms.[13] Even before the US invasion, Harith al-Dhari condemned the US threat to Iraq,[14] considering it a duty to resist the coming invasion.[15] This nationalist attitude of the AMS has been translated into the rejection of any form of cooperation with the United States and their sponsored political institutions that are part of the "political process," whether in the form of the Interim Governing Council installed in July 2003,[16] the installation government of Ayad Allawi in June 2004,[17] or the meeting of the National Conference in August of that year as a precursor to the general elections scheduled for January 2005.[18] This overall image as a force of steadfast resistance has been enhanced by the projection of the history of the leaders of the AMS as part of the nationalist struggle for independence. However, its nationalist stand has also led it to reject a transnational organization like Al-Qaida in Mesopotamia not only for its indiscriminate killing of Iraqi citizens, especially Shia, but also because Abu Musab al-Zarqawi was a "non-Iraqi and a foreigner" and had "other goals than the national resistance."[19]

The position the AMS has adopted to counter its rivals is to regard itself as standing above the political parties as "a religious authority and an authority on Islamic law" (*marja'iyya diniyya wa shar'iyya*).[20] In this manner, the AMS asserts the age-old claim of the ulama that they, through their religious knowledge, should assume moral and legal authority over the believers, expressed succinctly in Harith al-Dhari's own words as a task to "bring the Sunni community under one roof."[21] In that sense, the AMS, according to its spokesmen, is "not a political party, nor a movement." Rather it "contains political parties" and leaves room for "a diversity of opinions."[22] On the other hand, the AMS does acknowledge its political role and it is clear that the AMS has a political program and strives for political power, as is apparent in Harith al-Dhari's expression that it is the "national and religious duty of the ulama [to] lead the people on the right path."[23] The only reason that the AMS does not openly present itself as a political party, Harith al-Dhari claims, is that "the AMS refuses to be a political party at the present moment, because to do so would mean to legitimate the present political situation."[24]

The major political breakthrough of the AMS occurred during the first crisis in Falluja in April 2004. The AMS took advantage of this opportunity by firmly supporting the local insurgents, propagating the notion that it was a popular revolt, while mobilizing its mosque infrastructure to collect food and medical help.[25] Such clear support for the resistance marked a major change in the relationship between Sunni political forces and the insurgency. Not only did the active support of the AMS for the resistance during and after the Falluja crisis provide it with a more elaborate ideological justification of the right to resist, addressing the general feelings of injustice and the outrage Sunnis felt after the fall of the Baath regime and the subsequent discrimination by the United States, it also lifted the ideological rhetoric of the resistance, which had been mainly formulated in tribal terms of honor, to a much higher ideological level.

Through its ideological input and its access to the regional and international media, the AMS turned Falluja symbolically into the Sunni Stalingrad against the US occupation. Tactically, this move enabled the AMS both to counter the US propaganda that tried to discredit the resistance as terrorism, as well as acquire ideological hegemony over its rivals, especially the Iraqi Islamic Party, whose image was tarnished by its membership in the Interim Governing Council, even though it had opposed the decision to attack Falluja and had resigned from the Allawi government.[26] For the AMS, this was a major opportunity to try to become the spokesman for the Sunni resistance.[27] In character with its claims to ideological leadership, it made a self-conscious attempt to "direct" (*tarshid*) the political concepts the resistance had adhered to until then.[28] To underscore this claim, the AMS stated that it regarded itself as "spiritually" (*ruhan*) close to the resistance but that it did not claim to be its political leadership.[29]

■ The AMS Ideology of Resistance

During the following year, the AMS made a serious attempt to construct an ideology with which it tried to appeal to the armed insurgency.[30] Muhammad Ayyash al-Kubaysi expressed the ideas of the AMS most systematically in a series of twenty articles under the title *On the Jurisprudence of Resistance and Jihad*, which were partially published in the Jordanian weekly of the Muslim Brotherhood, *Al-Sabil*.[31] In January 2006, *Al-Sabil* published the whole collection as a booklet, which is also being distributed by the AMS as their program. Five topics stand out in particular in the ideology of the AMS; with its mix of issues, the AMS has been able to address different constituencies forming the insurgency—Arab nationalists, tribal adherents, and Salafists.

First, the ideological legitimacy of resistance was initially couched by the AMS in a non-Islamic discourse of international law, in order to appeal to a large Arab public. In a debate on a television program of Al-Jazeera, just after the fall of Falluja in November 2004, when the whole of Anbar province was in uprising and it was clear that the armed resistance was there to stay, Muhammad Ayyash al-Kubaysi stated that every population, whether they were Vietnamese or Arab, non-Muslim or Muslim, had the right to armed resistance against the forceful occupation of its country. As it was a human right, it was not necessary to call for a jihad or issue a fatwa to sanction it.[32] In fact, the AMS preferred the term resistance (*muqawama*) to that of jihad or mujahidin. As in the Palestinian case of Hamas, from which AMS borrowed the Islamo-nationalist terminology of rejecting a foreign occupation (*ihtilal*) and boycotting its institutions, including elections, as part of "Oslo," the term *resistance* became the central frame of reference.[33]

However, despite this effort to appeal to a larger following, the AMS used a religious legitimatization as well and adopted Salafist terminology to promote the jihad. In a direct attack on the Islamic ummah by the unbelievers, Muhammad Ayyash al-Kubaysi claims there is no place for "leniency," "pliability," and a peaceful spreading of the call (*da'wa*). The dire situation in Iraq demands armed resistance and all efforts of the ummah should be subordinated to jihad.[34] In typical Salafist terminology, resistance has become a struggle against the tyrant and foreign occupation and has become a "personal obligation" (*fard 'ayn*) that can only be ignored at the risk of denying the unity of God, *tawhid*.[35] Underlining the glory and the necessity of resisting the enemy, Muhammad Ayyash al-Kubaysi states that joining the *muqawama* is a duty of the times (*wajib al-waqt*). This supremacy of resistance and the necessity of sacrifice also implies redefinition of *wala' wa-l-bara'* (love and hate in the name of God)—another Salafi concept— and a redrawing of the lines between to whom one belongs and whom one is against.[36] All those wavering in their support for the jihad, for instance, should be regarded as cowards, egoists, and weaklings, and should be rejected,[37] while all those willing to sacrifice themselves with a "strong faith" and for a "noble goal" should be embraced for the love of God.[38]

Third, the AMS regarded as part of its function in directing the resistance the making of a distinction between the legitimate Sunni resistance against the US occupation and the indiscriminate terrorism of more radical groups like those of al-Zarqawi, whose actions were increasingly directed against Shia Iraqis who were regarded as rejectionists. In numerous communiqués, the AMS condemned terrorist attacks against "innocent people."[39] The official position of the AMS was that both Iraqi civilians and military belong to this category.[40] This term even applied to the recruits of the national security forces, who were mostly Shia and were increasingly used by the United States against the Sunni resistance. Muhammad Ayyash al-

Kubaysi stated that according to Islamic law, they are Iraqi "citizens" and therefore "cannot be executed without legal proceedings." A US soldier is, however, a legitimate target because he is part of the occupation.[41]

Fourth, the AMS was highly successful in translating growing resistance against "occupation" into a policy of uncompromising boycott of all political institutions as long as the United States has not drawn up a timetable for the withdrawal of their troops. By regarding "true democracy as impossible under the occupation," the AMS for a long time fundamentally undermined the attempts of the IIP to take part in the political process. It further discredited the United States by accusing it of deliberately instigating sectarian strife (*al-fitna al-ta'ifiyya*).[42] From the moment of the installation of the Interim Governing Council and its proportional representation of different ethnic and religious groups, the AMS accused the United States of introducing a form of political representation that undermined the Iraqi nation,[43] which should be regarded as a deliberate means of destroying national unity by playing the sectarian card.[44] Outraged by the claim that the US presence prevented a civil war, the AMS promoted the view that the United States was in fact the source of the problem and the reason for civil strife, and that Iraq's religious and ethnic communities could solve their problems by themselves and "live peacefully together," if US forces left.

Fifth, in line with its counterframe that Iraq was a united nation, the AMS cleverly used the insurgency in Falluja to propagate its Arab and Islamic program of unity between Shia and Sunnis. This strategy was especially directed with an eye to Muqtada al-Sadr, who, as the rival of the pro-Iranian SCIRI, was regarded as a pro-Iraqi nationalist. Besides this aspect, the AMS also used this as a means of splitting the Shia into rival factions and weakening them. On the practical and political levels, the framing objective of national unity was transformed by the AMS into a Sunni-Shia campaign of solidarity during the spring and summer of 2004 in the form of coordination of guerrilla actions, organizing common demonstrations against the US occupation, and promoting the program of a common struggle for Iraqi unity.

▪ Hegemony of the AMS

The threefold strategy of the AMS to boycott the US-sponsored political process, support the insurgency politically and ideologically, and to try to form an alliance with the dissident Shia leader Muqtada al-Sadr, as part of its aim to establish a national armed resistance, appeared to be quite successful during the spring and summer of 2004.

Several factors worked to the AMS's advantage and its campaign to boycott the general elections scheduled for January 2005. First, the general elections were announced at a moment when the first assault on Falluja in

April had failed and the second assault was about to be launched in November, just after the reelection of President Bush. To make sure that none of its Sunni rivals would waver in their boycott of the US-sponsored political institutions, the AMS cleverly launched a campaign to honor the name of Falluja and the other cities of Anbar province that were facing the brunt of the US counterinsurgency campaign. In addition, it stepped up efforts to give voice to the resistance and its legitimacy in fighting against the occupation as the "honorable and nationalist resistance."[45]

Despite the confrontation with the great bulk of the Shia as represented by SCIRI and the Al-Dawa Party, which joined to form the United Iraqi Alliance, and which had gained the support of Grand Ayatollah Ali al-Sistani, the AMS continued to support national unity. The AMS also strove to maintain good relations with Muqtada al-Sadr, who, it was claimed, had been betrayed, like the Sunnis in Falluja, by the Shia leaders who collaborated with the United States. To consolidate this alliance, the AMS erected Sunni-Shia organizations like the Iraqi Nationalist Forces in Uprising Against the Occupation and the Charter of Understanding and National Action, whose seven resolutions were signed by sixty organizations and individuals of all sects and ethnic groups in Iraq.[46] The final factor that worked to the advantage of the AMS was the unwillingness of the United States to speak to the insurgency. Unwittingly, Secretary of State Powell's statement condemning the insurgency because "they're terrorists, they're murderers, and they have no interest in free, fair elections" helped the cause of hardliners such as the AMS.[47]

With the Falluja crisis broadcast every night and the upsurge in the insurgency, the AMS's rivals were unable to counter its rhetoric. The best the Iraqi Islamic Party, as well as influential leaders such as Adnan al-Dulaymi, the head of the Sunni Waqf Endowment (Diwan al-Waqf al-Sunni), could do was to argue in favor of postponing the elections for half a year.[48] Eventually, they succumbed to the pressure of the circumstances. By the end of December 2004, they announced their decision to boycott the elections, although the IIP explicitly stated that it would not withdraw from the political process.[49] With the exception of Sunni moderates such as Ahmad Abd al-Ghaffur al-Samarra'i, who remained opposed to the boycott until the very end, the boycott was complete a few weeks before the elections.[50]

The boycott turned out to be a complete success for the AMS. Once the votes were counted in February 2005, only 17,000 of as many as 250,000 eligible voters from Anbar province had voted, or 0.2 percent of all voters.[51] Less than 50 percent of eligible voters nationwide had voted. Only 17 Sunnis had managed to acquire seats in the 275-seat parliament. In contrast, the Shia list, the United Iraqi Alliance, won 150 seats, while Muqtada al-Sadr's supporters, despite his rejection of the elections, obtained 23 seats.

This was a remarkable achievement for the AMS, as the United States had scored a major propaganda success by having organized free elections in Iraq for the first time in history. Adopting the US presentation of the elections as a victory for democracy, the international media lauded the democratic attitudes of the Shia and condemned the Sunnis as spoilsports or worse.

The price the AMS paid for its success was, however, high. Tens of its members were assassinated that winter,[52] and even the AMS leadership was not spared, both Harith al-Dhari and Bashar al-Faydhi losing a brother to assassins' bullets.[53] On the national level, the price for opting out of the political process was even higher. As Grand Ayatollah Ali al-Sistani, supported by the main Shia parties, SCIRI and the Al-Dawa Party, called for "massive participation" in the elections, and one *'alim* considered nonparticipation "treason of a national right," issuing a fatwa regarding voting as a personal duty (*fard 'ayn*),[54] the rift between Sunnis and Shia deepened. Occurring at the same time as the second attack on Falluja, Sunnis felt betrayed and the insurgency against the United States increasingly turned into a sectarian struggle between Sunnis and Shia.

■ Return of the Political Process

The predominance of the AMS was short-lived. It proved to be much harder for the AMS to maintain a united Sunni front and continue its pressure on its rivals once the elections had taken place and the mechanism of politics reasserted itself. A crucial factor in changing the Sunni strategy was that the new Shia-Kurdish-dominated parliament would go ahead and draw up a permanent constitution and present it in August, in spite of the widespread Sunni insurgency. As a sign of the changing mood, the imam of the Umm al-Qura Mosque, Shaikh Ahmad Abd al-Ghaffur al-Sammara'i, who had been adamantly opposed to the boycott of the elections, organized a meeting between attendants at Friday prayers and a spokesman of the Ministry of Religious Endowments five days after the elections. During this meeting, he asked the congregation to participate in the next elections, scheduled for December 2005.[55] In the meantime, Muhsin Abd al-Hamid, secretary-general of the IIP at the time, met with representatives of the UIA, during which he confirmed the earlier policy of his party, stating that "we have not withdrawn from the political process."[56] A further breach of unity occurred when it was announced that a new political body, the General Conference of the Iraqi People (Al-Mu'tamar al-'Amm li-Ahl al-Iraq), was founded in order "to prepare joining the process of drafting the permanent constitution and the broad Sunni participation in the next elections."[57]

During the next months, the boycott crumbled rapidly. On April 1, Ahmad Abd al-Ghaffur al-Samarra'i read a fatwa signed by sixty-four Sunni clerics and scholars that encouraged Iraqis to join the security forces to protect the country and their own interests, otherwise the Shia would take them over exclusively.[58] On May 20, 2005, one thousand Sunni shaikhs, clerics, and political leaders from Baghdad and nearby cities convened to form a new Sunni political alliance, the Sunni Bloc (Al-Takattul al-Sunni), which was a first step toward the establishment of the Iraqi Consensus Front in October.[59] This step was regarded by many observers as the end of the two-year boycott by the Sunni community of the political process. Typical of the Sunni horror of the direction the political process had taken and the sense of urgency to influence events was the remark of Adnan al-Dulaymi: "We think it is time to take steps to save Iraq's identity, its unity and independence. Iraq is for all, and Iraq is not sectarian."[60]

The argument in favor of joining the political process was finally decided when the UIA succeeded in forming a government at the end of April with the unified Kurdish list. They immediately took over government institutions, filling them with their own followers, thereby underlining the increasing marginalization of the Sunnis. At the same time, the strategy of the AMS collapsed when it became clear that Muqtada al-Sadr had his own agenda and that his Shia affiliation and personal political ambitions prevailed over his political alliance with the AMS. Since the elections, Muqtada al-Sadr limited his Sunni relations to intermediating between the SCIRI leaders and the AMS, whose relationship had deteriorated dramatically after the AMS accused the SCIRI's militia, the Badr Brigade, now acting under the guise of government security forces, of acting as death squads and killing Sunni clerics.[61] However, by then, even moderate Shia held the AMS responsible for the increasing conflict between Sunnis and Shia.[62] The fact that the AMS only addressed the issue of Abu Musab al-Zarqawi's terrorism in September 2005, when it condemned him personally in one of its communiqués, did not enhance its standing among Shia.[63]

▪ *Tawafuq* as a Political Concept and Strategy

The major breakthrough for the political process occurred when in October 2005, the Iraqi Consensus Front (Jabha al-Tawafuq al-'Iraqi, or the Tawafuq) was formed. The ICF consisted of three groups: (1) the Sunni Waqf Endowment, with its former head, Adnan al-Dulaymi, who led the General Conference of the Iraqi People (Al-Mu'tamar al-'Amm li-Ahl al 'Iraq); (2) the National Iraqi Dialogue Council (Majlis al-Hiwar al-Watani al-'Iraqi), led by Khalaf al-Ulyan; and (3) the IIP, led by Tariq al-Hashimi, who had succeeded Muhsin Abd al-Hamid. The ICF was founded in order to participate in the elections of December 2005, despite the fact that the position of the Sunnis had deteriorated further when the constitution was adopted in October. Against the wishes of the Sunnis, the permanent constitution did not recognize the Arab character of Iraq, accepted the possibility of a highly decentralized form of federalism, and did not guarantee an equitable distribution of oil.

The political concept of *tawafuq* (consensus) lies at the heart of the political thinking and strategy of the ICF to redress this imbalance. Largely as a continuation of the IIP, the ICF forms an interesting alternative to the inflexible strategy of the AMS of boycotting the political process. The program of the IIP, published just after the invasion of Iraq, gives a general overview of the basic ideas of the ICF. Besides being based on the "education of the soul" and the "strengthening of morality," it is directed to the reign of "justice" and the principle of "equality" before law. Parliamentary democracy, tolerance, and nonviolence are furthermore regarded as the basis of politics.[64] In its first introductory communiqué, issued on April 20, 2003, the IIP confirmed these ideas when it announced that it was opposed to "fanaticism" and "extremism" and that it accepted "pluralism" (*ta'addudiyya*) in order to stimulate the growth of civil society.[65] Its "enlightened Islamic project" is comparable to the liberal program of the London branch of the Syrian Muslim Brotherhood, led by Ali al-Bayanuni,[66] and the recent program of the Egyptian branch of the Muslim Brotherhood.[67]

The image of a modern political party is further underlined in the regular communiqués the IIP has disseminated by means of its website over the last three years. They portray a party that accepts the necessity of political negotiations and compromises and takes responsibility for its actions, although it is aware of the severe consequences that might ensue from negotiating with the United States and the political forces benefiting from its presence. With the installation of the Allawi government in June 2004, for instance, the party announced that it "decided to take part [in the government] because our absence would be worse than our presence."[68] While acknowledging that political participation in the Allawi government had exposed them "to suspicion, vilification, and accusations,"[69] the IIP only resigned from it belatedly, after the destruction of Falluja in November,[70] while it joined the boycott of the elections in December 2004 only with the deepest misgivings.[71] It participated again in the political process by taking part in the negotiations in the constitutional committee, but as the major deals had already been made when the Sunnis joined the committee, it was not able to achieve much. Not until the very last moment before the referendum on the constitution in October did it succeed in attaining the incorporation of article 142, which called for the installation of a special committee after the next general elections to review the constitution. The IIP gained political clout when it won the surprising number of forty-four seats as part of the Iraqi Consensus Front during the general elections of December 2005.[72] By that time, the ICF had acquired a temporary and conditional mandate from the Sunni voters to push back the Shia steamroller and discredit its political principles and fight for Sunni political demands. As during the referendum, the insurgency allowed the Sunni population to vote during the general elections at the end of 2005.[73]

The ICF interpreted this electoral victory as a mandate to stop the Shia steamroller, the UIA, which had won 138 seats in January. It warned that after the dictatorship of Saddam Hussein, Iraq now faced another trap, that of majority rule, which would allow the UIA to impose a new dictatorship of numbers.[74] Instead it advocated that the new Iraq should be built on the principle of national consensus, *tawafuqiyya*.[75] This principle consists of the rejection of sectarianism, the buildup of mutual trust and consent through negotiations, appointment and promotion on the basis of merit, and the strict imposition of checks and balances on the power of the prime minister. The ICF argued that *tawafuqiyya* would end the marginalization of the Sunni community, force the Shia alliance to withdraw its maximum program of decentralization and monopolization of the nation's wealth, and promote national reconciliation. Ultimately it would be the basis for negotiations with the insurgency.

The direct ideological form the confrontation between the ICF and the Shia United Iraqi Alliance took was the clash between the principle of "national exigency" (*al-istihqaq al-watani*) in times of crisis versus the principle of the division of power based on the election results (*al-istihqaq al-intikhabi*).[76] Once this principle had been accepted, it was assumed that other steps in the political process would follow suit. After the formation of a "government of national unity" based on consensus, Kurds and Shia would recognize the legitimacy of the Sunni insurgency and recognize the injustice of the indiscriminate de-Baathification process, leading to reconciliation and renewed constitutional negotiations.[77]

During the first five months of 2006, the ICF managed to promote its program remarkably well. Several elements worked to its advantage and enhanced its bargaining position. First, the US attitude toward the Sunnis turned in their favor as fear of increasing Iranian power in Iraq grew and the United States realized that it could not beat the insurgency and that a coalition government of all groups was necessary to keep the country together. Second, the Kurds joined the ICF to force Prime Minister Ibrahim al-Ja'afari to step down. Third, the ICF was able to increase its power when the Baathist National Iraqi Dialogue Front (Al-Jabha al-'Iraqiyya li'l-Hiwar al-Watani) of Salih al-Mutlaq, which had gained eleven seats, in addition to the Nationalist Iraqi List (Al-Qa'ima al-'Iraqiyya al-Wataniyya) of Ayad Allawi, at twenty-five seats, joined it to form the Political Bloc (Al-Kutla al-Siyasiyya) with eighty seats in parliament.[78] With the Kurds, they formed an even more powerful force. With this added clout, the ICF was able to put forward its program of consensus. In order to limit the power of the prime minister, several proposals for supervising councils were put forward that would ensure the application of the principle of *tawafuqiyya*, eventually taking the form of the Security Council (Hay'at al-Majlis al-Aman).[79] This council was regarded as a means of controlling the crucial ministries of defense, interior, and national security.[80]

The Future of the Political Process

Since the attack on the Golden Mosque in Samarra in February 2006 and Iraq's descent into a full-fledged civil war, it is difficult to say whether the political process has a future before a certain level of war weariness will have been reached. Whatever form the poltical process takes, its eventual success will depend on the inclusion of some accommodation with the Sunnis, who in their desperation will otherwise prevent the Kurds and the Shia from enjoying the benefits of the new decentralized Iraq, especially the income from oil if it is not shared. Based on research from Arab sources, it seems that the Sunni current in favor of participation in the political process has been quite creative in divesting itself from its position as a minor, marginalized, and negligible factor in the Iraqi political arena since the US-led invasion. In the first half of 2006, it changed from toeing the line and accepting the form of the political process as Bremer had defined it (proportional representation and total neglect of the Sunnis and destruction of their national project)—or as the Shia Alliance had reinterpreted and reappropriated it as a Shia-Kurdish majority strategy for far-reaching decentralization (majority rule and systematic discrimination of Sunnis)—to formulating its own political principles of *tawafuqiyya* (consensus and inclusion). This enabled it to unite the ranks of the moderate Sunnis, include a secular Shia like Ayad Allawi, and build bridges to the Kurdish leaders, in order to enter negotiations with the UIA. The ICF has also been successful in pushing aside, at least for the time being, its main political rival, the AMS, which was the initiator and motor of the political boycott; in fact forcing it to comply with its own definition that it is not a political party. Finally, it succeeded in removing the SCIRI leader, Jabir Bayan Sulagh, from his post as minister of the interior, held responsible for Shia death squads operating under the clout of the Interior Ministry. The very fact that its members speak as ministers or as vice president makes a huge difference.

However, the ICF has also encountered severe setbacks. It has not been able to split the UIA and build cross-sectarian bridges, although the Fadila Party temporarily withdrew from the Shia list. Nor has the political concept of *tawafuqiyya* been accepted by the UIA, which has steadfastly maintained that all ministerial portfolios should be divided in accordance with the electoral results and not on the basis of national unity and consensus, or merit. If the UIA has accepted the principle of a government of national unity, it did so with the conviction that the Shia should play the dominant role in it and that it would strictly adhere to the provisions of the permanent constitution, which until mid-2006 it had refused to consider revising. Even the Security Council, on which ICF and the Iraqi List had pinned their hopes as a consensus-building body, will probably be based on proportional representation, although its decisions will be based on a two-thirds majority.[81] In fact, the principle of *tawafuqiyya* has been reduced to the Ministries of Security, Interior, and Defense, which were only appointed three weeks after the cabinet had been formed. Perhaps as damaging were also problems the ICF encountered with its allies. During the hard and prolonged struggle for the division of cabinet portfolios, the broad Sunni–moderate Shia coalition with the Iraqi List broke down. While the ICF received one of the two vice presidents—for Tariq al-Hashimi—with only five minor ministries, it was disappointed that it received only one more than the Iraqi List of Ayad Allawi, with which it was in competition.[82] Even more threatening was the internal split with the Baathist leader Salih al-Mutlaq, who refused to join the cabinet, and with the group of Shaikh Khalaf Ulyan, one of the ICF's coalition partners, who walked out of parliament during the vote of confidence on the cabinet, calling it a "sectarian government."[83]

If the weakened Sunni support and the split within the ICF does not augur well for the future inclusion of moderate Sunni elements, the initial reactions of the Sunni insurgency stress the conditional and provisional character of the ICF's political mandate. Despite President Jalal Talabani's conciliatory statements that he would welcome talks with any insurgency group that is willing to take part in the political process and does not have Iraqi blood on its hands,[84] Prime Minister Nuri al-Maliki's statement in parliament that he would "crush terrorism" does not seem promising for the strategy of the Tawafuq to integrate the insurgency into the political process.[85] Recent attempts to convince the insurgency to lay down its arms have failed. Those talks that have been initiated, like those in Amman, seem to be with the minor groups.[86] Responding to Tariq al-Hashimi's announcement on May 15, 2006, that negotiations with the insurgency were already under way, five major groups immediately issued a communiqué, stating that negotiations at this point were "untimely."[87] The Army of the Mujahidin even accused the ICF of intending to split the insurgency.[88] Even more negative were the reactions of the insurgents following the presentation of the new government on May 20.[89] The assassination of Tariq al-Hashimi's brother at the end of April underlined the precarious existence of politicians and their families.

For the ICF to succeed in firmly establishing a legitimate basis for the political process and bridge the gap between political process and the armed insurgency, let alone stop the insurgency, it must deliver on the major political issues that preoccupy the Sunni community concerning the equitable division of oil wealth, greater centralization of power, the Arab character of

Iraq, termination of the US occupation, the dismantling of the Shia death squads, and the release of Sunni prisoners. It must salvage the intangible sense of honor that the Sunnis have lost after the US invasion, by forcing other groups, which have benefited the most from their arrival, especially the Shia, to make concessions. Moreover, its leader, Tariq al-Hashimi, will have to convince his community that what he regards as the "hidden occupation," the Iranian presence in Iraq, is more threatening than the US military's "open occupation."[90] Given the unfocused nature of the insurgency and its tenuous relations with the ICF, this will be a difficult task.

Has the ICF been successful in attaining its goals since the beginning of the new parliamentary session in September 2006? As before, the results are mixed. Although it did not succeed in blocking the vote on the law on the formation of regions that UIA leader Abdul Aziz al-Hakim eventually managed to push through parliament in September, it did succeed in postponing the enactment of the law for eighteen months.[91] At the same time, it was successful in forcing the UIA to accept the establishment of a constitutional committee in accordance with article 142 of the constitution that the IIP had succeeded in adding at the last moment of constitutional deliberations in October 2005. This committee, which is to review the constitution and submit its recommendations within a year, works on the basis of consensus, not majority vote. It could block the formation of a Shiite super region of nine southern, predominantly Shia provinces that Abdul Aziz al-Hakim calls for and revise the trend toward decentralization enshrined in the "permanent constitution" of August 2005. A similarly important success was the compromise that will strengthen the central government by giving it the right of veto over all contracts made between oil companies and existing (Kurdistan) and future regions. This draft law, presented in January 2007, is regarded as a major breakthrough for the Sunnis and the strengthening of the central state.[92]

It is doubtful, however, whether these compromises will lead to anything. The escalation of violence between Sunnis and Shia puts the entire political process in jeopardy and makes it increasingly irrelevant. It also has led to greater internal clashes within both communities, positing moderate against more radical Sunnis and pro-Iranian against Arab nationalist Shia groups. Typical of the new polarized situation within the Sunni community is that while in November 2006, the Iraqi interior minister issued an arrest warrant for Harith al-Dhari, the leader of the AMS, for being involved in terrorism,[93] a month later, the leader of the IIP, Tariq al-Hashimi, was welcomed by US president Bush at the White House as vice president of Iraq. The two Sunni currents will have to come closer together to devise a common Sunni political program if the Sunnis want to succeed in retaining some form of central government. However, the internal divisions within the Sunni and Shiite communities also make cross-sectarian compromises possible. Political compromises between moderates on both sides can prevent the all-out eruption of full-scale civil war.

▨ Notes

1. L. Paul Bremer III with Malcolm McConnell, *My Year in Iraq: The Struggle to Build a Future of Hope* (New York: Simon and Schuster, 2006), 49.

2. For the insightful account of the humiliation of Sunnis and the psychological crisis it led to as one of the major motives for the insurgency, see Ahmed S. Hashim, *Insurgency and Counter-Insurgency in Iraq* (London: Hurst, 2006), Chapter 2, "Origins and Motives of the Insurgency," 59–124, and Chapter 5, "Ideology, Politics, and Failure to Execute: The US Counter-Insurgency Campaign," 271–344, and especially the section "Ideological Lens Versus Political Pragmatism," 276–288. See also my "'Defending Our Honor': Authenticity and the Framing of Resistance in the Iraqi Town of Falluja," *Etnofoor* 17, nos. 1–2 (2005): 23–43.

3. See especially Toby Dodge's analysis of the extreme, narrow basis of the Baath regime in his *Iraq's Future: The Aftermath of Regime Change* (London: Routledge, 2005), 45–46. His conclusion is that "[t]his was not a 'Sunni-dominated' state: by the 1990s it was a state ultimately ruled by and for Saddam's family" (p. 46). See also Phebe Marr, "Comments," *Middle East Policy* 7, no. 4 (October 2000): 87.

4. For a short article on the Association of Muslim Scholars see my "The Association of Muslim Scholars in Iraq," *Middle East Report* 237 (winter 2005): 12–19. For a more extensive version see my "Muslim Politics Under Occupation: The Association of Muslim Scholars and the Politics of Resistance," *Arab Studies Journal* 13, no. 2 (fall 2005) and 14, no. 1 (spring 2006): 92–112.

5. See Hashim, *Insurgency*, 178–179; and Michael Eisenstadt and Jeffery White, "Assessing Iraq's Sunni Arab Insurgency," *Policy Focus* 50 (December 2005): 33–35, published by the Washington Institute for Near East Policy. In their report, they adopt the official low estimates of the US forces of around ten thousand fighters with twenty thousand direct supporters. However, the potential recruitment is far higher, from hundreds of thousands to at least tens of thousands of "angry Iraqis." They calculate that the number of Iraqis "involved" one way or the other is around one hundred thousand (pp. 8–11).

6. International Crisis Group (ICG), "In Their Own Words: Reading the Iraqi Insurgency," *Middle East Report* 50 (February 15, 2006): 10–13; Hashim, *Insurgency*, 170–176; Amatzia Baram, "Who Are the Insurgents? Sunni Rebels in Iraq," *USIP Special Report* 134 (April 2005); Dodge, *Iraq's Future*, 14.

7. ICG, "In Their Own Words," 18. This ambivalence is also reflected in the polls held among members of the Sunni community. While between 45 percent and 85 percent of the respondents in Sunni areas expressed support for insurgent attacks on US forces, other surveys show that no more than 30 to 40 percent of the Sunni Arabs believed they would be able to improve the situation and 35 to 50 percent had little confidence in their ability to effect change. See Eisenstadt and White, "Assessing Iraq's Sunni Arab Insurgency," 9–10.

8. Toby Dodge, "Negotiating with the Iraqi Insurgency: Dilemmas and Doubts," *IISS Strategic Comments* 12, no. 1 (February 2006), www.iiss.org/stratcom.

9. ICG, "In Their Own Words," 8–13, and Hashim, *Insurgency*, 184–188.

10. See for the background of the AMS, *Al-Sharq al-Awsat*, 20 April 2004.

11. The website of the AMS is www.iraq-amsi.org. The website of the AMS has been refurbished after July and August 2005, so that most of its articles can no longer be found there. Its communiqués are, however, still on the website from number one.

12. The website of *Al-Basa'ir* is www.basaernews.i8.com.

13. Farhad Khosrokhavar, *Suicide Bombers: Allah's New Martyrs* (London: Pluto Press, 2005), 70–148; and Fawwaz Gerges, *The Far Enemy: Why Jihad Went Global* (Cambridge: Cambridge Univ. Press, 2005), 43–79.

14. *Bayan 'ulama al-'Iraq bi-sha'n al-'azmat al-'Iraqiyya* (Communiqué of the Ulama of Iraq on the Iraqi Crisis), issued by the Leaque of Iraqi Ulama on 4 November 2002, www.islamonline.net/Arabic/doc/2002/11/article0.SHTML.

15. *"Ulama al-Iraq: Muwajahat al-ghazat fard 'ayn"* (Ulama of Iraq: Resistance Against the Invasion Is a Personal Duty), 25 March 2003.

16. *Bayan* (No. 1) *hawl ma yusmi bi-'Majlis al-Hukm* (Communiqué No. 1 Concerning the So-called Interim Governing Council), 16 July 2003, www.iraq-amsi.org.

17. *Bayan* (No. 41) *hawl tashkila al-hukuma* (Communiqué No. 41 Concerning the Formation of the Government), 9 June 2004, www.iraq-amsi.org.

18. *Al-Sharq al-Awsat*, 29 July 2004. The boycott of "foreign" political institutions or institutions that legitimate "occupation" has also a strong parallel with the boycott of Hamas in the Palestinian elections as part of the rejection of the Oslo Agreements.

19. *Al-Sharq al-Awsat*, 6 October 2004. The critical attitude to Jihadi Salafi in general, despite the adoption of some of its tenets, is reciprocated by a critical analysis of the AMS. See *'Hay'at 'Ulama al-Muslimin' fi mizan al-tawhid wa-l-jihad* (The Association of the Muslim Scholars in the Balance Concerning Tawhid and Jihad), published on www.tawhed.ws.

20. Interview with Harith al-Dhari by *Al-Arabiyya* (no date, but probably just before the general elections in December 2005).

21. This has been repeated during the years, one of the last times during the *Al-Arabiyya* interview with Harith al-Dhari.

22. www.swissinfo.org , 29 April 2005.

23. Interview with Abd al-Salam al-Kubaysi in *Al-Sabil*, 7 October 2003. *Al-Sabil* weekly is an important source for research on the AMS. Its website is www.assabeel.info.

24. Interview in *Al-Ahram Weekly*, reposted by San Francisco Bay Area Indymedia, 21 January 2005.

25. Interview with Harith al-Dhari in *Al-Sabil*, 18 May 2004.

26. For remarks on the IIP, see *Al-Sabil*, 18 May 2004.

27. See, for instance, an interview with Abd al-Salam al-Kubaysi, who stated: "The AMS was independent and that is why the resistance trusted it." *Al-Sabil*, 18 May 2004.

28. Interview with Muhammad Ayyash al-Kubaysi in *Al-Sabil*, 1 February 2005.

29. Interview by *Al-Arabiyya* with Harith al-Dhari, cited above.

30. For an analysis of the diversity of the Sunni resistance, see Baram, "Who Are the Insurgents?" 10–12.

31. The series, *Min Fiqh al-Muqawama wa-l-Jihad*, was published between May and July 2005 and consisted of twenty articles dealing with a variety of issues relating to Islamic law and the Sunni resistance. The first ten articles were published in *Al-Sabil*, the rest were put on the internet site of the AMS.

32. Transcript of the Al-Jazeera program, *Al-Shari'a wa-l-Hayat* (Islamic Law and Daily Life) in which Muhammad Ayyash al-Kubaysi participated, broadcast on 28 December 2004. During this program Muhammad Ayyash al-Kubaysi stated: "I do not think there is a *'alim* or thinker in the world who forbids a people whose land is occupied from defending itself. A case like this does not need a *fatwa* and is not the subject matter for *ijtihad*."

33. For comparisons with Hamas, see Beverley Milton-Edwards, *Islamic Politics in Palestine* (London: I. B. Tauris, 1996), 181–198; Jean-Francois Legrain, "Palestinian Islamism: Patriotism as a Condition of Their Expansion," in *Accounting for Fundamentalisms: The Dynamic Character of Movements*, vol. 4 of the Fundamentalism Project, ed. Martin E. Marty and R. Scott Appleby (Chicago: Univ. of Chicago Press, 1996), 413–427.

34. Muhammad Ayyash al-Kubaysi, "Mujahidin am Du'a?" (Mujahidin or Preachers?), in *Min Fiqh al-Muqawama wa-l-Jihad*, Part 11, 4 May 2005, www.iraq-amsi.org.

35. "Al-Muqawama wa-'aqida tawhid" (The Resistance and the Creed of the Unity of God), in *Min Fiqh al-Muqawama wa-l-Jihad*, Part 3, originally published in *Al-Sabil*, 1 March 2005.

36. "Al-Muqawama wa wajibat al-waqt" (The Resistance and the Duty of the Times), in *Min Fiqh al-Muqawama wa-l-Jihad*, Part 10, originally published in *Al-Sabil*, 26 April 2005.

37. "Al-Muqawama wa-l-munafiqin al-judud" (The Resistance and the New Hypocrites), in *Min Fiqh al-Muqawama wa-l-Jihad*, Part 8, originally published in *Al-Sabil*, 12 April 2005.

38. "Al-Muqawama . . . al-ihtilal . . . wa-harb al-mustalahat" (The Resistance, the Occupation, and the War of Words), in *Min Fiqh al-Muqawama wa-l-Jihad*, Part 4, originally published in *Al-Sabil*, 29 March 2005.

39. *Bayan* (No. 18) *hawl ahdath fi-l-mudun al-'Iraqiyya* (Communiqué No. 18 Concerning the Incidents in Iraqi Towns), 15 February 2004, www.iraq-amsi.org. See also interview with Umar Ghalib, spokesman of the AMS, who stated that the AMS "rejects all forms of terrorism," in *Al-Sharq al-Awsat*, 15 February 2005.

40. Interview with Harith al-Dhari by *Al-Arabiyya*, broadcast on 11 December 2005.

41. Interview with Muhammad Ayyash al-Kubaysi in *Al-Sabil*, 1 February 2005.

42. See for example *Bayan* (No. 21) *hawl al-'itida' 'ala al-Rawda al-Kazimiyya* (Communiqué No. 21 Concerning the Aggression on Al-Rawda al-Kazimiyya), 28 February 2004, and the communiqués on the attacks on Karbala and Kazimiyya, 23 March 2004, or the attack on Najaf, 4 April 2004.

43. *Bayan* (No. 1) *hawl ma yusmi bi-Majlis al-Hukm* (Communiqué No. 1 Concerning the So-called Interim Governing Council), 16 July 2003, www.iraq-amsi.org.

44. "Al-Muqawama wa-l-waraqa al-ta'ifiyya" (The Resistance and the Sectarian Card), in *Min Fiqh al-Muqawama wa-l-Jihad*, Part 12, 11 May 2005, www.iraq-amsi.org.

45. These are the words of Muthanna al-Dhari, in an Al-Jazeera program titled "Religious Authorities in Iraq," January 11, 2005.

46. See www.iraq-amsi.org, January 18, 2005.

47. *Los Angeles Times*, 26 December 2005.

48. *Al-Sharq al-Awsat*, 28 November 2004.

49. See the declaration in favor of joining the elections by Ahmad 'Abd al-

Ghaffar al-Samarra'i in *Al-Sharq al-Awsat*, 25 December 2004. See the announce-ment of IIP of its boycott of the elections in *Al-Sharq al-Awsat*, 26 December 2004, and the announcement of Adnan al-Dulaymi's boycott of the elections, www.iraq-amsi.org, January 4, 2005.

50. *Al-Sharq al-Awsat*, 25 December 2004.

51. *Los Angeles Times*, 5 February 2005.

52. In September 2005, the AMS disclosed a report in which it computed that since the US invasion of Iraq, and especially since the fall of Falluja, 107 Sunni ulama had been assassinated, 163 ulama had been arrested, and 663 Sunni mosques had been destroyed or taken over. See www.islamonline.net, September 25, 2005.

53. *Al-Sharq al-Awsat*, 23 November 2004.

54. *Al-Sabah*, 23 October 2004.

55. *Los Angeles Times*, 5 February 2005.

56. Ibid.

57. *Al-Hayat*, 23 February 2005.

58. *New York Times*, 2 April 2005; www.washingtonpost.com, April 2, 2005.

59. *New York Times*, 22 May 2005.

60. *Washington Post*, 22 May 2005. See also *Los Angeles Times*, 22 and 23 May 2005.

61. Scott Peterson, "Iraq's Religious Factions Make Calls for Restraint," *Christian Science Monitor*, 23 May 2005.

62. Debate with Harith al-Dhari on Al-Jazeera, May 7, 2005.

63. Condemnation of al-Zarqawi in *Bayan* (No. 157) *al-mut'allaq bi-l-tasrihat al-akhira li-Abi Mus'ab al-Zarqawi* (Communiqué No. 157 Concerning the Recent Statements on Abu Musab al-Zarqawi), 15 September 2005, www.iraq-amsi.org.

64. See its program, *Man Nahnu?* (Who Are We?), on its website, www.iraq-party.com.

65. *Bayan* (No. 1), *ilan al-Hizb al-Islami al-Iraqi* (Communiqué No. 1, Announcement [of the existence] of the IIP), 20 April 2003, www.iraq-amsi.org.

66. See the program of the Syrian Muslim Brotherhood led by Ali al-Bayanuni, *Al-Mashru' al-Siyasi li-Suriya al-Mustaqbal. Ru'ya Jama'at al-Ikhwan al-Muslimin fi Suriya* (The Political Program for the Future of Syria: The View of the Society of the Muslim Brotherhood in Syria), on its website, www.ikwan-muslimoon-syria.org.

67. *Mubadara Jama'at al-Ikhwan al-Muslimin li-l-islah al-dakhili fi Misr* (The Initiative of the Society of the Muslim Brotherhood for the Internal Reform of Egypt), published on 3 March 2004, on the website of the Egyptian Muslim Brotherhood, www.Afaqarabia.com.

68. *Bayan* (No. 22), *bi-khusus tashkil al-hukuma al-jadida al-intiqaliyya* (Communiqué No. 22 Concerning the Formation of the New Interim Government), June 6, 2004, www.iraq-amsi.org.

69. *Bayan* (No. 33), *intikhabat murashshahi al-mu'tamar al-watani* (Communiqué No. 33 Concerning the Election of the Candidates of the National Conference), 27 July 2004, www.iraq-amsi.org.

70. *Bayan* (No. 50), *bi-khusus al-insihab min al-hukuma al-mu'aqqata* (Communiqué No. 50 Concerning the Resignation of the Interim Government), 9 November 2004, www.iraq-amsi.org.

71. *Bayan* (No. 56), title is unclear, December 27, 2004, www.iraq-amsi.org.

72. *Al-Sharq al-Awsat*, 27 October 2005.

73. For the communiqué of six major insurgency groups in support of the elec-tions against the constitution, see Islam Online, www.islamonline.com, August 22, 2006. During the referendum in October and the general elections in December the

insurgent groups in general refrained from attacking ballot boxes and supported the election campaigns.

74. See the program of Tawafuq, *Barnamijuna al-siyasi* (Our Political Program), on the website of the Iraqi Consensus Front, www.altawafuk.com.

75. For an interesting analysis of the concept of *tawafuqiyya* by Jabir Habib Jabir, see in *Al-Sharq al-Awsat*, 19 February 2006.

76. The opposition between these two principles has defined the political struggle between Shia and Sunnis since the general elections in December 2005. See examples for the content of these terms in *Al-Sharq al-Awsat*, 25 April 2006.

77. For the different demands, see interviews with Ayad Allawi in *Al-Sharq al-Awsat*, 1 February 2006; and the interview with Salih al-Mutla in *Al-Sharq al-Awsat*, 11 February 2006.

78. *Al-Sharq al-Awsat*, 27 January 2006. For the formal formation of the Political Bloc, see *Al-Hayat*, 15 February 2006; and *Al-Sharq al-Awsat*, 10 February 2006.

79. See the interview with Kurdish negotiator Fu'ad Ma'sum in *Al-Sharq al-Awsat*, 20 February 2006.

80. *Al-Hayat*, 26 March 2006.

81. *Al-Hayat*, 11 May 2006.

82. *Al-Sharq al-Awsat*, 1 May 2006.

83. For earlier remarks on the sectarian character of the government by Salih al-Mutlaq, see *Al-Sharq al-Awsat*, 12 May 2006. For more on Salih al-Mutlaq's political demands, see interview with Talabani in *Al-Sharq al-Awsat*, 16 May 2006 and 19 May 2006. See also the critique of Shaikh Khalaf al-Ulyan in *Al-Hayat*, 23 May 2006.

84. *Al-Sharq al-Awsat*, 1 May 2006.

85. See the remarks of Nuri al-Maliki, *Al-Hayat*, 21 May 2006.

86. *Al-Sharq al-Awsat*, 2 May 2006.

87. See also the article on the response of the five groups in Islam Online, www.IslamOnline.com, 16 and 17 May 2006.

88. See the *bayan* of the Jaysh al-Mujahidin, *"Radd 'ala da'wa Tariq al-Hashimi"* (Answer to the Call of Tariq al-Hashimi), 16 May 2006.

89. For the comments of the insurgency, see *Al-Hayat*, 23 May 2006. The Shura Council of the Mujahidin stated it would hit the new government "as hard as possible" and that it considered the new government "apostates" and that it was legitimate to kill its members. The Battalions of the Revolution of 1920 stated that "there is no life, no power and honour except in the jihad in the way of God." For an analysis of the relations between the government and the insurgency, see the article by the Jordanian journalist with excellent connections with the insurgency, Yasir al-Za'atara, in *Al-Hayat,* 24 May 2006.

90. Interview with Tariq al-Hashimi in *Al-Arabiyya*.

91. See the articles in the *Washington Post* covering this issue: "Sunni Bloc Denounces Legislation to Split Iraq," 11 September 2006; "Sadr Holds Out Against Plan to Divide Iraq," 12 September 2006; "Federalism Plan Dead, Says Iraqi Speaker," 13 September 2006; "Iraqi Parties Reach Deal Postponing Federalism," 25 September 2006; and "Parliament Approves Measure Allowing Autonomous Regions," 12 October 2006.

92. "Draft Law Keeps Central Control over Oil in Iraq," *New York Times,* 20 January 2007.

93. "Shiite-Led Iraqi Ministry Seeks Arrest of Top Sunni Cleric," *Washington Post,* 17 November 2006.

7

Shia Militias in Iraqi Politics

Juan Cole

AMONG THE MORE pressing problems in contemporary Iraq is the role of the ethnic and sectarian militias. These paramilitaries provide local security at a time of guerrilla war and criminality on a vast scale. But they also can form death squads and engage in their own excesses. They deny the new state its monopoly on the use of force, a key definition of state success. This chapter focuses on Shia militias, specifically the Badr Corps paramilitary of the Supreme Council for the Islamic Revolution in Iraq (SCIRI). How did the Badr Corps gain its current power in southern Iraq? What security and political roles has it played? Is it a force for stabilization or destabilization in the new Iraq?

Using the Badr Corps as a case study, this chapter will argue that such militias have too much in the way of specialized, sectarian interests, along with a long history of seeking political power, to be compatible with state building in post-Baathist Iraq. The Badr Corps is among the more disciplined of the militias, but even it poses severe security problems in places such as Basra, and seems to have been involved in death-squad activities in Baghdad.

■ The Badr Corps in Iraqi Politics

The Badr Corps of the Supreme Council for the Islamic Revolution in Iraq was formed in the 1980s in Iran among Iraqi exiles from radical Shia parties seeking to overthrow the Baath regime from abroad.[1] The Shia form over 60 percent of the Iraqi population but have historically been repressed by the Sunni Arab minority. The secular, Arab nationalist Baath Party that came to power in a 1968 coup was dominated at its upper echelons by Sunni Arabs and had persecuted activist Shiites. Badr fighters were trained by the Iranian Revolutionary Guard, and came to be ten thousand to fifteen thousand strong. They conducted guerrilla strikes and suicide bombings against

Baath targets all through the 1980s and 1990s. Their cells inside Iraq played a vigorous role in the failed uprising of spring 1991, after Saddam Hussein's defeat in Kuwait at the hands of the international coalition led by the United States.[2]

As the Bush administration made it clear it would invade Iraq to unseat Saddam Hussein, expatriate Iraqi parties had a choice of cooperating (and being rewarded in the new order) or of remaining on the sidelines. Ayatollah Muhammad Baqir al-Hakim agreed to talk to the US government, though he hoped they would back his Badr Corps to fight and take Iraq, just as Washington had taken Afghanistan by backing the Northern Alliance. Al-Hakim was deeply dismayed to discover that the United States instead planned to invade and occupy Iraq with its own army, and to rule it by fiat thereafter. He nevertheless continued to keep in close contact with the US government and never could bring himself to break with it.

Given the close ties between Badr and the Iranian regime, some of the militia's leaders disagreed with Muhammad Baqir al-Hakim's alliance of convenience with the United States. A dissident faction of SCIRI released a communiqué, in March 2003, complaining that al-Hakim had packed the organization's council with yes-men and remarking, "[W]e support the Badr Brigade leaders in their latest initiative in which they rejected Baqir al-Hakim's unilateral policies and denounced his move to throw himself into the lap of the Americans."[3] Since the titular Badr leader was Abdul Aziz al-Hakim, this report raises the question of whether he differed with his older brother on policy.

Despite some internal dissension, most Badr units became committed to joining in the war effort against Saddam. They began doing maneuvers at their base at Darbandikhan in Iran, near the border with Iraq. Badr fighters came first of all into Kurdistan, where the Kurds welcomed them as allies. In late February 2003, "ten truck loads" of Badr fighters are said to have crossed over from Iran, deploying in Khaniqin and Penjwin.[4] On March 16, on the eve of the war, the major Iraqi opposition parties that maintained paramilitaries met in Kurdistan to set up a joint military command that included the Badr Corps, the Kurdish *peshmerga*, and other forces. A Kurdish leader gave a telephone interview with the Kuwaiti daily *Al-Watan* in which he insisted that the paramilitaries "will play a major role" in the overthrow of the regime.[5] SCIRI figure Muhsin al-Hakim gave a press conference in Tehran just after the United States invaded, in which he affirmed, "The Badr Corps will continue its activities in northern and central Iraq, as well as in Baghdad and important southern cities."[6]

In late March, aware of the Badr infiltration, US secretary of defense Donald Rumsfeld identified the group as a cat's paw of Iran and threatened to have the advancing US military treat them as enemy combatants. SCIRI spokesman Muhsin al-Hakim denied that Badr was an extension of the

Iranian Revolutionary Guards.[7] The regime fell in April, but the United States and Britain still did not have effective control of the center-north of the country, giving an opening to the Badr fighters. Presumably having come down to nearby Diyala province from Kurdistan, in April the Badr Corps battled the remnants of the Baath military for the city of Baquba, northeast of Baghdad, which US Marines had not yet entered. A Kurdish newspaper reported:

> Every night there are clashes near Badr Army headquarters. Sometimes the fighting lasts two hours, and most of the time people are killed and injured. The people of Baquba are not satisfied with the presence of the Badr Army. In a recent development, a group was formed asking all political parties in the area to cooperate with it in order to force the army out. It is worth mentioning that the Badr Army was prevented from entering the liberated areas but it infiltrated into some other areas and carries out its political activities.[8]

In mid-April, the Kuwaiti daily *Al-Watan* warned that its source was saying that "elements of SCIRI's Badr Brigade have entered certain areas in the southern city of Al-Kut in civilian dress and have mingled with the population. He estimated their number at 9,000." The source expressed fears that the Iran-backed paramilitary would next attempt to infiltrate Basra province.[9] The numbers mentioned are certainly exaggerated, but that the Badr was coming into Iraq is perfectly plausible. By April 25, the US military was making a concerted effort to detain Badr Corps combatants, seeing them as proxies of Iran.[10]

Badr fighters quickly discovered that they were not the only Shiite paramilitary. Young men in the Shiite slums loyal to young clerical firebrand Muqtada al-Sadr of Kufa established patrols, dominated mosques and clinics, and ran protection rackets. They were eventually dubbed by Sadr the "Mahdi Army." They were loyal to the memory of Grand Ayatollah Muhammad Sadiq al-Sadr, killed by Saddam in 1999, and they ridiculed the al-Hakims for having fled Iraq for the safety of Iran in the Baath period. They largely kept SCIRI and Badr out of east Baghdad, which they dubbed "Sadr City," and competed for influence in southern provinces such as Maysan. Yet, by avoiding clashes with the United States and utilizing the contacts established along their rat lines, which they had used to infiltrate Iraq from Iran, the Badr Corps established itself as a stronger and more mature force in much of the south than the Mahdi Army.

With the fall of Saddam, SCIRI and Badr leaders began returning to Iraq. The corps commander, Abdul Aziz al-Hakim, came to Najaf in mid-April. On May 10, Ayatollah Muhammad Baqir al-Hakim crossed from Iran to Basra, where he addressed ten thousand admirers at a stadium. The British military offered him protection, fearing that he might meet the same fate as Abdul Majid al-Khu'i, who returned to Iraq from London with coalition backing and was cut down by a mob in Najaf on April 10. Al-Hakim insisted on being guarded by Badr Corps fighters.[11]

In mid-May, US civil administrator L. Paul Bremer issued an order demanding that all armed groups in the country give up their heavy weapons and apply for permits to carry light arms. The Agence France-Presse interpreted this decree as the dissolution of all militias save the Kurdish *peshmerga*.[12] In fact, the United States never had the troops available to enforce a ban on owning light weapons, so only the ban on heavy weapons was effective, and then only with regard to carrying them in public. Ayatollah Muhammad Baqir al-Hakim rather disingenuously replied that the Badr Corps had no weapons![13] In any case, in late May, US military commanders reported that Badr members were "playing by the rules" and seemed to pose no threat.[14]

In a May 31, 2003, interview on Al-Jazeera, the anchor asked Abdul Aziz al-Hakim whether Badr would give up its heavy arms. He replied in the affirmative:

> As you know, the Badr Corps had been working against the criminal Baathist regime of Saddam Hussein. After the collapse of this regime, there is no justification for the Badr Corps to keep its heavy weapons. Therefore, it left these weapons. The Badr Corps intends to work in the fields of construction, keeping security, and supporting the Iraqi people in their political demands of establishing a national Iraqi government that is elected by the Iraqis.[15]

He rejected, however, US demands that the Badr Corps disarm completely, abandoning even its light weaponry, and complaining that it was unfair to make such a demand of the Shia while allowing the Kurdish *peshmerga* to retain their arms: "There should be no discrimination between the Iraqis, although we are proud of our Kurdish brothers."

On June 5, L. Paul Bremer's staff told the Arab press about a plan to disarm the Badr Corps and said it would not be incorporated into the new army. He said that armed groups would be given an amnesty until June 14 to turn in their heavy weapons and would only be allowed to retain pistols and hunting rifles if kept at home.[16] SCIRI leader Ayatollah Muhammad Baqir al-Hakim became forthright in continuing to defend a role for an armed Badr Corps. In his first major Friday prayer sermon in Najaf after the fall of Saddam, on June 6, 2003, he replied to the proposal for disarming the militias, saying that "criminal groups should first be disarmed. The followers, henchmen and remnants of the regime who are still armed and are committing crimes should be disarmed first. Looting gangs must be disarmed. These gangs are wreaking havoc in the land."[17] Also in early June, al-Hakim gave an interview with *Der Spiegel* in which he said that Badr no longer needed tanks or artillery, but would continue to deploy light weapons. Indeed, he said, Iraqis in general needed such weapons for self-defense. He wondered how the United States could allow armed bands, including Saddamists, to roam with weapons but wanted to disarm the Badr Corps, which was "an integral part of the Iraqi people."[18]

The United States' need for armed Kurdish allies in the north led them to face difficulties in arguing for disarming the militias of the Shia south, since such a policy was clearly invidious. Tensions between the United States and the Badr Corps continued to flare up from time to time. On June 7, the US military announced that it had detained twenty members of the Supreme Council and the Badr Corps who were making their way into Iraq from Iran.[19] Typically, such captured figures were released fairly quickly.

SCIRI leadership, for all its impatience to be rid of the United States and Britain, imposed strict discipline on the Badr fighters. In late July, Muhammad Baqir al-Hakim gave an interview in which he said that he supported peaceful resistance to the US occupation so as to convince them that Iraqis were perfectly capable of managing their own affairs. He darkly hinted that if the United States did not respond to Iraqi demands, "it will be a different story." He complained that Iraqis suffered insecurity at US hands, and could not even leave money at home because the foreign troops would steal it. He "categorically denied any connection between the Badr troops and the ongoing armed Iraqi resistance."[20]

As security and services deteriorated in southern Iraq, some observers became alarmed about Badr's ambitions. In mid-August, riots broke out against the British in the large southern port city of Basra, over lack of fuel and services. A Kuwaiti daily reported that the Badr Corps had become a state within a state and was responsible for the killing of several truck drivers: "It has begun powerfully organizing its ranks in order to establish hegemony over the southern regions of Iraq, encompassing the area from southern Baghdad to the Faw Peninsula." It accused the corps of recruiting ex-Baathists and criminal elements in order to establish a powerful army, and of funding itself by car theft rings: "Reliable sources tell *al-Watan* that the commander of the Corps now dominates entire districts of Basra and that he is readying 'prisons and special sites' wherein he will imprison all those who attempt to stand in his way." Badr stood accused of requisitioning trucks and tankers and stealing tools and equipment.[21] While at the time this report might have read as breathless, in light of subsequent events it seems plausible. On August 25, Kuwait's *Al-Watan* reported that coalition forces were planning to move against Badr in Safwan and elsewhere in the south.

If the coalition did entertain such plans, they were derailed by an enormous explosion. On August 29, 2003, guerrillas assassinated Muhammad Baqir al-Hakim with a massive truck bomb in front of the shrine of Imam

Ali in Najaf, as he was exiting Friday prayer ceremonies. Hundreds of members of the Badr Corps immediately headed for Najaf. A Middle East wire service reported, "The witnesses told the MENA correspondent that hundreds of the brigade's elements were seen in military fatigues bearing weapons and rocket propelled grenades (RPGs) and assembling in different places in Baghdad before heading for Najaf."[22] They were said to be threatening revenge. The assassination produced a crisis in the relationship between the United States and its allies among the Shia religious parties, a threat the United States could ill afford at a time when the Sunni Arab guerrilla movement was growing.

The very next day, SCIRI and its allies, according to the *New York Times*, pressed the United States on the "possibility of forming a large Iraqi paramilitary force to help improve security in the country." The United States appears seriously to have considered the idea of setting up such a force, thousands strong, which would eventually patrol Iraqi cities as US troops withdrew. The Iraqis insisted that they could form such a force in just over a month. Dexter Filkins quoted a participant in the talks, Mudhar Shahkawt, as saying, "The situation has changed, and there is a new receptiveness to the idea. . . . This force could move inside the cities and allow coalition forces to withdraw to places outside."[23] Shiite leaders worried that they would not be able to keep control of the Shiite masses, enraged by the blasphemous killing of a prominent ayatollah outside their holiest shrine. Followers of Muqtada al-Sadr blamed the US military for the blast, and demanded that they leave Iraq.

Even though the idea of a combined Shia militia force for the south was quickly shelved, as the feared massive unrest among Shiites did not materialize, the United States appears to have backed off pressuring the Badr Corps after this incident. Its commander, Abdul Aziz al-Hakim, emerged as the new leader of SCIRI, ensuring that it would continue to enjoy the support of its civilian parent party.

In late October 2003, the political adviser of the Badr Corps, Muhsin al-Hakim, announced that it had become an Iraqi reconstruction organization. Henceforward, he said, the group would be known as the Badr Organization. He maintained that the militia no longer had any heavy arms to turn over. The new focus on reconstruction would involve a "structural change." It seemed clear, however, that Badr would not change its stripes too radically. The spokesman admitted, "Security is one of the requirements of development and the Badr Organization will participate actively in order to achieve development."[24] Moreover, only the previous day *Al-Adalah*, the newspaper of the Supreme Council for the Islamic Revolution in Iraq, had carried an editorial arguing that "Only the Mujahidin [i.e., Badr] are capable of maintaining the Iraqi people's security."[25] The new emphasis on development would position the organization to receive monies earmarked for that purpose, at the same time that its leaders appear to have hoped such activities would soften their image. In this regard, they may have learned something from the Pentagon, which was having its troops do development work as well.

As Badr became involved in politics, it began to reach out to possible constituencies. A paraphrase of a 2003 article in SCIRI's official newspaper informs us that "the tribes in holy al-Najaf held their first conference in coordination with the branch of the Badr Organization in the city on December 16" and that "many political, social, and cultural figures attended the conference." Among the issues addressed in the speeches given was "the effective role the Iraqi tribes are supposed to assume at this stage in the history of the country."[26] The rural tribes are armed and organized on a kinship basis, and if Badr was looking for new members, they would have been prime recruits.

Badr was already beginning its transformation into a political party in its own right. In late December 2003, an Arab journalist who visited the small city of Samawah in the south reported that its municipal council "was totally dominated by the *Da'wah* party, the Supreme Council for Islamic Revolution in Iraq, and the *Tha'r Allah* group of the Badr forces."[27] Badr Corpsmen were said in January 2004 to be dividing up policing and security duties in Samawah with Al-Dawa Party activists.

This sort of situation existed in many small towns and villages in the Shia south, as came to light in early March, when British troops in the small town of Qal'at Salih south of Amara were fired on by a Badr fighter, who took refuge in the Badr Organization offices. They followed him there and arrested all the activists within, but then a town crowd gathered to protest and set their vehicle on fire. Four British troops were killed in the melee, and, it was said, a civilian woman. Such firefights between the British and Badr were rare, but the real moral of the story was the obvious loyalty of the townspeople to their militia.[28] Throughout 2004, Sunnis charged that Badr was engaged in a secret, dirty war of assassination against former Baathist officials and other perceived enemies.

By late 2004, Abdul Aziz al-Hakim was boasting that the Badr Corps had one hundred thousand men under arms (almost certainly a vast exaggeration), and he proposed that they be deployed to guard polling stations during the January 30, 2005, elections. Informally, this may have been done in some of the Shia south, where violence was kept to a minimum. Sunni Arab critics raised alarms about the offer, pointing to what they considered the group's terrorist past and implying that Badr guards for the elections were a surefire way to ensure that SCIRI and the Badr Corps stole the elections.[29] The Badr Organization ran as a party in its own right, as part of the United Iraqi Alliance, the coalition put together by Grand Ayatollah Ali al-Sistani. It held a small bloc of seats in the federal parliament, as part of the ruling coalition (the UIA gained 51 percent of seats).

The UIA victory gave SCIRI control of the Ministry of the Interior, which in Iraq was long responsible for domestic spying and repression. The new minister, Bayan Jabr—a nom de guerre for Baqir Sulagh—was a Turkmen SCIRI activist long resident in Damascus with strong ties to Badr. He inducted large numbers of Badr fighters into the new units of special police commandos, which were given names such as the Scorpion Brigade and the Wolf Brigade. Under Jabr, the interior ministry also pushed for the Badr Corps to dominate the police in cities such as Amara in the south.[30] In the January 2005 elections, the Badr Organization also won seats on the provincial councils. In the Shiite holy city of Najaf, the new elected governor hailed from the Supreme Council for the Islamic Revolution in Iraq, and the deputy governor was from Badr. Everywhere the Badr Organization won provincial council seats it became an ally for the federal Interior Ministry in facilitating the recruitment of Badr fighters into the official police force. This process occurred in Basra, Najaf, Karbala, and elsewhere, though its exact details are murky. The police chief of Basra gave an interview in the summer of 2005 in which he admitted that much of his force was of dubious loyalty and mainly oriented to militias and religious parties.

In the negotiations over the formation of a new government in spring of 2005, after the victory of SCIRI and Al-Dawa in the national polls, Kurdish MP Arif Tayfur complained that SCIRI was pushing for the Badr Corps to have the sort of security duties in the south that the *peshmerga* or Kurdish militiamen had been given in Kurdistan.[31] Since the Kurds refused to allow federal troops on their soil and depended for security wholly on the *peshmerga*, which they recognized as the official armed forces of Kurdistan, the analogy suggests that Abdul Aziz al-Hakim was already envisaging a wide-ranging role for Badr.

The special police commandos with a Badr background had been trained by the Iranian Revolutionary Guards, and they were increasingly accused of engaging in death-squad tactics against those they suspected of belonging to or aiding the Sunni Arab guerrilla movement. Men dressed, at least, as special police commandos began invading Sunni neighborhoods and even mosques and kidnapping the men within, who often later appeared in the streets dead, with a bullet behind the ear. In April and May of 2005, a major dispute broke out when the hard-line Salafi Association of Muslim Scholars (AMS) openly accused Badr of running anti-Sunni death squads from the Ministry of the Interior. SCIRI and Badr officials angrily denied the charges, and violence threatened to erupt.[32] Ironically, an emerging crisis was somewhat defused when young clerical leader Muqtada al-Sadr stepped in to mediate between the two.[33]

The special police commandos set up secret prisons where they tortured suspected guerrillas. US forces invaded one of these prisons in late summer 2005 and released its inmates, who showed clear signs of abuse, torture, and starvation. In contrast, Badr fighters appear not to have been able to infiltrate the ranks of the new Iraqi army in any numbers.

Having become a force in southern Iraqi politics, the Badr Organization, like SCIRI, increasingly saw itself as a regional political force, based in the south. Its leader, Hadi al-Amiri, therefore backed a provision in the new constitution drafted in summer 2005, which allowed the formation of provincial confederacies (several of Iraq's eighteen provinces could band together to establish a joint administration and increase their weight vis-à-vis Baghdad).[34] Provincial confederacies, modeled on the Kurdish Regional Government in the north, would be able to claim 100 percent ownership of all future petroleum and other natural resource finds, denying them to the weak federal government. The likelihood is that such provincial confederacies, if founded, will be theocratic mini-states under the dominance of Shiite religious parties such as SCIRI and Al-Dawa.

Such a loose federalism was opposed by the other Shia forces, the Al-Dawa Party, and the followers of Muqtada al-Sadr. In September of 2005, Mahdi Army militiamen clashed with Badr fighters in Najaf and Karbala, raising alarms of an intra-Shiite war. Grand Ayatollah al-Sistani and other Shia notables stepped in, however, to calm the dispute, which subsided.

In the run-up to new elections on December 15, 2005, the United Iraqi Alliance admitted the Sadr bloc, promising it that an effort would be made to allot it thirty seats. After the elections, in which the UIA won 46 percent of seats, the Sadrists made an alliance within the coalition with the Al-Dawa Party. SCIRI and Badr lost their dominance within the UIA, as a result. They were unable to get their candidate, Adil Abdul Mahdi, nominated for prime minister. The UIA first chose Ibrahim al-Ja'afari, who proved unacceptable to all the other major parties and to the United States. The UIA therefore relented and replaced him with another Al-Dawa leader, Nuri "Jawad" al-Maliki, who had long been in exile in Damascus.

When, in late February 2006, guerrillas blew up the Al-Askariya Shrine in Samarra, the site of the tombs of the tenth and eleventh Imams and a place associated with the messianic twelfth Imam for Shiites, communal violence broke out on a scale seldom seen in modern Iraq. Shia mobs roamed Baghdad's streets looking for Sunni Arabs to kill. Over 100 Sunni mosques were attacked, several being burned to the ground and dozens damaged. In early March, a United Nations envoy charged that Badr had been involved in hundreds of killings and assassinations.[35] In contrast, Abdul Aziz al-Hakim and Hadi al-Amiri used the Samarra attack to defend the Badr Corps, suggesting that had it been allowed to operate freely instead of being repressed under US pressure, and had it been guarding shrines like the Askariyyah, the desecration would never have occurred.

After a late March US raid on a Sadrist religious center, or Husayniya, which went awry and resulted in the deaths of several civilians, al-Amiri even at one point became so bold as to demand the expulsion from Baghdad of US ambassador Zalmay Khalilzad, who had decided to mollify the Sunni Arabs by reining in Badr.[36] This demand went too far, and, given the fact of US power in Iraq, damaged Badr's case rather than helped it. It was not repeated. Badr Corps fighters were accused of again using death-squad tactics against Sunni Arabs in the weeks that followed. In one specific incident, Interior Ministry special police commandos, mostly Badr Corps fighters, attempted to invade a largely Sunni Arab Baghdad district, but were repulsed by local Sunni neighborhood militiamen.

As the new government was forming in spring of 2006, the continued prominence of militias in Iraq had become a central issue in high politics. Al-Maliki pledged to disband them and to allow their members to be recruited into government security forces. The Badr Corps and its dominant position in the special police commandos was an issue that inspired a great deal of politicking, with attempts made to ensure that SCIRI lost control of the Ministry of the Interior. In late April, reports surfaced that large reconstruction contracts, as well as bribes to permit the work, had been granted to Badr and other militias.[37] In contrast to the al-Maliki approach, the ex-Baathist secularists Salih al-Mutlaq and Ayad Allawi agreed that the militias had to be disbanded, but rejected the idea of incorporating organizations such as Badr into the new security forces.[38] In any case, both the Supreme Council and Sadrist leaders disingenuously denied that their militias any longer existed as such, saying that they were popular political forces.

In late spring 2006, the militia issue was broached with special urgency in the southern port city of Basra, which witnessed a wave of assassinations in April and May (one every hour for the previous month, according to the Iraqi government). Some of the assassins appear to have been Marsh Arab tribesmen who had come into the city after the fall of Saddam, and their victims seem to have included political rivals. Iraqi government sources reported that the police mostly refused to attempt to apprehend the perpetrators, fearing reprisals from their tribesmen. Sources told the Iraqi newspaper *Al-Zaman* (May 16, 2006) that Basra was in chaos and dominated by militias and lawless gangs. Automobiles with darkened windows cruised the streets, armed militiamen within, imposing their law on the city. These sources blamed Kuwait and Iran for the situation, alleging that their intelligence services were funding and arming the Iraqi militias for their own purposes (the allegation is probably that Iran was funding the Badr Corps). Tribal firefights between the Marsh Arab Al-Bait Sa'idah tribe and the Bani Mansur were common—as were feuds between the Bani Ammar and Al-'Ashur. The sources said that Basra was without authority save that of the militiamen. The major political parties, they said, were unable to dampen down the violence because they were so divided against one another (this allegation is probably a reference to the divisions on the city council between the Fadila Party and SCIRI).

The governor of Basra, Muhammad Misbah al-Wa'ili of the Fadila Party, attempted to fire his police chief. He complained that the Basra police had not undertaken a single investigation of the hundreds of assassinations. He further charged that some in the Iraqi border patrol and the army had suspicious ties to the assassins. Al-Wa'ili also insisted that two clerical representatives of Grand Ayatollah Ali al-Sistani were involved in the collapse of security. This dispute between governor and police chief had overtones of a conflict between the Fadila ("Virtue") Party and the Badr Corps, which had a privileged position inside the Basra police force because of the influence of the SCIRI-controlled Interior Ministry in 2005 and 2006.[39]

In early May, persons dressed as Iraqi policemen lured the head of the Al-Karamisha Marsh Arab tribe in Basra into a trap and killed him. In the aftermath, the furious tribesmen warred with police and with Shia militias in several districts of the port, at a time of vacuum in municipal government. Majid al-Sari, adviser to the minister of defense, reported that Al-Karamisha tribesmen came out into the streets of the city heavily armed, and killed eleven policemen in the course of an attack on a police station in the Dayr quarter to the south of the city.

They also burned down two buildings used in the Intisar district of the Dayr quarter by the Supreme Council for the Islamic Revolution in Iraq. The hostility of the Karamisha to SCIRI and their torching of that party's district headquarters suggest strongly that they believed the policemen who attacked their chief had actually been Badr Corps. The assassination, in turn, may have itself been vengeance for Karamisha operations against Basra police, themselves often recruited from militias such as the Badr Corps and the Mahdi Army. Two organizations, Rebels of the Uprising and the Revenge of God (Tha'r Allah, a branch of the Badr Corps), staged demonstrations on successive days against Governor al-Wa'ili in protest against the collapse of security in the city. Here we see another Badr connection and increasingly can conclude that these events derived from a growing feud between the Karamisha and Badr, both as the latter was organized within the police and as an independent militia. A Basran living in Jordan e-mailed me in late May that reports from the city spoke of the tribes battling Iranian-influenced elements. Since native Iraqis often coded Badr as an Iranian cat's paw, this allegation is further evidence of the character of the struggle.[40]

In late May and early June 2006, Prime Minister Nuri al-Maliki attempted to deal with the situation in Basra. He visited the city and consulted with its notables and politicians. He established a provincial security council with representatives of all the major political factions in the city, including SCIRI and Badr, and declared a state of emergency, placing troops of the newly formed Iraqi Tenth Division at major checkpoints. These steps do not appear to have restored security to the city, though the severe crisis of May 2006 passed. The party and tribal militias remained armed, active, and involved in massive smuggling of petroleum, which fueled their turf wars. In summer and fall of 2006, several firefights broke out between the Badr Corps (or Badr Corps–dominated police forces), not only in Basra but also in Amara and Diwaniyah, other important cities of the Shiite south.[41]

■ Conclusion

The full extent of Badr paramilitary control of the Shia south is difficult to estimate. It has rivals, such as the Mahdi Army of Muqtada al-Sadr, which predominates in east Baghdad (Sadr City). In Basra, the paramilitary of the Fadila (Virtue Party) also has influence in the police. But in much of the south, especially Najaf, Karbala, Diwaniyah, Nasiriyah, Samawah, and large swathes of Basra, the Badr Corps seems likely to provide what local security there is. The United States had proved unable to disarm it or curb its influence. In part, they failed because they depended heavily on the *peshmerga* in the north and so lacked credibility when they demanded that the Shia give up their paramilitaries. In part, the United States was threatened by the Sunni Arab guerrilla movement and could not afford to move dramatically against the Shiite militias, lest they lose their major Arab ally. And in part, their inability to ensure security in cities like Najaf, and the consequent assassination of Muhammad Baqir al-Hakim, made a powerful argument to local political forces for their need for the Badr Corps.

If Badr has turned to death-squad tactics on a grand scale, it has, however, become more of a security problem than a security solution. At the same time, given how beholden the United Iraqi Alliance is to parties with strong paramilitaries, it remains to be seen if it has the political will to curb them. And, given that the United States dissolved the regular Iraqi military and that it will take years to form a new one, it is not clear that the new political class could survive a single day were it not guarded by its paramilitaries. Insecurity has become both the mother and the child of the chaos in Iraq, and the Badr Corps will not go gentle into that good night.

The narrative presented above suggests that the Badr Corps as a stand-alone militia poses significant and ongoing challenges to restoring security and building the new Iraqi state. Where there is a clear Shia majority and SCIRI political dominance, as in Samawah, it is possible that Badr's peace-keeping efforts are a positive force. In any case, the multinational forces have withdrawn from Muthanna province where Samawah is located, and so there may be few alternatives for the local population to dependence on

Badr or on a police force infiltrated by Badr. In such small-town, all-Shia settings, the Badr Corps appears to have behaved in a relatively disciplined and positive manner.

But where there is a mixed population, as in Baghdad, the Badr Corps has been involved in ethnic cleansing campaigns and death-squad activity against Sunni Arab forces and populations. Even in largely Shiite Basra, it has engaged in faction-fighting with other Shia militias and with Marsh Arab tribal gangs. Even when Badr elements have been regularized, as with their induction into the special police commandos of the Interior Ministry in 2005 and 2006, they continue to function as a rogue element, corrupting the national police and pursuing private vendettas. They also are likely vectors of continued Iranian influence-peddling in Iraq, often of an unhelpful character.

In conclusion, it has to be argued that the Badr Corps and other sectarian militias are for the most part a negative factor in Iraqi security and state building. In some limited contexts, they might contribute to local security by policing neighborhoods. But for the most part, they have behaved in ways that exacerbated sectarian tensions and decreased security for the entire population, and this has been true whether they functioned as independent militias or were integrated into official Iraqi security forces, mainly local police or the Interior Ministry special police commandos. The best thing that could be done with Badr Corps fighters is to decommission them as a paramilitary force and give them government desk jobs in the civilian bureaucracy. It would be dangerous to simply dissolve the Corps and leave its members unemployed. But they are not suitable recruits for the new Iraqi military and police, given their background and long experience as a specifically sectarian guerrilla force. The same conclusion would apply to the Mahdi Army of Muqtada al-Sadr, which is even less professional and disciplined than the Badr Corps. Ultimately, the Iraqi army and police will have to be built from scratch.

■ Notes

1. For the historical background of modern Iraqi Shiism, see Pierre-Jean Luizard, *La formation de l'Irak contemporain* [The Formation of Contemporary Iraq] (Paris: Editions du Centre National de la Recherche Scientifique, 1991); Yitzhak Nakash, *The Shi'is of Iraq* (Princeton, NJ: Princeton Univ. Press, 1994); Meir Litvak, *Shi'ite Scholars of Nineteenth Century Iraq* (Cambridge, MA: Cambridge Univ. Press, 1998); Juan Cole, *Sacred Space and Holy War: The Politics, Culture, and History of Shi'ite Islam* (London: I. B. Tauris, 2002); Faleh Abdul-Jabar, ed., *Ayatollahs, Sufis and Ideologues* (London: Saqi Books, 2002); Salah al-Khursan, *Hizb al-Da'wa al-Islamiyya: Haqa'iq wa watha'iq* [The Islamic Dawa Party: Facts and Documents] (Damascus: Al-Mu'assassa al-'Arabiyya li'l-Dirasat wa'l-Buhuth al-Istratijiyya, 1999); Keiko Sakai, "Modernity and Tradition in the Islamic Movements in Iraq," *Arab Studies Quarterly* 23, no. 1 (winter 2001): 37–52;

Mahan Abedin, "Dossier: Hezb al-Daawa al-Islamiyya: Islamic Call Party," *Middle East Intelligence Bulletin* 5, no. 6 (June 2003), at www.meib.org/articles/0306_iraqd.htm; Hanna Batatu, "Shi'ite Organizations in Iraq: Al-Da'wah al-Islamiyah and al-Mujahidin," in *Shi'ism and Social Protest,* ed. Juan Cole and Nikki R. Keddie, 179–200 (New Haven: Yale Univ. Press, 1986); Joyce N. Wiley, *The Islamic Movement of Iraqi Shi'as* (Boulder, CO: Lynne Rienner, 1992).

2. Juan Cole, "The United States and Shi'ite Religious Factions in Post-Ba'thist Iraq," *Middle East Journal* 57, no. 4 (autumn 2003): 543–566; Juan Cole, "The Iraqi Shiites: On the History of America's Would-Be Allies," *Boston Review* (fall 2003), online at www.bostonreview.net; Mahan Abdedin, "Dossier: The Supreme Council for the Islamic Revolution in Iraq (SCIRI)," *Middle East Intelligence Bulletin* 5, no. 10 (October 2003), at www.meib.org/articles/0310_iraqd.htm.

3. "Splinter Faction of Iraqi Opposition Group Criticizes Chairman Al-Hakim's Policy," *Al-Quds al-'Arabi,* 10 March 2003, Foreign Broadcast Information Service (FBIS).

4. "Iraqi Opposition Islamist Force Deployed in the Kurdish Region," *Hawlati* (Kurdish), 26 February 2003, FBIS.

5. "Al-Mu'aridah al-'Iraqiyyah tushakkil Qiyadah Maydaniyyah Mushtarikah," *Al-Watan* (Kuwait), 16 March 2003.

6. "Iran: Iraqi Islamist Leader Says Opposition Preparing to Meet in Kurdistan," *Tehran Iranian Students News Agency,* 21 March 2003, FBIS.

7. "Iran: Mohsen Hakim Denies Relations Between Badr Corps in SCIRI Group, IRGC," Tehran, IRNA in English, 0927 GMT, 29 March 2003, FBIS.

8. "Iraq: Kurdish Paper Reports Effect of War on Town of Ba'quba," *Hawlati* (Kurdish), 26 April 2003, BBC Monitoring Middle East.

9. "Badr Brigade Elements, Iranians Reportedly Enter Iraq's Al-Kut, Basra Provinces," *Al-Watan* (Kuwait), 17 April 2003, FBIS.

10. "Iran-based Iraqi Shiite Group Accuses US of Arresting Military Leaders," Agence France-Presse, 26 April 2003.

11. "Ba'd 23 'amman fi al-manfa, al-Hakim ya'ud ila al-'Iraq bi Himayat Faylaq Badr," *Al-Watan* (Kuwait), 11 May 2003.

12. "US Lifts Sanctions on Iraq as Guerrilla Violence Flares," Agence France-Presse, 28 May 2003.

13. "Iraq: SCIRI Leader Denies Military Wing Possesses Weapons," Voice of the Mujahidin Radio, in Arabic 1600 GMT, 27 May 2003, BBC Monitoring.

14. "Marine Commander Says Pro-Iran Forces in Iraq Appear to Pose No Threat," Associated Press, 30 May 2003.

15. "Iraq: SCIRI Leader Explains Decision to Abandon Heavy Weapons," Al-Jazeera TV, Doha, in Arabic 1340 GMT, 31 May 2003, FBIS.

16. Nasir al-Nahr, "Ta'limat Amrikiyyah Jadidah li naz' al-Silah," *Al-Sharq al-Awsat,* 7 June 2003; "Iraqi Sources on Plans to Build New Army, Disarm Badr Corps," *Al-Hayat,* 5 June 2003, BBC Monitoring, 6 June 2003.

17. "SCIRI Chairman Rejects US Proposal to Appoint Iraqi Council," Al-Jazeera TV, Doha, in Arabic 1716 GMT, 6 June 2003, BBC Monitoring International Reports, 7 June 2003.

18. "Amerika ist parteiisch," *Der Spiegel,* 7 June 2003, interview with Muhammad Baqir al-Hakim.

19. "Iraq's Top Shiite Group Says 20 Members Arrested by US Troops," Agence France-Presse, 7 June 2003.

20. "Shiite Leaders in Iraq Call for Resisting America Peacefully," *Al-Majallah* (London), 20 July 2003, FBIS.

21. "Faylaq Badr: Dawlah Dakhil al-Dawlah al-'Iraqiyyah," *Al-Watan*, 18 August 2003.

22. "Armed SCIRI Activists Heading for Al-Najaf, Vow Revenge for Leader's Death," MENA (Cairo), 30 August 2003.

23. Dexter Filkins, "After the War: Security; US and the Iraqis Discuss Creating Big Militia Force," *New York Times*, 29 August 2003.

24. "Iran: SCIRI's Badr Corps Officially Becomes Iraqi Reconstruction Organization," Tehran Mehr News Agency, 28 October 2003, at www.mehrnews.ir/en/NewsDetail.aspx?NewsID=33709.

25. "Selection List: Iraqi Press 29 October 2003," FBIS.

26. *Al-Adalah*, December 2003 (Arabic) in "Iraqi Press Highlights 3 January 2004," FBIS.

27. "Al-Sharq al-Awsat' fi al-Basrah: Mushahadat Jadidah bayna al-Nas wa al-Amkinah (1 min 2)," *Al-Sharq al-Awsat*, 27 December 2003.

28. "Muwajahah Musallahah bayn al-Quwwat al-Baritaniyyah wa 'Anasir min 'Faylaq Badr' fi 'Amarah," *Al-Sharq al-Awsat*, 7 March 2004.

29. Zafir Sa'd, "Abd al-Aziz al-Hakim wa al-Khiyar al-Amiriki," *Al-Bayyinah*, Radical Sunni Web "encyclopedia" entry, circa 24 December 2004, at www.albainah.net/index.aspx?function=Item&id=4046.

30. Tom Lasseter, "Iranian-Backed Militia Groups Take Control of Much of Southern Iraq," Knight Ridder, 26 May 2006.

31. "Salam al-Maliki: al-Ta'khir Mu'amarah," *Al-Sharq al-Awsat*, 21 March 2005.

32. "Al-Majlis al-A'la: Ittisalat mukaththafah ma'a al-Marja'iyyat al-Sunniyyah li Naz' Fatil Fitnah," *Al-Zaman*, 21 May 2005; "Al-Hakim Yad'u al-'Iraqiyyin ila al-Talahum wasat tasa'ud al-Tawatur al-Ta'ifi," *Al-Sharq al-Awsat*, 21 May 2005.

33. "Muqtada al-Sadr yabda' Wasatah bayna Hay'at Sunniyyah wa Shi'iyyah Mutalasinah," *Al-Sharq al-Awsat*, 23 May 2005.

34. 'Ala' al-Lami, "Fidiraliyyat Faylaq Badr tanza' al-Qina,'" www.beirut.indymedia.org, 19 August 2005.

35. "Mab'uth Dawli: Faylaq Badr wara' mi'at al-I'damat fi al-'Iraq," *Al-Sharq al-Awsat*, 4 March 2006.

36. "Maqtal 40 'Iraqiyan . . . wa Munazzamat Badr Tutalib bi Tard Khalilzad," *Al-Hayat*, 28 March 2006.

37. "I'mar al-'Iraq," *Akhbar al-Basrah*, 24 April 2006.

38. "Iraq: Al-Maliki, Al-Sistani Statements on Militias Prompt Opposition, Evasion," Open Source Center Analysis: Iraqi Media, 11 May 2006, World News Connection.

39. " . . . Khilafat Shi'iyyah-Shi'iyyah tufajjir al-wad' fi al-Basra," *al-Hayat*, 19 May 2006.

40. "Eight Iraqi Police Killed After Tribal Leader Slain," Agence France-Press, 15 May 2006.

41. "Rival Militias Threaten Stability of Iraq's Shiite South," Associated Press Worldstream, 26 October 2006.

8

Kirkuk as a Peacebuilding Test Case

Joost R. Hiltermann

ON THE EVE of US intervention in Iraq in March 2003, many expected that Kurdish *peshmerga* forces would press for advantage and make a grab for Kirkuk.[1] The Kurds have claimed Kirkuk—both the city and the governorate—as their birthright since the early 1960s, from which date Iraq's republican regimes launched various Arabization campaigns to extend their control over this oil-rich region.[2] As a result, Kirkuk's Kurds and Turkomans faced dispossession and expulsion.[3] In the late 1980s, Arabization reached its lethal conclusion with the Anfal campaign, in which tens of thousands of Kurdish villagers were machine-gunned to death and buried in mass graves.[4] But now, in 2003, the Kurds' opportunity had come, as the Saddam Hussein regime was about to be brought down by the United States, a country that had protected them and allowed them to govern themselves since the 1991 Gulf War.

Some feared, however, that a Kurdish takeover of Kirkuk would trigger intervention by neighboring Turkey.[5] To Ankara, the Kurds' ambition for Kirkuk is fueled not by their self-proclaimed historical rights to the area but by their quest for independence, which Kirkuk's oil wealth would facilitate.[6] In the event, Turkey was forced to watch from the sidelines, finding itself marginalized after its parliament denied the United States the right to use its territory as a launching pad for invading Iraq from the north.[7]

■ **The Kurdish Bid for Kirkuk**

Racing in from Erbil and Suleimaniyeh in early April 2003, the *peshmerga* reached Kirkuk even before US Special Forces teams and immediately set about pacifying its population. Soon the United States, consolidating its grip on the country, took formal control and under its jurisdiction established a provincial council drawn from the region's main communities—Kurds, Arabs, Turkomans, and Christians—giving a roughly equal share to each.[8] De facto, however, the Kurds were in control. Led by their two principal parties, Massoud Barzani's Kurdistan Democratic Party (KDP) and Jalal Talabani's Patriotic Union of Kurdistan (PUK), they extended their writ over Kirkuk's administrative institutions and security forces, claiming their aim was to reverse decades of injustice. In 2006, they dominated the army and police while running their own intelligence and security services. They also dominated the local civil service, having placed their own people in key positions, paying their salaries out of the budgets of the (parallel) Kurdish Regional Governments in Erbil and Suleimaniyeh.[9]

The Kurds' bid to take Kirkuk by stealth has led to serious frictions between them and the other communities in a situation that has become increasingly inflamed by armed insurgency and rampant criminality. Kirkuk's Arabs, Turkomans, and Christians reject the Kurdish claim as inspired singularly by a thirst for oil wealth;[10] the Turkomans even present a counterclaim based, like the Kurds', on continuous habitation and, moreover, a historical Turkoman majority in Kirkuk city.[11] The Kurds' desire to make Kirkuk the capital of the Kurdish region, in particular, constitutes a red line for all these communities, as it does for Turkey and the two other neighboring states, Iran and Syria. But such a scenario has become conceivable following Iraq's adoption of a new constitution in October 2005. Article 140 of the constitution prescribes a process—census and referendum—and a deadline—December 2007—by which the status of Kirkuk is to be determined. Kurdish political leaders, who have encouraged displaced Kirkukis to return, realize that they are in a good position to win a referendum based on a simple-majority vote in the governorate, and they have therefore pushed hard for the constitution's full and prompt implementation.[12]

On paper, Kurdish chances look good. In reality, the most likely scenario is further violence and, as the Kurds press ahead with their plans, even civil war and military intervention. The fragile postwar alliance between Kurds and Shia, who have dominated the country's successive governing organs since 2003, would be shattered. This would come on top of Iraq's other crises—unremitting insurgency, pervasive lawlessness, deepening sectarianism, endemically weak institutions—that together could trigger the country's bloody breakup. This is not in the interest of either the international community or the neighboring states. These have every interest, therefore, in finding a peaceful solution to the Kirkuk question through negotiation and compromise.

■ Deploying National Power in the Service of Absorbing Kirkuk

The PUK and KDP emerged from the Baath regime's ouster as among the strongest political actors in the new Iraq. Well organized, strategically aligned, and enjoying both popular Kurdish support and US backing, they managed to seed Iraq's interim institutions with their top cadres and thus shape the nation-building agenda. Their two leaders, Massoud Barzani and Jalal Talabani, used their positions on the twenty-five-member Interim Governing Council (2003–2004) to influence the drafting of the interim constitution, the Transitional Administrative Law (TAL), signed in March 2004, including article 58, which prescribes a reversal of Arabization (see below), and article 61 (C), designed to accord the Kurds veto power over the permanent constitution.[13]

In the run-up to the January 2005 general elections, the Kurdish parties' power was such that they had become indispensable for the transition's success. A Sunni Arab boycott then reinforced their growing power by inflating their representation at both the national and provincial levels and thus turned them overnight into the kingmakers of Iraqi politics.

Building on their newly won electoral strength, they set about shaping the country's new constitution. Their ambition, both in politics and in constitutional negotiations, has been to maximize the possibility of their future peaceful secession by extending their region's boundaries and enhancing its powers and access to resources. The success of this strategy is expressed most vividly in article 140, a key provision concerning Kirkuk that absorbs the TAL's article 58 and expands on it by setting both a process and a timetable for resolving Kirkuk's status. Moreover, the TAL's article 53 (C), which prevented Kirkuk, along with Baghdad, from joining a region, does not appear in the new constitution; in theory, this deliberate omission will enable Kirkuk's incorporation into the Kurdish region by popular referendum.

Surpassing their electoral success at the national level, the Kurds swept the provincial council elections in Kirkuk in January 2005 and thereby dramatically changed the local political landscape. The Kurdish list collected almost 60 percent of the vote, giving it twenty-six of the forty-one council seats, an absolute majority. An amalgam of Turkoman and Sunni Arab parties took the remaining seats. Strikingly, not a single party representing a non–ethnically based platform made any headway. The Kurdish victory in Kirkuk has not translated into an ability to dictate policy, however, but into stalemate. While Arabs and Turkomans participate in council discussions, as soon as decisions have to be voted on they absent themselves so as not to legitimate the results, and the Kurds are left with decisions reached—by default—unilaterally that they cannot implement.[14]

The key component of the Kurds' strategy of peacefully seizing—in their view, regaining—Kirkuk and other territories they claim has been a process they refer to as "normalization," essentially a methodical reversal of Arabization. The notion was elaborated in the TAL's article 58, the text of which constitutes holy writ to the Kurds. It has the following elements:

- The return of displaced residents, who should have their lost properties restored or receive compensation;
- A provision under which persons settled in these areas by the former regime "may be resettled, may receive compensation from the state, may receive new land from the state near their residence in the governorate from which they came, or may receive compensation for the cost of moving to such areas";
- The creation of employment opportunities to aid those who suffered job discrimination;
- Cancellation of the "nationality correction" law;
- A request for the Presidency Council's recommendations on how to undo the results of the former regime's manipulation of administrative boundaries;
- Deferral of a permanent resolution of these "disputed territories" until after ratification of the permanent constitution.

In January 2004, shortly before the TAL's adoption, the Coalition Provisional Authority (CPA) established the Iraq Property Claims Commission (IPCC) to help restore confiscated properties to their original owners and adjudicate competing claims.[15] In Kirkuk, its work has been slow but steady. The main problem for the Kurds, however, is not the restoration of confiscated properties but the return of displaced persons to homes that were destroyed, in both the city and the countryside.[16] To them, this therefore made article 58 a more powerful instrument than the IPCC in reversing past wrongs.[17]

The new constitution embraces the notion of normalization and also provides, without any detail, a process by which the status of these territories is to be settled. Article 140(2) states:

> The responsibility placed upon the executive branch of the Transitional Government stipulated in Article 58 of the Law of Administration for the State of Iraq for the Transitional Period shall be extended and conferred upon the executive authority elected in accordance with this constitution, provided that it completes normalization, a census, and a referendum in Kirkuk and other disputed territories to determine the will of their citizens before 31 December 2007.[18]

Wielding their "constitutional weapon," Kurdish leaders have pressed their political partners to get on with "normalization" in Kirkuk and elsewhere. Their efforts, however, have encountered active resistance from Arabs and Turkomans in Kirkuk, as well as from a broad sector of Arab opinion in Iraq, including powerful elements of the central government. And just as no steps were taken by the Allawi and Ja'afari governments to implement de-Arabization under the TAL's article 58,[19] so the Kurds expressed fears that the constitutionally elected, Shia-dominated government formed in spring 2006 likewise would do little to implement the new constitution's article 140. They noted, in particular, the fact that the new government was headed by the Islamic Al-Dawa Party's Nuri al-Maliki, whose emergence as prime minister (replacing Al-Dawa leader Ibrahim al-Ja'afari) had been brokered by the Sadrist movement. Both Al-Dawa and the Sadrists have taken a hard line on Kirkuk, asserting its essential Iraqiness.

Because there has been no tangible progress in implementing de-Arabization through established institutions, the Kurds have made every effort to effect changes on the ground in Kirkuk unilaterally without appearing to violate the letter or spirit of the TAL or the constitution. They have the funds and capacity to settle a great number of displaced Kirkuki Kurds in the Kirkuk countryside, with the help of foreign governments that have supported village rehabilitation. But the absence of significant central government funding has complicated and delayed the removal of Arab newcomers (al-'Arab al-Wafidin) through compensation and resettlement.

With additional numbers, Kurdish leaders believe they can win a Kirkuk referendum, based, as the constitution mandates, on a simple-majority vote.[20] But matters may not be so easy.

■ Constraints on Kurdish Ambitions

Politically and militarily strong, enjoying a moment of internal peace, and backed by the United States, the Kurds indisputably have made serious headway in their ambition to incorporate Kirkuk into their federal region, both de jure and de facto. Moreover, Kurdish leaders have expressed steely confidence that their strategy will succeed and have convinced their followers, who have criticized the process as too slow, that success is just around the corner, namely by the end of 2007.

It is therefore easy to overlook that the Kurds face serious constraints. First of all, while they have enjoyed relative political strength in the immediate aftermath of the regime's ouster, the Kurds remain—in the final analysis—a minority in Iraq and, in the event of their independence, a landlocked entity utterly at the mercy of its neighbors for protection, trade, and access to markets. The Kurdish region receives 17 percent of Iraq's national budget, uses the Iraqi dinar as its currency, and taps into the national power grid for most of its electricity needs. If the current low-intensity conflict in Iraq escalates into a full-blown civil war, the Kurds would lose these connections with no easy substitutes, while potentially facing a refugee crisis.[21] It is for this reason that Kurdish elite consensus fears an Iraqi civil war rather than welcoming it as a prelude to Kurdish independence.[22] Moreover, even should the Kurds gain control over Kirkuk's oil wealth, current realities dictate that Kirkuki crude will have to be refined in Baiji in the Sunni Arab heartland and shipped through eastern Turkey for export via that country's Mediterranean port city—and hydrocarbon hub—of Ceyhan. As events since April 2003 have shown, insurgents have found it easy to sabotage the flow of oil by attacking pipelines and tanker trucks.[23]

The Kurds' dependence on Baghdad also finds expression in the difficulty Kurdish leaders face in effecting the constitution's implementation or, with a Shia-dominated national assembly in place, pushing through legislation favorable to their aspirations. The implementation of article 140 may prove to be particularly complicated, as it requires the active cooperation of both the central government and Kirkuk's other communities, all of whom may withhold it. While having accepted the constitution, Iraq's Shia majority broadly opposes the Kurds' bid for Kirkuk and may use procedural wrangling to postpone indefinitely any definitive resolution of the Kirkuk question. It would be helped in this by the vagueness of article 140. Who, for example, will have the right to vote in a Kirkuk referendum and, just as critically, which authority will have the right to answer this question? Also, who will organize a Kirkuk referendum? And who will decide whether to organize a single referendum covering the entire governorate (certainly the Kurds' choice) or two separate polls for the city and surrounding areas (a Turkoman preference, given their affinity to the city)? The political will to draft the necessary rules may simply be lacking, except on the Kurds' part, who may be incapable, however, of imposing their own preferred rules. Furthermore, even if a referendum, or a series of referendums for all the territories claimed by the Kurds, is organized, Arabs and Turkomans, anticipating defeat, may boycott it, or participate but reject its results, in either case undermining its legitimacy.[24]

Secondly, the Kurds' internal divisions have served to place a crimp on their ambitions, while giving ammunition to their detractors who (gleefully) point at internecine conflict as evidence of the Kurds' inability to govern their own region. While it is true that the KDP and PUK succeeded in forging a shared vision of the Kurds' place in the new Iraq and have deployed this vision, as well as strong internal discipline, to score political successes in Baghdad, their efforts at reunifying their parallel governments—a legacy of the parties' mid-1990s civil war—have proceeded at a snail's pace, as mutual mistrust continues to run deep and wounds of conflicts past still fester.[25] As new challenges and points of contention present themselves—political dominance in Kirkuk, for example, and access to Kirkuk oil—will Kurdish leaders be able to hold on to their conviction that only a strategic KDP-PUK alliance can help them retain control over their respective spheres of influence?

Furthermore, Kurdish ambitions do not enjoy broad international support. As the Kurds have learned from experience, the support of its US patron is fickle and contingent. US strategic interests lie with strong central states such as Turkey, and Washington has historically used the Kurds as no more than helpful pawns in regional power plays. While it has remained largely neutral on the Kirkuk question—being preoccupied with developments further south—Washington is unlikely to support Kurdish ambitions up to the point of alienating Turkey, its long-time strategic ally.[26] Moreover, as long as hope remains that Iraq can be stabilized, the United States will pursue a peaceful solution in Kirkuk that accommodates the main concerns of all principal players—the Kurds, Turkey, and Baghdad. This has been not only its policy since April 2003 but is an overriding interest, as chaos in Kirkuk resulting from a Kurdish takeover would further undermine Washington's efforts to rebuild Iraq.

Of the neighboring states, each of whom has its own Kurdish minority and attendant pressures, none would tolerate independence for Iraqi Kurdistan, and they therefore all oppose a Kurdish seizure of Kirkuk. Iran and Syria have been happy to let Turkey do the heavy lifting, however. Syria has been in the international doghouse, and this has circumscribed its ability, though not lessened its desire, to influence developments in Iraq. Its principal asset has been the Iraqi insurgency, which has been active in Kirkuk and could potentially turn up the heat. Iran's strategy has been (even before 2003) to keep the Kurdish leadership on the defensive by supporting certain Islamist groups and seeding the region with its agents.[27] The Pasdaran's security arm for northern Iraq, the Karargeh Ramazan, has offices in Suleimaniyeh and Erbil, as does the country's intelligence service, the Ittala'at. Iranian agents have been accused of funding or otherwise facilitating recent attacks on Kurdish leaders.[28] Moreover, Iraq's Shia-led government, Iran knows, will act as a brake on Kurdish ambitions.

Turkey has been the most visible player on the Kirkuk question. Although Ankara makes no claim on Iraqi territory, the Kurdish region, as part of *vilayet* Mosul, was an integral component of the Ottoman Empire, and the region's Turkoman population is considered kin deserving of Turkish protection.[29] But if Turkey faced little international opprobrium for its efforts to contain Kurdish nationalism through its Khabur border choke-point in the 1990s, the Iraqi regime's removal and its aftermath changed the equation dramatically. The emergence of a US-Kurdish alliance forced Turkey to seek improved relations with Iraqi Kurds and accept the notion of a Kurdish federal region within Iraq, previously a red line.[30] Still, Turkey would not want to see such a Kurdish entity gain control over Kirkuk's oil resources. As long as its ambition to join the European Union remains unconsummated—as it well might for some years—it fears that its own Kurdish population will draw inspiration and support from their brethren across the border rather than turning toward the economic benefits expected from EU membership. A Kurdish seizure of Kirkuk, by law or by force, would therefore constitute an immutable Turkish red line. Ankara has been working actively to thwart the Kurdish quest through diplomatic means and could cause a lot of harm to Kurdish interests in Kirkuk through coercive diplomacy—closing the border, shutting down the oil pipeline, or deploying special forces for targeted operations.[31] Turkey could also decide to play the Turkoman card and foment violence against Kurdish rule.

In Kirkuk itself, the Kurds have encountered stiff resistance to their plans from the Arab, Turkoman, and Christian communities. Interviews with a range of community leaders indicate they strongly resent de facto Kurdish control and vigorously oppose Kirkuk's formal incorporation into the Kurdish region.[32] The Kurds' much-heralded charm offensive in Kirkuk has consisted mainly of restating their supposed entitlement to Kirkuk rather than a campaign to convince Arabs and Turkomans that they would benefit from Kurdish rule.[33] Some community leaders have openly suggested they may resort to violence.[34] While they do not have an effective fighting force capable of standing up to the Kurds' firepower, they do have the ability, supported by foreign sponsors, to sabotage Kurdish dominance in Kirkuk and generally make the Kurds' lives there very unpleasant.[35]

These factors combined suggest that a Kurdish takeover of Kirkuk, by constitution or by force, may be a lot more complicated than most Kurds seem to believe.

■ Kurdish Takeover Scenarios

There are essentially three different ways in which Kirkuk could fall to the Kurds, and each way will have its own consequences for local peace and stability.

1. *By constitution.* In this scenario, created by the Kurds through their influence over the political process in Baghdad and their input into the country's new constitution, the Kurds would count on Kirkuk falling into their lap through the constitution's full implementation. "Normalization"— the return of displaced Kurds, removal of Arab newcomers, and restoration of predominantly Kurdish districts to Kirkuk governorate—should be completed by March 31, 2007, Kurdish leaders say. Then a population census should be held in Kirkuk and other claimed areas by July 31, followed by a referendum, or separate referendums, in these same areas by November 30, thus completing the constitutionally mandated process on schedule.[36] Given that a referendum is won by a simple-majority vote and that the Kurds expect to have an absolute demographic majority in these areas well before the referendum (especially if the pre-1968 Kirkuk governorate boundaries are restored), nothing could prevent a Kurdish victory, according to the Kurdish view. The Kurds say that Kirkuk will thus come to them in a legal and democratic fashion that cannot be argued with.

The problem with this plan is that it is rejected by Kirkuk's other communities and is embraced only half-heartedly by the central government. Kirkuk's Arabs and Turkomans say there is nothing democratic about the procedure prescribed by the constitution, because the Sunnis did not substantively participate in its drafting, and the Kurds have stacked the deck.[37] Community leaders have indicated that even if it comes to a referendum—many hope that the central government will block this eventuality by creating procedural problems—they may boycott it as unfair and/or reject its results as biased.[38] Some have indicated their readiness to take up arms and fight any Kurdish attempt to take Kirkuk by referendum.[39]

It is impossible to predict today that the inevitable outcome of the implementation of the constitution is civil war in Kirkuk, but it can be assumed with reasonable confidence that there will be active opposition to any attempt by the Kurds to seize Kirkuk through procedures in which none of the other communities have invested. If this happens, the Kurds may have to resort to their bottom line, which is to take Kirkuk by force.

2. *By force.* There are two ways in which the Kurds may be compelled to deploy military power to take Kirkuk. One is if their preferred way—by constitutional implementation—is rejected and meets with violence. The other is if the constitution is not implemented at all, either because of active central-government opposition to the constitutionally mandated process or because Iraq dissolves into civil war and effectively no central government remains that could implement the constitution. Sensing the futility of proceeding with a referendum lacking Baghdad's fiat, the Kurds may simply press ahead to declare Kirkuk theirs, drawing the governorate's boundaries unilaterally (excluding, for example, Hawija district) and deploying forces to protect these. One can even imagine, in a civil-war scenario in Iraq, that the sizable Kurdish population of Baghdad will be expelled by hostile militias,[40] triggering a refugee crisis that Kurdish leaders may seek to address by forcibly removing remaining Arab newcomers from Kirkuk and offering their homes to displaced Baghdadi Kurds. This will strengthen their hold on Kirkuk town, in addition to lending a veneer of legitimacy to Kurdish actions.

Given the Kurds' military superiority, and assuming no US veto of such Kurdish actions in the case of all-out civil war in Iraq, the Kurds should be able to take full control of Kirkuk governorate (minus the Arab areas) and incorporate it into Kurdistan unilaterally.

The problem with this scenario is that it will deprive the Kurds of the substantive legitimacy they need to rule effectively. Even if their opponents cannot mount a significant military challenge in the short term, they will be able, through sabotage and political violence, to make life difficult for the Kurds in Kirkuk. Already, many displaced Kirkuki Kurds are refusing to return to Kirkuk because of fears of rampant crime, political violence, and chaos, not to mention the absence of adequate educational and health facilities.[41] And even if Turkey exercises restraint and keeps its forces on its side of the border, it may well encourage insurgent activity against the Kurds in Kirkuk.

This, in short, is not a scenario that the Kurds should pursue; indeed, it is one they should do everything in their power to avoid.

3. *By default.* There is another way in which Kirkuk may fall to the Kurds, one in between the use of law and the use of force. In this scenario, the Kurds would simply continue doing what they have been doing since they arrived in April 2003: incrementally extend their political, institutional, and military control over Kirkuk governorate and other areas they claim and thus create a fait accompli.

The problem for the Kurds is that while this may give them effective control over Kirkuk, it will not allow for the area's formal incorporation into Kurdistan. But it may minimize the threat of insurgent violence, as the Kurds may succeed in dividing their opponents, especially if they agree to share formal power with the Arab and Turkoman communities, as some Kurdish leaders have indicated they might.[42] Everything depends, in other words, on how the Kurds manage their endeavor. As one Kurdish intellectual put it: "I can't win elections for them. But I can give them positions in government and administration."[43]

This may well be the best way for the Kurds to proceed. However, it will leave the status of Kirkuk unresolved. Pressed at home to act more forcefully, Kurdish leaders may have no choice but to take unilateral steps to incorporate Kirkuk.[44] And this, again, may lead to open violence.

▪ How to Tackle the Kirkuk Question

The status of Kirkuk cannot be resolved peacefully if it does not accommodate the core concerns of all of Kirkuk's communities and their primary sponsors. This will require a decision by the Kurdish leadership, which has been the dynamic, most assertive actor, to step back from its maximalist demands. There is some basis for believing that it may do so, as such a step lies in the Kurds' fundamental interest. The Kurds have no interest in having endemic instability and violence within their region. Instead, their fundamental interests are to preserve their post-1991 gains, protection from the central state and neighboring countries (to prevent a return to the atrocities of the past), the opportunity of wealth accumulation, and a window toward future independence.

For now, the Kurds face a basic choice: Do they wish to remain a part of Iraq, or not? If the answer is yes, then the Kirkuk question will be dramatically decreased in importance and can be settled via negotiations. The Kurds would still want to have access to Kirkuk's natural resources and have guarantees that Kirkuki Kurds have sufficient protection, but these matters can be taken care of in a revised constitution backed by international guarantees.

The problem is, however, that the Kurds seem to be saying yes while at the same time investing great efforts in bringing Kirkuk into Kurdistan. This inevitably raises the suspicion among Iraqis that while the Kurds are saying yes, they are thinking no. This only serves to harden positions all around.

If the Kurds, as they say, want Kirkuk only because historically Kurds have lived there, and even have constituted a majority in the countryside, then they run up against competing claims of the other communities that appear to have no less value. If the Kurds want Kirkuk in order to prevent a repeat of the atrocities of the past, then there are ways of providing the necessary protections for Kirkuki Kurds short of incorporating Kirkuk into Kurdistan. It is, however, only because the Kurds desire independence that they feel they *must* annex Kirkuk.

The Kurds' insistence on implementation of the constitution's article 140 suggests, therefore, that the answer to the question is no. It is perhaps worth stating that the Kurds have a strong case—on the basis of ethnicity, language, and culture, as well as past struggle and suffering— that they are entitled to their independence. They have failed so far, however, to present an equally persuasive case that they are entitled to exclusive control over Kirkuk.

All indications are that the Kurds cannot take Kirkuk, by law or by force, without unleashing civil war, or that they can subsequently retain it without facing perennial challenges to their rule and endemic instability. They have, of course, the option of declaring independence within the current boundaries of the Kurdish region, that is, without Kirkuk; in this case they could count on the support of many Iraqis. But to the Kurds this would make little sense. And so we return to the original question: Whatever the Kurds may want in their hearts, and many agree they fully deserve, is it realistic to strive for independence when they are not in a position to acquire basic resources or local, Iraqi, regional, and international support?

If Kirkuk's status cannot be resolved peacefully the way the Kurds want it, then alternative ways must be explored to settle the Kirkuk question, at least during an interim period. Whatever its final disposition—as there is no guarantee that things will proceed as recommended below—it should be emphasized that both Kirkuk's history as a mixed region and current realities limiting everyone's ambitions suggest that according Kirkuk governorate the status of a federal region is likely to offer the most durable solution to the conflict. Such a solution is preferred by no one but may address the core concerns of all without overstepping existential red lines— a solution, in other words, that perhaps all could accept once they individually reach the understanding that they cannot achieve their maximalist demands.[45]

According the governorate of Kirkuk the status of a stand-alone federal region (either including or excluding districts removed under Arabization) would put it on a par with Baghdad.[46] Additionally, however, power in Kirkuk should be shared between its principal communities during the interim period. The international community, represented by a United Nations envoy specifically designated for this purpose, should facilitate the establishment of such a federal region in Kirkuk, assist in resolving the status of other disputed territories, and create mechanisms both for determining who, on the basis of past expulsion, has the right to return to Kirkuk and other Arabized areas, and for resolving these territories' permanent status. The precise modalities of such an interim arrangement will have to be worked out by Kirkukis themselves, in coordination with the central government and the Kurdistan regional government.

De facto, the Kurds will control Kirkuk and share in its natural wealth, much as they will partake in Iraq's huge oil and gas resources.[47] An interim solution will give Kurdish leaders time to prepare their people for the painful compromises that will have to be made to facilitate the most optimal arrangement: a peaceful, protected, and well-endowed Kurdish region within a federal Iraq that shares Kirkuk with its other communities. The alternative—violence, civil war, and foreign intervention—is a solution no one should desire.

▪ Notes

1. This chapter is based primarily on interviews conducted by the author for the International Crisis Group in Iraq, Turkey, and Jordan in 2004–2006.

2. Dr. Nouri Talabany, a Kirkuk native who has written widely on the subject, declared that "Kirkuk is not a Kurdish city but it is a part of Kurdistan. The boundaries of Kurdistan are very clear: It is the original Wilayet Shahrazour of Ottoman times. It always had minorities but it was always known as a Kurdish wilayeh." Interview with the author, Erbil, March 18, 2005. See also, Nouri Talabany, *Arabization of the Kirkuk Region* (Uppsala: Kurdistan Studies Press, 2001). On the political side, an official of the Patriotic Union of Kurdistan (PUK) has articulated the Kurdish claim to Kirkuk as follows:

> Kirkuk governorate is historically and geographically a part of Kurdistan. We have fought for Kirkuk for forty years and have entered it twice, in 1991 and 2003. We have been victimized because of Kirkuk: in Halabja and in the Anfal campaign. These atrocities suggest we need our own Kurdish region, which must include [in addition to the current three Kurdish governorates] Sinjar, Zammar, Sheikhan, Makhmour, Khanaqin, as well as a reconstituted Kirkuk governorate. (Author interview with a senior PUK leader, March 17, 2005)

See also, International Crisis Group (ICG), "War in Iraq: What's Next for the Kurds?" *Middle East Report* 10 (March 19, 2003), www.crisisgroup.org.

3. For Kurdish views, see Talabany, *Arabization of the Kirkuk Region*; and Patriotic Union of Kurdistan, *Ethnic Cleansing Documents in Kurdistan*, in three parts (Kirkuk, 2004). For a Turkoman view, see Arshad Al-Hirmizi, *The Turkman Reality in Iraq* (Istanbul: Kirkuk Foundation, 2005). For additional sources on Arabization, see John Fawcett and Victor Tanner, *The Internally Displaced People of Iraq* (Washington, DC: Brookings Institution, October 2002), at www.brookings.edu; and Human Rights Watch, "Iraq: Forcible Expulsion of Ethnic Minorities" (March 2003), www.hrw.org.

4. Human Rights Watch, *Iraq's Crime of Genocide: The Anfal Campaign Against the Kurds* (New Haven: Yale Univ. Press, 1995). The original report (1993) is at www.hrw.org/reports/1993/iraqanfal.

5. Gareth Evans and Joost Hiltermann, "The Kurds: A Catastrophe Waiting to Happen," *International Herald Tribune*, March 20, 2003.

6. Interviews with Turkish policymakers, 2004–2006.

7. International Crisis Group, "Iraq: Allaying Turkey's Fears over Kurdish Ambitions," *Middle East Report* 35 (January 26, 2005): 6, note 37, www.crisisgroup.org.

8. In May 2003, US military commanders in Kirkuk established a thirty-member council, giving each community, regardless of its demographic size, six seats and allocating an additional six seats to "independents" who, in the event, were five Kurds and one Christian. See ICG, "Iraq's Kurds: Toward an Historic Compromise?" *Middle East Report* 26 (April 8, 2004): 11, www.crisisgroup.org.

9. Interviews with Kirkuk community leaders, April 5, 2006.

10. Interviews in Kirkuk, April 5, 2006.

11. See, for example, al-Hirmizi, *The Turkmen Reality in Iraq*.

12. Interviews in Erbil and Suleimaniyeh, March–April 2006. Article 131 of the constitution states: "Every referendum mentioned in this constitution will succeed if approved by a majority of the voters, unless otherwise stipulated."

13. The Transitional Administrative Law (TAL) can be found at www.cpa-iraq.org/government/TAL.html. Art. 61 (C) reads: "The general referendum will be successful and the draft constitution ratified if a majority of the voters in Iraq approve and if two-thirds of the voters in three or more governorates do not reject it." The phrase "three or more governorates" was generally understood at the time (March 2004) as a code for the three predominantly Kurdish governorates of Suleimaniyeh, Erbil, and Dohuk, and the article was added at the request of the Kurdish negotiators. Regardless of its original intent, however, it became a weapon for Sunni Arabs who used it in their quest to defeat the constitution in the October 2005 referendum. They fell short just eighty-five thousand votes in one governorate (Nineveh), having obtained a two-thirds majority in two others (Salah al-Din and Anbar). See www.ieciraq.org.

14. Interviews with community leaders in Kirkuk, April 5, 2006, and March 22, 2005. See also, Soran Dawde, "Kirkuk Council Split on Roles," *Iraqi Crisis Report* 121 (April 18, 2005), www.iwpr.org.

15. CPA regulation no. 12 of June 24, 2004, at www.cpa-iraq.org.

16. ICG, "Iraq: Allaying Turkey's Fears," 2–3.

17. By contrast, to the Turkomans the Iraq Property Claims Commission (IPCC) holds more value, as their community was subjected to confiscation more than the destruction of their homes.

18. Because of numerous late changes to the constitution, different drafts have

circulated that have served to confuse. The draft submitted to popular referendum on October 15, 2005, can be found at www.ieciraq.org/final%20cand/Draft%20Constitution_2005%5B1%5D.09.20_En.pdf. However, this version does not include the last-minute changes concerning the constitution's early review and therefore has incorrect numbering. The available translations into English tend to be of poor quality. The original Arabic text of a close prefinal draft can be found at www.iraqigovernment.org.

19. At the beginning of July 2005, Kurdish leaders unleashed a torrent of criticism at the Iraqi leadership over the lack of progress in implementing art. 58, with both the Kurdistan Regional Assembly and Kurdish deputies in the Transitional National Assembly threatening the Ja'afari government that if it failed to act, they would seek to bring it down. As reported in *Al-Ta'akhi* (a Kurdistan Democratic Party daily, in Arabic) and *Kurdistan Newe* (PUK daily, in Kurdish), and reproduced in the Institute for War and Peace Reporting, *Iraqi Press Monitor*, July 5, 2005, at www.iwpr.net, and "Kurds Pressure Jaafari for Kirkuk," Cihan News Agency, July 8, 2005.

20. Interviews with Kurdish officials, Erbil and Suleimaniyeh, March–April 2006.

21. Kurdish officials have expressed fear at the fate of Baghdad's large Kurdish population in the event of civil war. Even aside from possible Kurdish refugees, a full-blown civil war in Iraq is pushing Iraqi Arabs and members of minority groups into a relatively stable Kurdish region. Throughout 2006 and the beginning of 2007, the region witnessed the arrival of significant numbers of Iraqi professionals, including doctors, who were escaping the threat of killing, robbery, kidnapping for ransom, and intimidation in cities such as Baghdad and Mosul. Many were assimilated Kurds who still had relatives in Kurdistan; others had no such relations but found the Kurdish leadership welcoming because of the skills they brought to a region that was long deprived of them. Interviews in Erbil, March 2006.

22. Interviews with Kurdish leaders, opposition politicians, and independent intellectuals in Erbil and Suleimaniyeh, March–April 2006.

23. See, for example, James Glanz and Robert F. Worth, "Attacks on Iraq Oil Industry Aid Vast Smuggling Scheme," *New York Times*, June 4, 2006.

24. Interviews with community leaders in Kirkuk, April 5, 2006.

25. On May 7, 2006, KDP and PUK leaders announced their reunified government, more than fifteen months after Kurdish regional elections. Yet four key ministries—Interior, Peshmerga Affairs (Defense), Finance, and Justice—were to remain separate for the period of at least a year, with parallel ministers in Erbil and Suleimaniyeh and committees established to advise on ways of reunifying them. See Joost Hiltermann, "Kurd Leaders Must Maintain Unified Front," *Boston Globe*, May 10, 2006.

26. Although US-Turkish relations dipped following the Turkish parliament's decision in March 2003 to refuse US troops the right of transit to Iraq, they were undergoing significant improvement in spring 2006 as recognition of mutual interests in the region prevailed. Interviews in Istanbul and Ankara, May–June 2006.

27. There was wide speculation among Kurdish officials about whether Iran might have had a hand in the popular uprising in Halabja, the scene of the 1988 Iraqi chemical bombardment, on March 16, 2006, the day of the annual commemoration. Interviews in Erbil and Suleimaniyeh, March–April 2006; and Joost Hiltermann, "External Forces on Iraq's New Government: The US and Iran Should Put Their Interests Aside and Work Together to Stabilize Iraq," *Christian Science Monitor*, April 19, 2006.

28. The attempted assassination of senior PUK official Mullah Bakhtiar and the almost simultaneous attack on the PUK's Ministry of Peshmerga Affairs compound in Suleimaniyeh in November 2005 have been attributed to an Iranian agent, who was found with a weapons cache and materials needed for the construction of a car bomb, and who reportedly admitted to having been sent by the Pasdaran (Islamic Revolutionary Guard Corps). Interview with a Kurdish official, Suleimaniyeh, April 3, 2006.

29. Interview with a senior policy adviser to the Turkish government, Ankara, June 1, 2006.

30. ICG, *Iraq: Allaying Turkey's Fears*, 7–8.

31. Interview with a Turkish analyst, Ankara, June 1, 2006.

32. Interviews in Kirkuk in 2005 and 2006.

33. Kurdish officials have repeatedly stated they intend to persuade Kirkuk's other communities that they would be better off under a Kurdish government than under Baghdad's rule. This argument has failed to resonate with either Kirkuk's Arab population (both indigenous Arabs and settlers) or even with the Turkomans, who also suffered from the dictatorial regime's depredations but all the same have expressed no confidence in the Kurds being any better. Interviews in Erbil, Suleimaniyeh, and Kirkuk in 2005 and 2006.

34. Interviews in Kirkuk in 2005 and 2006.

35. In April 2006, Kurdish shop owners in Kirkuk claimed they had been forced to close their businesses, due to threats and violence, and complained that the Kurdish parties had made no effort to protect them. Interview, Kirkuk, April 5, 2006.

36. Interview with a KDP official, Erbil, April 1, 2006. These dates are contained in the governing accord that forms the foundation of the Iraqi government that was established in May 2006. See "Iraqi Premier Designate's Policy Statement to Council of Representatives," *Al-Iraqiyeh Television* (in Arabic), May 20, 2006.

37. They have a point: Because Sunni Arabs absented themselves from the January 2005 elections, they were underrepresented in the Transitional National Assembly from whose ranks the constitution-drafting committee was chosen. Fifteen unelected Sunni Arabs were added to the committee later, but the entire committee itself was sidelined when the KDP, the PUK, and SCIRI moved constitutional negotiations to their party headquarters and leaders' homes, where all key decisions were taken. See ICG, *Unmaking Iraq: A Constitutional Process Gone Awry, Middle East Briefing* 19 (September 2005), at www.crisisgroup.org/home/index.cfm?id=3703&l=1; and Jonathan Morrow, "Iraq's Constitutional Process II: An Opportunity Lost," *USIP Special Report* 155 (November 2005), at www.usip.org/pubs/specialreports/sr155.html.

38. Interviews with a Turkoman and a Christian leader, Kirkuk, April 5, 2006.

39. Interview with a Sunni Arab leader, Kirkuk, April 5, 2006.

40. Interview with a Kurdish parliamentarian, Erbil, March 30, 2006.

41. Interviews with Kirkuki Kurds living in Erbil, 2005 and 2006.

42. For example, interview with a senior PUK leader, Suleimaniyeh, March 27, 2005.

43. Interview with a Kurdish parliamentarian, Erbil, April 1, 2006.

44. To the Kurds, a solution to the Kirkuk question short of its incorporation into the Kurdish region will be very difficult to accept. They say that even Mustafa Barzani, in the 1970s, rejected a regime offer to place part of the Kirkuk governorate within the Kurdish autonomous region, and that no subsequent Kurdish leader could therefore accept an even lesser compromise (interview with a Kurdish aide to the late Barzani, Ottawa, May 11, 2006). Their stance, however, is the result of Kurdish

leaders' own historically high expectations and their repeated attempts to realize their maximum ambition. Moreover, in their public discourse Kurdish leaders have actively encouraged their followers to believe that Kirkuk is a Kurdish heirloom whose return to its rightful owners is long overdue. There has even been public grumbling about Kurdish leaders' assent to the December 2007 deadline, which for too many Kurds comes far too late. As one Kurdish official put it: "We concentrated so much on Kirkuk, we would lose face if we now lowered our position. This is the problem" (interview, Erbil, April 6, 2006).

45. Not only will the Kurds have to make painful concessions. To the Turkomans, the town of Kirkuk has historically been Turkomani in character. Today they will have to accept the fact of Kurdish domination there, something they clearly resent. The situation for Kirkuk's Arabs may be even more difficult, as things—rightly—will not return to the way they used to be under the previous regime, when they were Arabization's primary beneficiaries. Not only will they now have to accept de facto Kurdish domination but they may additionally have to settle for Kirkuk being taken from the central government's control. This is an understandable outcome, however, given the Kurds' reasonable demand for a situation in which they will never again be subject to expulsion and mass killing as a result of their coincident ethnicity and residence in an oil-bearing region.

46. In fact, Iraq's interim constitution, the TAL, offered the basis for a temporary arrangement for Kirkuk by according it the same status as Baghdad. Art. 53 (C) states in part: "Any group of no more than three governorates outside the Kurdistan region, with the exception of Baghdad and Kirkuk, shall have the right to form regions from amongst themselves." In the permanent constitution, Baghdad's status as a stand-alone federal region was retained.

47. Like many of Iraq's oil fields, the Kirkuk field has been poorly maintained (even mistreated), relies on outdated technology for extraction (vertical versus horizontal drilling), and is gradually depleting. Over time, in other words, the value of Kirkuk's oil fields, and therefore of Kirkuk as an oil-bearing region, will diminish. Compare this with the oil and gas wealth that experts say exists in the Kurdish region and one could argue that Kirkuk's incorporation into Kurdistan will not add significant value.

PART 2

Toward a Stable Peace

9

Forging an Inclusive and Enduring Social Contract

Nicholas "Fink" Haysom

A STARTING POINT for assessing the need and possibilities for an inclusive and enduring social contract in Iraq is to place this need, and its likelihood, in the current context. One simple but effective way of describing this context is to share a journey from Iraq to Kuwait. Flying by helicopter between Erbil and Baghdad reveals the unmistakable signs of the agricultural sector in disarray and decay. Iraq now imports its food, whereas previously it was a food exporter. Flying into Baghdad low over the city, one is immediately aware of the urban decay and the disintegration of public facilities. Baghdad's public services have all but collapsed. Most streets are manned by militias or checkpoint guards as the city endures a conflict that has turned ever more vicious and cruel. An insurgency has transformed itself into a sectarian intercommunity conflict that is a civil war in all but name.

If one must exit Baghdad to Baghdad International Airport, it would require a trip down "Route Irish," which is a reminder that the technologically most advanced and trained army in the world is engaged in a war against a fragmented insurgency, an engagement that it is not winning. It is clear that there is no military solution to Iraq's conflict. Flying over southern Iraq into Kuwait one might be reminded that on the road below a significant amount (in some estimates as high as 40 percent) of Iraq's oil exports are leaking across the border.[1] Driving from the military base in Kuwait into Kuwait City, one confronts very long convoys of petrol tankers driving back into Iraq, importing refined petrol at considerable expense to the Iraqi public, which would be duly sold in the internal market at an uneconomic subsidy that costs more than the combined expenditure on health and education.[2]

An inclusive social contract agreed across the fault lines that divide Iraq is a necessary condition for a long-term peace. A "social contract" signifies a broad agreement between the political elite and the major sectarian

143

factions they represent, on the terms under which they can live together—a modus vivendi. Self-evidently, this does not exist. But it is possible. This is not simply an assessment of a hardened optimist. The broad outlines of what such a social contract must necessarily provide are identifiable even now: a substantial measure of autonomy for Kurdistan (that is, without a significant deviation from current arrangements), a decentralized or federal arrangement for the rest of Iraq, provided there is the equitable sharing of natural resources, and the development of rule of law and parliamentary institutions, which guarantee constitutional promises, particularly with respect to the human rights provisions contained in the constitution. In addition, an appropriate framework for subordinating the military and militias to civilian control and authority and the establishment of institutions to entrench accountability are needed.

There are many ways of imagining the constitutional formulations and institutions that could secure these conditions. However, for any of the possible formulations to be successful it must meet one difficult but necessary condition: the three main Iraqi communities must be willing to accept it. Whatever degree of autonomy the constitution allows for regions, and for Kurdistan in particular, whatever the form of state, the critical question is how to facilitate the necessary consensus, how to agree on formulations that the different Iraqi groups can live with, whatever their aspirations may be. This draws us directly into consideration of the conditions that would make both this consensus possible and the social contract sustainable.

◼ Point of Departure: The 2005 Iraqi Constitution

First, it needs to be stressed that Iraqis as a whole have already agreed on a constitution that is to govern their relationships, and so it is necessary to say something about that constitution and the process under which it was crafted. This chapter focuses on the constitution as the core of the social contract that Iraq has crafted and must still elaborate and review. At the same time, it acknowledges that the social contract goes beyond the constitution itself to include political practices, laws, and other manifestations of an agreement between the Iraqi people as represented by their political elites.

The 2005 Constitution: The Legacy of the Process

In another paper, we have analyzed in detail and benchmarked the constitution-making process.[3] In brief, the constitution-making process, while able to demonstrate some positive attributes on the credit side, also reflects a real deficit in other areas. Although it underwent a process in which it achieved a significant majoritarian endorsement, at the same time a distinct and significant community (Sunni Arabs) emphatically rejected it. This was a community that had been subject to a measure of exclusion from participation in the process resulting, among other things, from their boycott of the January 2005 elections. The constitutional drafting process was, as an Iraqi commentator wryly remarked, subject not to a set of "sacred principles" commonly agreed upon by all the parties, as had been the case in the South African process, but instead was subject to "sacred timelines" driven both externally and internally.[4] Those timelines would, notwithstanding the best efforts of the Constitutional Drafting Committee, seriously limit public participation, as well as the necessary deliberation that should go into an enterprise of this kind. The design of the process would, at the end, demand not a full consensus to adopt the constitution but a legally sufficient one: that is, a consensus between the Shia and Kurdish communities.

Patterns of voting in both the national elections and the constitutional referendum reveal a starkly divided society, and the constitution-making process, if it manifested a harsh deficit, did so particularly in the project of nation building. While acknowledging that the security context was always going to have an impact on the constitution-making process, it should also have underscored the importance of constitution making as nation building. Constitution making is necessarily a divisive undertaking in all societies. It requires communities to assert their communal identities and their sectional needs. It is for this reason that constitution-making processes should also place emphasis on the nation-building dimension: that is, identifying common aspirations and the fact of a shared destiny. There is a relationship between process and product, and the Iraqi process produced a text that reflected the unbalanced negotiating table around which it had been debated and drafted.

Engaging with the Text of the Present Constitution

It is necessary, then, to say something about the substance of the current constitution. On the credit side, its character is democratic, it provides for extensive decentralization, it enshrines an extensive bill of rights, and it clearly subordinates the military to civilian authority. However, we have set out elsewhere in greater detail what we would regard as the six most pressing areas in the constitution requiring reconsideration or elaboration.[5] These are summarized below.

As a general observation, the constitutional text has been most deeply influenced by the drive for autonomy by the Kurdish community and, in the end, it accurately reflects the minimum demands of that community for reincorporation into the Iraqi state. However, it is the extension of the Kurdish autonomy demands into the framework of governance throughout the country that is cause for concern. The generalization of these Kurdish demands into a national system of government is reflected in those portions of the text that divide the responsibilities and rights of federal government vis-à-vis subnational units. These provisions can be characterized as providing for an underresourced and underpowered federal government and a framework that allows for a territorial division of the state, weak national institutions, and an incomplete resolution of national identity issues. Unfortunately, those who had the interest and capacity to argue these issues were simply not present in sufficient strength during the negotiations.

We could make a number of specific recommendations that address the main problems with the constitutional text, which could lead to both an ineffective central government and ineffectual regional governments.[6] First, the division of powers list (articles 110 to 115) should be reformulated in order to create a more effective equilibrium between the powers of the federal and regional levels. Also, the regional preeminence clause (article 115) could be adjusted as there is a practical need for the preeminence of national authority in certain critical circumstances, such as the treatment of concerns affecting the whole country.

The formation of regions, a major point of concern for most Sunni Arabs and many other Iraqis, needs to be spelled out more clearly. Currently the system offers an "all-or-nothing" choice between rapid autonomy and near powerlessness.[7] The current procedure could be reformulated to reflect the acquisition of powers by future regions on the basis of democratically ascertained desire, fulfillment of preset capacity benchmarks, and through a process of principled negotiations with the federal level, particularly in regard to the division and allocation of government assets.

Iraq needs a framework of governance that clearly identifies the role of regional and central institutions, minimizes friction, and harmonizes the functioning of the various governments and government institutions. The role of the Federation Council needs to be clarified. Such an institution could be central in balancing region-center interests and integrating regions into the responsibility of managing and formulating the national interest. A chapter dealing with the structures (as opposed to the powers) of regional government has been excised from the final text. We would recommend the reintroduction of a chapter requiring at least satisfaction of basic principles of accountable, regional government.

More than anything else, Iraq needs an equitable and manageable framework for ensuring a fair distribution of the benefits of its natural resources and to lay the basis for prosperity throughout the nation. Under the constitution as it stands, natural resources are effectively to be managed by the region.[8] They are not in the exclusive federal list of powers, and to the extent that current resources are jointly managed, it is the region that will be preeminent. Meanwhile, regions would have exclusive rights over new oil and gas ventures. The constitution leaves the mechanisms for shared management to a forthcoming hydrocarbon law. There are many ways to achieve this. For example, a possible solution is the creation of a national oil company, with branches in the regions, and an independent oil and gas commission. Indeed, this is the direction that the current draft hydrocarbon law seems to be taking, including a mechanism for the national sharing of oil revenues. Any discussion of the fair division of the benefits of natural resources would have to take into account Iraq's dependence on oil and, most importantly, that the constitution deprives the central government of taxation powers in regions.[9]

Finally, we would want to believe that the Iraqis are capable of resolving the identity-related issues in a more inclusive way. These issues have been punching way above their jurisprudential weight in the constitutional debate and could find resolution in both constitutional and nonconstitutional ways. The same could be said for the contentious issues of de-Baathification and the settlement of disputed regional boundaries. Badly managed, these issues, especially the resolution of the status of Kirkuk, are waiting like primed explosive devices on the constitutional highway.

■ The Constitutional Review

In order to accommodate Sunni reservations on the constitution, a last-minute amendment was adopted, article 142, which allowed for a constitutional review process to be carried out for four months after the formation of a new parliament. It was clear at the time of writing that the review would not be completed as envisaged within the four months, but it might still lead to an engagement on the terms of the constitution over a more extended period. At the time of writing, the review would only commence before the end of 2006 and could extend well into 2007. There is division both between and within parties on the approach to it. The crucial question, however, is what the prospects are for reorganizing the terms of the social contract, given the firm political postures of the various parties.

Some preliminary remarks are in order as regards the process of the constitutional review. First, reviewing the constitution and establishing consensus will indeed be difficult. Those who were winners in the process, in particular the Kurdish community, have already expressed their reluctance to reopen the terms of the deal struck in 2005, at least inasmuch as it affects Kurdistan's autonomy. However, it is also true that there has been considerable amelioration of the views regarding autonomous states outside Kurdistan by some of the factions and tendencies across Arab Iraq, and specifically within the (Shia) United Iraqi Alliance (UIA). More than this, as regards the concrete implementation of the constitution and the framing of a practical system of governance, many of the constitutional positions will need to be elaborated and reviewed. Considerations of practical implementation will demand a fresh look at the text.

Second, one very evident characteristic of the constitution is the extent to which it defers concrete issues of implementation and even issues of substance, which would usually be framed within a constitution, to subsequent legislation. In this regard, there is scope for a substantial reformulation of the social contract, which can take place through implementing legislation. Focused and technical examination of the necessary practicalities of implementation is more likely to yield consensus than the simple sectarian win-lose political propositions that dominate the political discourse.

A third observation would be that there is not likely to be a "big bang" process to peace, consensus, and reconciliation. It is the normalization of politics and the gradual establishment of a framework of governance that will yield concrete results, which will in turn promote the national consensus Iraq needs. It will be rather like a tide slowly running out. In this regard, if it happens at all, the collaboration necessarily implied in the functioning of a government of national unity could create the common purpose necessary to recognize the problems facing Iraq and to agree on structures of governance to deal with them. This is what happened in the deeply divided government of national unity in Burundi.

A Peace Accord to Build the Climate for Reconciliation

One of the conditions for this gradual, trust-building normalization of Iraqi political life will be the active presence of peace and an interruption in the cycle of violence that now threatens to engulf the political process. Since the destruction of the Shia al-Askariya shrine in Samarra on February 22, 2006, the violence has further intensified with thousands of tit-for-tat killings in the days following the bombing, along with the destruction of many Sunni mosques. It is estimated that up to one hundred thousand people fled their homes in the six months following the bombing. Some previously mixed areas of Baghdad, such as Dora, are rapidly becoming homogeneous as people not from the local majority community receive threats to leave.

The conventional wisdom that has been dominant in Iraq would suggest that the violence itself can only be tackled through the forging of a long-term political settlement. There is now cause to rethink this seemingly self-evident assertion. In a recent study tour to South Africa, Iraqi delegates took note that in that country, when it was also facing a threat from a spiraling cycle of violence—notable in KwaZulu-Natal and in the industrial heartland—the negotiators had quite deliberately diverted their attention away from the long-term political settlement in order to focus on an intervention that would bring the spiraling violence under control. This was the National

Peace Accord, which was based on the logic that the violence itself was an impediment to securing a long-term peace agreement. Indeed, it was the same realization during the Sudanese peace talks that led the Sudanese People's Liberation Army to declare a unilateral cessation of hostilities when it became clear that the negotiations were being held hostage by battlefield fortunes.

In Iraq, considered attention has been given to a violence mitigation initiative, along the lines of those mentioned above, and to the conditions that would allow such an initiative to have a marked impact on the rising levels of intercommunity violence rather than become yet another lame public pronouncement by leaders in support of peace and nonretribution, which achieves nothing on the streets. Taking note of the markedly different circumstances in Iraq, such as the presence of international forces and the absence of disciplined structures linking political leaderships and militia rank and file, this chapter argues that on comparative practice and experience, the minimum conditions for such an initiative to work would be as follows:

1. A clear commitment from the political and nonpolitical leadership to reduce violence through the public signing of an accord and the formation of structures to implement it;
2. Local structures to apply appropriate measures to mitigate violence at the level of individual neighborhoods and to hold the parties present in those areas accountable to their obligations in the accord;
3. The accountability of the police and other security forces to these structures;
4. The involvement of civil society, business, and other elements of society to lock political parties into their obligations.

By mid-2006, a violence mitigation initiative along these lines was under development for the capital, under the name of the Baghdad Peace Accord. It was unlikely to stop the violence overnight, nor to influence directly the criminal and Al-Qaida elements, but it was hoped that it might play a role in checking the growth and then gradually reducing the sectarian killings and displacements. In addition, such an initiative might allow for the growth of popular involvement, across sectarian lines in a grassroots peace movement. There was considerable enthusiasm from Iraqis across the country's many fault lines for such an initiative.[10] This initiative was suspended during the sharp upturn of sectarian violence in Baghdad in late 2006, and the apparent favoring of an intensified military response by all sides including the Multinational Force–Iraq (MNF-I). But the time may yet come to dust off the shelved plans to implement a civil remedy to intercommunity violence.

■ Problems Facing the National Unity Government and Their Implications

Violence is only one of the conditions destabilizing Iraq and negatively impacting intercommunity relations and prospects for reconciliation. However, the violence both feeds and is fed by other damaging conditions. These are: (1) a shattered economy with massive unemployment, (2) the lack of a framework for effective governance and a disintegration of public service delivery, (3) rampant corruption, and (4) the absence of a genuinely national leadership able to overcome and rise above the fault lines of Iraq.

Thus, for example, in the oil sector, there is an inadequate framework for the overall management of the sector, there is massive leakage (theft and smuggling), no adequate policing agency to monitor the sector, and few prospects of investment in a sector desperate to repair its decaying infrastructure. The income that is derived from the oil sector (97 percent of all export earnings)[11] is spent, inter alia, on a fuel subsidy that exceeds social expenditures on health and education combined. Without an effective framework, including a workable interpretation of the constitutional provisions, it is difficult to see how this Iraqi asset can shift from being a "curse" to being a "blessing" contributing to the improvement of social conditions. The same can be said for the collapse of administrative infrastructure, not only in the governorates but also in Baghdad. As social conditions deteriorate, the impact can be felt in rising crime, emigration, intercommunity tension, and street violence.

These are complex and interrelated, yet urgent, areas that need to be tackled: the need to reduce violence, the need to improve social conditions, and the pressing need to find a framework for governance that can operate as a social contract between Iraq's communities. They must all be tackled simultaneously, hopefully each contributing to gradual progress in other areas.

On the constitutional front, the center of gravity in the UIA seems to have moved away from the more radical decentralist solution of a single powerful southern region to a more nationalist vision. There have also been tentative indications that Sunnis might enter into a political dialogue based on a better understanding of federalism in order to shape it into a form they feel more comfortable with.[12] While from the Kurdish side there is a strong recognition that Kurdistan cannot be an island and that it too requires a stable Iraq, whatever its relationship to Baghdad, its leaders must position themselves in the negotiations in a way that best secures this outcome.

What is required for a marked shift toward the necessary political and community collaboration, which would create a basis for this progress, is for the political elite to look over the edge of the abyss and see what the alternative to a negotiated settlement looks like. Since the Samarra attack, at least some leaders have done that and have seen how horrid that alternative is.

▓ Notes

1. United Nations Assistance Mission for Iraq (UNAMI) Office of the Constitutional Support Unit, *Executive Summary of the Oil and Gas Resource in Iraq Multiparty Dialogues*, unpublished report, April 4–6, 2006. See also Abdulatif al-Mawsawi Azzaman, "Smuggling and Sabotage Drain Oil Industry, SOMO Says," *Iraq Economy*, 18 April 2005, available at www.iraqieconomy.org/home/infra/oil/performance/20050418/, quoting Dhiyaa al-Bakaa, the head of State Organization for the Marketing of Oil, according to whom "smuggling operations cost the industry 5–10 percent of revenues and several times that percentage is lost due to sabotage. The country's loss due to smuggling and sabotage is estimated at billions of dollars." See also "Attacks on Iraq Oil Industry Aid Vast Smuggling Scheme," *New York Times*, 4 June 2006, available at www.iht.com/articles/2006/06/04/africa/web.0604smuggle.php, citing US and Iraqi officials, according to whom 30 percent of imported gasoline is promptly stolen and resold abroad by smugglers.

2. Comments by Kamal Field, Iraqi deputy minister of finance, UNAMI Seminar on Oil and Gas, April 5, 2006.

3. UNAMI Office of the Constitutional Support Unit, "The Making of the Iraqi Constitution and Evaluation of the Process," unpublished report, December 2005.

4. Interview with Sunni negotiator Salih al-Mutlaq, 6 March 2006.

5. UNAMI Office of the Constitutional Support Unit, "Critical Review and Analysis of the Iraqi Constitution," unpublished report, December 2005; and "Issues for Consideration by the Proposed Constitutional Review," unpublished report, February 2006.

6. Constitution of Iraq, art. 110 to 115; 121.

7. Constitution of Iraq, art. 119.

8. For a more detailed discussion—not necessarily in agreement with the arguments put forward here—see Brendan O'Leary's chapter in this volume.

9. Constitution of Iraq, art. 110 read together with 115, 121.

10. This initiative was still being prosecuted as of August 2006, by which time it was running parallel to Iraqi prime minister al-Maliki's broader reconciliation proposals.

11. UNAMI Office, "Executive Summary of the Oil and Gas Resource." See also "Iraqis Look at Cuts in Payroll," *Los Angeles Times*, 6 June 2005, available at www.iraqieconomy.org/home/macro/unemployment/press/20050606/, quoting Laith Kubba, the Iraqi government's main spokesman, according to whom "because of sabotage, the country failed to fully fund its 2004 budget and is in danger of falling further behind in 2005. Oil exports amounted to 95 percent of Iraqi revenue last year, making the economy particularly vulnerable to any drop in oil prices." See also "Iraq Too Dependent on Oil, Must Diversify—Govt.," Reuters, 4 June 2005, available at www.iraqieconomy.org/home/macro/gen/press/20050604/view?searchterm= oil%2040%, quoting Laith Kubba, according to whom:

> 95 percent of Iraq's national income is dependent on oil and that's an oddity. If we take a country like Saudi Arabia, it's 60 percent, and in another oil producing country it might be 40 percent. Iraq is in an exceptional situation. It proves that the Iraqi economy is dependent—people wait for someone to give them money, but there isn't real production. The idea of waiting and thinking that improvement will come only from the government is over.

12. See Roel Meijer's chapter in this volume.

10

Making Federalism Work

David Cameron

IN CLASSICAL LIBERAL THEORY, individuals escape from the state of nature and enter civil society by agreeing to a social contract that establishes legitimate political power from which all will benefit and by which all will be bound. Similarly, in classical federal theory, autonomous political communities freely join together to form a new, complex polity from which all will benefit and by which all will be bound. The constitution is federalism's social contract.

Contemporary federal experience is rather different. Instead of the image of free peoples coming together to build something better, the picture today is often of warring communities, locked in a political relationship from which they cannot escape. Federalism, in such melancholy situations as these, often presents itself as each community's reluctant second choice—a system designed to make an unsatisfactory situation habitable.

The challenges confronting the founders of contemporary federations are therefore rather different from what classical theory assumes. Instead of showing the federating communities the mutual benefits that justify coming together in a new federal union, federal lawgivers are often faced with the bleaker task of taking something apart, of replacing an existing political union that has ceased to be just or viable with a more complex political association constructed on the foundation of pluralism. In the contemporary world, the federal moment seems as often as not to arrive toward the end of acute civil conflict, when a grudging realization emerges among the combatants that the old regime cannot stand, but that the utter collapse of the state is not tolerable either. Federalism, then, appeals to a country or an international order that is struggling with ethno-cultural conflict, separatist movements, and terrorism. It may be countries such as Sudan, Sri Lanka, and Iraq that prove to be the cradles of federalism in the twenty-first century.

Certainly, Iraq fits neatly into this picture. A unitary state, ruled for decades by a tyrant, Iraq's invasion and the destruction of its dictatorship have exposed deep internal diversities not apparent to the casual outside observer of the former regime. For reasons internal, regional, and international, neither the continuation of a centralized, unitary state, nor its replacement by several new sovereign states, is thought acceptable; between the two, federalism beckons, not really the preferred choice of any, but possibly the second choice of all. Given the pluralistic composition of Iraqi society and the goal of introducing a legitimate political order, it is evident that the successful reconstitution of Iraq will necessarily involve a kind of double consent: the consent of individual Iraqi citizens, and the consent of the diverse ethno-religious communities that compose Iraqi society.

Iraqis, operating under the most difficult imaginable circumstances, have traveled part way along this path. They have negotiated a liberal and federal constitution, which, despite its many flaws, offers the only available footing on which to develop common political institutions and practices. The constitution has received popular consent through a referendum process that, while controversial, nevertheless ultimately attracted broad public participation. The continued strength of the insurgency and the continued presence of the coalition forces, however, reveal the distance yet to be traveled before the emerging constitutional order receives the broadly based acceptance that lies at the foundation of most legitimate political systems.

This chapter addresses the following question: How can Iraqis make use of the federal system created by the 2005 constitution[1] to mediate competing interests in a peaceful manner? Given that the task of establishing an Iraqi federation is in its infancy, our reflections on federalism will not simply relate to how it could be used in the future but what it may actually become. The 2005 constitution does not, in reality, "create federalism"; it sets the federal process in motion, a process which, it is assumed, will lead to a functioning federal system. Iraq is not in fact a federal country yet: Kurdistan existed before the 2005 federal constitution and it exists today; no other federal regions exist; none of the major federal institutions is up and running. Thus, Iraq's constitution has a range of alternative, potential federal futures embedded within it; our job in this chapter is to explore what some of these might look like and how they might contribute to the construction of a peaceful political order.

Iraq has created its foundational document, but how does a political community foster the coming into being of a genuine, living constitution and so, in a sense, create itself? The 144 articles of the 2005 constitution are the product of tough negotiations and hard-won compromises. But their real meaning is opaque and will only be revealed over time.

- Will the constitution trigger constitutionalism? Will it foster over time the emergence of constitutional norms and practices that will be increasingly accepted as just, legitimate, and authoritative? How might that happen? How might such a sane process of constitutional development be rationally supported and explicitly encouraged?

- Will the country's key federal institutions, yet to be built, contribute to the practical development of a functioning federal system?
- Will the radical decentralization envisaged by most critics of the 2005 constitution in fact be realized in the coming years?
- Will Iraqi federalism moderate or deepen the divisions currently plaguing Iraqi society?

As we speculate about the future role of federalism in this chapter, comparative experience suggests a distinction worth drawing. Students of constitutional government have often remarked on the surprises that the future holds in store for any given set of constitutional arrangements; what the founders of a federation thought they were doing often turns out to have little apparent bearing on the actual shape of the federation generations hence, and it frequently seems clear, looking back, that no one could have successfully forecast the actual evolution of that society at its beginning. The United States began as a decentralized federal system and is now heavily centralized; Canada, however, started its federal life with a highly centralized constitution and it is now the most decentralized federation in the world—or the second most decentralized, after Switzerland.[2] Of one thing we can be certain, then: things will happen in the future in federal Iraq that no one will have predicted today.

Yet an acknowledgment of this reality should not blind us to another, which is analytically distinct. A federal system can take root in a society and can perform its constitutional functions even while the evolution of that society and its federal order follow a course that was unanticipated and even unwanted at the beginning. Indeed, it may be that it is *because* the federal system is doing its work effectively that the unanticipated and the initially unwanted are brought into being. International security pressures, a changing marketplace, shifting community aspirations, political leadership, evolving social structures, and new technologies will create an environment different from that which prevailed at the founding of a political regime, and to which that regime, if it is to survive, must respond. Thus, the test for Iraq is not whether it follows a specific course, like a railroad track, into the future, but whether—whatever direction Iraq's journey takes—the federal constitution serves to assist, support, and legitimize the public processes by which Iraqis make their collective choices over time.

■ The 2005 Constitution: An Evaluation

Despite the continuing power of the insurgency and the sectarian violence, Iraq has experienced a deepening constitutional process. The elections of

January 2005, the negotiation of the constitution in the summer of that year, the referendum of October 15, which ratified the constitution, and the second general elections in mid-December—all attest to a functioning political and constitutional process, albeit one that is new and raw and displays many imperfections. The gradual drawing in of Sunni participation is a notable indicator of the growing power of the constitutional and political arena. However, the casual disregard for deadlines during the constitutional talks, the last-minute injection of article 142 into the constitutional draft (designed to mollify the Sunni community just prior to the referendum), the five months it took to form a government after the December 15, 2005, election, not to mention such things as private militias, clothed in the incipient authority of the state, are all signs that Iraqi constitutionalism is in its earliest stages of development.

The utility of the federal constitution in mediating future conflict will depend on two things: what is in the constitution and how it is used. While few would contest that the negotiation of the 2005 constitution is an impressive accomplishment, achieved under forbiddingly difficult conditions, equally no one would argue that the constitution is without flaws. Identifying its flaws as well as its formal character is the prelude to reflecting on the role it might play in the country in the years ahead. The following are some of the important federal characteristics of the 2005 constitution: incomplete, unclear in places, decentralist in its formal structure, and asymmetrical and, by design, evolutionary.

• *Incomplete.* Much constitutional work remains to be done. The 2005 constitution is a gigantic work site; it sets out a magnificent work plan for future Iraqi legislatures and governments. Clearly, a constitution or basic law cannot be expected to do everything, so it is perfectly appropriate that it should contemplate some future legislative action to flesh out its content and give effect to its general provisions. But there are some things that need to be dealt with as part of the original constitutional settlement, for example: the creation of the Federation Council (articles 65 and 137); the composition and work of the Federal Supreme Court (article 92 [2]), as well as the Higher Juridical Council (article 90); and the procedures for the formation of regions (article 118). All of this remains work yet to be done, all of it arguably should have been done as part of the original drafting, and all of it will be of material significance in defining the future concrete reality of federalism in Iraq.

• *Unclear.* In many cases, it is simply not clear what is intended by the constitutional text; alternatively, the relationship between one provision and another is ambiguous. For example, the difference between a governorate and a region is not specified. It is apparent that the intention of the drafters is that regions will have higher status, greater powers, and a more senior position in the federation than will governorates, otherwise why make such a fuss about the difference? The constitutional recognition of Kurdistan as a region, with all its existing authorities, makes it clear that a region is to be very different from a governorate. Yet in many sections of the constitution, the governorates have a status and authority similar to, or in some cases the same as, regions.[3] On the other hand, article 122, which explicitly deals with the powers of the governorates, suggests an essentially administrative function under the general authority of the federal government.[4] As for oil and gas, apart from the ringing declaration in article 111 that they are "owned by all the people of Iraq in all the regions and governorates," it is by no means clear what the drafters intended with respect to the management of these critical resources.[5]

Then there is Baghdad. Why the distinction between municipal borders-cum-capital on the one hand and administrative borders-cum-governorate on the other? Article 124 (3) states that the capital cannot merge with a region. But can the governorate of Baghdad, with its administrative borders, form a region on its own or merge with other governorates to form a yet larger region? If so, what does that mean? With about a fifth of the population of the country, it might seem anomalous democratically to insist that Baghdad remain as a governorate in the charge of the national government; on the other hand, as a regional government with the powers available to it under the constitution, it could pose a significant threat to national authority. Baghdad, as the federation's capital, will be where political, official, business, and civil-society leaders of the country's diverse communities meet and work together. It is not just another city, but the country's largest metropolitan center with a critical national mandate. It is possible that the curious formulation of article 124 is meant to express the combined national and local realities of Baghdad, but a fuller and clearer articulation of these dual roles is needed, mandating the city to fashion policies and programs reflecting its national status, for example, in the provision of minority-language education and other public services.

• *Decentralist.* The 2005 constitution exhibits a pronounced decentralist bias. The constitution sets out a relatively short list of exclusive federal powers and a list of shared powers.[6] All powers not stipulated as exclusively federal or shared are to be powers of the regions or the governorates. Paramountcy, where powers are shared, goes to the regions and governorates. Giving paramountcy to the subnational units in a federation is highly unusual. With well over 90 percent of public revenues in Iraq deriving from the oil and gas industry, permitting regional legislation to trump federal will place great power in the hands of the federation's subnational units and raises questions about the redistributive capacity of the national government.

There is also the fact of Kurdistan. The predominantly Kurdish part of northern Iraq is recognized by the constitution as a region, and under article

141 the legislation, policies, court decisions, and contracts passed or approved by Kurdish authorities since 1992 will be considered valid until amended or annulled by the region, "provided that they do not contradict with the constitution." What the Kurds have they will hold. The substantial autonomy that the Kurdish region has achieved will likely become the gold standard for other ambitious Iraqi regional governments.

In addition, setting aside Baghdad, the absence of any constraint on the consolidation of governorates into large regions holds out the possibility that three large, ethno-culturally defined regions, in addition to Baghdad, may emerge, reflecting the basic territorial fault lines dividing the Kurdish, Shia, and Sunni communities in the country. A Shia region, containing over half of the population of Iraq and controlling the richest existing oil fields, would be a force to be reckoned with, for any national government. What is more, comparative experience suggests that a three-unit federation (plus Baghdad) is likely to be inherently unstable: it would accentuate and reify the division of the Iraqi population into Shia, Sunni, and Kurd, at the expense of the other forms of diversity and pluralism and at the expense of national identity; it would exacerbate sectarian tensions, encouraging the flight of minorities from the three main regions and reducing the willingness of regional majorities to protect the remaining minorities within their midst; it would restrict the potential for shifting and cross-cutting political alliances among regional governments; it would make interregional resource redistribution more difficult.[7] Nigeria, for example, began as a three-region federal republic in 1963, but because of the instability that created, quickly found it necessary to multiply the number of subnational jurisdictions; today the Nigerian federation is composed of thirty-six states and a federal capital territory.

• *Asymmetrical and Evolutionary.* The constitutional model, as it currently exists, is highly asymmetrical. Kurdistan is currently the only federal region. The rest of Iraq is composed of the administrative governorates that are an inheritance of Iraqi history. However, the constitution contemplates the formation of an unspecified number of regions in the future. It will be possible for a single governorate, or a group of governorates, to form a region by holding a referendum as specified in article 119.[8] Interestingly, though, what are called "the executive procedures to form regions" are to be legislated by the Council of Representatives, within six months from the date of its first session. If there are to be constraints or criteria guiding the creation of regions, such as those that shape the establishment of autonomous regions in Spain, they will presumably fall within this federal legislation. This regionalization component of the constitution creates a powerful dynamic that in all likelihood will shape federal Iraq in its early years, and for many years to come. It is likely to be more deeply structural in its impact than most of the other institutions and legislation that will follow the ratification of the constitution as part of the implementation process.

▦   Turning to the Future:
The Shaping of the Federal Idea

If Iraq is to be free, it will be federal. Its territorially based communities will permit nothing less. Thus, the federal idea is not so much useful in Iraq as inevitable. Beneath the needed political balancing of shared and self-rule lies Iraqi society itself: What balance will be struck by Iraqis between national patriotism and loyalty to community, tribe, and sect?

Much recent political discussion is premised on Iraq being composed of three blocs—Shia, Kurd, and Sunni—but of course this is not really true. There are many minorities, some of them mentioned in the constitution,[9] which do not see themselves as a part of any of these three. As well, there are ideological, tribal, professional, demographic, and urban-rural differentiations that shape Iraqi citizenship. There are secularists and Islamists. And there are, inevitably, divisions aplenty *within* the three blocs; the Kurds, for example, spent years fighting one another, as well as Saddam, and the five months the country spent forming a government after the December 2005 elections offer an object lesson to anyone seeking to understand the deep diversities that characterize Iraqi society. Phebe Marr, in Chapter 3, provides a comprehensive survey of the competing views of various political, religious, and ethnic groups in Iraq, noting that there is little convergence among the country's political leaders. Roel Meijer traces the influence and relationship between three key currents within the Sunni community in Iraq in Chapter 6, while Juan Cole, in Chapter 7, locates the role of the Badr Corps militia within the landscape and interests of the broader Shia community.

Thus it is a mistake to rely reflexively and exclusively on a simple three-community understanding of Iraq. In the further constitutional development of Iraq, it will be useful to adhere to the proposition that there is safety in *diversities*. There are risks associated with the institutionalization of a single pattern of diversity, namely, the three-bloc framework that is so widely utilized. Safety and stability are more likely to be found, not by locking in on and privileging these three communal identities, but by structuring a federation that is, as far as possible, permissive—by building a federal system that permits many forms of identity, including the national, to achieve expression. A unitary political structure is not possible in Iraq, but a rigidly tripartite federal structure is not desirable.

▦   Fixing the 2005 Constitution

The principal procedural weakness of the 2005 constitution is that it was formed largely without the participation and consent of the Sunni community. The main substantive deficiency of the 2005 constitution has to do with its provisions on federalism. The article 142 amending process gives Iraqi lawgivers an opportunity to address both of these issues.[10] Thus, if the constitution is to make a contribution to the moderation of future conflict in

Iraq, the first order of business is to broaden its legitimacy and to fix its provisions on federalism. On the substantive side, there are three main areas that require attention. The first is rectifying the imbalance in power between the center and the regions. This requires clarifying and strengthening the jurisdiction of the federal government, making it clear that it has a central role in national leadership and redistribution, and giving it the explicit authority to raise the revenues, especially from the gas and oil industry, necessary to finance its activities. The second is establishing key federal institutions, in particular the upper house and the Supreme Court. And the third is clarifying the distinction between regions and governorates, while outlining the procedures by which a governorate or governorates form a region. If the opportunity is creatively seized, the amending process could both extend the national consensus on the constitution to include the disaffected Sunni community and also improve the workability of its federal provisions. These two results would better equip the country to offer effective government and to begin to implant a constitutional culture. The construction of these federal institutions and processes will itself be a significant part of the practical implementation of democratic constitutionalism—or the reverse, if things go badly. Federal institutions and processes will be built and used, at one and the same time, and this process will continue well beyond the 142 amendment period.

■ Three Scenarios

Looking ahead, how might the future unfold, and in what way might the federal system exacerbate or, alternatively, relieve the tensions and conflicts Iraq is experiencing? In order to think more critically about what may transpire, three alternative scenarios are sketched out below, not in the belief that one or the other is likely to chart the actual future constitutional development of Iraq but rather to suggest the range of quite different possibilities the country confronts. Excluded from consideration in what follows are the more doleful possibilities that imply the failure of the constitutional experiment in Iraq: civil war and the breakup of the country; or civil war leading to the emergence of a new dictatorship.

Scenario 1: Partial Federalism

This possible future reflects the present reality: a highly autonomous Kurdish region, whose position and prerogatives are recognized in the constitution, existing in conjunction with the rest of the country, for which the central state is responsible. The existing governorates outside of Kurdish Iraq continue to exist, but they remain administrative units, not autonomous subnational jurisdictions in a functioning federation. Baghdad continues to be the political focal point for Arab Iraqis, while Kurds increasingly with-draw into their northern region and occupy themselves with the building of a quasi-sovereign political community. This scenario rests on the fact that what currently exists is in fact the default position: Kurds at present enjoy a highly autonomous regional government; Iraqis elsewhere find it very diffi-cult to agree on reforms and proposals for change. Thus, while the emer-gence of federal structures in the rest of the country is prefigured in the con-stitution, on this scenario it simply does not happen, and the country struggles on in this netherworld, caught between the historical experience of a centralized, unitary state and the promise of a decentralized federation.

A situation such as this could prevail for some time to come. Traditions of constitutional government are virtually nonexistent in Iraq, and we have seen that, in the absence of a shared culture of constitutionalism that can discipline political behavior, Iraqis have done what they have had to do to make the system work. This "government by deals" has filled in the blanks and gaps in the country's constitutional structure and, in some cases, has simply supplanted constitutional rules and provisions.

Were this scenario to occur, the nature and character of conflict would be largely determined by the preferences and strategies within the Shia community. The Kurds would stand aside from national politics, although the issue of outright secession could arise at a later point. The Sunnis would be comfortable with the concentration of politics in the national capital, at least until they began to experience the reality of minority status in a majoritarian political system. But how would the Shia react? Some might discover the pleasures of being a majority in a quasi-unitary system and aspire to effectively run the country from Baghdad. To the extent that this occurred, conflict would be mediated in Baghdad through the central politi-cal institutions. Other Shia, however, might react differently; if the national management of the oil and gas resources concentrated in the south was per-ceived by the people of the south to be unjust or exploitative, a regional protest movement could arise, insisting on regional decentralization as pro-vided for in the constitution. This would create severe stress within the Shia community itself.

Scenario 2: A Radically Decentralized Federation

The second scenario builds on the conventional understanding of the consti-tution as establishing or prefiguring a highly decentralized federal system with: a limited list of exclusive federal powers; a weak or indeterminate revenue-raising capacity; a regional residual power; regional paramountcy over shared powers, including apparent regional dominance over the man-agement and development of oil and gas; the absence (apart from Baghdad) of any limit on the consolidation of governorates into regions; a federal electoral and party system that seems destined to yield relatively weak coalition governments in Baghdad; the existence and example of a powerful and autonomous Iraqi Kurdistan; and a degree of international representation for the regions and governorates.

In this scenario, Iraqis fulfill the apparent intent of the constitutional drafters. Self-rule trumps shared rule, and the country runs a real risk of fragmentation. What might happen within this scenario? Looking out over the next ten years, there are really two possibilities.

The first has the predominantly Shia governorates creating one super-region whose government asserts control over the rich oil and gas fields in the southern part of the country. Long treated as second-class citizens within their own country, the Shia would concentrate their energies over the next several years on consolidating their hold over their territory and its resources. The Kurds continue to do the same in the north. The Sunni, without significant resource endowments, are forced in self-defense to create their own region, despite their understandable preference for a strong national government. This sectarian regional consolidation leads to an acceleration of population shifts, as Shia and Sunni move to those parts of the country in which members of their community are in a majority. The smaller minority groups feel increasingly marginalized and vulnerable. The federal government, and federal institutions in general, remain weak and fail to develop as a focus of citizen loyalty, and the country's ablest and most ambitious politicians gravitate to the regions, rather than to Baghdad. In a decade, the country's capacity to survive is in serious question.

This federalism of sectarian consolidation is probably the worst and most dangerous path Iraq could follow. It pits community directly against community, with little in-built leavening or moderation; it encourages the formation of mutually exclusive identities, buttressed by population shifts; it fosters a kind of zero-sum game, with limited potential for shifting alliances and the expression of diverse interests; it is likely to attract the interest and possibly the involvement of neighboring countries, which see their interests engaged in the playing out of Iraq's sectarian conflict. This is the institutional expression of the single framework of diversity described above.

There is, however, another version of this scenario of radical decentralization that is more benign. It is built on the reality of multiple diversities—ethno-religious, regional, economic, and simply political. The process of region formation in this version reflects these diversities and yields a federation of multiple units, several in each of the Sunni and Shia parts of the country. The Kurdish region remains intact, as it does in all imaginable futures, but it becomes part of a highly decentralized six-, or eight-, or ten-unit federation. The high degree of regional autonomy may foster thoughts of separation in some parts of the country, but these will be counterbalanced by the loose and shifting sets of relationships that offer many different pathways to membership and participation. The main risk for Iraq in this version of scenario 2 is that the national government may simply be too weak to hold the federation together. If Baghdad's leadership and redistributive capacity are feeble and uncertain, or selectively exercised, the stronger units within the federation may over time lay claim to greater and greater degrees of autonomy.

Scenario 3: The Emergence of a Balanced Federation

The third scenario sketches out a possible future in which the central authority manages to assert and retain control over the national life of Iraq and acts as a forceful counterbalance to the regional tendencies embedded in the society and reflected in the formal structure of the constitution. It could be grounded in possible article 142 amendments that rebalance federal and regional power, but it does not depend on that. Instead, it relies on a number of other factors, perhaps the most important being the interests and ambitions of politicians and officials committed to careers on the national stage.

The holding of national elections and the drafting of the constitution in 2005 have already produced a generation of political leaders whose experience is national, not regional or local. Except in Kurdistan, they stand alone; there are, as of the moment, no rival regional governments or regional politicians, endowed with popular mandates, leaguing with one another to wrest power from Baghdad. If politicians in the national capital, despite their many differences, develop a common interest in protecting and developing their power in the federation, what resources do they have at their disposal to pursue this ambition?

One could argue that the authority given to them in article 109 to "preserve the unity, integrity, independence, and sovereignty of Iraq and its federal democratic system" is sweeping and offers them a solid foundation on which to contest the authority of the regions. Several of the exclusive powers listed in article 110—national security, including the armed forces; fiscal policy; the preparation of the "national budget of the State"; drawing up the "general and investment budget bill," what the Americans call interstate commerce—could, if interpreted expansively, support a national government with considerable clout in the federation.

Then there are some of the things on the Council of Representatives "to do" list: establishing the procedures for the formation of regions, creating the Federation Council, and setting up the Supreme Court.

New regions cannot be formed until the Council of Representatives, under article 118, passes a law setting out "the executive procedures" to be followed. While this is to be done within six months of the date of the first

Council of Representatives session, if one looks at the track record of the legislature so far, and the many other things it has to do, it seems quite likely that that will not happen on schedule. Each month or year of delay permits the federal political leadership to develop a stronger and clearer sense of itself and its own interests and a concomitant caution about the creation of unduly powerful regional governments. Since the Kurds already have their region up and running, and recognized in the constitution, they can afford to be philosophical about the nature and pace of the regionalization process elsewhere.

These procedures could be drafted to facilitate or retard the emergence of the regional level of government in the federation. They could establish conditions relating to size and to governmental and financial capacity that would delay the move of governorates to regional status. They could equally, if the national government so chooses, make the position of governorates more attractive vis-à-vis regions than they might otherwise be. In the absence of sitting regions, the federal government could, in conjunction with the existing governorates, assert vigorous control over the management and development of the oil and gas resources of Iraq.

The Council of Representatives has the entire responsibility for setting up the second chamber—membership, conditions, powers, and "all that is connected with it" (article 65). What might the legislature choose to do? Let us suppose, under this scenario, that it designed a second house composed of directly elected members from the regions and governorates. If the experience, for example, of the United States Senate is anything to go by, these politicians might become competitors of the regional governments, with a mandate to speak for the interests of the region they represent in the national capital. This arrangement would be quite different in its effects than if the representatives were people chosen by regional executive bodies and accountable to them.

Finally, there is the Federal Supreme Court. Its establishment also falls within the purview of the federal Council of Representatives. The council will decide the composition, nomination, and work of the country's top court, which will oversee the constitutionality of laws, interpret the provisions of the constitution, and settle disputes among governments. The Council of Representatives could decide to reserve the right of appointment to itself in the hope that a court could be created that is more sympathetic to the requirements of the center. The nature of the appointments, which will be heavily dependent on the nomination procedures, can be expected to have a material effect on the interpretation of the Iraqi constitution and, in consequence, on the shape of the Iraqi federation itself.

Combined with all the things the federal government can do, or delay doing, there is the emerging regional reality, particularly in the areas of the country in which the Shia are a majority. Initial critiques of the 2005 constitution anticipated the possible emergence of a Shia super-region, which would assemble all of the predominantly Shia governorates into one large, powerful subnational jurisdiction. Yet opinion within the Shia community is diverse and dynamic. Shia voices, after all, seemed not to be so sure about the benefits of a decentralized federation at the beginning of Iraq's constitutional talks, thinking, understandably, that as the majority community they would do well for themselves with a controlling position in the national capital of a fairly centralized system. Then, the prospects of a super-region appeared to be attractive to some. At the same time, however, there was discussion in the three southernmost governorates, richly endowed with oil and gas resources, about the merits of forming a single regional government structure.

Thus, there is debate and division within the community about strategy and goals. This suggests that the creation of a single super-region may not be as easy or as unproblematic a process as some imagine. There could, then, be delays and surprises relating to region formation coming from the regional as well as the national side.

At its outer limit, this scenario describes a process in which the federal government delays the creation of regions, while it gathers political and financial strength to itself. It uses its head start over the regions (except for Kurdistan) to assert control over the oil and gas resources in southern Iraq. Supported by the ambitions of national politicians, it aggressively exploits its areas of exclusive jurisdiction and entrenches its revenue-raising capacity, aided by a sympathetic court that it has created. In addition, it creates a second chamber designed to act as an alternative and a competitor to regional governments, so that there are significant voices, other than those of the heads of subnational governments, articulating the regional aspirations of the country at the center.

In ten years' time, under this scenario, Iraq emerges as a balanced federation. The center is reasonably well-equipped with the power and resources to manage Iraq's multiple diversities and to hold the country together. Conflict is dispersed and institutionalized within a complex pattern of intergovernmental relations.

■ Conclusion

We do not know what the future of Iraq holds, or what the character of federalism in that country will be, but the aforementioned scenarios are helpful in sketching out a fairly wide band of potential future constitutional development within which—barring catastrophe—one might expect the federation of Iraq to evolve. One could imagine any of the scenarios unfolding within the framework of the 2005 constitution of Iraq. They help us to understand that Iraqi federalism could develop in quite different ways, depending on circumstances and political will and on the nature and needs of Iraq's "federal society." Clearly, the scenario most likely to lead to deep and unmanageable conflict is the three-unit system with radical decentralization. The scenario most likely to accommodate Iraqi pluralism, maintain national unity, and direct political conflict into constitutional channels is the third, namely, a federal system similar to other successful decentralized polities in which self-rule and shared rule are balanced.

Each of the scenarios assumes that Iraqi Kurdistan will continue as an autonomous region within Iraq. Whether the Kurds are inclined to draw back into their region and minimize contact with their fellow citizens will likely depend on the extent to which the center performs, or fails to perform, functions that matter for Kurds in the northern part of the country. An energetic federal government will foster active Kurdish participation at the center; a weak and ineffectual federal government will likely accentuate the desire for self-rule. Almost any scenario will have the Sunni community supporting a strong federal government. As things stand, their needs cannot be satisfactorily addressed in the absence of vigorous national leadership and a robust federal capacity for redistribution. As we have seen, it is the Shia population, concentrated in the southern half of the country, that will have the most complex strategic decisions to make.

Our review of the 2005 constitution in this chapter suggests that in no sense have Iraqis constructed a constitutional straitjacket for themselves. The federal process that the constitution initiates is open and, to a substantial degree, indeterminate; as such, it offers a complex array of political resources and constraints to all of the major players in the country. Much is unresolved; much remains to be done. It is for Iraqis themselves, in succeeding years, to build the future most suited to their interests and aspirations. If the institutions and mechanisms of federalism help them to do that, if they successfully contain Iraq's political development within constitutional channels, they will be doing their job, whatever specific course the country follows. Federalism is, after all, properly understood as an instrument of constitutional government, not as an end of political association.

■ Notes

1. I am using the UN/US/UK/NDI consolidated translation of the constitution (unofficial), January 25, 2006.

2. Years ago, K. C. Wheare rated Canada's constitution, the British North America Act of 1867, as at best "quasi-federal."

3. Oil and gas are to be managed by the federal government and both producing regions and governorates (art. 112). The same rule applies to the management of antiquities and other national treasures (art. 113). Regions and governorates are

equally the subject of national fiscal redistribution (art. 121 [3]). Offices in embassies and diplomatic missions will be established to serve both regions and governorates (art. 121 [4]). All powers not stipulated as exclusively federal belong to the authorities of the regions and governorates, and priority with respect to those powers shared between the two orders of government shall be given to both the regions and governorates (art. 115), and yet, when the shared competencies are described in art. 114, it is said that the sharing is between "the federal authorities and regional authorities." That this ambiguous phrase may be meant to include governorates is suggested by the first and sixth subsections of art. 114, which state that customs and education policy are fields shared between both regions and governorates that are not organized in a region.

4. Subsec. 2 states: "Governorates that are not incorporated in a region shall be granted broad administrative and financial authorities to enable them to manage their affairs in accordance with the principle of decentralized administration, and this shall be regulated by law."

5. The positioning of the oil and gas clause is of interest. It, and art. 113 relating to antiquities, come immediately after the provision outlining exclusive federal authorities and immediately before the provision detailing competencies that are to be shared between the federal and regional authorities. The structure of the oil and gas provisions might suggest that they should be read as implying exclusive federal authority: the resource is owned by all Iraqis, and the federal government shall undertake its management, along with the producing governorates and regions. On the other hand, the section could be read as describing a shared power: the federal government cannot act alone, as it can with respect to its exclusive authorities, and—as for the development of new fields—the federal government, with the producing regional and governorate governments, *shall together* formulate the necessary strategic policies. If the translation is precise, this formulation is setting out a comanagement obligation to which all relevant governments must accede. If the latter interpretation is correct, then presumably the field of oil and gas falls under the regional paramountcy provision of the constitution; regional (and governorate?) legislation will trump federal law in the case of a conflict between the two.

6. While most exclusive federal powers assign responsibility for "executing" or "regulating," some do not, or at least do not do so explicitly. See, for example, parts of art. 110, subsec. 3, and subsec. 7 and 8. This could be particularly significant with respect to the regulation of the country's water resources, where there are potential conflicts between art. 110 (8), which speaks of water as an exclusive federal power, and art. 114 (7), which speaks of water as a shared power.

7. See the discussion of this issue in Yash Ghai and Jill Cottrell, "A Review of the Constitution of Iraq," 27–28, www.law.wisc.edu/ils/glsi/arotcoi.pdf.

8. Although it is not entirely clear, it would seem to require a single referendum in the interested governorates, not separate referendums in each; "one or more governorates" (plural) would hold "a referendum" (singular), art. 119.

9. See, for example, the references in the preamble and in art. 2, 3, and 4.

10. Art. 142 requires the new legislature to establish a committee to review the constitution and, within four months of its creation, to recommend amendments. These amendments, as accepted by the Council of Representatives, will be put for approval to the people of Iraq in a referendum, using the same decision rules as applied in the previous constitutional ratification process. A close reading of the 142 provision suggests that the overall process of constitutional amendment might take a good deal longer than originally thought, because there is no time limit on how long the Council of Representatives may take between when it receives the proposed amendments and when it approves them.

11

Liberal Consociation and Conflict Management

John McGarry

TWO DOMINANT and broad prescriptions are offered for stopping Iraq's conflict. The first is integrationist. Integrationists see Iraq's current problems as based on sectarianism and ethnocentrism, usually seen as of recent origin, rather than rooted in age-old hatreds, and usually said to stem from the "invasion" of 2003, though they are also recognized to have been facilitated by Saddam's privileging of sectarian and tribal loyalties. The US-led coalition, it has been argued, came to Iraq with a superficial groupist, primordialist, and atavistic reading of the country, one which downplayed the crosscutting ties that bound Iraqis together. The coalition provided an advantage to sectarian and ethnocentric leaders, and the descent into civil war began. These leaders then negotiated a sectarian and unfair constitution, which has further polarized matters.[1]

Integrationists, accordingly, stress the commonalities that Iraqis share and argue for nation building. They call for a strong, centralized, and ethnically impartial Iraqi state. They insist that the decentralizing provisions in the recently negotiated constitution be "overhauled," "fundamentally changed," or "totally revised," and argue that if this is not done, it will break Iraq apart, plunge the region into war, and provide a boon to international terrorism.[2] "Rather than being the glue that binds the country together," a report of the International Crisis Group warns, the constitution "has become both the prescription and the blueprint for its dissolution."[3] Broad integrationist sentiment is dominant among Iraq's small "centrist" parties and is popular among Sunni Arabs, at least those who have given up on a return to the status quo ante. It is the preferred public position of all surrounding Arab states and of Turkey, where it is associated with the founding philosophy of the Turkish state. It is the most popular prescription in the West, among supporters of the 2003 invasion, in the Bush administration and elsewhere, and among the invasion's critics. In spite of this popularity, integrationists see themselves as losing the battle to the forces of sectarian and ethnic division.

The second approach focuses on the accommodation of Iraq's different communities. It is consociational. It is labeled by its critics as "primordialist," "tribalist," "atavistic," "sectarian," "ethnocentric," and "partitionist," and by its supporters as "realist" or "pluralist."[4] The consociational approach was tacitly at work in the decision by the Coalition Provisional Authority (CPA) to appoint a broad-based Interim Governing Council (IGC) in the summer of 2003, and again in the 2005 constitution, which confirmed autonomy for the region of Kurdistan and offered a number of other protections to Iraq's diverse communities. The consociational approach has also informed proposals to partition Iraq into three states, one for each of its Kurdish, Shia Arab, and Sunni Arab communities and, more recently, to decentralize Iraq along these same lines.[5]

These contrasting ways to contain Iraq's conflict have produced a vigorous debate. Integrationists accuse consociationalists of exaggerating the monolithic nature of communal and ethnic groups and of downplaying an Iraqi identity. In giving power to the very ethnic and sectarian politicians responsible for the conflict, and by reifying identities that are in fact fluid and contingent, consociationalists are said to have made matters worse. Group-based thinking in Iraq, it is argued, "is a static caricature that does great damage to a complex, historically grounded, reality"[6] or betrays a "sublime artificiality" and ignorance of the historical record.[7] By contrast, consociationalists see the current civil war, and election results, as evidence that Iraq is deeply divided, with a divided past. They believe that these divisions cannot be easily overcome in the near future and that there is a need, therefore, for accommodation, autonomy, or partition. Consociationalists accuse integrationists of ignoring the reality of divisions on the ground and of exaggerating the basis for unity. They think that integrationist prescriptions will produce the disasters that integrationists seek to avoid.

In this chapter, I argue that integrationist prescriptions have several flaws and that Iraq's integrationists, ironically, exaggerate the monolithic nature of consociational approaches. While some consociationalists are guilty of the errors to which integrationists allude, not all are. The main division in consociational approaches is between those who favor a corporate consociation and those who favor a liberal consociation,[8] or between those who prefer "predetermination" and those who prefer "self-determination."[9] A corporate or predetermined consociation accommodates groups according to ascriptive criteria, such as ethnicity or religion, and rests on the assumption that group identities are fixed, and that groups are both internally homogeneous and externally bounded.[10] Since corporate consociations privilege ascriptive identities, it becomes difficult for politicians with intragroup or transgroup identities to thrive. A liberal or self-determined consociation, by contrast, rewards whatever salient political identities emerge in democratic elections, whether these are based on ethnic or religious groups, or on subgroup or transgroup identities. Liberal consociations also take care to ensure that the rights of individuals as well as groups are protected. While the leading academic consociationalists are invariably exponents of liberal consociation, integrationists and other critics of consociation almost always identify it with corporate arguments.

An important part of Iraq's new constitution is consistent with liberal consociational principles, and I shall argue that if Iraq's next generation is to be free of conflict, the 2005 constitution needs to be defended and, particularly where it is incomplete or vague, developed in a liberal consociational direction.

■ Iraq's Constitution: Self-Rule and Shared Rule

Iraq's new constitution creates a federation. Federations have elements of both self-rule, in which the federation's units enjoy autonomy, and shared rule, through the federal government.

Federal Self-Rule

There are two important issues on the question of self-rule: the nature of the self or community that is to be given *self*-rule, and how much self-*rule* this community should enjoy. To the first question, integrationists commend autonomous regions based on administrative or territorial principles, rather than on ethnic or religious principles. In Iraq, they have argued for a federation based on the existing eighteen governorates.[11] The governorate boundaries are preferred because they are purely administrative regions, rather than the focus of historic or ethnic loyalties and, indeed, this had been the rationale for establishing them. It is thought that internal boundaries based on governorates would be more consistent with nation building, as they would stress citizenship over ethnicity or communalism, and because they would spread communal and ethnic groups across different regions, giving rise to intragroup divisions and crosscutting loyalties. Integrationists also argue that it is virtually impossible to create ethnically homogeneous federal units in Iraq and that an ethnically based federalism would inevitably condemn local ethnic or non-ethnic minorities to discrimination and second-class citizenship and would be a source of injustice as well as instability.[12]

Iraq's recent constitution deviates from the eighteen governorates' model by recognizing Kurdistan, which is presently comprised of three governorates and fragments of other governorates, as a federal region. Integrationists have generally come to accept this, although hardly enthusiastically.[13] However, they continue to object to two other parts of the constitution that also break with the model of administrative federalism: the provision that allows Kirkuk to join Kurdistan, should a majority of its population decide to do so, in a plebiscite to be held by December 2007; and that which allows all governorates, except Baghdad, to amalgamate to form "regions, following a referendum in each governorate."[14] The concern is that these provisions will promote ethnic or communal federalism, with associated dangers of ethnocentrism or sectarianism and breakup.

For corporate consociationalists, the internal boundaries of Iraq's federation should be organized ascriptively. There should be a tripartite federation of Kurds, Sunni Arabs, and Shia Arabs. This is the approach that was argued for in a *New York Times* article by Senator Joseph Biden and Leslie Gelb. A similar arrangement, they point out, was tried by the United States in Bosnia-Herzegovina under the Dayton Accords, when separate units of self-government were established for Bosniaks, Croats, and Serbs, respectively. The result was a decade of relative peace, and now that memories of civil war are fading, Bosnians are beginning to rebuild their central government.[15]

Both approaches have flaws. The main problem with integrationist (administrative) federalism in Iraq is that it seeks to prevent communities that want to enjoy *collective* self-government from doing so. It is not at all clear that such an approach would promote unity or peace. An attempt to stop Kirkuk uniting with Kurdistan, after an affirmative plebiscite, or to prevent such a plebiscite from being held, would probably increase violence rather than reduce it. The difficulty with the corporate consociational approach, on the other hand, is that it requires ascriptive communities to adopt collective self-government in advance of clear evidence that all of the relevant communities seek it. It is not yet clear that Iraq is divided into three parts, whether like Bosnia-Herzegovina or Caesar's Gaul. While there is "near unanimity" among Kurdish political leaders and much of the populace on a Kurdish identity, and therefore on the need for collective autonomy, the same cannot be said with respect to Shia and Sunni Arabs.[16] There are intra-Shia divisions, between those with primarily a Shia identity, particularly supporters of the Supreme Council for the Islamic Revolution in Iraq (SCIRI), and those with more of an Iraqi identity, predominantly the Sadrists and Al-Dawa Party. Some Shia, a minority, are more centralist than decentralist, and there are well-known divisions on the question of a Shia super-region in the south.[17] It may be that Sunni Arabs come to embrace a desire for collective self-government, but they do not do so yet, as their support for the eighteen governorates' model suggests.

Given these facts, a liberal consociational approach seems prudent, one that leaves it to local democratic constituencies to decide if they want to amalgamate or not. This is the approach taken in the constitution. Kirkuk can choose to join Kurdistan if its people want. Governorates in other parts of the country are permitted to unite, forming regions, if there is democratic support in each governorate. In this case, a twin democratic threshold is proposed: a vote within a governorate's assembly and a referendum. It is therefore possible for Biden and Gelb's tripartite solution to be implemented, if there is support for it, but it is not mandatory. It is also possible for Shia-dominated governorates that do not accept SCIRI's vision to remain separate, and indeed for any governorate that may be, or may become, dominated by secularists to avoid inclusion in a *sharia*-ruled Shiastan or Sunnistan.

There is another reason why the constitution's provisions on *self*-rule may be more conducive to stability than those recommended by corporate consociationalists, other than that they are more consistent with democratic preferences. Federations that have only two or three regions are less stable than those with many.[18] Two-region federations are especially prone to collapse, as the experience of Czechoslovakia, pre-1971 Pakistan, and Serbia and Montenegro suggests, because there are no opportunities for overlapping alliances and the two units tend to be ranged against each other on every issue. But three-unit federations are also suspect, as the opportunities for shifting coalitions are still slim. Bosnia-Herzegovina's survival is not proof against this, as it is widely believed to be held together by the international community. It is, therefore, an advantage of Iraq's constitution that it allows for the possibility of multiple federal units, without mandating it.

The second important question on self-rule concerns its extent, that is, how decentralized should Iraq's federation be? Integrationists' chief criticism of the new constitution is that it has established "probably the weakest federation in the world."[19] They insist that only a centralized government with strong "capacity" can perform vital nation-building tasks, hold the country's fissiparous regions together, defeat the insurgency, fend off avaricious neighbors, particularly Iran, and protect minorities throughout the state.[20] They argue that this is not only desirable but politically popular. Reidar Visser describes "today's situation" in Iraq as involving a "dualism" of weak regional identities combined with a "quite robust Iraqi nationalism."[21] In this collection, Toby Dodge argues that there is a "*widespread wish* for a strong unitary state centered on Baghdad" (my italics) and claims that a collective appreciation of the state's administrative capacity would contribute to a "collective sense of identity that can rival or even replace sub-state, centrifugal political mobilization."[22] The corporate consociational view associated with Gelb and Biden, by contrast, argues for decentralization. They extol the virtues of the Dayton Accords, which provided for a decentralized federation in Bosnia-Herzegovina, and which even allowed "Muslims, Croats, and Serbs to retain separate armies."[23] This is seen by Biden and Gelb as the most effective way to prevent sectarian violence and, paradoxically, to maintain a united Iraq.

There are problems with both positions, but particularly the first. The chief difficulty with the integrationist approach is the considerable evidence that important constituencies in Iraq oppose centralization and have a weak or nonexistent Iraqi identity. To argue that there is "widespread" support for a Baghdad-centered unitary state arguably does more damage to Iraq's "complex reality" than the claim that it is based on three communities. Support for decentralization is strongest among the Kurds. Not only did they suffer terribly from the last strong state in Baghdad but they have enjoyed unprecedented stability and prosperity in their autonomous zone since 1991. In two elections in 2005, almost all Kurds gave their support to parties that called for the preservation and possibly the expansion of Kurdish self-government. In the October 2005 referendum on the constitution, which by the integrationists' own admission provided for extensive decentralization, the three Kurdish-dominated provinces voted overwhelmingly in favor (Dohuk—99.13 percent; Suleimaniyeh—98.96 percent; Erbil—99.36 percent).[24]

To the extent that the Kurdish community is divided on the issue of decentralization, the fault line is between a younger generation that wants independence and an older one, prepared to accept a decentralized Iraq. This is why balanced integrationists, like Kanan Makiya, generally preface their remarks regarding the need for a centralized Iraq, "except for Kurdistan."[25] Such qualifications are missing from Dodge's account. Kurdish support for decentralization means that centralization cannot happen, at least not within the constitutional order. This is because the Kurds possess an effective veto over constitutional change that is against their interests.[26]

There is also evidence that most Shia oppose a strong centralized state, although, arguably, Shia views are more fluid than Kurdish attitudes. Many in this community, like the Kurds, have bad memories of Iraq's last unitary state, and their worst nightmare is a strong Baghdad-centered state falling under Sunni Arab or Baathist control. If there is indeed "widespread" support for centralization, why then did the Shia-dominated governorates support Iraq's constitution in the recent referendum, with levels of support averaging more than 90 percent, and why was the constitution supported by 79 percent of Iraqis overall?[27]

A second important problem with the integrationist position on centralization is the necessary assumption, sometimes left implicit, that it will involve an impartial central government, what Dodge describes as a "shared vision of the future."[28] There is important comparative experience that suggests that this is not the only form a centralized Iraq might take, or even the most likely one. When Eastern Europe democratized in the 1990s, the almost universal pattern was for the dominant community in each of its states to seek to "nationalize" the state in its own image and to exclude others.[29] The result was ethnically based discrimination, policies of coercive assimilation, the abolition of previously existing arrangements for self-government, and, in some cases, ethnic cleansing. There followed what Brubaker has described, following Lord Curzon, as an "un-mixing of peoples," the migration of several million people from minority groups seeking more hospitable havens in other states; a considerable number of civil wars (in Croatia, Bosnia, Macedonia, Moldova, Georgia, Russia, and Azerbaijan); and the de facto secession of several regions (Trans-Nistria, Abkhazia, South Ossetia, Nagorno-Karabakh, and, before its forced reincorporation into Russia, Chechnya).[30]

In Iraq, support for the impartial and secular vision championed by integrationists is concentrated in the "centrist" parties, including that led by Ayad Allawi. However, these parties are overwhelmingly Arab in composition and support. An additional difficulty is that they are politically marginalized. Centrist parties won less than 10 percent of the vote in the elections of December 2005. They have, in Marr's words, "too little support to play much of a role in the political dynamics of the future."[31] The most enthusiastic and numerous supporters of a centralized Iraq are not the centrists, but the parties based on Iraq's Sunni Arab community. However, support for centralization here is mostly ethnocentric in nature and based on nostalgia for an Iraq that Sunni Arabs controlled since its creation. It also appears related to the belief among Sunni Arabs, widespread until recently, that they are a majority of Iraq's population, as high as 60 percent in some estimates.[32] Even Sunni Arabs' calls for a government based on technocrats and a "professional" army are not as impartial and civic as they may seem, as Sunni Arabs dominated both the technocratic and army officer class under Saddam.

This leaves the Shia centralizers, including those associated with Muqtada al-Sadr and the Al-Dawa Party. This group may expand as fears of a Sunni-controlled center recede. Much of its support for centralization, however, is based on the typical reflexes of a majority under conditions of democratization—the same pattern that developed in Eastern Europe. Some Shia centralizers aspire to control a centralized Iraq and use it to promulgate Shia religious values. These are values that Sunni Arabs, Kurds, and secularists will find it difficult to live with, to put it mildly.[33] It is hardly exaggerated, then, to argue that there is no guarantee that a centralized Iraq would evolve in the benign neutral way envisaged or implied in integrationist accounts, even if there was "widespread" support for it.

The corporate consociational or tripartite approach associated with Biden and Gelb has the virtue of being closer to much more of existing political opinion in Iraq, because the referendum and election results suggest that there is widespread support for decentralization, not centralization. However, while integrationists, who believe there is a strong Iraqi identity, seek to impose a one-size-fits-all centralized system on the whole country, corporate consociationalists appear to want a one-size-fits-all decentralized model. This cannot easily accommodate Sunni Arabs, who embrace a vision of Arab or Iraqi nationalism, or those Shia Arabs who reject regionalism. This criticism of the corporate approach is suggested by integrationists who argue that the constitution represents a "Kurdish agenda to which Shiites signed on,"[34] that is, its provisions for decentralization reflect primarily Kurdish preferences. It would indeed be unfair if all of Iraq was decentralized to the extent sought by the Kurds for Kurdistan, just as it would be unfair if all of the United Kingdom was decentralized to the extent sought by the Scots for Scotland, or Canada's federal government was weakened throughout the country just because the Quebecois sought a weak federal presence in Quebec.

However, Iraq's constitution actually eschews both the one-size-fits-all preference of integrationists and corporate consociationalists in favor of a bespoke, flexible, or asymmetrical federalism tailored to whatever (legitimate) preferences exist, or come to exist, among Iraq's democratic constituencies. In this respect, it takes a liberal consociational approach that is focused on democratic preferences rather than on predetermined ethnic or communal categories. At least four parts of the constitution are relevant here.

First, while the constitution allows governorates to become regions, which have more authority and power, it does not require them to do so. Nor is changing from a governorate into a region simply a decision to be taken by the governorate's politicians, who might arguably have a vested interest in assuming more powers. First, article 119 requires a referendum and leaves open the possibility of other hurdles to be decided later by Iraq's federal legislature. Second, article 121 gives regional authorities the right to amend the application of federal legislation in that region, if this legislation is outside the exclusive authority of the federal government. This means, conversely, that a region is free to accept federal legislation in areas of shared jurisdiction. Third, article 126 provides for any region, with the consent of its legislative assembly and the majority of its citizens in a referendum, to surrender some or all of its powers to the federal authorities by constitutional amendment. Finally, while article 115 of the constitution gives paramountcy to regional (and governorate) governments in disputes with the federal government over shared powers, a governorate or region could decide to accept federal intrusion rather than to dispute it.[35]

There are thus several channels in the constitution that will permit any part of Iraq to defer to the government in Baghdad if it chooses. Governorates can retain their status as governorates, rather than become regions; regions or governorates can accept federal legislation in areas of shared jurisdiction; and both can consent to transfer some of their constitutional powers to the federal government. Thus, areas that are dominated by Shia Arab and Kurdish decentralizers can have what they want, while those

Shia and Sunni Arab regions that want to be governed from Baghdad can also have their preferences met. It would be possible under the constitutional order for all of Arab Iraq to be ruled centrally from Baghdad, should they so decide.[36] What is ruled out is the imposition of a centralized Iraq on a community that rejects it (the integrationist preference popular among Sunni Arabs)[37] and the imposition of a weakened relationship with Baghdad on a community that rejects this (as implied by the corporate consociational approach). Moreover, the constitution allows decisions regarding both decentralization and centralization to be taken now or later. Sunni-Arab-dominated Iraq can choose centralization now and opt for more autonomy later, should it find that centralization means unacceptable intrusions from Shia-controlled security services or a Shia-Kurdish-dominated army. Such flexible asymmetry is desirable, and particularly in contexts, as in Sunni Arab and Shia Arab Iraq, where, arguably, there has not been enough experience of democratic politics to test long-term preferences, and when it is not certain how a decentralized or centralized Iraq will evolve.[38]

One common and important integrationist objection to decentralization that allows regions to be dominated by particular communal or ethnic communities is that this will contribute to the abuse of regional minorities. The liberal consociational response to this is twofold. First, minorities will exist under integrationist-preferred institutional arrangements also, whether in a federation with internal boundaries that are organized on administrative or territorial principles or in a unitary state. There is no compelling evidence, particularly from Iraq or the surrounding region, that minorities are better protected in administrative/territorial federations or unitary states. Second, the abuse of regional minorities can and should be prevented through the promotion of liberal consociational principles at the regional level and through the promotion of regional and federal bills of rights.

Iraq's constitution offers some protection to regional minorities, but it is incomplete. The constitution provides for a wide-ranging bill of rights with statewide effect, which, among other things, outlaws discrimination on the basis of ethnicity or religion (article 14). Small minorities that are unlikely to be able to control governorates or regions, such as the Turkmen, Syriacs, and Armenians, have been extended the right to educate their children in their mother tongue in "governmental educational institutions" (article 4). The Turkmen and Syriac languages are also given official status in the "administrative units in which they constitute density of population" (article 4). Article 125 of the constitution, under the chapter heading "Local Administrations," guarantees "the administrative, political, cultural, and educational rights of the various nationalities, such as Turkomen, Chaldeans, Assyrians, and all other constituents."

Many of these constitutional protections for local minorities are poorly or vaguely worded and should be strengthened, at least in the enabling legislation, if not in the constitution itself. It will be particularly crucial, given the wide-ranging provisions for decentralization in Iraq's constitution, that local minorities are protected, not just in Iraq's constitution, *but within regional constitutions also.* The promotion of the rights of regional minorities is an area where outsiders, and in particular the United States, can help. Encouragement and incentives should be given to the governments of regions and governorates to incorporate generous provisions for their minorities, including Turkmen and Arabs in Kirkuk, Kurds in Mosul, and numerous communities in Baghdad.

Federal Shared Rule

The main debate over Iraq's political institutions has focused on the question of centralization versus decentralization. Neither integrationists nor those who prefer a corporate consociational approach have given as much attention to institutional arrangements *within* the federal level of government. Yet how Iraq's different communities and regions share power within its federal-level institutions will arguably determine whether loyalty to the federation can be developed and if the state will survive intact.

When integrationists consider federal institutions, they usually insist that the federal government be "strong," possess "capacity," and be able to act "decisively." Makiya criticizes not just the constitution's division of powers between the federal government and the regions, but also the separation of powers at the federal level between the president, prime minister, and legislature, which he sees as contributing to conflict and indecisiveness.[39] Others call for a "technocratic" government, that is, one that is professional as well as isolated from sectarian passions and corruption. Before the constitution's adoption, some suggested the need for a strong executive presidency on the US model, which would be capable of both stabilizing and unifying the state.[40] Other integrationists have criticized the proportional electoral system used for Iraq's federal elections for facilitating ethnic and communal fragmentation.[41] When considered along with their views on centralization, Iraq's integrationists appear to endorse a classic "demos-enabling" majoritarian federation, albeit one that is impartial among its different constituencies, that is, a federation that both concentrates power at, and within, the federal level of government.

Corporate consociationalists, by contrast, favor federal institutions that share power proportionately among ascriptive, or predetermined, communities. This is the model implicit in Biden and Gelb's belief that Iraq has much to learn from the Dayton Accords. The Dayton Accords not only divided Bosnia-Herzegovina into three autonomous communities, dominated by Bosniaks, Croats, and Serbs, respectively, they also created corporate consociational institutions within Bosnia-Herzegovina's federal government. It is presided over by a rotating presidency, based on one Bosniak and one Croat from the Federation of Bosnia-Herzegovina and one Serb from Republika Srpska.[42] The indirectly elected upper chamber of the federal legislature is comprised of five Bosniaks and five Croats from the Federation of Bosnia-Herzegovina and five Serbs from the National Assembly of Republika Srpska.

Again there are limits to both integrationist and corporate consociational approaches. As Iraq's current political leadership is overwhelmingly based on communal or ethnic groups, there is a danger that strong majoritarian institutions of the sort recommended by integrationists would exclude minorities, such as the Kurds, Sunni Arabs, or others. Some integrationists seek to prevent ethnically partisan majoritarianism by institutional rules that privilege centrist politicians.[43] However, this would be unacceptable to the currently dominant political leadership and would therefore encounter a serious implementation problem. It would also not be as ethnically neutral as integrationists tend to assume, as few Kurds in particular support centrist parties.

Corporate consociational arrangements are also unfair and unstable, but for different reasons. They are *unfair* because they privilege certain ascriptive identities and exclude those who hold other group identities or no group identity. Thus, in the case of Bosnia-Herzegovina, citizens who do not want to define themselves ethnically, or are not Bosniak, Croat, or Serb, are barred from the highest offices of the state. The institutions also convert Serbs who live in the Federation of Bosnia-Herzegovina, and Bosniaks and Croats who live in Republika Srspka, into second-class citizens, as they cannot become members of the rotating presidency or win seats in its upper chamber.[44] Corporate consociational institutions are *unstable*, not just because they cause resentment among the excluded but because they are not flexible enough to accommodate demographic shifts even among the included.

This latter problem was particularly obvious in Lebanon, the experience of which is often cited to counsel against consociation in Iraq. Lebanon had corporate consociational features in its legislature, which after 1943 awarded seats to Christians on a six-to-five ratio, regardless of their actual share of the population. As it became increasingly clear that Christians were a declining minority, these privileged arrangements contributed to resentment among non-Christians, the Shia in particular, and also the Druze. The Ta'if Accord of 1989, which accompanied the end of the Lebanese civil war, dealt with this problem rather unsatisfactorily: it failed to remove this corporate feature from Lebanon's consociation, but simply reduced the Christians' share to a still-inflated 50 percent.[45]

Liberal consociation avoids the problems of both integrationism and corporate consociationalism. Its emphasis on inclusion gets around the danger of exclusion associated with integrationist majoritarianism. It is based on elites who are popular rather than on centrists who are not. Liberal consociation avoids the dangers of corporatism by accommodating leaders with democratic mandates, rather than leaders of ascriptive communities. It avoids privileging particular "group" identities while remaining responsive to demographic (electoral) shifts. Liberal consociationalists value consensus and stability over decisiveness in divided societies because they believe that decisiveness without consensus can lead to disaster.

Again, the provisions of Iraq's constitution relating to shared rule have the flavor of a liberal consociation. Its federal executive is a hybrid presidential-parliamentary executive, but most executive authority is held by a Council of Ministers, headed by a prime minister. During the transitional period, there is a three-person Presidential Council with a president and two vice presidents, elected by a two-thirds majority in the Council of Representatives. This weighted majority has the effect of making it likely that the Presidential Council will be broadly representative, although it does not require that any member of the Presidential Council come from a particular ethnic or religious group. The Presidential Council then charges the nominee of the largest party in the Council of Representatives with forming the Council of Ministers, which must be approved by majority vote (article 76). Although this rule suggests a majoritarian cabinet,[46] the fact that the prime minister cannot be appointed until the Presidential Council is elected means that any party or parties with more than one-third of the votes in the Council of Representatives has leverage in the negotiations that lead to cabinet composition. The clout of smaller parties is also helped by the fact that certain types of legislation require weighted majorities. Hence, if a government is to successfully pursue its entire legislative agenda, it will have to be more broadly representative than the majoritarian rule that applies to the cabinet's composition would suggest.

Other features of Iraq's political system point in the same direction. Its proportional-representation, party-list electoral system makes it unlikely that there can be a one-party government or that a majority in the legislature (Council of Representatives) can be constructed from a plurality in the electorate, as happens in countries with plurality electoral systems, including the United States, Canada, and the United Kingdom.[47] Proportional representation (PR) is criticized by integrationists in Iraq for promoting national fragmentation.[48] However, as it provides for the fair democratic expression of whatever constituencies exist in a state, it should be considered conducive to fairness, stability, and democratic inclusiveness.[49] Ironically, PR is far more likely to facilitate the election of nonsectarian (secular) political parties in Iraq's current circumstances than the rival plurality or majoritarian electoral systems associated with integrationist thinking. It is also more likely to promote intraethnic or intrareligious group divisions through party fragmentation, another integrationist goal.

The likelihood that the federal government will want to enjoy reasonable relations with regions, particularly given the number of jurisdictional responsibilities that are shared and the fact that there is regional paramountcy in cases of dispute, also creates incentives for an executive that is representative of different regional constituencies. The effect of these various institutional provisions is apparent already. The Presidential Council is currently comprised of a Kurdish president, and Sunni and Shia Arab vice presidents. The prime minister is a Shia Arab, while his two deputies are Kurdish and Sunni Arab. The cabinet roughly reflects the country's diversity.[50]

Indeed, if Iraq's executive arrangements are problematic, it may be because they are insufficiently consociational. They do not, after all, offer *guarantees* of inclusiveness, as many consociational systems do, including those in Belgium, Bosnia-Herzegovina, and Northern Ireland. Iraq's constitution permits the possibility of a federal cabinet that is drawn entirely from its Arab majority, or even its Shia majority. This is arguably more likely after the four-year transitional period, when the Presidential Council is to be replaced by a single-person presidency, which can be established by a simple-majority vote, if two-thirds support is not available.[51] This means both that the presidency will no longer be able to mirror roughly Iraq's diversity, as it will be based on a single person rather than three, and that the legislative threshold necessary to start executive formation will be lowered.[52] These arrangements are consistent with a recent argument in the academic literature that while special antimajoritarian devices may be called for during transitional periods, they are both unnecessary and undesirable afterwards.[53] But one cannot know in advance when Iraq will have made the transition to a stable polity, and at this point, four years seems like a rather optimistic projection.

There are other executive models that Iraqis might have considered, or might still consider. One of these is to retain the three-person Presidential Council, and the two-thirds rule required for its establishment, beyond the transitional period. This would be a relatively easy change. More radically, and less likely, Iraqis could opt for a more powerful, and possibly larger, executive Presidential Council, which would replace the current hybrid presidential-parliamentary executive, the membership of which would be drawn from the different *regions* of the country. This was the model that operated in Yugoslavia under Tito, and it was the attempt by Serbia to take over its federal council that helped to foment the country's breakup. It was not the existence of the council that broke Yugoslavia apart, as an integrationist might argue, but the fact that it became unrepresentative of Yugoslavia's diversity. Switzerland also has a representative (seven-person) presidential council.

Another option would be to have a fully inclusive parliamentary executive that is automatically drawn from the legislature by a mechanical rule, such as d'Hondt. Under this, all significant parties in the legislature would be entitled to a proportional share of seats in the cabinet. One advantage of d'Hondt, in addition to guaranteeing an inclusive executive, is that it would have avoided the political squabbling over executive formation that led in early 2006 to a three-month delay in the establishment of Iraq's government. D'Hondt would also create obstacles to a dominant party monopolizing a number of strategic portfolios. This is because it permits the largest party to pick the first cabinet portfolio, but then allows all smaller parties entitled to portfolios to have their first pick, before allowing the largest party its second pick.[54] This feature would help to deal with Sunni Arab concerns about both the key Interior and Defense ministries falling into the hands of the United Iraqi Alliance.[55] Neither Iraq's current arrangements for appointing its federal executive or the changes suggested here privilege particular identity groups. They are open, in principle, to ministers from any identity group and those from none. They are more likely in practice, in contemporary Iraq, to reward secular parties than the majoritarian alternatives. They are not subject to some of the most serious and common charges that are leveled against consociation.

Another complementary way to protect Iraq's minorities would be to ensure the proper design of two important federal institutions that are named in the constitution but not yet established: the Federation Council and the Supreme Court. Both institutions typically perform in federations what Al Stepan has described as a "demos-constraining" function, that is, they prevent the state's federal demos, or dominant community, from riding roughshod over its regional demoi.[56] A Federation Council, or federal second chamber, performs such a function because it is typically based on regional rather than popular representation and because it has antimajoritarian decisionmaking rules for at least some purposes. One way for Iraq to proceed would be to allow the Federation Council to be appointed by the regional (or governorate) governments or even, as in Germany, to be comprised of members of those governments. This would both give the regions a stake in the center and help to make the Federation Council the locus for negotiations among the regional governments and between the regional governments and the center. There is no other mechanism for intergovernmental relations in the current constitution, and if the Federation Council does not perform this role, some other institution will have to. The Federation Council, in addition to possessing a role in passing legislation and constitutional amendments, could be given some voice in appointments to federal institutions, including the Supreme Court, as happens with the US Senate.

The Supreme Court is given three functions that will make it a pivotal institution for protecting Iraq's diverse communities and individuals (article 93). First, it is tasked with "interpreting the provisions of the constitution," including its various minority-protection provisions. Second, it will umpire disputes between the government of the federal demos and those of the regional demoi. Third, it is responsible for "overseeing the constitutionality of laws and regulations," that is, it will decide if legislation of the federal and regional legislatures complies with the constitution's rights-protection clauses. The liberal consociational approach to Supreme Court appointments is to ensure that they are regionally (not ethnically) representative and that the appointment power is spread across the state's constituencies. One way to proceed here would be to adopt one Canadian practice while rejecting another. The practice to emulate is that part of Canada's Supreme Court Act that stipulates that three of its nine Supreme Court justices come from Quebec. In Iraq, it would make sense for one-fifth of Iraq's top court to come from Kurdistan and the rest to come, proportionately, from other regions. The practice to avoid is Canada's unusual tradition of concentrating the appointment power in the hands of the federal government, which is tantamount to allowing one side to a conflict to pick the referee. The alternative is to give the Federation Council input into Supreme Court appointments or, failing that, the regional governments directly.

■ Conclusion

Supporters of integration and corporate consociation both appeal to the international community, in particular to the United States, to assist with their suggested prescriptions. Integrationists ask outsiders to play a leading role in changing the constitution in a way that strengthens the central government and weakens the forces of regionalism. Donald Horowitz notes that "departing colonial powers left their imprints on new constitutions all over Asia and Africa and many of these proved durable. It is the time for the US to do the same [in Iraq]."[57] Kanan Makiya argues in a *New York Times* opinion piece that a committee of (external) expert constitutional lawyers should "make the necessary amendments" that are required within the federal level of government and warns that for democracy to emerge in Iraq, it "must be saved from the irresponsibility of the Iraqi parties and voting blocs that are today killing it."[58] The International Crisis Group and the US-based Iraq Foundation are also skeptical of the local political class and call on the United States to throw its weight behind Iraq's nonsectarian forces.[59]

For Biden and Gelb, by contrast, the United States should proceed as it did in Bosnia-Herzegovina with the Dayton Accords: it should intervene to partition Iraq into three ethnic or communal enclaves. This is said to represent a "third way" between the "staying the course" and "bringing the troops home" options, one that would "wind down our military presence responsibly while preventing chaos and preserving our key security goals." To cement the deal, the United States should offer the Sunni Arabs (unspecified) "irresistible sweeteners," an "offer they cannot refuse."[60]

Liberal consociational advice is different. From this perspective, the primary task for outsiders is to work with Iraq's democratically elected politicians and to support the internally negotiated constitution, while recommending and offering advice on constructive changes within the process for constitutional amendments. Support for the constitution is merited on the grounds that while it does not satisfy the first preferences of any of Iraq's communities, and is opposed by Sunni Arabs in particular, it represents a reasonable compromise among conflicting agendas. The liberal consociational approach further suggests that the international community should assist in building the "capacity" of regional (and governorate) governments, and not just the capacity of the federal government, as integrationists recommend. Regional governments should be given assistance with the training of internal security and police services. Outside aid should be tied to the development of regional constitutions that are respectful of both individual and minority rights and that promote intraregional power sharing. Outsiders should also use their diplomatic weight to ensure that the informal mechanisms for power sharing within the federal government, including the allotment of key ministerial portfolios, are implemented in a way that all communities can accept, now and in the future. Finally, expert advice should be offered to Iraqi politicians on best constitutional practices with respect to the design of those crucial institutions that have yet to be established, in particular the Supreme Court and Federation Council. Again, the aim here should be to ensure liberal and pluralist inclusion.

No one would suggest that the creation of liberal consociational institutions will guarantee Iraq's stability and survival. This will require the defeat of the neo-Baathist and jihadist insurgencies. It will also require a commitment to democratic pluralism that is not yet apparent among all of Iraq's communities, and particularly those who were ascendant under the old order. However, liberal consociation offers a more reasonable and evenhanded response to Iraq's complex reality than the alternatives on offer.

▨ Notes

1. According to Said, "[I]nternational actors have not been innocent bystanders. They have contributed to sectarianism in many ways, including by subscribing to a 'realist' narrative that argues that Iraq is an artificial state; that the groups comprising it were only held together by tyranny, and that disintegration is a by-product of liberation from authoritarianism. This narrative, which is antithetical to nation-building, has been embraced by sectarian politicians in Iraq and has found its reflection in post-invasion policies, including the dissolution of the army and the new constitution." Yahia Said, "Federal Choices Needed," *Al-Ahram Weekly*, March 2006, weekly.ahram.org.eg/print/2006/784/sc6.htm. Daloglu accuses the United States of enforcing an "ethnic and sectarian calculus onto the infrastructure of the Iraqi Governing Council," while the International Crisis Group (ICG) argues that it prized "communal identities over national-political platforms." See, respectively,

Tulin Daloglu, "End Sectarian Violence," *Washington Times*, 17 April 2006; and the International Crisis Group (ICG), "The Next Iraqi War? Sectarianism and Civil Conflict," *Middle East Report* 52 (February 27, 2006).

2. The words in quotation marks are from the following works, respectively: Kanan Makiya, "Present at the Disintegration," *New York Times*, 11 December 2005; Donald Horowitz, "The Sunni Moment," *Wall Street Journal*, 14 December 2005; and ICG, "The Next Iraqi War?" i.

3. ICG, "The Next Iraqi War?" 11.

4. For examples of the consociational approach, see the series of chapters in Brendan O'Leary, John McGarry, and Khaled Salih, eds., *The Future of Kurdistan in Iraq* (Philadelphia: Univ. of Pennsylvania Press, 2005).

5. Leslie Gelb, "The Three-State Solution," *New York Times*, 25 November 2003; and Joseph Biden and Leslie Gelb, "Unity Through Autonomy in Iraq," *New York Times*, 1 May 2006.

6. Toby Dodge, Chapter 2 of this volume.

7. Reidar Visser, "Iraq's Partition Fantasy," *Open Democracy*, May 19, 2006, 1, www.openDemocracy.net.

8. Brendan O'Leary, "Debating Consociation: Normative and Explanatory Arguments," in *From Power-Sharing to Democracy: Post-Conflict Institutions in Ethnically Divided Societies*, ed. Sid Noel (Toronto: McGill-Queen's Univ. Press, 2005), 15–16.

9. Arend Lijphart, "Self-Determination Versus Pre-Determination of Ethnic Minorities in Power-Sharing Systems," in *The Rights of Minority Cultures*, ed. Will Kymlicka (Oxford: Oxford Univ. Press, 1995), 275–287.

10. For an integrationist criticism of this approach, see Rogers Brubaker, *Ethnicity Without Groups* (Cambridge, MA: Harvard Univ. Press, 2006).

11. Makiya, "Present at the Disintegration"; Adeed Dawisha and Karen Dawisha, "How to Build a Democratic Iraq," *Foreign Affairs* 82, no. 3 (2003): 36–50; Dawn Brancati, "Is Federalism a Panacea for Post-Saddam Iraq?" *Washington Quarterly* 25, no. 2 (2004): 14; Andreas Wimmer, "Democracy and Ethno-Religious Conflict in Iraq," *Survival* 45, no. 4 (2003): 124.

12. Andreas Wimmer points out that "federalization may heighten, rather than reduce the risks of gross human rights violations, especially for members of ethnic minorities living under the rule of the majority government in a federal unit." "Democracy and Ethno-Religious Conflict in Iraq," 123. Also see Imad Salamey and Frederic Pearson, "The Crisis of Federalism and Electoral Strategies in Iraq," *International Studies Perspectives* 6, no. 2 (2005): 1999.

13. See Makiya, "Present at the Disintegration," and the ICG, "The Next Iraqi War?" ii.

14. Art. 119, in the constitution of Iraq, unofficial translation made available by the Forum of Federations (Ottawa).

15. Biden and Gelb, "Unity Through Autonomy."

16. See Marr's contribution to this volume, Chapter 3.

17. Integrationists often point to intragroup divisions in order to criticize consociationalism, and in Iraq, they point to internal divisions among both Kurds and Shia Arabs. However, while the Kurds clearly have internal party-based divisions, these exist alongside a consensus on the question of collective self-government. The Kurdish perspective is that internal divisions can be managed within a self-governing Kurdistan. There is not yet a similar consensus on collective self-government among Shia Arabs.

18. Ronald L. Watts, *Comparing Federal Systems* (Montreal: McGill-Queen's Univ. Press, 1999), 113–114.

19. Horowitz, "Sunni Moment."

20. See Dodge's contribution to this volume in Chapter 2.

21. Visser argues that Iraqi nationalism remains "flourishing" and that "even today, in a climate of growing sectarian terrorism calculated to obliterate the idea of coexistence, many Iraqis stubbornly refuse to reveal their ethno-religious identity when interrogated by western journalists. Many simply say they are Iraqis." Visser, "Iraq's Paritition Fantasy."

22. See Dodge's chapter in this volume.

23. Biden and Gelb, "Unity Through Autonomy."

24. See the referendum results by province online at news.bbc.co.uk/2/hi/middle_east/4374822.stm#map.

25. Visser, "Iraq's Partition Fantasy," also acknowledges that the Kurdish desire for autonomy is more widespread than elsewhere but argues that there are intra-Kurdish divisions on the question.

26. Art. 126 (4) of the constitution states that it may not be amended "if such amendments take away from the powers of the regions" except by the approval of the concerned region's legislature and its people voting in a referendum. Art. 142, which suspends art. 126 for the transitional period, states that constitutional change requires the support of a majority of voters and must not be rejected by two-thirds of the voters in three or more governorates. As the Kurds make up the overwhelming majority of voters in three governorates, this translates into a Kurdish veto.

27. One integrationist response, which I have heard from Rend Rahim al-Francke, president of the Iraq Foundation and a leading Iraqi integrationist, is that Iraqi voters did not know what they were voting for.

28. See Dodge's contribution to this volume.

29. See Jack Snyder, *From Voting to Violence: Democratization and Nationalist Conflict* (New York: W. W. Norton, 2000); and Rogers Brubaker, *Nationalism Reframed* (Cambridge, MA: Cambridge Univ. Press, 1995).

30. Rogers Brubaker, "Aftermaths of Empire and the Unmixing of Peoples," *Ethnicity and Racial Studies* 18, no. 2 (April 1995): 189–218.

31. See Marr's contribution to this volume.

32. ICG, "The Next Iraqi War?" 32. It is likely that this myth has been shattered by recent election results, which should eventually force a Sunni Arab reconsideration of the merits of centralization.

33. Also see Marr's contribution to this volume.

34. Horowitz, "Sunni Moment."

35. Constitution of Iraq. It may appear unthinkable that regional politicians would ever surrender jurisdictional responsibilities or miss the opportunity to acquire more, but there is evidence to the contrary from the comparative experience. In Canada, only Quebec has opted to take up its own pension plan, and all other Canadian provinces have been happy with the federal plan. There are many other examples, under Canada's practice of asymmetrical federalism, of Quebec being the only province to exercise a degree of autonomy that is available to all provinces.

36. This is one reason why Laith Kubba, personal adviser to ex–prime minister Ibrahim al-Ja'afari, supports the constitution. He believes it provides for a centralized Arab Iraq linked to a decentralized federacy of Kurdistan. Personal communication with the author.

37. My point here is that each of Iraq's communities has the right to choose how they should be governed, but not the right to choose how others should be governed. The current preference of many Sunni Arabs is for all of Iraq, including Kurdistan and the Shia south, to be ruled from Baghdad. This is an illegitimate pref-

erence, as it would involve imposing centralization on communities that do not want it. However, it is legitimate for all communities to aspire to a fair distribution of revenues from Iraq's natural resources. Contrary to the conventional wisdom, this does not entail a centralized federation, with Baghdad in charge of oil and gas. As in Canada, it is quite possible for a decentralized federation, one in which the regions own and control natural resources, to equalize public services across the state. I have not addressed the constitutional provisions on the distribution of natural resources in this chapter. For more on this, see my colleague Brendan O'Leary's chapter (Chapter 12) in this volume.

38. Integrationists should like flexible arrangements for asymmetrical decentralization, as it seems suited to their view that identities, and associated political aspirations, are fluid.

39. Makiya, "Present at the Disintegration."

40. Brancati, "Is Federalism a Panacea," 18.

41. See Salamey and Pearson, "The Crisis of Federalism."

42. Constitution of Bosnia and Herzegovina, 1995, article 5.

43. See Donald Horowitz, *A Democratic South Africa: Constitutional Engineering in a Divided Society* (Berkeley: Univ. of California Press, 1991).

44. These arrangements also work at cross-purposes with the international community's expressed aim of encouraging Bosnia-Herzegovina's ethnically cleansed to return home.

45. Although critics of consociation everywhere cite the example of Lebanon to buttress their arguments, it is not at all clear that the Lebanese precedent supports their interpretation. Consociation maintained peace in Lebanon for most of the period between 1943 and the outbreak of civil war in 1975, and it is instructive that the Ta'if Accord went back to (modified) consociational arrangements. The weaknesses of Lebanon's consociation had something to do with its corporate features, and the civil war was largely a result of the destabilizing influence of the Israeli-Palestinian conflict, which produced a significant influx of Palestinian refugees, rather than consociation.

46. The majoritarian decisionmaking rule for cabinet composition does not represent the triumph of the integrationist principle of impartiality. Rather, it reflects the preference of the Shia majority for an executive that it could control.

47. The electoral system is not a part of the constitution, but the constitution stipulates in article 49 that any election should provide for the "representation of all components of the Iraqi people," which suggests a PR system. Any electoral system that is not based on PR, such as the single-member plurality or alternative-vote systems that are favored by integrationists, would have the effect of underrepresenting minorities, particularly small minorities, and could be subject to court challenges.

48. Salamey and Pearson, "Crisis of Federalism."

49. See Brendan O'Leary, "Power-Sharing, Pluralist Federation, and Federacy," in O'Leary, McGarry, and Salih, *The Future of Kurdistan in Iraq.*

50. The cabinet's thirty-six members include nineteen Shia Arabs, eight Sunni Arabs, eight Kurds, and one Christian.

51. Constitution of Iraq, art. 70.

52. The two deputy premierships also disappear after the transitional period.

53. Donald Rothchild, "Reassuring Weaker Parties After Civil Wars: The Benefits and Costs of Executive Power-Sharing Systems in Africa," *Ethnopolitics* 4, no. 3 (2005): 247–267; Ian O'Flynn and David Russell, *Power-Sharing: New Challenges for Divided Societies* (London: Pluto Press, 2005).

54. See Brendan O'Leary, Bernard Grofman, and Jorgen Elklit, "Divisor

Methods for Sequential Portfolio Allocation in Multi-Party Executive Bodies: Evidence from Northern Ireland and Denmark," *American Journal of Political Science* 49, no. 1 (2005): 198–211.

55. D'Hondt would have to be supplemented by a rule that prevents opportunistic party fragmentation aimed at seizing key portfolios.

56. Al Stepan, "Federalism and Democracy: Beyond the U.S. Model," *Journal of Democracy* 10, no. 4 (1999): 19–34.

57. Horowitz, "Sunni Moment."

58. Makiya, "Present at the Disintegration."

59. ICG, "The Next Iraqi War?" Rend Rahim al-Francke, the director of the Iraq Foundation, made a clear appeal along these lines during her talk at a conference in Ottawa in February 2006.

60. Biden and Gelb, "Unity Through Autonomy."

12

Federalizing Natural Resources

Brendan O'Leary

JOHN KENNETH GALBRAITH, one of Canada and the United States' major public intellectuals, advised us to consider whether there is a "conventional wisdom" on any matter of public policy. Where there is, he urged that its easy embrace should be resisted and that it be scrutinized as to what interests it served, whether vested or confused. There is a conventional wisdom on Iraq. It is that Iraq should be integrated and centralized if it is to avoid multiple disasters in addition to those it has recently experienced. A centralized state, it is held, is necessary to end the current insurgency (properly insurgencies), combat crime, hold the country together, promote a civic national identity against ethnocentric and sectarian elites, defend the state against its neighbors, prevent Iraq from becoming a haven for the export of international jihadism, and allow the US-led coalition to withdraw its troops.

The sources of the conventional wisdom are widespread, and the interests that sustain it cannot be fully analyzed here. It is encouraged both by pro-US and anti-US sentiments. US Republicans and Democrats, French republicans, and the European left all favor a strong state in Iraq, albeit for different reasons. The conventional wisdom is regionally entrenched in much of the Middle East, at least in those states to the west and southwest of Baghdad and north and west of Diyarbakir, and not just those that have an interest in Iraq as an Arab state. The conventional wisdom is extensively represented in this volume.

A central corollary of the conventional wisdom is that Iraq's central authorities should be firmly in control and ownership of its natural resources, and of the revenues from these resources, now and in the future. Baghdad's control of oil and gas is seen as a sine qua non for centralization. For most supporters of the conventional wisdom, the most glaring failure of the 2005 constitution is that it fails to achieve this imperative. As a result, the International Crisis Group has called for a "total revision of key articles concerning the nature of federalism and the distribution of proceeds from oil sales" and argues that revenues from natural resources be "centrally controlled."[1] The conventional wisdom usually judges the constitution as a partisan document with provisions on natural resources that privilege Kurdish and Shia Arab regions, while collectively punishing Sunni Arabs for the sins of the Baathists. Kanan Makiya has described the constitution as a "punitive" document that penalizes Sunnis "for living in regions without oil." The constitution suggests, allegedly, that the "state owes the Sunnis of the resource-poor western provinces less than it does the Shiites and Kurds."[2] Yahia Said, another centralist, has argued that the constitution means that "Baghdad and the non-oil-producing regions will be at the mercy of the oil-producing ones."[3] The International Crisis Group has warned that if Shia Arabs construct a nine-province Shia region, as permitted by the constitution, it would "leave the Sunni Arab community landlocked and without oil."[4] Donald Horowitz, explaining Sunni alarm at the constitution, traces that fear to a provision that "seems to tie the distribution of future oil revenues to the location of the resource in one region or another. Iraq's oil is in the Kurdish north and Shiite south."[5] Many who believe the conventional wisdom see control over natural resources as at the heart of the struggle for Kirkuk. Why else, the argument goes, does Kurdistan want to incorporate Kirkuk, if not for the fact that it sits on top of some of the world's largest oil fields?

Some supporters of a centralized Iraq, in which Baghdad controls natural resources, argue with breathtaking early revisionism that the constitution actually mandates their preferred world. This appears to be the curious position of the oil minister, Hussain al-Shahristani, appointed in 2006, who claimed on assuming office that the federal government's (alleged) control over exploration extended to all oil fields in the country, including those that are not yet in production.[6] The Turkish government has taken a similar line, seeking through its official spokesmen to play down the extent to which Iraq's constitution gives any control over oil to Iraq's regions.[7]

This chapter analyzes and defends the federalizing provisions on natural resources in Iraq's constitution of 2005. After the subjects of violence and security, the ownership and allocation of the revenues from natural resources are undoubtedly the most controversial political questions in contemporary Iraq, and in this book. The argument advanced here rejects the conventional wisdom and emphasizes the centralizers' failure to learn from Iraq's history. Iraq, it is maintained, can become and remain democratic, united, and at peace with its neighbors only as a pluralist federation, and this imperative requires decentralization and cooperation between regional and federal governments. The case for a pluralist federation has been made at length elsewhere, both by me and colleagues of mine,[8] and is also addressed in John McGarry's contribution to this volume, with which I agree.

The constitution's provisions on natural resources, I maintain, are appropriate for a pluralist federation, coherent, and politically and morally defensible. A centralized Iraq, with Baghdad in charge of its oil and gas, would repeat the institutional arrangements that made Iraq a prison for a significant share of its population and a threat in the region. A centralized Iraq presided over genocide at home and precipitated wars of expansion. The decentralized 2005 constitution, by contrast, precludes no community from equitable treatment, differing markedly in this respect from the status quo ante, in which the Baathists pocketed oil money, and disproportionately benefited Arabs, especially Sunni Arabs. The new constitution provides for an adequately resourced federal government in Baghdad, but not one that owns and controls oil and gas. It does not link Kirkuk's future territorial status to that of oil and gas, a major accomplishment of the negotiations. Contrary to the ill-informed thinking of the Iraqi federal oil minister, the constitution does not hand control over exploration in new fields to Baghdad. It does not necessarily leave Sunni Arab–dominated regions without their own future oil. And the constitution provides for an important federal role in perhaps the most important natural resource of all: water. This chapter defends these claims and is underpinned by an important political warning. The constitution's federalizing provisions, especially as regards natural resources, cannot be substantively renegotiated. That is because Kurdistan enjoys a veto over any such proposed amendments and, if necessary, will use this blocking capacity.

◼ Natural Resources in the 2005 Constitution: Water, Oil, and Gas

Let us start with water, the natural resource that perhaps will be of greatest importance in the long run for the peoples of Iraq, the land of the two rivers, which is heavily dependent upon the mountains, streams, and rivers of Kurdistan.[9] The Euphrates flows from Kurdistan in Turkey and through Kurdistan in Syria, and major tributaries in the Kurdistan region of Iraq mightily amplify the Tigris. One must first observe that there were no fundamental difficulties in negotiating the relevant clauses for water, and that the consensus that they express may suggest that a loose pluralist federation may be able to work. Article 50, the constitutional oath of the members of the Iraqi Council of Representatives, places an obligation on the members to "ensure the safety of [Iraq's] land, sky, *water*, wealth, and federal democratic system" (my emphasis). Water, however, is federalized in a manner that is different from oil and natural gas.

Article 110, which specifies the "exclusive" competencies of the federal government, includes, at subsection 8, "planning policies relating to water sources from outside Iraq and guaranteeing the rate of water flow to

Iraq and its just distribution inside Iraq in accordance with international laws and conventions." This provision plainly grants the federal government exclusive responsibility for policy related to water flowing from outside Iraq into it and provides for a federal role in ensuring both the rate of flow within Iraq and in internally just distributions. This clause may fairly be interpreted as giving Mesopotamia (or the predominantly Arab parts of Iraq)[10] a federal stake in the rivers that begin in Kurdistan and as warranting the federation an international lead role in negotiating water responsibilities with Iraq's neighboring states.

Article 114 of the constitution, which specifies shared competencies, where both the federal government and the regional governments may legislate (and which are subject to regional supremacy as we shall see), enumerates at section 7, "to formulate and regulate the internal water resources policy in a way that guarantees their just distribution, and this shall be regulated by a law." This article must be read in conjunction with article 115, which grants supremacy to regional law, and with article 121 (2), which grants regions the power of nullification over federal laws outside of the exclusive competencies of the federal government. Article 115 does not require extensive commentary:

> All powers not stipulated in the exclusive powers of the federal government belong to the authorities of the regions and governorates that are not organized in a region. With regard to other powers shared between the federal government and the regional government, priority shall be given to the law of the regions and governorates not organized in a region in case of dispute.

Nor does article 121, which is a provision under the chapter dealing with "Powers of the Regions," with which article 115 should be read, require the services of a constitutional lawyer:

> (1) The regional powers shall have the right to exercise executive, legislative, and judicial powers in accordance with this constitution, except for those authorities stipulated in the exclusive authorities of the federal government. (2) In case of a contradiction between regional and national [read "federal government"] legislation in respect to a matter outside the exclusive authorities of the federal government, the regional power shall have the right to amend the application of the national [read "federal government"] legislation within that region.

In the light of these two articles, which powerfully express regional legal supremacy in domains outside of the exclusive competences of the federal government, how should we read the apparent clash between the "exclusive" competence of the federal government to plan for "just distribution" of water inside Iraq (article 110, section 8), with the "shared competence" of the federal government and the regional governments for "just distribution" for "internal water resources policy" (article 114, section 7)?

The most straightforward—and intended—construction is as follows: The federal government has exclusive competence for *planning* the external dimensions of water policy. The federal government is under a constitutional obligation to plan a just distribution within Iraq. But any regional government is entitled to nullify (or modify) within its region any application of the law as regards "just distribution," since the determination of "just distribution" is specified as a shared competence. The relevant articles express the technical acknowledgment of Iraq's interdependence as regards water and grant the federal government the minimum necessary planning authority, but they also express the historic distrust of Baghdad governments by Kurdistan—and ensure that the Kurdish Regional Government can veto any law that in its judgment does not match international law and conventions on "just distribution."

The Bremer dinars, the currency that may be L. Paul Bremer III's most lasting contribution to the new Iraq, include a graphic that represents a beautiful waterfall at Gali Ali Beg, in Kurdistan. The waterfall is not named on the currency and is not named as being in Kurdistan. And the Bremer dinars do not use both Kurdish and Arabic—changes that are mandatory under the 2005 constitution. But the waterfall on Bremer's currency may be taken as a metaphor for the treatment of water in Iraq's constitution. The relevant clauses recognize interdependence but also the hidden power and importance of Kurdistan. They balance federal and regional interests, but prevent the former usurping and trumping the latter. They obligate the federal government to follow international law and conventions in planning distribution or else it will face the nullification of the relevant statute by the Kurdish Regional Government. Given the present and future importance of water resources for Iraq's urban populations, and for agriculture, the necessary interdependence between water policy and hydroelectric power, and Saddam's past abuse of central authority to build huge dams without any degree of local consultation or planning, these articles and subsections express a principled bargain—one which ensures that regions can block misbehavior by the federal government.

The "law" that must be made, though it is a shared competence, is subject to article 110, section 8, and therefore the planning law must be a federal law, but nothing in the constitution prevents regions from modifying or nullifying the law's provisions as regards "just distribution"—provided they do so within the conventions of international law. Regional and federal courts will have to develop the requisite expertise in these domains since the relevant law's constitutionality may be challenged both by citizens and regions. The constitution also exclusively allocates "planning" to the federal government. By implication, where there are regions, the organizational implementation of the federal law shall be the responsibility of the regions unless they choose to share responsibility with federal bureaucracies.

In the broad-based coalition government formed in Baghdad in May 2006, a Kurd, Abdul Latif Rashid, was given responsibility for the federal ministry of water, whereas an Arab, Hussain al-Shahristani, was given responsibility for the federal oil ministry. That is one of many examples of the difficult and exquisite political balancing that is required in contemporary Iraq. One may fondly hope that this example augurs well for the future flourishing of political accommodation. But if so, the oil minister, at least judging by his first significant press outings, would appear to need a thorough briefing on the implications of the constitution's provisions on oil and gas.[11] What follows attempts to provide exactly that.

Let us start with article 111, to wit, "oil and gas are owned by all the people of Iraq in all the regions and provinces." This article is certainly not straightforward, but its construction is best understood as follows. First, it does not explicitly indicate how this provision is to be regulated, or by whom. It is deliberately *not* a subclause of article 110, that is, the preceding article that specifies the exclusive competencies of the federal government. That is certainly deliberate, as a comparison with the relevant article in the Transitional Administrative Law (TAL) makes clear.[12] Therefore, it follows that oil and gas ownership are *not* within the defined list of exclusive competencies of the federal government. Article 111 must therefore be read in conjunction with article 115, which specifies that all other unstipulated powers belong to the regions (and governorates not organized in a region) and that where competencies are shared, and there is a clash, regional laws prevail; it should also be read in conjunction with article 121 (2), which specifies that outside of the domain of exclusive competencies regions have a general power of nullification.

Article 111 is also *not* specifically listed among the shared competencies of the federal government and regional governments (these are specified in article 114). Therefore, there should be no presumption that article 111—or article 112, which I shall examine presently—must be treated as a wholly shared competency, that is, one for which both the federal and regional governments are permitted to legislate. The federal government, by implication, can only automatically legislate for governorates that are not regions.

This construction establishes that article 111 is subject to the supremacy of the law of any established region—which for the present simply means Kurdistan—as the negotiators intended. But does article 111 have any other constitutionally constraining meanings? Yes, in my view. There cannot be any exclusive non-Iraqi ownership of oil and gas. There is, however, no statement saying that ownership has to be *exclusive* to Iraqis; the article just requires that all Iraqis must be owners of all the oil and gas—

though presumably not that in all cars or trucks on roads between Basra, Baghdad, and Hawler (Erbil).

A reading of article 111 as a requirement that oil and gas be exclusively owned by Iraqis, or exclusively governed through a single public corporation, may contradict article 112, which, as we shall see, commends the "most advanced techniques of market principles and encouraging investment." Any reasonable court may presume that article 111 prohibits non-Iraqis from having more than 49 percent of equity in any oil and gas enterprise, but it should also presume that article 111 does not prohibit foreign direct investment, or equity sharing, in which Iraqi governments (note my use of the plural) would have a golden share. Presumptively, article 111 may suggest that some benefits from ownership must flow to all Iraqi citizens and territories—subject, of course, to articles 115 and 121 (2), which specify regional supremacy, including over article 111.

Finally, article 111 does not, in any way, mandate the continuation of a centralized, vertically integrated industry; indeed it must be read as expressly removing oil and gas ownership from the exclusive competencies of the federal government.

The next critical article is 112, which has two parts:

> (1) The federal government, with the producing governorates and regional governments, shall undertake the management of oil and gas extracted *from present fields*, provided that it distributes its revenues in a fair manner in proportion to the population distribution in all parts of the country, specifying an allotment for a specified period for the damaged regions which were unjustly deprived of them by the former regime, and the regions that were damaged afterwards in a way that ensures balanced development in different areas of the country, and this shall be regulated by a law. (2) The federal government, with the producing regional and governorate governments, shall *together* formulate the *necessary* strategic policies to develop the oil and gas wealth in a way that achieves the highest benefit to the Iraqi people using the most advanced techniques of market principles and encouraging investment [my emphasis].

How should we understand article 112? First, its provisions are also subject to articles 115 and 122 (2), which authorize regional legal supremacy. That is because, inter alia, article 112 is not part of the list of exclusive competences of the federal government and because the natural construction, which now follows, presupposes regional supremacy. Article 112 (1) makes it plain that the federal government's constitutionally prescribed role is *managerial*. It does not—and this is consistent with the reading just given of article 111—require that the federal management role take the form of managing a single public corporation. Moreover, the federal government's managerial role is confined to currently exploited fields. Equally vital, the federal government's managerial role is *shared* with the respective regions and governorates where production takes place. But the Arabic version of this article subtly implies a lead role for the federal government in management as regards article 112 (1). This interpretation is not contested by Kurdistan, provided, of course, it is not abused.

Article 112 (1) also makes it constitutionally mandatory that the federal government (and the regional governments) plan a per capita formula for the distribution of revenues from oil and gas production from currently exploited fields. So, contrary to one element of the conventional wisdom, Sunni Arabs and Sunni Arab–dominated regions or governorates are not cut out of revenues from currently exploited fields. Far from it; no Iraqi is. One should also recall that at present, all of Iraq's oil and gas revenues flow from currently exploited fields. However, the per capita formula may, by statute, be modified by time-limited support for regions deprived under Saddam and "damaged after." An "allotment," which dictionaries treat as a synonym for quotas, shares, rations, grants, allocations, allowances, and slices, and (informal) "cuts"[13] will be specified by law to go to the regions unjustly underdeveloped under Saddam (read: Kurdistan and Kirkuk governorate, and the nine southern governorates), as well as regions "that were damaged afterwards." Any allotment has to be time limited, and it has to be consistent with a "balanced" development strategy. Therefore it would be unconstitutional for the Iraqi authorities wholly to dwarf the per capita allocations by the allotment reparations. Sensible advice to the Sunni Arab community would be to focus on developing a statute that places a premium on the per capita revenue allocations and that limits the period of reparations. That offers them far better prospects of collective reassurance than nonnegotiable demands to restructure the constitution.

Which are the regions that "were damaged afterwards"? I do not think, knowing the negotiators' intentions, this phrasing refers to the Sunni Arab–dominated governorates, which have been damaged by the actions of insurgents and the counterinsurgency operations of the federal authorities and coalition forces—though it would be open to Kurdistan and the new federal government to interpret the clause in that generous spirit. It is my understanding, by contrast, that the clause was intended to cover southern governorates that were damaged after a period of development under Saddam (during the Iran-Iraq War and after the Shia intifada) and Kurdistan (which did not gets its fair share of Iraq's revenues during the period between 1992 and 2003, and which was outside the grip of the regime from 1992).

Article 112 is also important because of what it does not say. Its complete silence on future (or presently unexploited) oil and gas fields removes the warrant of any role for the federal government in their *management,* as well as over legislative competence. The injunction on future policy planning specified in article 112 (2) has an important "*together*"—and the Arabic version is equally clear on this. The "together" implies a full regional veto as regards the content of article 112 (2), even though the federal government has a tacit lead managerial role in article 112 (1).

So how then should the substance of article 112 (2) be constructed? It places an obligation on regional governments and governorate governments to formulate necessary strategic policies together with the federal government. The necessary policies flow from Iraq's membership in the Organization of Petroleum Exporting Countries (OPEC). It would be odd if Iraq's regions were to develop completely different exploitation and pricing policies. Iraq's OPEC membership, as long as that is maintained, may reasonably be held to necessitate regional—and producing governorate—agreements on production quotas. But necessity does not dictate a single vertically integrated oil or gas industry; and necessity does not require regions to link their new (or old) fields to existing Iraq-wide pipelines. Regions are constitutionally free to have their own investment strategies, oil and gas industry infrastructures, and exploration strategies. They are free to deem "necessary" whatever they wish with the federal government, and to revise such judgments. Unquestionably, it was the intention of the negotiators, and this intention is textually achieved, to grant future supremacy in ownership and management to the regions (and governorates) over unexploited fields of oil and gas. That is what article 112 (1) and (2), together with articles 115 and 121, accomplish. Article 112 (1) and (2) must be read together: the obligation to achieve the "highest benefit to the Iraqi people" is confined to policy as regards "present fields." Regions are not, by implication, required to make any federal-wide distribution of benefits from new fields of oil and gas. Nothing stops them from agreeing to that; but they are not obligated to do so. President Barzani of the Kurdish Regional Government has, however, indicated the willingness of his government to commit to such distributive arrangements, provided others (especially in the south and Baghdad) do so.

■ In Defense of These Arrangements

The constitutional provisions governing three key natural resources—water, oil, and gas—are wholly consistent with the vision of a pluralist federation. In addition, contrary to integrationist conventional wisdom, they permit a sufficiently empowered and resourced federal government. There will be a sufficient revenue base, from present oil and gas fields, for a workable federal government, including enough for it to meet its significant security obligations in the short and medium term. Iraq's present fields have long lives ahead of them. As and when regions develop outside Kurdistan, there will be a corresponding reduction in the revenues of the federal government, especially if the regions exercise their constitutional right to monopolize internal security. In the long run, the federal government, which lacks the *independent* power to tax, will have to develop revenues from other sources, which will require the consent of the regions if duties other than those on imports and exports are to be levied. That is as it should be. The constitution spells the death warrant of a highly centralized Iraq, but it delays the execution—to enable the regions to grow and to enable the federal government to establish with them the new political order.

The arrangements are both just and gradualist. The justice has already been elaborated: there is a constitutional obligation to have per capita allocation of revenues from existing fields to all regions and governorates, and there is a constitutional obligation to redress past misallocations. The gradualism of the arrangements is less well known. In 2007, fully 100 percent of Iraq's oil revenues will flow from current fields; it is reasonable to project that 90 percent will do so in 2017 and that 80 percent will do so in 2027. There will therefore be a slow adjustment from a time when all oil revenues from currently exploited fields fund all of Iraq's governments to a time in which there will be an Iraq of regions with greater revenues from the to-be-exploited fields. This gradual shift will enable appropriate development strategies for both the future resource-rich and the future resource-poor regions. Well-run governorates and regions will plan according to their respective futures and tailor their cloths appropriately—economic diversification planning should start now. There will also be opportunities for exploration *throughout* Iraq, because all three major communities predominate in some territory where there are good prospects of new fields—Baghdad, which should become a region itself, also straddles good prospects. What matters politically is that the historically underdeveloped regions have constitutional assurances that Iraq's future will not be like its past. These arrangements are exactly the necessary components of a constitutional order that will prevent the type of overcentralized, rentier oil state, which led Iraq to disaster.

The constitutional arrangements on natural resources also enable a creative settlement of the status of Kirkuk. The constitution enables Kirkuk governorate to vote to join the existing Kurdistan region by December 2007—and the other disputed territories have the same right. The votes are there for Kirkuk's incorporation into Kurdistan lawfully (judging by the outcomes of the January and December 2005 elections and by the outcome of the constitutional referendum in October 2005). Moreover, the full implementation of article 58 of the Transitional Administrative Law will ensure that there will be more pro-Kurdistan voters to vote for this change of status by December 2007—as the right of return of expelled persons will be implemented, as it should be. But what is insufficiently known is that the constitutional settlement of 2005 creatively and deliberately separates deciding the final territorial status of Kirkuk governorate from the questions of the ownership, management, and revenues of the Kirkuk oil field.

Under article 112 (1), the Kirkuk oil field shall be federally managed, in conjunction with *either* the Kurdish Regional Government, *or* the Kirkuk governorate (*or* both), and the revenues distributed according to the statute discussed above that must have both a per capita formula and a balanced development requirement. Therefore, *it is not true that if the Kurdistan region unifies with Kirkuk governorate that the rest of Iraq loses all stake in Kirkuk's oil field. It is not true; it is false.* The better this constitutional fact is appreciated, the greater the likelihood that the heat can be taken out of the referendum on Kirkuk's territorial status. Recognition of this fact by responsible international organizations, nongovernmental organizations (NGOs) such as the International Crisis Group, the government of Turkey, and Arab governments in the Middle East is a consummation devoutly to be desired.[14] Kurds will not be holding their breath, but the Kurdish Regional Government has done the right thing, by law, by prudential judgment, and by justice.

◼ Conclusion

Praise for the constitutional settlement of natural resources enables me to conclude by commending both realism and principled conduct. The bargain of 2005 as regards natural resources is part of a coherent and principled remaking of Iraq as a pluralist federation that can work, and deserves a chance to work. The constitution obligates a per capita allocation of oil revenues from currently exploited oil fields across Iraq, and does not prevent any agreement among regions to share wealth from new fields. That the constitution can work is, of course, no proof that it will. Those who voted "no" and bombed "no" to the constitution persist in their campaigns. Ethnic and sectarian killings and expulsions are rife in mixed cities and governorates. But realism also requires me to warn that article 126 (4) of the constitution empowers Kurdistan's voters and the Kurdistan region with the powers to block any amendments to the constitution, especially those that weaken any region's competences—unless that region's parliament and people consent. No one should expect Kurdistan to accept any constitutional amendments that are detrimental to its interests.

The constitution confirms Iraq's reality. It is primarily divided into four main parts: Kurdistan (including Kirkuk), Baghdad, a Shia Arab–dominated south, and a Sunni Arab–dominated west and center. The territorial politics of Mesopotamia itself are undecided. If it wishes, the United Iraqi Alliance can preside over the formation of one large southern region, or two, or more such regions. For now, neo-Baathist Sunni Arab elites, jihadist religious fanatics, and the followers of Muqtada al-Sadr among the Shia cling zealously to the vision of a centralized Iraq. Oddly, the "international community," with or without the United States, tends to empathize with—or support—the centralizing objectives of this mostly reactionary and mostly divided minority. In doing so, they falsely equate pluralist federation with wholesale disintegration and thereby feed vicious circles of misinterpretation. They also encourage neo-Baathism.

The constitution normatively establishes a pluralist, democratic framework acceptable to Kurdistan and the majority of Shia Arabs and (overtly) harms no others' rights in a democratic political order. It provides incentives for Sunni Arabs to accept new democratic realities—in those parts of Iraq in which they comprise majorities within governorates they are free to decide exactly what levels of self-government they wish to exercise and which powers they wish to leave to the federal government, or to share with it.[15] Conceding all the nostalgic demands of Sunni Arab leaders is both unacceptable and impossible for the overwhelming majority of Iraqis—Kurds and Shia Arabs—and simply will not happen inside any democratic framework. Iraq may have no future; but if it is to have a democratic future, it has to be along the lines of the constitutional settlement of 2005, including its provisions for federalizing natural resources.

▓ Notes

1. International Crisis Group (ICG), "The Next Iraqi War? Sectarianism and Civil Conflict," *Middle East Report* 52 (February 27, 2006): ii.

2. Kanan Makiya, "Present at the Disintegration," *New York Times*, 11 December 2005.

3. Yahia Said, "Federal Choices Needed," *Al-Ahram Weekly*, March 2006, weekly.ahram.org.eg/print/2006/784/sc6.htm.

4. ICG, "The Next Iraqi War?" ii.

5. Donald Horowitz, "The Sunni Moment," *Wall Street Journal*, 14 December 2005.

6. *Financial Times*, 24 May 2006.

7. "Turkey Wary of Iraqi-Kurd Plans to Export Oil," Nicosia, Deutsche Presse-Agentur, 27 June 2006, f28.parsimony.net/forum68059/messages/4187.htm.

8. See the chapters in Brendan O'Leary, John McGarry, and Khaled Salih, eds., *The Future of Kurdistan in Iraq* (Philadelphia: Univ. of Pennsylvania Press, 2005), particularly Chapters 1–4.

9. Quotations from the text of the official constitution given below—and the numbering of sections, articles, and subclauses—follow the unofficial United Nations translation, kindly made available to me by Jonathan Morrow of the United States Institute of Peace. Throughout I have checked the pertinent meanings with other advisers to Kurdistan's negotiators, including those who have a command of Arabic and Kurdish that I cannot remotely match, and with those whom I advised during the 2005 negotiations. Some articles were negotiated in English before being rendered into Arabic—and then back into English through the UN translation. Only poetry has been lost in these retranslations. Nicholas Haysom of the United Nations agreed at the conference that produced this volume that I had constructed these provisions reasonably; he agreed, in particular, with my readings of the provisions for oil and gas. I am grateful for that acknowledgment, though I do not presume that he agrees with the rest of my arguments.

10. I use Mesopotamia to refer to those parts of contemporary Iraq that are not Kurdistan, Kirkuk governorate, or the "disputed territories," that is, as a synonym for Arab-dominated Iraq.

11. *Financial Times*, 24 May 2006.

12. Art. 25 (E) of the Transitional Administrative Law made "managing the natural resources of Iraq" one of the exclusive competences of the Iraqi Transitional Government and declared, as part of that subclause, that they belonged "to all the people of all the regions and governorates of Iraq" (see Appendix 2, *The Future of Kurdistan in Iraq,* 324). The textual contrast with the permanent constitution is stark.

13. Since the clause was negotiated in English and translated into Arabic, it is fair to look at both the English and Arabic wordings—and also at the authorized Kurdish version of the constitution.

14. Elsewhere I have argued that what Iraq desperately requires in addition to its worthy constitution is tailor-made, urban power-sharing arrangements in its mixed cities, embedded in regional constitutions or laws for the relevant governorates—in Mosul, in Nineveh, or a northwestern or central region; in Kirkuk, within a unified Kurdistan region, and, of course, in Baghdad.

15. See John McGarry's chapter (Chapter 11) in this volume.

13

US Policy and Diplomacy

James Dobbins

THE UNITED STATES has few good options in Iraq. The presence there of US troops incites resistance. Their absence could open the way for a broader civil war. In these circumstances, US policymakers continue to be left with the unhappy choice of either making things worse slowly, by staying, or quickly, by going.

President Bush has chosen the middle course, promising, on the one hand, to stay long enough to establish a representative Iraqi government capable of holding its own against the centrifugal forces threatening to break up the country, but also promising to draw down US forces as quickly as Iraqi police and military units can be stood up. This policy has encountered criticism from both sides, some urging a more rapid, less conditioned withdrawal, others arguing for a more robust longer-term commitment.

■ Divergent Critiques

Those advocating accelerated withdrawal suggest that the early departure of US troops would encourage Iraq's political leaders to apply themselves more seriously to the process of reconciling contending factions, suppressing the insurgency, and governing the country. Perhaps—but experience suggests otherwise. If history is any guide, a state as badly divided and weakly governed as Iraq will, if left to its own devices, probably descend further into open civil war. And it will likely remain there for some time, the level of violence waxing and waning from one year to the next, until some outside power or group of powers intervenes to restore order. This has been the experience over the past couple of decades of Lebanon, Yugoslavia, Congo, Cambodia, Mozambique, Angola, Sierra Leone, Liberia, Sudan, Somalia, El Salvador and Haiti.[1]

If this analysis is correct, the options confronting US policymakers may be to: (1) stay and stabilize Iraq now; (2) leave and come back later, possibly after millions of Iraqis have been killed or driven from their homes; or (3) leave, stay out, and cede the task of securing Iraq to others, most notably Iran and Turkey, both of whom would find it hard to avoid being drawn into the vacuum created by a collapse of the Iraqi state.

■ Vietnam or Yugoslavia?

Most critiques of the Bush administration's approach to Iraq rely upon analogies either to Indochina or the Balkans. Those favoring the former urge adoption of lessons derived from the post-Tet US pacification program in South Vietnam.[2] The latter school argues that the war in Iraq resembles more the ethnically based conflicts in the former Yugoslavia than the ideologically based insurgency in Vietnam.[3] The Indochina school argues for a "hearts and minds" campaign focused on protecting the local populations, affording them better government, and ultimately winning their cooperation in marginalizing violent extremists. The Balkans school rejects the "hearts and minds" objective, arguing that Iraqis are not fighting for good government but for government dominated by their sectarian group. Both critiques tend to see the Kurdish and Shia militias as greater long-term threats to Iraqi unity than the less numerous Sunni insurgents and both therefore urge that the United States shift the weight of its operations from hunting down insurgents in the Sunni heartland toward establishing secure areas, initially in Baghdad and the Shia south.

Those arguing from the Balkan model differ among themselves regarding the wisdom of promoting further devolution of authority in Iraq away from the central government toward ethnically defined regions. Some argue that such a process could be stabilizing, as proved ultimately to be the case in Bosnia.[4] Others fear that the results would more likely resemble the breakup of Yugoslavia, producing heightened violence, massive population transfers, ethnic cleansing, and genocide.

Both the Indochina and Balkan analogies provide valid insights. The search-and-destroy operations favored by US commanders for the first several years in Iraq clearly produced more insurgents than they killed or captured. The administration has, consequently, moved to a "seize, hold, and build" approach reminiscent of the pacification campaign in post-Tet Vietnam. In order to implement that strategy, US troops are slowly relearning long forgotten counterinsurgency skills.

It is also true that ethnic tensions in Iraq are reminiscent of those that led to the breakup of Yugoslavia. Shia and Kurdish militias do present a growing threat, if not to US forces, then certainly to the unity of Iraq. Some repositioning of US and Iraqi forces to ensure greater control over the country's center of gravity, Baghdad, where 20 percent of the population lives, and where the Shia, Kurd, and Sunni communities are thoroughly intermixed, may well be desirable. On the other hand, those favoring further devolution of power from the center toward three ethnically based regions may well be moving with the tide of history, given the polarizing effect of the last two elections.

In one critical respect, however, the situation in Iraq is different from either Vietnam or Yugoslavia, and that is at the level of coalition forces. The United States simply does not dispose of a force large enough to successfully carry out either a Vietnam-style pacification campaign or a Balkans-style peace enforcement operation. The United States put five hundred thousand troops into South Vietnam, a country then with roughly less than half the current population of Iraq. The North Atlantic Treaty Organization (NATO) put a total of some one hundred thousand troops into Bosnia and Kosovo, societies that in combination are less than one-fifth the size of Iraq. There is no prospect whatsoever of the United States achieving comparable troop densities in Iraq. On the contrary, given that the US military presence in Iraq has become increasingly unpopular with both the US and Iraqi publics, troop levels will likely follow a downward, not upward, trend over the next year.

■ Prospects for Iraqization

US concerns have naturally focused on the Sunni extremists and their foreign allies because these are the only groups regularly targeting US forces. But Kurdish militias are engaged in ethnic cleansing designed to reestablish their dominance over the city of Kirkuk and the northern oil fields. Shia militias are organizing death squads and intimidating the Sunni population in mixed areas like Baghdad. All of the sectarian groups in Iraq have thus been resorting to terrorism to achieve their political purposes. This is not a war with the terrorists on one side and the United States on the other. It is a three-cornered civil conflict with terrorists in all three corners, and the United States increasingly in the middle, doing its best to channel this increasingly violent sectarian competition into more peaceful forms of political activity.

Of course, the United States has not remained entirely impartial in this contest. It has supported both Kurdish claims to autonomy and Shia claims to preeminence. The first is the product of Washington's earlier backing of the Kurds against Saddam, the latter of its aspiration for a democratic Iraq, a commitment that was entirely absent, only a decade earlier, from its liberation of Kuwait. US efforts have thus empowered the Shia majority, assured Kurdish autonomy, and helped build Iraqi security forces that reflect these choices.

After some false starts, the US efforts to recruit, train, and equip Iraqi army and police units are bearing fruit. The Iraqi army and, to a lesser degree, police are taking functions over from US soldiers. Iraqi soldiers and police have some advantages over US forces in waging a counterinsurgency campaign, specifically their greater access to the language and culture of the local population. These advantages may compensate for their comparative lack of firepower, defensive equipment, mobility, and sustainability. However, to the extent that Iraqi police and army units themselves assume a sectarian guise, they may have an even greater difficulty than the United States in winning the confidence of the population in mixed and Sunni areas of the country.

The National Guard and police are recruited in the localities in which they serve and thus reflect in their makeup the locally dominant sect, whether Kurd, Shia, or Sunni. Only the regular army is recruited on a national basis and organized into fully multiethnic units. This means that only about one-third of Iraqi national security forces are ethnically mixed and fully national in composition. The most recent Iraqi elections reinforced the coincidence between the country's political and militia leaderships. This might be interpreted as a good sign; it is probably better to have militia leaders, even highly irresponsible ones like Muqtada al-Sadr, inside the political process than outside it. Yet the presence of militia leaders in the political game greatly raises its stakes, allowing all sides to believe that they have other options if unable to achieve their objectives peacefully.

If, in the end, Iraqi national police and army units prove unable to secure their country, it will not be because they are inadequately trained or equipped but because they are not working for a government capable of inspiring them, paying them regularly, and using them wisely. At this point, therefore, the critical variable of success in Iraq is no longer the pace at which the United States can train and deploy new Iraqi security forces, but the quality of Iraq's next government. The Iraqi government under Ibrahim al-Ja'afari was widely perceived as incompetent, divided, corrupt, and abusive. If the al-Maliki government does not represent a marked improvement, even the best-equipped and -trained Iraqi army will not suffice to hold the country together.

■ Obstacles to Multilateralization

Critics of the administration have regularly called for greater internationalization of US nation-building efforts in Iraq, urging increased involvement of the UN, NATO, the European Union, and neighboring governments. This is, of course, easier said than done. The optimal time to have multilateralized Iraq's reconstruction was in the immediate aftermath of the invasion. At that moment, US prestige was high, no significant resistance had emerged, and the world still assumed that weapons of mass destruction (WMD) would be found. In those early months, however, the United States tended to see Iraq more as a prize won than a burden acquired. Steps were taken to ban French, German, and Russian companies from reconstruction contracts. President Bush rebuffed Prime Minister Blair's efforts to craft a central role for the UN. The United States chose to formally designate itself as an occupying power and to establish as the legal basis for its presence in Iraq the laws of armed conflict, rather than the United Nations Charter. Perhaps most importantly, the United States made no effort during those early months to create, as it had earlier with Bosnia and Afghanistan, a regional framework designed to involve Iraq's neighbors in decisionmaking regarding its future.

Holding together ethnically divided societies is hardly a new or unfamiliar task. Similar efforts were required to end the war in Bosnia in the mid-1990s and to install a successor to the Taliban regime in Afghanistan in late 2001. Iraq was not a more divided society than Bosnia and Afghanistan. Both of those states were in the middle of open, long-running civil wars when the United States stepped in. What makes Iraq different and particularly difficult is that in this case, for the first time, the United States has tried to pull a society back together without securing the cooperation, however grudging, of its neighbors.

In the mid-1990s, NATO nations discovered that they could not put Bosnia back together without the active cooperation of Serbian president Slobodan Milosevic and Croatian president Franjo Tudjman, the two men personally responsible for the genocide NATO was trying to stop. In late 2001, the United States recognized that it could not install a broad-based successor regime to the Taliban without the active support of those nations that had been tearing Afghanistan apart for several decades.

In the Balkans, the United States and its allies created the "Peace Implementation Council," which accorded all of Bosnia's neighbors a role in overseeing its transformation. With Afghanistan, the United Nations established the "six-plus-two" forum, bringing together all of that country's neighbors, along with the United States and Russia. It was this group that formally launched the process of forming a successor regime to the Taliban. Its principal member governments all participated actively in helping choose and install that government.

■ Democratization Versus Stabilization

In contrast to its earlier approach to nation building in Afghanistan, the administration's characterization of its objectives in Iraq has precluded any meaningful regional cooperation. The United States did not invade Afghanistan in order to remake that country into a model for Central Asia, nor did Washington state its intention to subsequently promote the democratization of all neighboring regimes. Had Washington announced such an intention, it would never have secured the support of Russia, Iran, Pakistan, Uzbekistan, and Tajikistan for the war, nor would it have had their help in shaping the subsequent peace. The stated US goal in Afghanistan was to ensure that the country never again became a launch pad for global terrorism. This was an objective all its neighbors could and did buy into.

In contrast, the United States did invade Iraq with the stated intention of making that state into a model for the Middle East, and with the promise that once this was achieved, the United States would then proceed to promote similar transformations in the political systems of all of Iraq's neighbors. This was not a vision any of those regimes was likely to embrace. Nor have they.

In weak, divided societies, local claimants to power always seek external sponsors. Faced with a failing state, neighboring governments always seek to develop local clientele and provide backing to one or another claimant to power. Much as one may regret and deplore such activity, neighbors can neither be safely ignored nor effectively barred from exercising their considerable influence. It has always proved wise, therefore, to find ways to engage them constructively.

None of Iraq's neighbors can match US influence in Baghdad, but several have the capacity to undermine its efforts to forge enduring power-sharing arrangements among the Shia, Sunni, and Kurdish communities. As long as the governments in Tehran, Damascus, Riyadh, Amman, Ankara, and Washington are pulling Iraqi politicians in divergent directions, no government of national unity is likely to stay unified for long.

As has been repeatedly demonstrated in the Balkans, democracy can mobilize a divided nation, but democracy alone cannot unite it. Quite the contrary: elections are polarizing events, particularly in societies riveted by sectarian conflict. In such circumstances, peace can only be secured through power-sharing arrangements that accord minorities a greater share in governance than their performance at the ballot box would normally justify.

By making Iraq the centerpiece of a larger effort to transform the Middle East, Washington has complicated its efforts to secure such an outcome. Democratization of Iran, Syria, Saudi Arabia, and Jordan, not to speak of Lebanon and the Palestinian territories, are all worthy goals, but not ones around which a regional consensus in favor of stabilizing Iraq can be formed. If stabilizing Iraq is the United States' most immediate priority, and if the support of neighboring governments is necessary, as experience elsewhere suggests it is, then these broader efforts at democratization need to be subordinated to the more immediate goal of stabilization. That does not mean abandoning attempts to promote democracy throughout the Middle East. It does mean, however, diminishing the prominence of the democratization campaign, while focusing US rhetoric and diplomatic activity upon the themes of power sharing, sovereignty, territorial integrity, and regional stability around which all the governments of that region can unite.

■ Establishing a Regional Security Dialogue

Stabilizing Iraq is not the US government's only interest in the Middle East. Washington must also be concerned with Syrian behavior in Lebanon, and Iranian behavior toward Israel, not to speak of Tehran's nuclear aspirations. Conversations with those governments over Iraq should not, therefore, be conducted in isolation, but should be designed to lead into a broader regional dialogue ultimately addressing all these other issues.

The Gulf is the only large area of the world that does not possess some framework for regular consultations on regional security issues. In the Western Hemisphere, there is the Organization of American States. In Europe, there is NATO. In Africa, there is the African Union. In Southeast Asia, there is the Association of Southeast Asian Nations (ASEAN). In Northeast Asia, there is the five-power forum created to address the North Korean nuclear program. Even in the midst of the Cold War, all the nations of NATO and the Warsaw Pact met regularly, in the context of the Conference on Security and Cooperation in Europe (CSCE), to debate their differences and address their mutual concerns. The absence of any such forum for dialogue in and around the Gulf makes what is already the world's most tense and dangerous region even more volatile than it need be.

Just as the United States has leveraged regional concern about North Korea's nuclear ambitions to forge a regional forum for security consultations among all the nations of Northeast Asia, so it now has an opportunity to leverage anxieties over Iraq's future to launch broader regional dialogue over security in and around the Gulf.

This dialogue might take several forms. At the most basic level, the United States might start talking to all the neighboring governments on a regular basis about Iraq. For these talks to produce an operative regional consensus, Washington would have to produce a vision of Iraq and its neighborhood likely to appeal to all the regimes in the area. This is not as hard as it might seem. All those governments favor a unitary Iraq, strong enough to maintain its territorial integrity, but not strong enough to threaten its neighbors. None favor federalism or the division of Iraq into strong autonomous regions (polling data suggest that the great majority of Iraqis, Kurds excepted, also support this vision). By deemphasizing its goal of regional democratization and emphasizing the themes of sovereignty, territorial integrity, stability, and power sharing, the United States could provide a program for Iraq that all of its neighbors and most of its citizens could buy into.

Beyond an intensified and enriched set of bilateral dialogues, the United States might propose periodic meetings of all the states bordering on the Gulf or maintaining forces in it to address issues of Gulf security. Initially, these sessions might serve to do no more than register and air various complaints, much as the Cold War CSCE dialogue did in its earliest days. Eventually, however, discussions might move on to negotiation of confidence-building measures and eventually even regional arms control, again on the CSCE model.

■ US, Regional, and International Roles

Neither the United States nor the Iraqi people want to see a larger or more extended US presence in Iraq. On the other hand, majorities in both countries also understand that a precipitate withdrawal could make a bad situation even worse. Proposals for future policy toward Iraq need to take account of the real constraints imposed by US and Iraqi opinion.

The policy of Iraqization represents the least bad option among a range of unhappy choices available to the United States. Staying in Iraq long enough to empower a broadly representative Iraqi government, and seeking to provide that regime the wherewithal to secure the country, is the only responsible course at this stage, given all that has gone before. On the other hand, leaving as quickly as Iraqi forces can take over from US troops is the appropriate response to the Iraqi public's antipathy to the US presence, and the US public's waning support for the commitment.

US counterinsurgency campaigns in Vietnam and stabilization efforts in the Balkans both provide enlightening analogies to the challenges faced today in Iraq. But commitments on those scales are not realistic options. The United States put five hundred thousand troops into South Vietnam, a country less than half the size of Iraq. NATO put over one hundred thousand troops into Bosnia and Kosovo, societies that in combination are less than one-fifth the size of Iraq. If the US commitment to Iraq is to be sustained, its role in the counterinsurgency campaigns of Central America in the 1980s may provide a better model, one in which the residual US role is largely confined to advice and material support.

Sectarian militias are, as Ambassador Zalmay Khalilzad has suggested, "the building blocks of civil war." In this respect, the Shia and Kurdish militias may be even more of a threat to Iraqi unity than the Sunni insurgents. It is not realistic to think, however, that the United States, at this late stage, is going to shoulder the burden of disarming and demobilizing these forces. That is a challenge that will have to be met primarily by the Iraqis, and primarily through political means.

US efforts to build Iraqi security forces are beginning to show measurable results. If Iraqization ultimately fails, it will not be because Iraqi forces are inadequately equipped or trained, but because the government they work for cannot win their trust and use them wisely. Building a government that can perform those functions should, therefore, be the top US priority. This can be achieved, in part, through efforts to build and train a cadre of civil officials, much as the United States and its coalition partners are doing with the Iraqi military and police. Improvements in Iraq's civil service, like those in its security forces, will avail little, however, if they continue to work for governments that are weak, divided, corrupt, and abusive.

Experience with other badly divided nations suggests that the task of uniting such societies is beyond the capacity of any one foreign power, even one as powerful as the United States. On the other hand, full-scale internationalization of the nation-building effort in Iraq is no longer feasible, if it ever was. Some greater effort nevertheless needs to be made to engage Iraq's neighbors in the process of stabilizing that country.

Iraqi political leaders will coalesce only if and when they receive convergent signals from their various external sponsors. Washington's high-profile commitment to regional democratization and its concomitant challenge to the legitimacy of all the neighboring regimes are working at cross-purposes with its effort to promote the formation of a government of national unity. Regional democratization, therefore, needs to be subordinated, at least for the next several years, to efforts to stabilize Iraq. The United States should leverage widespread anxiety over Iraq's future to promote the emergence of a forum for consultation among all the states of the region on issues of security in and around the Gulf.

Since Iraq is a weak, divided society headed toward open civil war, its security will inevitably be multilateralized. The only issue is what form this process will take. The effort to stabilize Iraq on the basis of a narrow, US-dominated coalition of the willing seems likely to fail. The choices then open to the United States are either to rapidly broaden this effort by inviting the neighboring governments to employ their influence to help stabilize the country or alternatively to watch while they use that influence to pursue their individual national agendas in ways that destabilize it.

The United Nations, the European Union, NATO, existing coalition members, and those who have stood aside can all play helpful roles in making the former scenario work, as can regional groupings such as the Arab League and the Organization of the Islamic Conference. Skillful US diplomacy can weave contributions from all these actors together, as was done in the latter half of the 1990s in the Balkans. In the end, however, it is the United States that created the current crisis, and it is the neighboring states that will have to live with its consequences. The rest of the world is inevitably going to look to these governments to take the lead in sorting it out. If they fail to do so, it is unlikely that any other collection of nations or international organizations will fare better.

■ Notes

1. All of these cases, except Lebanon and Liberia, are dealt with in either volume one or two of James Dobbins et al., *The RAND History of Nation-Building* (Santa Monica, CA: RAND, 2005).

2. Kenneth M. Pollack et al., "Switch in Time: A New Strategy for America in Iraq," *Saban Center Analysis* (Saban Center for Middle East Policy at the Brookings Institution) no. 7 (February 15, 2006).

3. Stephen Biddle, "Seeing Baghdad, Thinking Saigon," *Foreign Affairs* 85, no. 2 (March/April 2006).

4. Joseph Biden and Leslie Gelb, "The Bitter Fruits of War," *New York Times*, 1 May 2006.

14

Iraq's Arab Neighbors

Jon B. Alterman

IT WOULD SEEM INTUITIVE that Iraq's Arab neighbors would want the country's democratic transition to succeed. Long fearful of Saddam Hussein and the instability he caused, his removal held out the promise of a region that could breathe easier and concentrate on urgent issues of internal reform. Indeed, in the months preceding the US-led assault on Iraq, Gulf leaders were widely reported to have urged the Bush administration to take forceful action against Iraq, with the proviso that it should also be swift so as to avoid too many ripples in the region.

In the years following the fall of Saddam, however, regional instability has increased in many ways rather than diminished. Rather than facing the threat of Saddam's army and his missiles, Iraq's Arab neighbors now face starker challenges. For many, their populations are enraged by their governments' close cooperation with the United States, and the prospect of a new generation of well-trained and highly networked jihadi fighters returning home looms on the horizon. Sectarian rivalries flare anew, and Shia-Sunni tensions are higher than at any time since the Iranian revolution more than a quarter century ago. In addition, Iran's ascending influence in Iraq and more broadly in the region has made many uneasy, while others, such as Syria, have been emboldened. The fall of Saddam has not meant an end to fear for Iraq's Arab neighbors. In many ways, the fall of Saddam has merely shifted that fear. In some cases, Saddam's fall has even intensified it.

For many of Iraq's smaller neighbors, fear motivates governments more than hope. That fear often drives them into the arms of the United States, which alone among world powers can protect them from regional aggression. Iraq's liberation has not liberated these governments from their reliance on the United States, since Iran's rise swiftly followed Iraq's demise. What it has done, however, is make governments acutely aware of the fact that they are at the mercy of a US policy—toward Iran, toward Iraq, and more broadly—over which they have little influence, let alone control.

Among Iraq's Arab neighbors, there has been a range of attitudes toward US policy toward Iraq. Only Syria openly challenges US policy; the others support it to varying degrees. For the Gulf states that have traditionally sought US security guarantees, their formal alliances with the United States persist, albeit in varying forms. Jordan has continued the close security relationship it struck with the United States for more than a decade, reversing the attitude of neutrality it adopted in the 1991 Gulf War. In a way, Jordan has used its position with relation to Israel as a strategic asset comparable to the oil wealth of the Gulf. Thus, the stability of the current Jordanian regime has become a strategic interest of the United States.

As a general rule, the close bilateral relations that persist despite differences over Iraq underlines the extent to which few governments in the Middle East see any alternative to a close relationship with the United States. Throughout the region, only Syria and Iran can be said to be estranged, while all others seek either to make their peace with or profit from the relationship with the United States.

While events in Iraq raise anger and despair among the country's neighbors, events there have also reinforced the centrality of the United States to the security considerations of every country there. Saddam Hussein's removal did not mean more freedom for the crafters of foreign policy in the Middle East. Instead, it made their basic predicament clearer and diminished their hopes for a different order in the region.

▧ Iraq's Arab Neighbors and US Policy

At the outset, the Bush administration's ambitions in Iraq enjoyed little support among Iraq's closest neighbors. This coolness was not because the neighbors had any regard for Iraq's government, but rather because the Bush administration trumpeted how "inspirational" a new regime in Iraq would be to Arabs living under tyranny. "A liberated Iraq can show the power of freedom to transform that vital region, by bringing hope and progress into the lives of millions," the president told a friendly audience at the American Enterprise Institute in Washington a month before the US-led assault.[1] Bush left unspoken that many of the millions who would be inspired live under the thumb of governments allied to the United States. Those governments' cooperation would be vital to both wage the war and manage the consequences afterward.

The rhetoric of the administration's supporters outside of government heightened those governments' concerns still further by loudly proclaiming how deposing Saddam Hussein would provoke positive ripples throughout the Middle East. For some, the demonstration of US resolve would intimidate its foes, "making them recalculate the odds of defying a power that has demonstrated its intention to remain a permanent and dynamic regional player."[2] Others were blunter still. Former Central Intelligence Agency director R. James Woolsey told a UCLA audience just after Saddam fell,

> We will scare, for example, the Mubarak regime in Egypt, or the Saudi royal family, thinking about this idea that these Americans are spreading democracy in this part of the world. They will say, "You make us very nervous." And our response should be, "Good. We want you nervous. We want you to realize that now, for the fourth time in 100 years, this country and its allies are on the march, and that we are on the side of those whom you, the Mubaraks, the Saudi royal family, most fear. We are on the side of your own people."[3]

As far as Iraq's neighbors were concerned, they just wanted Saddam Hussein gone. Their interest in a success for the United States—especially the way the US government defined success and its consequences—was limited at best. As a group, Iraq's neighbors did not want a strong and united Iraq to emerge a beacon of freedom to the region. An inspirational Iraq could cause insurrection from within their countries, and a strong Iraq could threaten their borders. To a government, their interests would be much better served by an Iraq that remained relatively weak, too consumed by infighting to threaten its neighbors, and too mired in its own dysfunctional politics to inspire nearby populations.

In essence, these governments signed on for the military side of the US effort, but not the political one. Granting the US military basing rights, over-flights, support for reconnaissance operations, refueling, and other military functions helped maintain these countries' alliances with the US government. Yet these governments supported US efforts in order to preserve the status quo, rather than impose a new one. These governments have little interest in catastrophic failure in Iraq, but their interest in the broader goals that the US government has articulated is similarly limited. Long used to managing tensions in far from ideal conditions, the leaderships of the countries neighboring Iraq seek stability.[4]

It is perhaps surprising to them, then, that US actions in Iraq have not brought stability so much as shifted the most serious challenges most of them face from external threats to internal ones. While counterterrorism cooperation drives many of these countries closer to an alliance with the United States, and their strategic depth (or ability to survive an initial onslaught and ultimately repel an invasion) relies entirely on US support, much of the bilateral partnership remains hidden. On a public level, events in Iraq have driven most governments in the region to distance themselves from the United States and express concern that US actions are harmful to their interests.

■ Close Ties: Kuwait, Iraq, and the United States

Among the smaller Gulf states, three general trends are evident, typified by Kuwait, Qatar, and the United Arab Emirates. Kuwait is the most unabashed supporter of the United States, which liberated the country from Saddam Hussein in 1991 and whose support gives vital comfort to a small but wealthy country sandwiched between the two larger states of Iraq and Saudi Arabia. It is not an exaggeration to say that Kuwait exists today as a country because of the efforts of the US military, and the Kuwaiti government has not forgotten this fact. Kuwait maintains ten US bases on its soil and reportedly hosts approximately twenty thousand US soldiers. The rapidly expanding Camp Arifjan, located south of Kuwait City, is the main staging ground for all coalition troops in Iraq.[5] The facility replaces Camp Doha, the base that the US military hastily erected after the Iraqi invasion of Kuwait in 1990. Arifjan is designed as a permanent facility, and it is sprouting a variety of permanent structures—from lodging to covered storage for prepositioned materiel. In addition, Kuwait heavily subsidizes the oil and gasoline that US troops in the region use.

Kuwait has doggedly sought to deepen its bilateral relationship with the United States, being awarded "major non-NATO ally" status in 2004. That status facilitates the sale of surplus weapons, stockpiling of materiel outside of the United States, and allows additional antiterrorism funds to flow from the United States.[6]

For more than a decade after Saddam's 1990 invasion, Kuwaitis lived in mortal fear of another attack from Iraq. The downfall of Saddam's regime in 2003 allowed many Kuwaitis to breathe easier, since the principal external threat to the country had evaporated. Not only was Kuwait in the lead supporting the US-led invasion, but Kuwaiti businessmen aggressively sought to promote investment in post-Saddam Iraq, and the government established a fund of almost one billion US dollars for investment there.[7]

As violence mars the future picture for Iraq, and as the memory of Saddam recedes, Kuwaitis have two fears from beyond their borders. The first is the threat from a potentially nuclear-armed Iran. While Iran's relations with Kuwait are not hostile, as a small country Kuwait fears the growing influence of a regional neighbor, especially one with special ties to Kuwait's Shia population (about 15–20 percent of the total). Kuwait's other fear is that instability in Iraq will spill over into Kuwait, either through sectarian strife or from the establishment of an Iranian-influenced Shia state in the south of the country. As one journalist put it in an informal conversation, "We don't want Iran just fifty miles away."[8]

The fear of potential sectarian strife highlights the extent to which many of Kuwait's greatest fears now come from internal threats. Although a windfall from high oil prices, combined with a soaring stock market, have raised many Kuwaitis' standards of living, there is a doggedly persistent violent Islamist movement in the country, especially in tribal areas. While the threat level remains far below that of Saudi Arabia, several attacks against Western personnel occur every year in Kuwait.[9] The government is moving to exert more control over preaching in mosques and is trying Kuwaiti and Egyptian clerics for inciting youth to fight in jihad in Iraq. Finally, groups associated with Al-Qaida have pockets of activity in Kuwait, are stockpiling arms and explosive devices, and entering into occasional clashes with police. How much of these clashes represent the dying cry of these groups or the tip of the iceberg is unclear. Most Kuwaitis dismiss the idea that such militancy can threaten the government's survival. Still, they are part of a larger challenge of managing the expectations of a disaffected young population whose desires increase perhaps even more rapidly than the government's ability to satisfy them.

More, perhaps, than any of its neighbors, Kuwait acts as if it is a small boat tossed at sea. Kuwait is thrust between large and sometimes difficult neighbors, and the country remains uneasy. The only way it has any strategic depth at all is to rely on US forces to protect it, yet Kuwaitis often express frustration that they have little control over what the United States does in the region or how it sees the world. The difficulties the United States has faced in Iraq have made many Kuwaitis question both the wisdom and capacity of their most important ally, and such doubts occur precisely at the time that Kuwaitis are becoming preoccupied with potential threats from Iran. While Kuwaitis fully appreciate that there is no alternative to the United States in providing the country with strategic depth, there is far less enthusiasm for the bilateral relationship than there was five years ago. In addition, rising awareness of other global powers such as China—which one Foreign Ministry official observed has "positive positions on Arab issues"—suggests a desire to supplement reliance on the United States with ties to other countries.

■ Warm Relations with a Useful Irritant: Qatar, the United States, and Iraq

Qatar takes a more ambivalent stance, often seeking cooperation on the one hand while maintaining the perception of nonalignment. Qatar has a somewhat different strategic perspective than Kuwait, since its only land border is with Saudi Arabia, and it does not fear invasion. Qatar, however, has somewhat strained relations with the Saudi kingdom, especially since the emir deposed his father in 1996. Reportedly, Saudi intrigue seeks to threaten the current emir's hold on power, supporting his rivals and others in the country who wish to keep him in check.[10] Qatar is also notably more sanguine about Iranian nuclear intentions, reportedly objecting to proposed language in a December 2005 Gulf Cooperation Council (GCC) communiqué that would have referenced an Iranian proliferation threat to GCC security.[11]

In the last decade, the government of Qatar has sought to strengthen its internal position and to hold its external rival at bay, by building an even closer relationship with the United States. In the late 1990s, when US military bases in Saudi Arabia became increasingly controversial in that country, the Qatari government began to lay the groundwork to bring US bases to Qatar. The emir reportedly told US officials he hoped permanently to host ten thousand US soldiers in the country.[12] The Saudis' 2001 refusal to allow US forces to fly combat missions from Saudi bases in Afghanistan cemented the trend. The embodiment of this shift was the establishment of a US base south of Doha that same year to compensate for strictures over use of the Prince Sultan Air Base in Saudi Arabia. From Qatar, the US military established a Combined Air Operations Center with responsibility for counterterror air operations over Afghanistan and the Horn of Africa, and it assumed the leadership of the air campaign over Iraq in April 2003. It has grown into a multibillion-dollar project; at the same time, the United States has removed its personnel from the Prince Sultan Air Base in Saudi Arabia, turning it over to complete Saudi control.

Qatar has also sought to carve out an identity as a progressive country in the region. Its rulers speak frequently about democracy, and promote the small state—with a citizenry that probably numbers less than 150,000—as a model for development. Qatar has also invested huge amounts of money in becoming a regional education center, partnering with major US universities such as Cornell, Texas A&M, Georgetown, Virginia Commonwealth, and others to establish facilities there.

For all of its commitment to turn to the United States for military protection and educational advancement, however, Qatar is far from a US puppet. In particular, the aggressive news coverage of its satellite television station, Al-Jazeera, has proven a useful irritant in US-Qatari relations. It is, perhaps, ironic that this is so, and it is particularly ironic that the fiercest critics of Al-Jazeera in the US administration—generally among the Department of Defense—are also among those who are most dependent on Qatar's support for their posture in the region. US officials have complained bitterly about Al-Jazeera's airing of tapes from Osama bin Laden, as well as its news coverage of Iraq and the Arab-Israeli conflict. Al-Jazeera's role here is remarkably artful. The Qatari government professes an inability to control what the channel airs, yet the government's clear support for the station with tens of millions of dollars in annual subsidies, combined with persistent reports of royal engagement on strategic issues at the station, suggests considerable government influence over its programming.

What Al-Jazeera provides Qatar is a degree of distance from the United States, while providing the government deniability at the same time. Al-

Jazeera suggests Qatari independence, while the government of Qatar pursues an ever-deeper defense relationship with the United States. At the same time, Al-Jazeera provides the Qatari government with a tool it can use against Saudi Arabia and other regional rivals, modulating its coverage of issues involving neighboring governments and giving more or less prominence to regime opponents in its coverage. The genius in Qatar's use of Al-Jazeera is not the extent to which the channel is a precise tool of policy—it is not—but rather its effectiveness. The station allows the government both to become a significant regional player in its own right, while simultaneously permitting a closer relationship to the US military (which enhances Qatar's power as well).

Through this avenue, the war in Iraq has enhanced Qatar's position, because it has simultaneously allowed the country to deepen its relations with the United States and to assert its pan-Arab bona fides through broadcasting. At the same time, Qatar's relatively isolated geographic position and its small and largely homogeneous native population means that instability in Iraq in no way threatens the status quo in the country. The US base is sufficiently far from Doha that it is remote from most Qataris' daily life, but it allows the government to deepen its ties with the only country that can provide it with depth against whatever Saudi designs against it exist.

■ Silent Partnership: The United Arab Emirates, the United States, and Iraq

The third type of relationship is that pursued by the United Arab Emirates (UAE), which has simultaneously sought to build its own defensive capacity while deepening ties with a range of countries. Compared to Kuwait and Qatar, US military cooperation with the UAE has been almost silent; it is appropriate that the major UAE contribution to the war in Iraq is thought to be the basing of surveillance aircraft at Al-Dhafra Air Base outside of Abu Dhabi. Speaking at a press conference in Abu Dhabi in January 2005, Assistant Secretary of Defense Peter Rodman referred to "good quiet cooperation" between the United States and the UAE, and added, "I don't want to get into the specifics, but we are very pleased at the (military) cooperation that we have."[13]

While the UAE has a keen interest in Gulf stability, its interest in Iraq is secondary to its concern over Iran, with which it has a longstanding dispute over three islands in the Gulf. Relations between the two countries are not unremittingly tense, however. Tens of thousands of Iranians live in Dubai, and billions of dollars of Iranian assets are invested in Emirati businesses and real estate projects. Trade between the two countries is robust and slated to grow. A major bankroller of Saddam Hussein in his war with Iran, a key supporter of the anti-Soviet mujahidin in Afghanistan (and later the Taliban there), and a booster of senior Iraqi Sunni politicians such as Adnan Pachachi, the UAE pursues a strategy of diverse but quiet partnerships cemented by large amounts of cash. The country is reaching the end of a ten-year, US$15 billion defense modernization program. The country contracted for eighty modern F-16 aircraft from the United States at a cost of US$6.8 billion, an additional thirty-three Mirage 2000-9 aircraft from France (along with an agreement to upgrade thirty Mirage 2000-5 aircraft already in stock), and a full complement of high-tech missiles. In addition, the UAE is seeking a missile defense capacity, has extensive Russian- and French-supplied land forces, and it is aggressively building a navy that can operate both in the Gulf and the Indian Ocean.

The United States remains the UAE's most important military partner, and the two countries formed a joint military commission to facilitate cooperation and joint training. More than one thousand Emiratis train every year in the United States, and the country will need to almost double its supply of pilots by 2007.

In pursuance of its US relationship, the UAE offered training on its soil to hundreds of Iraqi troops and police recruits in 2004–2005. Emblematic of the way the UAE government seeks to cover many bases in its actions, much of the training was conducted by German forces on UAE soil, thereby establishing an avenue of participation for an open foe of the war and inoculating the UAE from charges that it was complicit in the US military occupation of Iraq.

Saudi Arabia's role is the most difficult to describe, and its balance the most difficult to maintain. Too proud to be as closely aligned as the Kuwaitis, too large to be as nimble as the Qataris, and too reliant on the United States to be as hedged as the UAE, the Saudi leadership has remained largely aloof from events in Iraq, at least on a public level. The strong influence of Sunni clerics on Saudi policy, and Saudi concern about its Shia minority in the kingdom's Eastern Province make Iraqi sectarian politics all the more inflammatory for the Saudis; the detection of at least some Saudi jihadis fighting in Iraq makes the specter of their returning to the kingdom to fight against the government all the more alarming. While there is not a single Saudi policy to emerge out of the war in Iraq, the broader bilateral relationship appears to be following a very clear line: strengthened bilateral participation on technical issues that remain below the public's radar and either silence or distance from US policies in public. Given the importance of the bilateral relationship to both countries, it is striking that in the years since the US invasion of Iraq, visible bilateral military cooperation has all but disappeared, US troops have withdrawn except for a small training mission, and Saudi Arabia is absent from most discussions of postwar planning in Iraq. Saudi Arabia is far too large, and far too important, to be inconspicuous in this regard, yet that appears to be exactly what the Saudi government is seeking to do.

■ Beyond the Gulf: Jordan and Syria

Outside of the Gulf, countries' options are more circumscribed. While oil wealth allows many Gulf countries to secure their own future, Jordan has relied on its strategic position as its chief asset in its relations with the United States. With a majority Palestinian population, few natural resources, and difficult borders on both its east and west, Jordan has often sought to do more with less. Accustomed from its days as a British mandate to forging close ties with outside powers, Jordan sought to maintain a nonaligned position in the 1991 Gulf War, partly in order to draw Iraqi support, and partly at popular demand. That orientation was costly to Jordan in terms of its relationship with the United States, and Jordan spent much of the 1990s rebuilding that relationship—signing a peace treaty with Israel in 1994 and deepening security and intelligence ties with the United States in the years following.

When war with Iraq was looming in 2003, Jordan chose a far different tack than it had in 1991. No longer seeking nonalignment, Jordan was perhaps the country closest to the United States after Kuwait. The United States flowed personnel and materiel through the country, and intelligence cooperation was remarkably close. Although not widely reported, Jordanian forces are thought to have been the eyes and ears of many of the initial US forays into Iraq, and US forces are thought to have entered Iraq covertly via Jordan even before hostilities began.[14]

In addition to helping Americans, Jordan also opened its doors to tens of thousands of Iraqi citizens fleeing chaos in that country. Real estate prices in Amman skyrocketed—more than tripling in many areas—and the stock exchange boomed. Jordan was a safe haven for many, and while some Jordanians struggled to make ends meet in an inflationary environment in which prices had risen 40 to 50 percent, many Jordanians were reaping windfall profits from the influx of Iraqis.[15]

Much of Jordanians' enthusiasm for the post-Saddam boom dissipated after suicide bombers from Iraq crossed the border and bombed three luxury hotels in Amman in November 2005. The country reversed its previous decision to leave the Iraqi border open to those fleeing the violence and privations of Iraq and began demanding passports from incoming refugees. The intelligence services began keeping a much closer watch on Iraqi expatriates. Perhaps most importantly, the mood shifted. Iraqis were suddenly a threat to Jordanians, rather than merely a challenge to the old order.

What the November 2005 Amman bombings did was reinforce notions of Jordanian fragility and to lead the country even more toward relying on the United States. The specter of a "Shia crescent" emerging in the Arab world, in King Abdullah's memorable phrase, further convinced the Jordanian government that only a close relationship with the United States could give the country strategic depth.

At the same time, events on the ground made such close bilateral ties more difficult to maintain. In particular, the Abu Ghraib scandal, continued US missteps in Iraq, and the concerted and very public US effort to force the collapse of a Hamas government in Palestine made the US government significantly less popular among Jordanians, making that partnership more difficult to maintain and defend in public. While it is difficult to assess the depth of support for radical movements in the country, anecdotal evidence suggests they may be gaining strength so long as their intended victims are Westerners rather than Muslims. One victim of this strategic tension was Jordan's "National Agenda," a far-reaching reform initiative whose drafting reflected the input of a wide swath of Jordan's liberal intelligentsia. The government delayed introduction of the plan for weeks, and then in the spring of 2006 quietly buried it. Rolling out a Western-style plan of modernization and reform had simply become more than the traffic could bear.

The Jordanian government's conundrum is one to which only external events can provide the solution. Just as the government has benefited massively from its role helping meet US policy goals in Iraq and in the Arab-Israeli arena, signs of diminishing US urgency in these areas—or at least diminishing energy put into regional support for US-led initiatives there—leaves their currency devalued. Meanwhile, the public is deeply disaffected. A long-running "Jordan First" campaign to persuade Jordanian citizens that their national interests need to take precedence over pan-Arab loyalties is likely inadequate for the task at hand. The country needs a genuinely populist gesture by the king, improved internal economic conditions, and some progress to point to among its neighbors that would demonstrate the wisdom of the government's course.

Syria remains the odd man out among Iraq's Arab neighbors, and it has seemingly sought to profit from its unique position. Rather than seek to ally with the United States, Syria has sought to profit from lining up against it. There are persistent reports that former members of the Iraqi regime sought sanctuary in Syria, as well as persistent reports that foreign fighters seeking to enter Iraq did so from the Syrian border. Traditional smuggling routes facilitated this movement, but they do not account for all of it. Indeed, in the early days of the war, foreign fighters used to leave on a bus that departed just a few blocks from the US embassy in Damascus. Syria has sought to use Iraq as a bargaining chip in a broader and largely tense relationship with the United States, and Iraq policy has become a kind of currency in this relationship in addition to being an irritant.

Syrian officials admit some puzzlement that their relationship with the

United States is not better. In the period after September 11, Syria provided extensive cooperation with US intelligence agencies on Al-Qaida-related issues. Syrian officials report their government provided the US government extensive information on terrorist activities and organizations, and on at least one occasion accepted the extraordinary rendition of a Syrian-born Canadian citizen suspected of involvement in terrorism.[16] Tension over Iraq, Arab-Israeli issues, and Syria's presence in Lebanon overwhelmed the counterterrorism cooperation, however. Following the assassination of Lebanese prime minister Rafiq Hariri in February 2005, amidst numerous signs of Syrian involvement, the United States recalled its ambassador to Damascus, and the position has remained vacant since. The US government has leveled numerous allegations of Syrian involvement supporting the Iraqi insurgency and, in particular, support for elements led by the Jordanian-born Abu Musab al-Zarqawi.[17]

For all of its tension with the United States, however, Syria surely benefits from the fact that Iranian-US tensions are of far more concern to the Bush administration. Iran's proliferation activities and the actions of Iranian allies in Iraq pose a far greater immediate threat to US interests than whatever Syria may do. Since the fall of 2005, Syria has shown more self-confidence toward the international community than it had before; a persistent hand in Lebanon since withdrawing troops in the spring of 2005, a crackdown on Syrian political dissidents in the spring of 2006, and a more defiant public stance are all signs that Syria is more comfortable about its international position.

While Syria superficially benefits from having far more independence and control over its relationship with the United States than most of its Arab peers, the cost of the policy upon which Syria embarked is quite high. Persistent US pressure against Syrian interests has diminished the little interest there was in investing in the country, and that pressure is also applied against Syrian-backed interests in Lebanon. The arrival of hundreds of thousands of Iraqi refugees into Syria has raised housing prices significantly and introduced a large population that is barred by law from seeking employment in the already impoverished country.[18] Syria presumably benefits to some degree from its relationship with Iran, although the subsidies most likely pale in comparison to the billions of dollars Syria obtained from helping Saddam Hussein smuggle oil through Syrian ports. Syria's calculation may be driven by the idea that Syria does better as a lone Arab holdout against US hegemony rather than a low-ranking also-ran in a crowded field; it may also have concluded that the United States will accept nothing short of the end of the current leadership. What seems most clear is that Syria has pursued a policy that needs to endure persistent pressure and challenge from the United States and its allies, and one with limited upside potential and significant downside risk.

■ **Conclusion**

While there is clearly no single Arab attitude toward Iraq—either among populations or governments—there are a range of things that Arab states could do collectively that would help improve conditions on the ground there. Among the most valuable, perhaps, are symbolic gestures that could help reassure those who feel left out of the current political process that they have not been abandoned. This particularly refers to Iraq's Sunni population, which enjoys significant sympathy in many of the surrounding states. Presumably this approach would come through the Arab League, which has exhibited periodic interest in taking a higher-profile role and has been attempting to find a role for itself more actively since late 2005.[19] Tailoring an approach that would not simultaneously antagonize Iraq's Kurdish population would make the task more difficult, but no less necessary; the key issue would be timing the League's intervention so that it would have the maximum effect on its intended audience, while being overlooked by those who feel threatened by it.

Surrounding states could also be more effective in stemming transnational support for the insurgency. While no government appears to be giving direct support to fighters in Iraq, that is a quite different thing from permitting such support to flow from nongovernmental sources. This will presumably become easier for governments to pursue as the insurgency targets fewer Western combatants and more Iraqi civilians; an inescapable part of this needs to be effective Iraqi national and Western government pressure to end death squad activity by Shia militias—either freestanding or incorporated into the Iraqi military and police—against Sunni civilians.

In the longer term, Iraq's neighbors could forgive the tens of billions of dollars in Iraqi debt that they currently hold and which they have little actual prospect of recovering. While the Paris Club has agreed to forgive 80 percent of Iraqi debt incurred under Saddam Hussein, two of Iraq's biggest debtors—Kuwait and Saudi Arabia—hold an estimated total of US$57 billion in debt, representing almost three times the total originally held by the Paris Club countries and 46 percent of the country's total indebtedness.[20]

Finally, Iraq's Arab neighbors could create a kind of contact group for Iraq that would create a seat at the table for all of the concerned countries, but most pointedly for the United States and Iran. Such a contact group was a valuable asset in postconflict discussions about Afghanistan, and it could provide a valuable (if belated) forum in which to promote common interests in Iraq. Such a forum would require Arab leadership to be effective, while at the same time requiring US participation.

Writing almost twenty years ago, Stephen Walt observed that threats were a far better determinant of alliance formation behavior than power, ideology, or some other motivating factor.[21] Iraq's aggressive behavior toward many of its neighbors led many of them into close alliances with the

United States, and emerging threats from Iran in the postwar environment have helped solidify their orientation. Indeed, one of the key surprises of the post–Cold War Middle East is that the demise of the Soviet Union has driven virtually every government in the region into the arms of the United States in order to guard against regional powers or internal opposition, at the same time that events on the ground—and their coverage in regional media—have bred more hostility toward the United States among broad publics than at any time since the 1967 Arab-Israeli war.

The postwar environment has also underlined the commitment of surrounding governments to the current shape of the Iraqi state, as all fear that its breakup would either inspire minorities within their own borders or bring hostile forces closer to home. As terrifying a prospect as Saddam Hussein was to many of them, the prospect of growing chaos in Iraq is more terrifying still.

The alliances that Iraq's Gulf neighbors maintain are often uneasy ones, born out of necessity and often kept out of the public eye. There are two ironies in all of this. The first is that a driving factor behind the US decision to go to war against Iraq was to protect these countries from persistent Iraqi threats, yet they have generally adopted a passive role toward shaping the post-Saddam environment in Iraq. Even more ironically, Iraq's demise has created opportunities for Iran, which these same governments see as a rising threat from which they seek US protection. Saddam's fall did not alter these countries' relations with the United States; instead, it merely shifted anxieties and underlined the very deep degree to which they have few alternatives to pursuing strong bilateral relations.

▨ Notes

1. President Bush's address to the American Enterprise Institute, February 26, 2003, http://www.whitehouse.gov/news/releases/2003/02/20030226-11.html.

2. Michael Scott Doran, "Palestine, Iraq, and American Strategy," *Foreign Affairs* 81, no. 1 (January/February 2002).

3. R. James Woolsey, address to UCLA conference of Americans for Victory over Terrorism, April 2, 2003, www.avot.org/article/20030402154900.html.

4. See Jon B. Alterman, "Not in My Backyard: Iraq's Neighbors' Interests," *Washington Quarterly* 26, no. 3 (summer 2003): 149–160.

5. Sandra Jontz, "Army Preparing to Close Camp Doha, Shift Operations to Other Kuwait Bases; Military Planners Relocating Troops Further from Civilian Population," *Stars and Stripes,* April 11, 2005, www.stripesonline.com/article.asp?section=104&article=27559&archive=true.

6. Joseph Rohe, "US Grants Kuwait 'Major Non-NATO Ally' Status," *Jane's Defence Weekly,* 7 April 2004.

7. Sanjay Suri, "Iraq: Few Enter the Door Kuwait Opens," *Global Information Network,* 12 February 2004.

8. Interview with a Kuwaiti journalist, Kuwait City, April 24, 2006.

9. Michael Knights, "Northern Gulf Vulnerable to Infiltration by Terrorist Groups," *Jane's Intelligence Review,* 1 October 2005.

10. See, for example, Oxford Analytica, "Qatar: Al-Thani Reformists Bolster Hold on Power," 24 April 2006.

11. "Gulf States at Odds on Iran," *Foreign Report*, 12 January 2006.

12. See the profile of Al-Udeid air base online at www.globalsecurity.org/military/facility/udeid.htm.

13. Lydia Georgi, "US Seeks to Formalize Military Links with the UAE," *Daily Star*, 13 January 2005.

14. Michael R. Gordon and Bernard E. Trainor, *Cobra II: The Inside Story of the Invasion and Occupation of Iraq* (New York: Pantheon, 2006), 164.

15. Jay Solomon, "Trouble Next Door," *Wall Street Journal*, 10 November 2005.

16. Jane Mayer, "Outsourcing Torture: The Secret History of America's 'Extraordinary Rendition' Program," *New Yorker*, 14 February 2006.

17. Alfred B. Prados, "Syria: US Relations and Bilateral Issues," CRS Issue Brief for Congress, Order Code IB92075 (March 13, 2006), 7–9.

18. Rhonda Roumani, "Iraqi Refugees Spur Housing Boom," *Christian Science Monitor*, 22 July 2005.

19. One might make the case that the Organization of the Islamic Conference, which includes the non-Arab neighbors of Iran and Turkey, would be a better legitimizing vehicle, although its non-Arab character would presumably dilute the mechanism's appeal to Iraqi Sunni Arabs while making it more palatable to Kurds. It would also more than double the number of participating countries.

20. Martin A. Weiss, "Iraq's Debt Relief: Procedure and Potential Implications for International Debt Relief," CRS Report for Congress, Order Code RL33376 (April 21, 2006), 4.

21. Stephen M. Walt, *The Origins of Alliances* (Ithaca and London: Cornell Univ. Press, 1987), 3.

15

Securing Iraq: The Mismatch of Demand and Supply

Nora Bensahel

WHEN THE UNITED STATES and its partners invaded Iraq in March 2003, they anticipated that an intense period of major combat operations would be followed by a relatively short postwar stabilization phase, and that they would be able to withdraw most of their forces by September.[1] Obviously, those withdrawals never occurred. The assumptions around which the plan was based proved faulty, and no contingency plans existed for alternate scenarios.[2] Law and order broke down almost immediately after the fall of Saddam. Widespread looting destroyed the country's infrastructure, including the facilities of the security forces, and the country's many arms caches were depleted of their stores. Supporters of the old regime joined forces with foreign fighters flowing across Iraq's porous borders, who were seeking a fight against the Western occupiers of Iraq. The ranks of the disaffected were soon swelled by those affected by the Coalition Provisional Authority's first two orders, which officially disbanded the country's security forces and prevented members of the Baath Party from holding positions in the new Iraqi government. Instead of being able to withdraw most of its forces by September 2003, the United States instead found itself battling a nascent insurgency.

Since that time, the number of international forces in Iraq has remained almost as high as it was during major combat operations. As Figure 15.1 shows, the number of international troops has ranged from 139,000 to 183,000 troops since the end of major combat operations. The vast majority of these troops are from the United States. Coalition contributions have varied over time, but have never constituted more than 17.3 percent of the forces on the ground, and in April 2006 accounted for just 13.2 percent of the total. As of April 2006, twenty-six countries participated in the coalition,[3] but most of their contingents were quite small and most operated under strict rules of engagement that prevented them from operating in anything but the most permissive security environments.[4] The United States has actively sought greater coalition participation, but few countries have been willing to send large force contingents into such an unstable security environment where they are likely to take casualties. Consequently, the United States largely dictates military operations in Iraq; US decisions about strategy, force levels, and missions determine the course of operations, for better or for worse.

This chapter seeks to understand the role that international security forces are likely to play in Iraq in the future. It starts by examining the missions that international forces are currently conducting. The next section discusses the demand for international forces across three of the most likely scenarios for Iraq's future and identifies what such forces would be required to do in each one. The chapter then turns to the likely supply of international forces—which countries will be willing to provide such forces and under what set of circumstances. It concludes by noting the mismatch between supply and demand and by observing that Iraq's future might be determined more by the willingness of the United States to continue supplying forces than by the demand for international forces that emerges from any of the scenarios.

Figure 15.1 Number of International Forces in Iraq, June 2003–April 2006

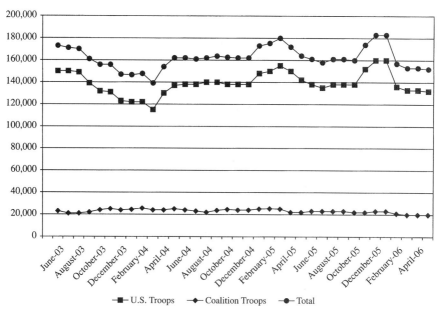

Source: Michael E. O'Hanlon and Nina Kamp, *Iraq Index* (Washington, DC: Brookings Institution, April 27, 2006), 20.

■ The Current Role of International Forces

The international forces that have been deployed in Iraq since 2003 conduct four broad categories of missions: offensive counterinsurgency operations, operational support, civic reconstruction, and security-force training. The lines between these categories are not neatly drawn, and individual units may be simultaneously involved in more than one category, but it provides a useful way to distinguish among their various missions.

Offensive Counterinsurgency Operations

US forces have been conducting offensive counterinsurgency operations ever since the insurgency first emerged, but their strategy has shifted and evolved over time. During 2003 and 2004, their strategy focused primarily on individual insurgents. Those who were identified while they were in the process of building, emplacing, or detonating explosives were often shot and killed; those suspected of direct involvement or active support of such activities were tracked down through raids, sweeps, and searches in order to bring them into custody. This strategy implicitly assumed a finite number of insurgents: the greater the number of insurgents caught and killed by the United States, the fewer would be left to engage in their nefarious activities. The April 2004 operations in Falluja serve as the best exemplar of this strategy: after four US contractors were killed and their bodies were gruesomely displayed to the world media, US forces used massive firepower to level sections of the city where the insurgents were suspected of operating. Once the city was cleared, however, US forces withdrew from the city, since their mission of destroying the insurgent base of operations had been achieved.

Over time, however, the limits of this strategy became clear. Between May 2003 and March 2006, the official estimates of the size of the insurgency ranged between fifteen thousand and twenty thousand personnel.[5] Figure 15.2, by contrast, shows the number of insurgents that were detained or killed each month during this same time period. Added together, this data shows that 63,470 insurgents were detained or killed—a number that is *three times* larger than the official estimates of the total size of the insurgency. Even after accounting for the inherent problems with such estimations, such a wide discrepancy suggests that the number of insurgents was not finite: as some were detained or killed, others emerged to take their place. Furthermore, Figure 15.3 shows that the number of insurgent attacks increased during this period of time and remained elevated despite the continuing detentions of so many insurgents. The evidence is therefore quite strong that the US strategy of detaining or killing individual insurgents was not successful and might well have been counterproductive.

In November 2005, the US National Security Council issued the *National Strategy for Victory in Iraq*, which identified a new approach for

**Figure 15.2 Total Number of Insurgents Detained or Killed,
May 2003–March 2006**

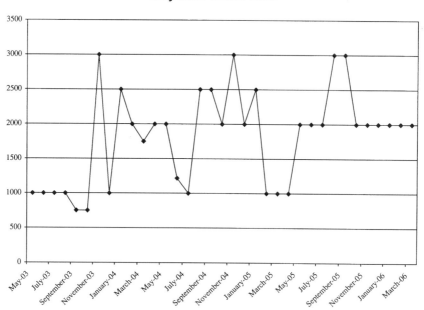

Source: Michael E. O'Hanlon and Nina Kamp, *Iraq Index* (Washington, DC: Brookings Institution, April 27, 2006), 17.

establishing security. Instead of focusing solely on individuals, the new strategy emphasized controlling territory through three steps. First, US, coalition, and Iraqi forces would *clear* areas controlled by the enemy, by capturing and killing individual fighters and denying them safe haven. Second, those forces would *hold* the areas that had been cleared rather than withdrawing, as they had done in Falluja in 2004, and would ensure that insurgents could not return and reestablish their activities. Third, they would *build* the Iraqi security forces and local institutions to the point where they would be capable of governing themselves effectively and, ideally, reduce public support for insurgents.[6] This clear-hold-build strategy was a radical departure from the previous approach, since it involved a long-term commitment to prevent insurgents from returning to areas where they had previously operated, rather than simply driving them out in the first place.

It is too early to tell whether this new strategy will be successful. Questions remain as to whether it has been fully implemented in Iraq to date. Operations such as in Tal Afar, for example, have been highly touted by the White House as an example of the new strategy in action.[7] Yet the

**Figure 15.3 Number of Daily Attacks by Insurgents,
June 2003–February 2006**

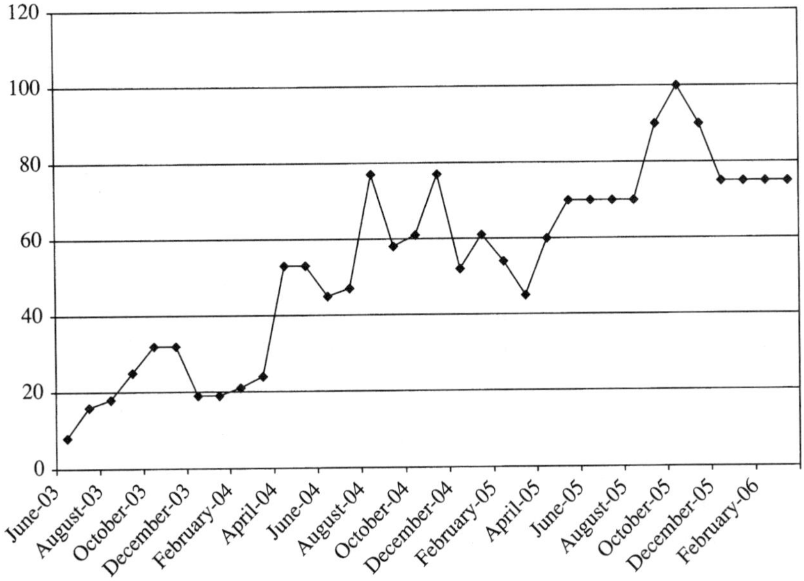

Source: Michael E. O'Hanlon and Nina Kamp, *Iraq Index* (Washington, DC: Brookings Institution, April 27, 2006), 22.

troops that conducted those operations in Tal Afar were rotated out of theater, and it remains unclear whether their replacements have been able to build upon their successes. Additionally, there have been few other examples of this strategy in action as of mid-2006. Nevertheless, the lessons of past counterinsurgency operations suggest that this strategy has a much greater chance of succeeding than one focused on individuals. By holding territory once it has been cleared, security forces can prevent insurgents from returning to their previous base of operations. By building and gaining the trust of the population, security forces can deprive insurgents of both the active and passive popular support that they require to conduct their activities. If properly implemented, this strategy seems more likely to reduce the insurgent activity than one focused primarily on individual insurgents.

Operational Support

The second type of activity that international forces have been conducting includes operational support to Iraqi forces. With the collapse of Saddam's regime and its security forces, Iraq found itself without some of the military capabilities necessary to defend its borders and to prosecute the counterinsurgency operations described above. Iraq essentially lacks an air force and cannot fly defensive missions around the country's borders or, more importantly, vital transport missions within the country. Its naval forces are generally limited to coastal operations, and the country completely lacks the technical intelligence systems that are an important part of counterinsurgency operations, border protection, and other military operations.

US forces have been providing operational support to the Iraqi military in these important areas since the fall of the regime and will likely continue to do so well into the future. All of these capabilities are expensive to build and maintain. During the occupation period, US decisionmakers determined that the highest military priority was building ground forces capable of ensuring security and conducting counterinsurgency operations, and the subsequent Iraqi government agreed with this prioritization. Since Iraqi capabilities in other areas are being built slowly, or in some cases, not at all, US forces have taken on many of these missions. Air support has proven particularly important. Air assets from the US Army and Air Force have provided operational support to Iraqi ground forces engaged in offensive counterinsurgency operations. They have also transported people, materiel, and supplies around the country, thereby providing a safer alternative to ground convoys that are vulnerable to attack by improvised explosive devices (IEDs). And they have provided valuable airborne command-and-control, reconnaissance, and surveillance capabilities that are prohibitively expensive (and, sometimes, prohibitively technical) for Iraq to procure or develop itself.

Civic Reconstruction

International forces have been involved in a wide variety of civic reconstruction activities in Iraq. In the immediate aftermath of major combat, US forces started taking on local reconstruction missions as a way to build goodwill and support among the local population. In May 2003, the US military established the Commanders' Emergency Response Fund (CERF), which provided money that division commanders could allocate at their discretion for local rebuilding and reconstruction efforts. These efforts were supposed to be temporary, since US planners expected that civilians working for the Coalition Provisional Authority (CPA) would arrive and take responsibility for what are essentially civilian missions. As it became clear that the CPA did not have the capacity to take the lead in civilian reconstruction, US forces took on more and more of these missions. The relatively ad hoc CERF program was formalized and renamed the Commanders' Emergency Response Program (CERP) and received an official appropriation as part of the November 2003 congressional supplemental.[8]

CERP funds enabled US military forces to conduct a wide range of civic reconstruction activities. Major General David Petraeus, then commander of the 101st Airborne Division, was one of the most proactive commanders in this area, establishing a wide range of civic services and reconstruction initiatives in the northern parts of Iraq.[9] Decentralization was the greatest strength of the CERP program, but also its greatest weakness: each commander could use the funds as he saw fit, but since some division commanders were not particularly eager to pursue civic reconstruction, missions varied considerably. Furthermore, policies adopted by one division were not necessarily adopted by others, which led to inconsistencies across the country. These inconsistencies posed real challenges for the CPA, and later for the Iraqi government, in their efforts to develop consistent national policies. Despite these challenges, the establishment of CERP is often cited as one of the greatest successes of the reconstruction effort, since it enabled local commanders to respond to local needs at their discretion and to avoid many layers of bureaucracy.

In November 2005, the United States announced a major new initiative to promote civic reconstruction by establishing Provincial Reconstruction Teams (PRTs) throughout the country. PRTs were first created in Afghanistan, to promote civic reconstruction outside of Kabul, and were widely seen as a success. US ambassador to Iraq Zalmay Khalilzad had previously served as ambassador to Afghanistan and had been impressed enough with the PRT model to recommend its adoption in Iraq. Each PRT in Iraq consists of approximately one hundred US civilian and military personnel and up to thirty local personnel, and its mission is to assist the provincial governments in developing governance and administrative capacity, promoting security, and fostering economic development. The first two PRTs were established in Nineveh and Babil provinces in November 2005, and more have followed since.[10]

As with the clear-hold-build strategy, it remains to be seen whether this initiative will fully live up to expectations. In particular, it is not clear whether the PRT model can be successful in regions that lack basic security. Proponents of the PRT initiative often cite the model's success in Afghanistan without noting that, until recently, the PRTs only operated in the relatively peaceful northern and western parts of the country. In December 2005, NATO agreed to expand the International Security Assistance Force (ISAF) in Afghanistan to cover the whole of the country and to establish additional PRTs in four southern provinces.[11] Yet NATO has had great difficulty recruiting force contributions for operations in these less secure areas, and these PRTs may not be able to achieve the same degree of success as they have in areas where the security situation is relatively stable. The PRTs in Afghanistan will serve as something of a bellwether for the PRTs in Iraq: if the PRTs in southern Afghanistan cannot thrive due to the security situation, then there is little hope that PRTs operating in the middle of a major insurgency in Iraq will achieve any lasting success.

Training Security Forces

International forces have been actively involved in training Iraqi security forces since shortly after the fall of Saddam's regime. The rapid military defeat in major combat operations, the extensive looting of government and military facilities, and the disbanding of the Iraqi army all combined to destroy the existing Iraqi security forces, which then had to be rebuilt from scratch. These efforts were fairly decentralized, uncoordinated, and not very successful during the first months of the occupation.[12] In the spring of 2004, Combined Joint Task Force 7 (CJTF-7), the military headquarters in theater, formally took responsibility for security-force training in Iraq. It established the Coalition Military Assistance Training Team (CMATT) and the Civilian Police Advisory Training Team (CPATT), which were responsible for training military and police forces, respectively.[13] After Iraq regained its sovereignty in June 2004, CMATT and CPATT both became part of the new Multinational Security Transition Command–Iraq (MNSTC-I), which reported to CJTF-7's successor, the Multinational Force–Iraq (MNF-I).[14]

These delays meant that training Iraqi security forces did not begin in earnest until more than a year after the fall of Baghdad. Progress since then has been slow, with some setbacks as well as advances, but generally moving in the right direction. The most frequently discussed statistic on this issue is the total number of trained forces. Figure 15.4 shows the number of trained Iraqi security-force personnel over time, reaching a total of 265,600 as of May 2006. These data, however, show only the *quantity* of trained forces and provide no information about their *quality*. For example, the downward spike in the number of trained police forces between June and July 2004 was caused by the increased training standards adopted by MNSTC-I.

A far better metric is the number of security force units that are capable of operating on their own, without any assistance or support from US and coalition forces. Here the numbers are less encouraging. In its May 2006 report to Congress, the Department of Defense reported that 71 out of 111 Iraqi army combat battalions (64 percent) were able to operate in the lead with coalition enablers or fully independently,[15] but the department did not provide the data necessary to distinguish between these two very different categories. Furthermore, the report also noted that in April 2006, only 25 percent of combat operations were conducted solely by Iraqi security forces—a lower number than in any of the previous four months.[16] The situation is even worse for the Iraqi police, where only six out of twenty-eight battalions (21 percent) had the security lead in their areas of responsibility.[17]

**Figure 15.4 Number of Trained Iraqi Security Forces,
July 2003–May 2006**

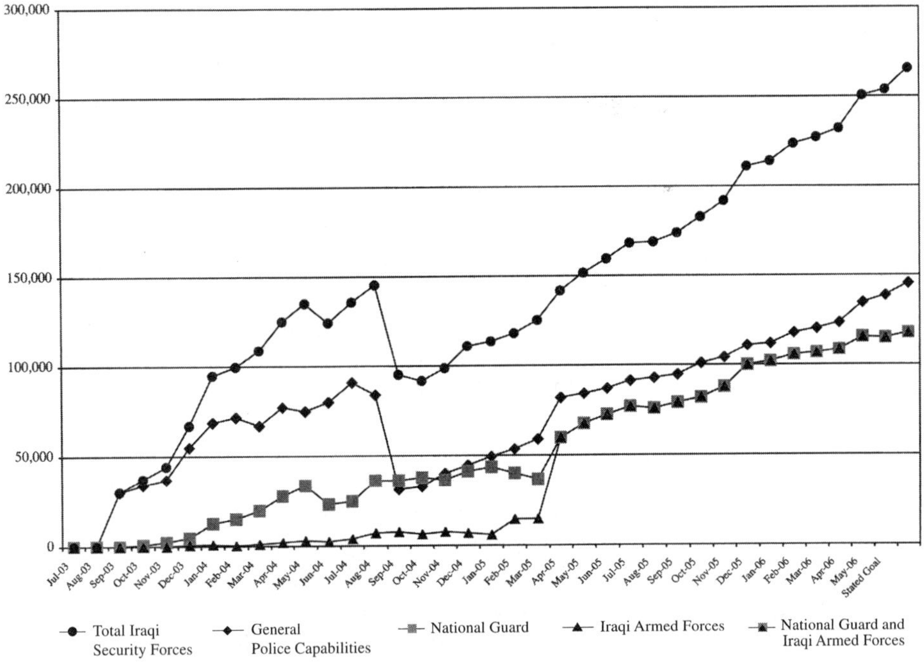

Source: Michael E. O'Hanlon and Nina Kamp, *Iraq Index* (Washington, DC: Brookings Institution, April 27, 2006), 25.

Note: The total number of Iraqi security forces also includes the border patrol, which is not represented in this chart.

These data suggest that international forces will be required to continue the training mission well into the future. Progress is being made, but even if current rates improve, it will still be a long time before Iraq can conduct most of its military and police operations without extensive international support. Furthermore, the US military is likely to continue to bear the bulk of the responsibility for this mission. MNSTC-I does include some international trainers, and NATO operates a small training mission,[18] but as with most of the other missions described above, these small international contributions mean that US forces will most likely retain primary responsibility for this mission.

■ The Demand for International Forces: Three Scenarios

The current situation in Iraq is so unsettled that it is difficult to make predictions about the future. The security situation remains unstable, with the insurgency continuing to rage despite US and Iraqi efforts to restore public order. Some political progress has been made, including the successful adoption of a constitution and national elections in 2005. But as continuing disagreements have plagued the new government, it remains to be seen whether it will be capable of adopting and implementing difficult governance decisions or whether it will remain a weak and limited institution. Perhaps most worrying, signs of increased sectarian tension have flared throughout 2006, most dramatically in the aftermath of the February bombing of the al-Askariya Mosque in Samarra.

The future role of international forces in Iraq obviously depends greatly on how these various trends play out. Since any specific prediction is likely to be incorrect, this chapter examines the three scenarios that seem most plausible as of mid-2006—muddling through an extension of current trends, partition, and civil war—and examines the different roles that international forces might be called upon to play in each one.

Scenario 1: Muddling Through

This scenario assumes that conditions in Iraq remain largely the same as they are today. In many ways, this is the best-case scenario that can be realistically hoped for, since Iraq is currently grappling with many deeply rooted problems that will not be easily resolved. The insurgency continues in this scenario, though the clear-hold-build strategy succeeds in establishing law and order in a handful of cities throughout the country. The Iraqi government proves itself to be capable of governing in some areas, and improves its ability to provide basic services for its residents, but cannot force sectarian militias to disband without risking a major backlash and a precipitous decline in popular support for the central government. Economic growth is uneven throughout the country, with rapid growth in the peaceful cities but flat or negative growth in the less secure areas of the country. The provision of essential services improves, but remains limited by continuing insurgent attacks on the country's infrastructure and constrained financial resources.

In this scenario, Iraqi security-force training would be the single most vital responsibility for international forces, since ultimately the viability of a democratic Iraqi state requires the central government to be able to provide basic law and order within its own territory. Until such a time as the Iraqi government develops those capabilities—a long-term project at best—international forces will be required to perform many of the same missions that they are conducting today, though their role would gradually wane as Iraqi forces and institutions gain the capability to take on increased responsibilities. International forces would still be required to conduct high-intensity counterinsurgency operations in the parts of the country that have not been secured, though over time the increasing numbers of trained Iraqi forces may be able to shoulder most of this burden. Operational support to the Iraqi forces and the Iraqi government would continue, particularly in areas such as air transport and airborne surveillance, where Iraqi capabilities will continue to be quite limited for the foreseeable future.[19] If any outside threat to Iraq develops, say through a buildup of conventional forces on Iraq's borders, international forces would likely be called upon to defend the country, since the Iraqi security forces are primarily focused on countering internal security threats. PRTs would help promote civic reconstruction in the cities that had been stabilized through the clear-hold-build strategy, but would be only marginally effective elsewhere in the country and might even be withdrawn from the most unstable provinces.

How many international troops would be required in this scenario? The total number would likely remain much the same as today, somewhere around 150,000 troops. In principle, that number could be reduced as Iraqi capabilities develop, but past experience suggests that the number of international troops does not decline in direct proportion to an increase in Iraqi capabilities. Iraqi capabilities have improved dramatically since the fall of 2004, for example, but as shown in Figure 15.1 above, the number of international forces in the country has remained unchanged or even increased since that time. It may be that Iraqi capabilities need to reach a certain threshold before international forces can be safely withdrawn and that the number of required international forces could drop precipitously at that point. The total number of international forces could be reduced before such a threshold is reached by redeploying and reconfiguring forces, or if the security situation improves around the margins. But even with the generous assumption that such developments could cut the number of required international forces in half from today's levels, that would still require approximately seventy-five thousand international troops to remain in Iraq for the foreseeable future.

Scenario 2: Partition

In this scenario, Iraq becomes partitioned into three separate entities.[20] A Kurdish entity would be established in the north, a Sunni entity would be created in the west, and a Shia entity would be created in the south. Baghdad might retain a special status, or it might be forcibly incorporated into the Shiite entity, which is likely to be the strongest of the three. Iraq might remain a single state in name in this scenario, but centralized powers would remain limited at best. It might have limited powers in coordinating foreign policy, border entries and exits, and perhaps some aspects of monetary policy (if Iraq retained a single currency), but it might also be a figurehead government that lacked even such limited powers. The Iraqi security forces would be disbanded, and each entity would build its militias into its own security forces. Each entity would retain control over its own natural resources. Any taxes paid to the central government would be nominal and would only support the government's administrative costs; the central government would have no capacity to redistribute wealth across the three entities.

In this scenario, international forces would most likely serve as peacekeepers along the borders of the three new entities. This scenario would probably involve large resettlements of populations; many people living in ethnically mixed areas would choose, either freely or through coercion and intimidation, to relocate to the entity dominated by their ethnic group. International forces might be called upon to provide safe passage to those in transit. They might also conduct peacekeeping operations along the borders between the new entities, much as NATO forces did in Bosnia after the Dayton Accords, to ensure that all of the entities comply with whatever agreements have been reached and that none try to gain territory or influence at the others' expense.

The role of international forces within each of the entities would vary across the entities, because each one would make its own decisions on what that role should be. The Sunni entity, for example, might want international forces to protect its borders and prevent incursions from the two stronger entities and possibly its external neighbors, while the Kurdish and Shiite entities might choose not to have any international forces within their boundaries. The role of international forces might also be determined by the terms of the partition, particularly if the United States participates in the negotiations. The United States might insist that any partition agreement include a large international presence monitoring the border between the Kurdish entity and Turkey, as a way to prevent Turkey from intervening to quell further Kurdish separatism. The United States might also press for international forces to monitor the border between the Shia entity and Iran, to ensure that the Shia entity remained a part of Iraq and did not simply become a de facto extension of Iran's borders.

Scenario 3: Civil War

If the trends toward increasing sectarianism continue, it is possible that the three main ethnic groups in Iraq—the Sunni, the Shia, and the Kurds—will take up arms against each other on a much wider scale than has been seen to date. Insurgent attacks would likely continue but would be targeted against sites that are particularly valuable to one of the ethnic communities, in the hopes that they would trigger ethnic reprisals. Militias associated with one of the three groups might also conduct attacks on such sites, hoping for the same outcome. One or two such attacks might not trigger widespread violence, but a continuing string of such attacks could easily trigger pressure for systematic retaliation against those responsible. Leaders of the major ethnic communities might be unable, or perhaps even unwilling, to forestall such retaliatory violence if popular passions become inflamed. Once unleashed, intercommunal violence would be extraordinarily difficult to stop. Any fragile bits of trust that have been built among the three groups would be shattered by such violence. As the violence spreads, it would quickly overwhelm the capabilities of the Iraqi security forces, and even those people who identify more as Iraqi nationals than as Sunni, Shia, or Kurd would be forced to seek protection from their respective ethnic groups. Left unchecked, such sectarian violence could engulf the country in a civil war.

International forces would make the greatest contribution in the early stages of such a scenario by trying to prevent the breakout of large-scale ethnic violence. Their most vital mission would be in the immediate aftermath of attacks on sites of symbolic value, first to maintain public order and then to conduct the forensic investigations needed to identify those responsible for the attacks. International forces would likely be seen as more honest brokers than Iraqi security forces in such a scenario, since they are more likely to be seen as impartial when ethnic tensions are running high. This would be particularly true for any attacks against the Sunni community, since the Iraqi security forces are composed largely of Shia and are suspected of being infiltrated by Shia militias pursuing their own agendas. International forces would have to take on many of the missions that are currently conducted by the Iraqi security forces: they would become responsible for neighborhood patrolling, cordon-and-search operations, and offensive raids against those determined to be responsible for such attacks. Operational support, civic reconstruction, and even security-force training would all become far lower priorities in such a scenario, as all available resources would be devoted to preventing ethnic violence from spreading.

Were a civil war to break out despite these efforts, international forces would most likely be withdrawn. It is hard to imagine that the United States, as the largest troop contributor, would take sides in a civil war and become embroiled in a massive internal conflict. US forces might retreat to Iraq's borders in an effort to maintain the territorial integrity of Iraq and to prevent sympathetic members from each ethnic group from entering the country and fueling the conflict, but even that indirect mission would be difficult to sustain as ethnic violence spread and intensified. Some of Iraq's neighbors might ask for external assistance in protecting their borders, but this would most likely consist of intelligence support and training of border police rather than a direct military presence. Partition might be the end result of any civil war, but by that time, international forces would most probably have been absent for a very long time. Any deployment of international forces to support a partitioned state would be an entirely separate military operation from the one currently under way, and the characteristics of such an intervention at that time would depend greatly on the specific chain of events in the civil war that led to partition.

■ The Supply of International Forces

For each of the three scenarios above, the discussion focused on the *demand* for international forces—the missions that international forces might be called upon to conduct. But what about the *supply* of international forces—the willingness of countries to deploy forces to conduct each of these missions? This is a much harder question to answer, since it is driven by political calculations rather than by military requirements. More specifically, the answer will be driven primarily by the political calculations of the United States. Since US forces make up the vast majority of forces on the ground, other countries will follow its lead; they may choose to withdraw their forces before the United States withdraws, but it is unlikely that they would choose to keep their forces in Iraq *after* a US troop withdrawal. Furthermore, it is hard to imagine that countries that have not yet contributed troops to operations in Iraq will suddenly choose to do so in the future, especially given widespread domestic opposition to the war throughout the world. Since the prospects for a broad internationalization of the troop presence in Iraq are weak at best, the United States will largely determine the supply of international forces for Iraq.

It is extremely difficult to make long-term predictions about the willingness of the United States to keep its forces in Iraq. The Bush administration has consistently reaffirmed its commitment to keep US forces in Iraq, despite increasing public support for withdrawal. The administration is clearly looking to reduce the numbers of troops in Iraq and has announced plans for future force withdrawals on several occasions, only to retreat from those plans when conditions on the ground made them unworkable. Yet the US presence in Iraq has become an increasingly important domestic issue, particularly in the aftermath of the 2006 congressional midterm election. The new Democratic majorities in both houses of Congress have been joined by many Republicans in calling for a new strategy in Iraq and timetables for troop withdrawals, and have vocally opposed President Bush's plans for a troop surge into Baghdad. The US role in Iraq seems likely to remain a major domestic issue in the United States as the 2008 presidential election approaches.

The willingness of the United States to supply forces for Iraq will also be affected by which of the scenarios described above comes to pass and the ways in which it unfolds. The United States is most likely to remain engaged in scenario 1. An extension of current trends would mean slow progress toward capable and effective Iraqi self-government, which is central to the Bush administration's vision of the future Middle East and which US public opinion may be willing to continue to support. It is much harder to imagine a sustained US military presence in either scenario 2 or 3. The partitioning of Iraq would be a political defeat for the Bush administration, and it would become increasingly difficult to rally public support for forces that would essentially be separating ethnic enclaves from each other. And it is hard to imagine that the United States would maintain any significant troop deployments in the event of a full civil war. The current level of sectarian violence has already prompted serious debates in the United States about whether US forces should remain in a country whose people are attacking each other; the outbreak of large-scale, organized, and sustained civil violence would likely cause a major, if not a complete, US withdrawal from Iraq.

■ Conclusion: The Mismatch Between Demand and Supply

Over the next year or two, the supply of international forces may prove to be the single greatest factor determining the future trajectory of Iraq. Demand for international forces is likely to remain high, regardless of which scenario emerges, since none of them includes a government that will be able to provide basic security and law and order any time soon. However, the supply of international forces—which for all intents and purposes means US forces—will remain constrained, at best, and is likely to decrease over time.

None of these trends bode well for the future of Iraq. One thing is clear, however: any major withdrawal of US forces in the foreseeable future would be disastrous and would precipitate an escalation of violence that would make scenarios 2 and 3 more likely. US and coalition forces are providing vital support for the Iraqi government in many ways: by training the country's security forces; by conducting offensive raids against suspected insurgents; by providing intelligence, transport, external defense, and other forms of operational support; and by assisting with civil reconstruction efforts that are improving the lives of the Iraqi people one project at a time. Withdrawing the troops below the minimum number necessary to fulfill these missions, whatever that number ends up being, would put the future of Iraq's national government at great risk and would increase the centrifugal forces that threaten to tear the country apart.

■ Notes

1. US plans assumed that the troops in place at the end of combat—which could be as high as 265,000 troops, depending on how long combat operations last-

ed—could be rapidly withdrawn, since the postwar security environment would be relatively benign and Iraqi security forces would be capable of addressing any postwar security challenges that did arise. The United States planned to withdraw most of its forces during the summer, planning to have only 30,000 remaining in Iraq by September 2003. See the discussion of the Hybrid Plan in Bob Woodward, *Plan of Attack* (New York: Simon & Schuster, 2004), especially p. 148; and Michael R. Gordon and Bernard E. Trainor, *Cobra II: The Inside Story of the Invasion and Occupation of Iraq* (New York: Pantheon Books, 2006), 459.

2. For more on prewar planning assumptions about postwar Iraq, see Nora Bensahel, "Mission Not Accomplished: What Went Wrong with Iraqi Reconstruction," *Journal of Strategic Studies* 29, no. 3 (2006).

3. As of April 2006, the twenty-six troop-contributing countries were: Albania, Armenia, Australia, Azerbaijan, Bosnia-Herzegovina, Czech Republic, Denmark, El Salvador, Estonia, Georgia, Italy, Japan, Kazakhstan, Latvia, Lithuania, Macedonia, Moldova, Mongolia, the Netherlands, Poland, Portugal, Romania, Slovakia, South Korea, Ukraine, and the United Kingdom. Nine of these countries were providing more than 500 troops; the other seventeen countries were providing a combined total of 1,140 troops. See Michael O'Hanlon and Nina Kamp, *Iraq Index* (Washington, DC: Brookings Institution, April 27, 2006): 21, www.brookings.edu/iraqindex (accessed June 2006).

4. The United Kingdom is one notable exception to this generalization; British forces have consistently conducted high-intensity counterinsurgency operations in the southern parts of Iraq as well as in and around Baghdad.

5. O'Hanlon and Kamp, *Iraq Index*, 18.

6. See National Security Council, "National Strategy for Victory in Iraq," www.whitehouse.gov/infocus/iraq/iraq_strategy_nov2005.html#part1 (accessed April 2006), 8 and 18–22.

7. See White House Office of the Press Secretary, "Fact Sheet: Strategy for Victory: Clear, Hold, and Build," March 20, 2006, www.whitehouse.gov/news/releases/2006/03/20060320-6.html (accessed April 2006).

8. CERP funds were limited to programs that addressed civic cleanup, education, electricity, food production and distribution, health care, irrigation, rule of law and governance, telecommunications, and water and sanitation. See Special Inspector-General for Iraqi Reconstruction, "Memorandum for Deputy Secretary of Defense: Management of Commanders' Emergency Response Program for Fiscal Year 2004," Report No. SIGIR 05-014, October 12, 2005, www.sigir.mil/reports/pdf/audits/SIGIR_Audit_05-014-Memo-CERP-2005-Letter.pdf#search='CERP%20funds%20Iraq (accessed April 2006).

9. See Michael R. Gordon, "101st Airborne Scores Success in Reconstruction of Northern Iraq," *New York Times*, 4 September 2003.

10. United States Embassy in Iraq, "Fact Sheet on Provincial Reconstruction Teams (PRTs)," February 23, 2006, baghdad.usembassy.gov/iraq/20060223_prt_fact_sheet.html (accessed April 2006).

11. These new PRTs are to be established in the Helmand, Kandahar, Uruzgan, and Zabul provinces. See North Atlantic Treaty Organization (NATO), "Revised Operational Plan for NATO's Expanding Mission in Afghanistan," www.nato.int/issues/afghanistan_stage3/index.html (accessed April 2006).

12. The Coalition Provisional Authority (CPA) was responsible for overseeing the rebuilding of the security forces, but its efforts were limited by a general lack of capacity and the fact that different individuals were responsible for the army and police training programs. The CPA also did not coordinate well with the military

forces in theater, which took on the police training mission and other military training missions by default. See Andrew Rathmell, Olga Oliker, Terrence K. Kelly, David Brannan, and Keith Crane, *Developing Iraq's Security Sector* (Santa Monica, CA: RAND, MG-365-OSD, 2005), 15–19.

13. Ibid., Chapter 3.

14. More information on MNSTC-I is available at www.mnstci.iraq.centcom.mil (accessed June 2006).

15. United States Department of Defense, "Measuring Stability and Security in Iraq," May 2006 Report to Congress, 47, www.defenselink.mil/home/features/Iraq_Reports/Index.html (accessed June 2006).

16. Ibid., 48.

17. Ibid., 57.

18. The NATO Training Mission–Iraq (NTM-I) was initially established in June 2004. It trained approximately one thousand Iraqi officers in Iraq and an additional five hundred officers in Europe during 2005 and expects to train the same number of personnel during 2006. See "NATO's Assistance to Iraq," available at www.nato.int/issues/iraq-assistance/in_practice.html (accessed June 2006).

19. In June 2006, US Air Force Chief of Staff General Michael Moseley noted that the Iraqi air force was still in the early stages of developing support capacities and had not yet started developing an attack capability. As for the continuing role of the US Air Force in Iraq, he stated, "I see nothing that tells us less intra-theater lift, or less intelligence, surveillance and reconnaissance or less strike support or less ability to do time-critical targets will manifest itself." Tony Capaccio, "Iraq to Need U.S. Air Force for 'a While,' Chief of Staff Says," Bloomberg.com, 13 June 2006.

20. In this scenario, partition occurs as a result of some deliberate decision by the Iraqi national government or by provincial leaders. Partition as the outcome of a lengthy civil war is discussed in the next section.

16

The Protection of Civilians

Pierre Gassmann

WHILE THE OCCUPATION of Iraq formally ended on June 28, 2004, armed conflict continues unabated, with opposing insurgents and extremist groups using indiscriminate, terrorist tactics against the Iraqi government and the Multinational Force–Iraq (MNF-I). Moreover, Iraq is on the brink of civil war pitting its ethnic and religious communities against each other. This chapter (1) highlights efforts by the international community to protect civilians in Iraq, (2) examines compliance by the warring parties with the laws of war, and (3) argues that this could best be achieved by basing the mandate of international security forces in Iraq on the principle of the "responsibility to protect."

■ Key Aspects of Protection of Civilians in War

Protection of civilians in war is defined as encompassing "all activities aimed at ensuring full respect for the rights of the individual in accordance with the letter and the spirit of the relevant bodies of law, i.e., human rights law, international humanitarian law, and refugee law."[1]

Interpreted restrictively, the protection concept covers the immediate need for civilians and for persons not directly participating in ongoing hostilities to be protected against the effects of warfare and other armed violence. More broadly, it includes the need for a safe and secure environment and the satisfaction of their basic physiological needs. Human rights advocates propose a broader meaning of protection, embracing, even in situations of armed conflict, all activities aimed at the achievement of all human rights. Some understand it as including the achievement of "human security, the protection of the vital core of all human lives," including political liberties and longer-term human fulfillment.[2]

Active protection demarches and activities of the international community include all types of pressure exercised on established civilian and military authorities and on armed nonstate actors to apply relevant national and international law: silent "humanitarian diplomacy" and attempts at persuasion to abide by the minimum standards of the law, monitoring compliance and forceful denunciation of violations, public appeals by human rights activists and humanitarian agencies, resolutions by the UN Security Council, the General Assembly, the Human Rights Commission (now the Human Rights Council), and other multilateral bodies. Protection activities can also mean direct assistance of international agencies to civilians, substituting for governments unable or unwilling to respond to the most urgent needs of their civilian population.

■ International Interventions to Protect Iraqi Civilians

Throughout Iraqi history, perhaps with the exception of Operation Provide Comfort for the benefit of an estimated two million Kurds fleeing from the ruthless repression of the Kurdish uprising by Saddam Hussein's army after the 1991 Gulf War, the protection of civilians in Iraq has not been a priority on the agenda of the international community. Whether under Ottoman or British domination, or whenever Iraqis had a chance to govern themselves, civilians fell prey to "the deployment of extreme levels of organized violence by the state to dominate and shape society."[3] The repressive violence of the Saddam regime did not, until the invasion of Kuwait, appear of major concern to any of the governments supporting Saddam Hussein's war on Iran. Neither did the gassing of thousands of Kurdish civilians in Halabja in 1988 or the extremely violent repression of the popular uprising in southern Iraq in 1991 spur the UN into action under Chapter VII of the UN Charter. The UN Security Council repeatedly took pains to express its concern about the humanitarian consequences of sanctions against Iraq.[4] However, it was ordinary Iraqis who suffered the most, while the regime, in complicity with UN officials as is now on the record, continued to live in revolting opulence.

Barely a day after the bombing of UN headquarters in Baghdad, Al-Qaida's Abu Hafs Brigade issued a detailed communiqué analyzing why it considered the UN and its representatives as enemies of the Iraqi people, and why it considered the UN a legitimate target of attack:

> Don't you recall that on July 9, 2002, the United States, Britain, and the United Nations suspended Iraq's request for cancer medicines and medicines for cases resulting from the body rejecting kidney transplants? Don't you remember who caused the deaths of more than one million Iraqis in an embargo that lasted 12 years?[5]

Many Iraqis share this critical appraisal of the UN's role. Most of them, perhaps with the exception of the Kurds, do not recognize the UN agencies' important contribution to the well-being of Iraqis and to the current political and constitutional processes. They see the UN as a political tool in the hands of the United States, an embodiment of the international community's neglect of their plight during the years of sanctions, and a source of continued vexation of Iraqi national pride through *special rapporteurs*, weapons inspectors, border observation missions, and damning resolutions of the Security Council. They perceive the UN as epitomizing the double standards applied by the international community. Iraqis are irate about what they see as the injustice and the severity of the UN's positions on Iraq as compared with the lenient attitude of the world body toward Israel's violent occupation of Palestine.

That the Security Council did not approve of the invasion of their country does not affect this view, especially as the UN later condoned, at the "request of the incoming Interim Government,"[6] the continued presence of the occupying forces in Iraq, albeit under a new denomination as Multinational Force–Iraq.

Ordinary Iraqis thus remain extraordinarily wary of the motives of the international community, including those expressed by the United Nations. In particular, few Iraqis will believe the argument that the United States and its coalition of the willing attacked and occupied their country because they were primarily concerned with the human rights situation and the fate of Iraqis under a repressive political regime.[7]

Rather than change the deep-rooted mistrust of Iraqis, the four years of occupation and nation building by coalition forces have reinforced their suspicion toward help from the international community. In the immediate aftermath of the occupation in the spring of 2003, many rejoiced at Saddam Hussein's demise, many harbored delusions of new freedoms and wealth, and many hopefully received the myriad of foreign contractors, NGOs, and UN staffers streaming into Iraq on the coattails of the coalition.

For some Iraqis, expectations have indeed been partly fulfilled, at least. In Iraqi Kurdistan within its current geographical boundaries, under an ever more autonomous administration, the economy is booming, and security is not a major issue. In the Shia south, material conditions are consistently improving, thanks, according to some observers, to a massive influx of Iranian funds into the strong Shia social networks and into public service projects.[8] The security situation may be more tense there than in Iraqi Kurdistan, and secularists may gripe about growing pressure from Shia zealots, but except for the small Sunni minority, there are no major, persistent, or immediate protection problems.

In Baghdad, however, in the Sunni heartland, and in many urban settings with substantial ethnic or sectarian minorities, the past four years have left most Iraqis thoroughly dispirited. Their expectations of a positive contribution by the international community to protect them from the ongoing violence and to improve their lives have been dashed.

Iraqis here see that the UN is essentially confined to Baghdad's Green Zone, while they suffer growing insecurity and lawlessness. They cannot but notice the apparent inability of the MNF-I to effectively counter the extremists among the insurgency and they are bewildered about the shifting policies of the MNF-I and the Iraqi government with regard to sectarian militias and their targeted violence. They still wait for the promised jobs and economic takeoff while the previous social safety net of the Baathist state is about to be dismantled. They observe the political wrangling at the central government level; they learn that funds for the reconstruction of Iraq have been spent, with little prospects of more to be forthcoming; they know about the graft and corruption that surrounds many reconstruction projects; and most importantly, they resent the new and severe constraints put on their social life, such as curfews and receding secular liberties.

Iraqis remember proudly how they had managed on their own the rehabilitation of their infrastructure, despite international sanctions, after the destruction wrought on the country by Operation Desert Storm and its aftermath, and they view the current reconstruction effort with disdain.[9]

Especially after the UN headquarters bombing of August 2003 in Baghdad, the coalition forces had high hopes that if not the UN then at least humanitarian NGOs and human rights groups would be well received by the Iraqi people. Before the war, many international NGOs and UN agencies had worked extensively in Iraqi Kurdistan; a few NGOs, mostly operating from Kuwait, and the International Committee of the Red Cross (ICRC) were even present in southern Iraq. Many important human rights groups and humanitarian agencies had lobbied intensely for rights during the Saddam years and had denounced the shameful passivity of the international community after the Halabja gas attack and its slow reaction to the repression of the Shia uprising in the south. During the buildup to the war, many agencies had publicly spoken out against the invasion. Most humanitarian operators anticipated the worst: tens of thousands of civilian casualties, millions of displaced people, and extensive shortages of food, medicines, and water. When the war came, they were ready and arrived in the immediate aftermath of the end of active hostilities.

Ordinary Iraqis welcome manifestations of Islamic charity from neighboring countries to their religious communities, even if the donations may conceal ulterior political or sectarian motives. They are at pains to believe that NGOs from industrialized countries have no hidden motives, that they are truly autonomous from their financing constituencies, that they are neither missionaries nor stooges of the occupying forces, or, as Secretary of State Colin Powell put it, "a force multiplier for us, such an important part of our combat team."[10]

In the aftermath of the bombing of the ICRC headquarters in Baghdad, on October 28, 2003, this author attempted to convince religious leaders of the ICRC's purely humanitarian motives and to seek their support in influencing their followers' perception. The answer, across the spectrum from Grand Ayatollah Ali al-Sistani to Harith al-Dhari of the Association of Muslim Scholars (AMS) was that they themselves understood and respected the neutrality, independence, and impartiality of the ICRC and that they would discreetly pass on the word. But, they said, it was not possible to guarantee the security of foreigners on Muslim soil under foreign military occupation.[11]

Notwithstanding the problem of their identification with the multinational forces, a dwindling number of international agencies continue to operate in Iraq but, for security reasons, most non-Islamic international organizations, the UN and NGOs alike, have moved their operational headquarters to Amman or Kuwait. Their expatriate presence outside of Iraqi Kurdistan and the Shia-controlled areas is practically nonexistent. Those that remain are, like private contractors, obliged to hire private security companies for their protection or to put themselves directly under the umbrella of the MNF-I. They have curtailed their activities and operate in "remote control," with only scant monitoring of the projects they are funding and managing, and they leave their Iraqi staff exposed to the growing insecurity. Most agencies would have to admit that they are far from realizing to the fullest their lofty mandates to provide protection and assistance to the Iraqi civilians.

The ICRC, the lead agency in matters of protection of civilians in war, had faithfully struggled during the Iraq-Iran War to fulfill its specific protection mandate on behalf of over one hundred thousand Iraqi prisoners of war in Iran. It had doggedly wrestled some important concessions from the Saddam regime in order to assist suffering Iraqis during the sanctions years. Its teams had hung on in Baghdad and other parts of Iraq during Operations Desert Storm and Iraqi Freedom. Yet after a massive deployment in May 2003, it quickly had to reduce its expatriate staff and suffered the same fate as the UN. The ICRC has not been able to comply with its specific mandate on behalf of the Iraqis languishing in Abu Ghraib and other places of detention. Due to security concerns for its staff, its visits to prisoners of the MNF-I are restricted to the detention facilities at Baghdad International Airport, in Iraqi Kurdistan, and in Bucca camp near Basra. It has never gained access to detention facilities run by the Iraqi Ministry of the Interior, nor has it visited the "holding areas" of the MNF-I throughout the country.[12]

In view of the faltering presence and performance of international agencies outside of Iraqi Kurdistan and the south, expectations among Iraqis in terms of active protection and assistance activities by international organizations are at a low point. These organizations are not willing to share the security challenges faced by the Iraqis left behind, because, as a matter of principle, most of them are unwilling to adopt the indispensable robust security measures that would allow them to stay. There is very little that they can effectively do to protect Iraqi civilians from their safe abodes in Kuwait and Amman, except attempt from afar to influence the conduct of hostilities of the warring parties by way of public opinion pressure.

■ The Conduct of Hostilities in Iraq and Protection of Civilians

The above section has dealt with the difficulties experienced by civilian international agencies in providing a measure of protection to Iraqi civilians. The public debate and the ongoing investigations into the death of Iraqi civilians following an attack by US Marines in November 2005 against the insurgent stronghold of Haditha[13] again brought to the fore the reality that the protection of civilians in war is very closely related to the conduct of hostilities by warring parties and to their compliance with two imperative tenets of the laws of war: the principle of distinction and the principle of proportionality.

International humanitarian law (IHL) explicitly spells out the principle of distinction between the civilian population and combatants and between civilian objects and military objectives. IHL also requires the protection of civilian livelihoods and respect for essential civil rights and humane treatment. In defining civilians, the law also seeks to remove as much ambiguity as possible by requiring that in case of doubt as to whether a person is a civilian, that person shall be considered a civilian, and that the presence within the civilian population of individuals who do not come within the definition of civilians does not deprive the population of its civilian character.[14]

The proportionality rule is codified in Protocol I to the 1949 Geneva Conventions. States have a legal obligation under Article 51 (5) (b) to refrain from attacks "which may be expected to cause incidental loss of civilian life, injury to civilians, damage to civilian objects, or a combination thereof, which would be excessive in relation to the concrete and direct military advantage anticipated."[15]

The principles of proportionality and distinction are the bedrock of universally applicable laws of war. They are considered as imperative norms even though they are subject to interpretation as a function of "military necessity."

■ Conduct of Warfare by the Insurgency and Sectarian Groups

The predominantly Sunni Iraqi insurgent groups conduct their war by attacking mainly the MNF-I and the Iraqi armed forces, including the Iraqi police forces. They also execute targeted attacks against civilian individuals or groups that they believe to be central to the continued occupation of their land. They foment sectarian violence and chaos to undermine efforts at political stabilization. They wage a war that "has more to do with the struggles of primitive tribes than with large-style conventional warfare"; "a war of listening devices and of car-bombs, of men killing each other at close quarters, and of women using their purses to carry explosives and the drugs to pay for them."[16]

Inasmuch as the insurgents consider the principle of distinction at all, they interpret the notion of active participation in hostilities in the broadest sense. Indeed, they deem that anyone abetting the occupation by working with, or exercising political rights within the framework of, the institutions created by the occupiers is a legitimate target. That view is compounded by justifications related to religious motives that demand a war effort against infidels and their apostate allies. In fact, "the willful ignorance of the principle of distinction is one of the primary operational strategies of the insurgents."[17]

In their fight against the overwhelming military might of the coalition forces, the insurgent groups measure proportionality not on the tactical level of each separate attack but rather with regard to the contribution that highly publicized acts of terror are making to weaken the resolve of the MNF-I and its Iraqi allies to pursue their political objectives.[18] The most extremist elements of the insurgency claim that Islam condones any means to achieve victory over the enemy, including suicide bombers and, as a corollary, the death of innocent Muslims.[19]

Some observers, such as the International Crisis Group, judge that a change of these radical attitudes is in the offing:

> The [insurgent] groups appear acutely aware of public opinion and increasingly mindful of their image. Fearful of a backlash, they systematically and promptly respond to accusations of moral corruption or blind violence, reject accusations of a sectarian campaign, and publicize efforts to protect civilians or compensate their losses. Some gruesome and locally controversial practices—beheading hostages, attacking people going to the polls—have been abandoned.[20]

However, unpredictable and devastating suicide bombings and the use of improvised explosive devices and mortars against military personnel and assets in densely populated areas continue to claim a heavy toll among a hapless civilian population.

The problem of targeted attacks of civilians by sectarian militias now appears to loom even larger than the civilian casualties from indiscriminate attacks by insurgent groups.[21] The International Crisis Group writes that "2005 will be remembered as the year Iraq's latent sectarianism took wings, permeating the political discourse and precipitating incidents of appalling violence and sectarian 'cleansing.'"[22] Rather than abating after the December 2005 elections, things took a turn for the worse. As sectarian attacks accumulate, Iraqis' perceptions are increasingly shaped along sectarian lines, with Sunnis and Shia seen not only as victims but also as the intended targets.

Article 9 (b) of the new Iraqi constitution of October 2005, much as article 27 (b) of the Transitional Administrative Law (TAL) of March 2004, explicitly forbids the formation of military militias outside of the armed forces.[23] The militias, however, appear stronger than ever. The Kurdish Regional Government commands the *peshmerga*, closer to an army than to a militia and said to number over one hundred thousand;[24] the Badr Organization, affiliated with the Supreme Council for the Islamic Revolution in Iraq (SCIRI), is reported to have over ten thousand members. The Mahdi Army of Muqtada al-Sadr is said to include between three thousand and ten thousand men.[25] Numerous other militia groups numbering in the thousands of militants, related to tribal and religious communities, are established at a local or regional level. Some of them directly participate in MNF-I–led operations.[26]

Today, the *peshmerga* and the sectarian and local militias even appear to outnumber the armed forces fielded by the central government. It is difficult to make precise estimates, as it remains unclear whether the official figures given for newly established and operational Iraqi army units in fact do include incorporated militias. Militia members (in particular from the Badr Organization) have partly been recruited into the Iraqi security forces. Their increasing presence there robs the government forces of the necessary credibility as an impartial instrument to ensure security for all Iraqis, regardless of their ethnic or religious origin. Their members' loyalty to the central government is questionable, and the MNF-I's control over their activities is doubtful.

The militias are manifestly condoned, if not sponsored, by some government ministries, and their exactions remain largely unchecked by the MNF-I. As a corollary to the continued weakness of the central government and the sectarian complicity of some ministries, regional as well as local administrations, and based on the impact of their violent targeted actions against ethnic and religious adversaries, insurgent groups and the militias—mainly the Badr Organization and the Mahdi Army as well as the *peshmerga*—have now become a major factor in providing security and protection for the civilian population among their constituents, along tribal, ethnic, and sectarian lines. As Robert Kaplan puts it: "[H]istory has taught the Iraqis to think of power not in any formal or legalistic sense but crudely, in terms of who actually wields the authority to help and the power to punish severely."[27]

■ Conduct of Counterinsurgency Warfare
by the MNF-I and the Iraqi Security Forces

The MNF-I and the Iraqi security forces are experiencing difficulties in complying with the principles of distinction and proportionality and their own rules of engagement (ROEs). A July 2005 version of the ROEs for the military police forces states that "if US or coalition forces *or innocent civilians* are being attacked or reasonably perceived to be in danger you are authorized to respond with deadly force without first employing less forms of force"; and "any persons demonstrating hostile intent or committing a hostile act may be engaged using necessary and proportional force, up to and including deadly force."[28]

International human rights groups and the insurgency regularly accuse MNF-I and the Iraqi security forces of responding to the insurgency in kind, "waging dirty war in coordination with sectarian militias, engaging in torture, and being impervious to civilian losses."[29] There are also numerous and documented complaints about force protection taking precedence over due care for civilians and about an excessive escalation of force at the slightest perception of threat against MNF-I forces and assets.[30]

The most common response to these accusations is that military units compelled to maintain law and order and simultaneously fight a strong insurgency, especially in an urban environment, face extremely ambiguous situations, and that anyone fighting among a highly resistant civilian population, or against a military force that is woven into the very texture of that population, faces such difficulties. In such contexts, soldiers operate in fear of being shot from the window of a house, or attacked by militia members or youth in civilian clothes. Hugo Slim asserts that "the risks and nerves involved in such encounters make the civilian idea, which might be cherished in theory, hard to hold on to and apply in practice."[31]

The way that Iraqis are described by the political taskmasters of the MNF-I does not make the principle of distinction by the military any easier to uphold, particularly for troops deployed in the Sunni heartland of the insurgency. It is the Sunni Arab population in particular that has for some time been identified by the MNF-I with the armed resistance against the occupation, while the insurgency itself is largely equated with its most extremist elements allied with Al-Qaida. As President Bush put it: "The rejectionists are by far the largest group. These are ordinary Iraqis, mostly Sunni Arabs."[32] In the Iraqi battle space, it is exceedingly difficult for any MNF-I soldier to differentiate between "rejectionists, Saddamists, and terrorists."[33]

The MNF-I's leaders, military thinkers, and planners realize that for the purposes of force protection alone, the application of due care in their interventions involving civilians is key to enabling the military to hold any area and to preparing the ground for the establishment of stable and loyal institutions. The MNF-I has detailed and complex procedures for the investigation of any incident involving civilian casualties.

Whatever the complexity of the situation on the ground, and however strong the temptation to abandon the idea of the possibility of distinction altogether and to "totalize the enemy once again and reduce everyone to a single and equal inimical identity,"[34] the MNF-I and Iraqi security forces are bound by provisions of international law, in particular human rights law and international humanitarian law, as confirmed by UN Security Council Resolutions 1546 and 1637, which circumscribe the framework for intervention.[35]

Concepts of the military role in protection are new and evolving. However, it is possible to identify a distinct move away from conceiving of protection only in terms of restraint in the use of force during war (according to the laws of war) and toward a more active concept, which sees civilian protection as a principal aim of intervention. This is in keeping with shifts in military-led protection operations, from protecting convoys and humanitarian actors to protecting people under imminent threat.[36] Evolving military doctrine, in particular related to peace enforcement operations under Chapter VII of the UN Charter, also tends to show greater concern for the protection of civilians.[37]

■ The Use of Force to Protect Civilians

The concept of protection of civilians in war also includes the enforcement of international human rights law through sanctions and international military intervention. To protect civilians from crimes against humanity and systematic and severe abuses of human rights has been an argument for the use of force well before now, but specifically ever since those crimes and rights have been codified. More recently, the protection argument has justified international interventions approved by the United Nations in northern Iraq in 1991 (Operation Provide Comfort), Somalia (Operation Restore Hope), and Sudan.[38] Protection of civilians in war has received a wider meaning in particular by the work of the International Commission on Intervention and State Sovereignty (ICISS), sponsored by Canada and cochaired by Gareth Evans and Mohamed Sahnoun. Their 2001 report establishes an international "responsibility to protect" (R2P) and defines the conditions under which states have the duty to use force in reaction to situations in which there is compelling need for human protection.[39] Security Council Resolution 1674 of April 28, 2006, is a direct outgrowth of the efforts of the ICISS.

The commitments of the 2005 World Summit as approved by the UN General Assembly read:

We are prepared to take collective action, in a timely and decisive manner, through the Security Council, in accordance with the Charter, including Chapter VII, on a case-by-case basis and in cooperation with relevant regional organizations as appropriate, should peaceful means be inadequate and national authorities are manifestly failing to protect their populations from genocide, war crimes, ethnic cleansing, and crimes against humanity. . . . We also intend to commit ourselves, as necessary and appropriate, to helping States build capacity to protect their populations from genocide, war crimes, ethnic cleansing, and crimes against humanity and to assisting those which are under stress before crises and conflicts break out.[40]

■ The MNF-I and the "Responsibility to Protect"

Security Council Resolutions 1546 and 1637 *ipso jure* declared and confirmed the end of occupation and the reestablishment of the sovereignty of the Iraqi state. It is now the Iraqi state that bears the primary responsibility for the guarantee of the constitutional rights of its citizens. However, the continued presence of over 150,000 foreign troops in the country, daily reports of violent confrontations with insurgents, as well as official reports,[41] confirm that without this international presence, the central government would not be able to carry out that task. Furthermore, there exists a large consensus today affirming that the Iraqi judiciary and Iraqi law-enforcement agencies are incapable of fully assuming that responsibility.[42]

As noted in a 2005 RAND report entitled *Establishing Law and Order After Conflict:* "In particular, the Iraqi Police Service (IPS), which must form the cornerstone of a secure, stable, and democratic society, remains unable to enforce the rule of law in most of the country. Until the IPS becomes capable of enforcing order, troops from the Multinational Force–Iraq, including the Iraqi military, will remain on the front line of Iraqi security, a situation acceptable neither to Iraqis nor to contributing nations."[43] In terms of international law, there is no doubt that the ultimate responsibility to protect lies with the Iraqi government and its fledgling law enforcement and security apparatus.

There is no genocide in Iraq, neither is there a substantial threat of genocide. There are, however, harbingers of systematic ethnic and sectarian cleansing, and there are massive violations of human rights as well as many instances that would qualify as crimes against humanity, namely repeated suicide bombings causing mass casualties. As of now, national Iraqi authorities are clearly failing to protect their civilians against these crimes and are in dire need of help to "build capacity to protect their population."

A discussion of the possible justification of an international military intervention, *hic et nunc,* to protect Iraqi civilians from their current plight cannot ignore that the invasion of Iraq in 2003, whatever its original reasons may have been, and the subsequent mismanagement of the military occupation and its aftermath, have substantially contributed to reaching the present extreme levels of violence. When a majority of Iraqis affirm to pollsters that they prefer the MNF-I to continue for a certain time in Iraq, they do not express an inordinate affection for the coalition forces and its political backers. Rather, they realize that if the MNF-I leaves, they, the Iraqis, will have to sort out for themselves the extraordinarily complex political situation created by the invasion and the regime change. They also know from experience that there would be far fewer resources to assist with the reconstruction of their country, and they anticipate the gruesome effects of unbridled civil war.

As it is, the MNF-I *is* in Iraq, at the behest of the Iraqi government, with the blessing of the United Nations and tasked with the promotion of "the maintenance of security and stability in Iraq to act in accordance with international law, including obligations under international humanitarian law."[44] Thus, the MNF-I has a clear "responsibility to protect," which it cannot relinquish unless it has provided Iraq with the means to assume its responsibilities vis-à-vis the civilian population on its own.

However, in most public utterances of the political leaders of the countries composing the MNF-I, there is a distinct trend toward advancing arguments that would eventually justify the withdrawal, or at least a massive drawdown, of MNF-I forces and that would justify a decrease of international commitment to Iraq. The two main arguments, albeit contradictory, pursue the same aim. On one hand, there is an insistent official emphasis on the rapidly improving capacity of the Iraqi government and its security forces to assume increasing responsibilities for the maintenance of law and order in Iraq, for the provision of a safe and secure environment for Iraqi citizens, and for the development of democratic institutions. Consequently, a massive withdrawal or reorientation of the MNF-I's commitment would not only be possible, but also justifiable.

On the other end of the political spectrum, analysts argue that the establishment of a sufficiently strong central government and loyal, operational Iraqi security forces is failing and that the continued presence of the international forces actually makes matters worse for Iraqi civilians, because it validates the motives of the insurgents and their use of indiscriminate warfare and incitement of sectarian violence. These analysts also contend that sectarian strife is an unavoidable outcome of institution building and democratic statehood. The examples of the horrendous human toll accompanying the separation of India and Pakistan, the British retreat from Iraq in 1932, and other examples of uncontrollable violence in other instances of civil wars are put forward to explain that the coalition forces, in the case of an all-out civil war in Iraq, would be left with no choice but to retreat to the sidelines, with the sole purpose of eventually protecting the country's borders to avoid a regional conflagration.

■ Toward a Transformation of
the International Presence in Iraq

Human rights arguments and the humanitarian concerns that were advanced to justify the invasion of Iraq, to liberate its people from a repressive and cruel tyrant, have all but disappeared from the political discourse about the future of Iraq. Domestic politics in the United States and other contributing nations of the MNF-I, as well as economic and geo-political interests, have a far greater weight in deciding on the duration, strength, form, and specific objectives of a continued international military presence.

Considering the overwhelming strategic and economic interests at stake, it is highly improbable that the coalition forces will leave Iraq any time soon, even if civil strife substantially worsens. The United States will almost certainly maintain a military presence in the country, to protect the supply of strategic oil resources in Iraq and the Arabian Peninsula, and to avoid major political upheaval in the region. It will certainly seek the collaboration of its present allies and of other partners to assist it in the task of building a relatively strong Iraqi central state within its current international borders, which can provide a safe and secure environment to its citizens and to international investors.

If the United States and its current major coalition partners were to restructure their military presence in Iraq on the model of Operation Enduring Freedom in Afghanistan and the International Security Assistance Force (ISAF) in Afghanistan, a multinational presence in Iraq with a peace-building and civilian-protection mandate, approved by the UN, would be conceivable. Evans and Sahnoun argue that to justify the use of force within the framework of an international "responsibility to protect," the UN Security Council should consider a number of criteria beyond the actual human rights situation.[45]

Evans and Sahnoun insist that the Council should examine the seriousness of the threat to international peace and stability and the existence of a well-defined purpose of the coercive action (such as separating warring parties, creating safe havens for civilians, and opening of humanitarian space). They also insist on the plausibility of the success of the use of force in stopping or mitigating the threat and on the proportionality of the military resources available to achieve the protection objectives. Evans and Sahnoun finally emphasize that the consequences of the use of force should not risk triggering a greater conflagration.

From the strict point of view of the protection of civilians in Iraq, it can be argued that a multinational force, in sufficient strength, with an appropriate composition including Muslim countries, and approved and supported by the neighboring countries of Iraq, could succeed in achieving protection-oriented coercive action. For this purpose, the force should be provided with the necessary resources to help the Iraqi state to proceed with security-sector reform and the strengthening of the judiciary and of law enforcement, so that it can effectively protect its citizens from the excesses of criminal, sectarian, and ethnic violence. That job will take years to achieve, and it has barely begun.

With regard to the proportionality of resources, a recent RAND study established a calculus suggesting that "international troop levels should be at least 1,000 soldiers per 100,000 inhabitants and international police levels should be at least 150 police officers per 100,000 inhabitants, especially when there is the potential for severe instability."[46] Applying these ratios to Iraq, a force well above the current strength of the MNF-I would be necessary.

Iraqis have shown that they are extraordinarily resilient and resourceful. They suffered an awful political regime in the past two decades, and for this they have paid a heavy price. In view of the broader objectives of promoting "freedom, democracy, and free market economies" in the region, following the Iraqi example, it appears inconceivable that, after having wasted billions of dollars on rebuilding Iraqi infrastructure with decidedly meager results, no new financial resources should be devoted to help Iraqis reconstruct their country and to build on their proven capability to marry a secular society with a profound respect for religious tradition.

The international community cannot leave the work undone that it has, albeit grudgingly, condoned. It may not be the protection of Iraqi civilians but rather the protection of strategic oil resources or the fear of greater regional turmoil that will lead the international community to the least harmful decisions. The latter will hopefully not only prevent a further generation of conflict but substantively contribute to protect Iraqi civilians as well.

▨ Notes

1. Sylvie Giossi Caverzasio, ed., *Strengthening Protection in War: A Search for Professional Standards* (Geneva: International Committee of the Red Cross, 2001), 19.

2. Alkire Sabina, "Conceptual Framework for Human Security," Working Paper prepared for the Human Security Commission, February 16, 2002, www.humansecurity-chs.org/activities/outreach/frame.pdf.

3. Toby Dodge, *Inventing Iraq: The Failure of Nation Building and a History Denied* (New York: Columbia Univ. Press, 2003), 169.

4. S/RES 666 (1990) adopted by the Security Council at its 2,939th meeting on September 13, 1990, www.casi.org.uk/info/undocs/gopher/s90/20.

5. www.warandpiece.com/blogdirs/000041.html, August 30, 2003.

6. S/RES 1546 (2004) adopted by the Security Council at its 4,987th meeting on June 8, 2004. daccessdds.un.org/doc/UNDOC/GEN/N04/381/16/PDF/N0438116.pdf?OpenElement.

7. See, for example, the remarks of US secretary of defense Donald Rumsfeld to the US Senate Armed Forces Committee on July 9, 2003: "There's no question but that this individual has created such fear on the part of the Iraqi people because

of his brutality and the numbers of—tens of thousands of people he's killed, and the willingness to use chemical weapons on his people and on his neighbors, that—that there is a fear, not just in Iraq, but in the region, that he—that we have to be certain that he is not going to be around." www.usiraqprocon.org/bin/procon/procon.cgi?database=5-M-Subs4.db&command=viewone&op=t&id=1&rnd=653. 9189622988547.

8. Nawaf Obaid, "Meeting the Challenge of a Fragmented Iraq: A Saudi Perspective" (Washington, DC: Center for Strategic and International Studies, April 2006), 16–18, www.comw.org/warreport/fulltext/0604obaid.pdf.

9. "A Tribute to Iraqi Ingenuity," riverbendblog.blogspot.com/, January 18, 2006.

10. Colin L. Powell, "Remarks to the National Foreign Policy Conference for Leaders of Nongovernmental Organizations," October 26, 2001, 66.249.93.104/search?q=cache:LXjRsgox564J:www.yale.edu/lawweb/avalon/sept_1 1/powell_brief31.htm+ngo+colin+powell+force+multipliers&hl=en&ct=clnk&cd=4 &client=safari.

11. Author conversations with Grand Ayatollah Ali Husseini al-Sistani, Najaf, February 28, 2004; Dr. Harith al-Dari, Umm al Qura, Baghdad, March 22, 2004; and many others.

12. Nada Doumani, ICRC spokesperson, ICRC interview, www.icrc.org/Web/Eng/siteeng0.nsf/html/audio-iraq-230206.

13. "In Haditha Killings, Details Came Slowly," *Washington Post*, 3 June 2006.

14. Geneva Conventions, Additional Protocol I, in particular Articles 29, 48, 50, 54, and 75; see www.icrc.org/ihl.nsf/7c4d08d9b287a42141256739003e636b/f6c8b9fee14a77fdc125641e0052b079.

15. Geneva Conventions, Additional Protocol I, Article 51(5)(b); see www.icrc.org/ihl.nsf/WebART/470-750065?OpenDocument.

16. Martin van Creveld, *The Transformation of War* (New York: New Press, 1991), 212.

17. Dr. Mahmoud A. Ould Mohammedou, *Report on a Roundtable on the Transformation of Warfare, International Law, and the Role of Transnational Armed Groups* (Cambridge, MA: Humanitarian Policy and Conflict Research, Harvard University, April 2006), 10, www.hpcr.org/pdfs/OccasionalPaper6.pdf.

18. On practices by insurgent groups and civilian casualties, see the United Nations High Commissioner for Refugees (UNHCR), *Country of Origin Information— Iraq*, October 2005, www.unhcr.org/cgibin/texis/vtx/home/opendoc.pdf?tbl=RSDCOI&id=435637914; and Anthony Cordesman, "Iraq's Evolving Insurgency and the Risk of Civil War" (Washington, DC: Center for Strategic and International Studies, April 26, 2006, revised working draft), www.reliefweb.int/library/documents/2006/csis-irq-26apr.pdf.

19. See Amir Taheri, "To Kill or Not to Kill Is the Issue," *Gulf News*, 9 June 2005, archive.gulfnews.com/articles/05/06/09/168387.html.

20. International Crisis Group (ICG), *In Their Own Words: Reading the Iraqi Insurgency* (Baghdad, Washington, DC, Brussels: International Crisis Group, 2006): i and ii, www.crisisgroup.org/library/documents/middle_east___north_africa/iraq_iran_gulf/50_in_their_own_words_reading_the_iraqi_insurgency.pdf.

21. Howard La Franchi, "US Seeks Options for Iraq, Finds Few Answers," *Christian Science Monitor*, 5 May 2006, www.csmonitor.com/2006/0505/p04s01-usfp.html.

22. ICG, "The Next Iraqi War? Sectarianism and Civil Conflict," *Middle East Report* 52 (February 27, 2006).

23. Text of the Iraqi constitution, available at www.washingtonpost.com/wpdyn/content/article/2005/10/12/AR2005101201450.html; and text of the Transitional Administrative Law (TAL), available at www.cpa-iraq.org/government/TAL.html.

24. Council on Foreign Relations, "Militia Groups" (Background Q&A), www.cfr.org/publication/8175/#2.

25. ICG, "The Next Iraqi War?"

26. Council on Foreign Relations, "Militia Groups."

27. Robert Kaplan, "The Coming Normalcy," *Atlantic Monthly,* April 2006.

28. Tony Rogers, "US MP Rules of Engagement in Iraq," July 21, 2005, on his website, tonyrogers.com/news/iraq_rules_of_engagement.htm.

29. ICG, *In Their Own Words.*

30. Human Rights Watch, "US Minimizes Civilian Casualties in Iraq" (New York: Human Rights Watch, March 17, 2006), hrw.org/english/docs/2006/03/16/iraq13022.htm; and Amnesty International, *Iraq: Amnesty International's Concerns with Regard to "Operation Swarmer,"* AI Index: MDE 14/011/2006 (Public) News Service No. 067, March 17, 2006, web.amnesty.org/library/Index/ENGMDE140112006?open&of=ENG-IRQ.

31. Hugo Slim, "Why Protect Civilians? Innocence, Immunity, and Enmity in War," *International Affairs* 79, no. 3 (2003): 481–501; also available at www .hdcentre.org/datastore/shaping%20opinion/Why%20Protect%20Civilians.pdf.

32. Ibid.

33. George W. Bush, "Strategy for Victory in Iraq," Speech given at the United States Naval Academy, Annapolis, MD, November 30, 2005, www.whitehouse.gov/news/releases/2005/11/20051130-2.html.

34. Slim, "Why Protect Civilians?"

35. "*Noting* the commitment of all forces promoting the maintenance of security and stability in Iraq to act in accordance with international law, including obligations under international humanitarian law . . . and to cooperate with relevant international organizations." S/RES 1546 (2004) adopted by the Security Council at its 4,987th meeting, on June 8, 2004, daccessdds.un.org/doc/UNDOC/GEN/N04/381/16/PDF/N0438116.pdf?OpenElement. "*Affirming* the importance for all forces promoting the maintenance of security and stability in Iraq to act in accordance with international law, including obligations under international humanitarian law, and to cooperate with relevant international organizations, and *welcoming* their commitments in this regard." Resolution 1637 (2005) adopted by the Security Council at its 5,300th meeting, on November 8, 2005, www.iamb.info/pdf/unsc1637.pdf.

36. Victoria Wheeler and Adele Harmer, "Resetting the Rules of Engagement: Trends and Issues in Military-Humanitarian Relations," Humanitarian Policy Group Research Briefing 23, March 2006, www.odi.org.uk/hpg/papers/HPGbrief21.PDF.

37. Victoria Holt, "The Responsibility to Protect: Considering the Operational Capacity for Civilian Protection" (Washington, DC: Henry L. Stimson Center Working Paper, January 2005), kms.isn.ch:80/serviceengine/FileContent?serviceID=PublishingHouse&fileid=6BFE9D0A-990F-4307-D2A0-5F30441CA4C3&lng=en.

38. S/RES/1556 (2004).

39. Gareth Evans and Mohamed Sahnoun, "The Responsibility to Protect," *Foreign Affairs* 81, no. 6 (November 2002).

40. A/RES 60/1, 2005 World Summit Outcome Document, October 24, 2005, daccessdds.un.org/doc/UNDOC/GEN/N05/487/60/PDF/N0548760.pdf?OpenElement.

41. General Accounting Office, "Rebuilding Iraq: Stabilization,

Reconstruction, and Financing Challenges," GAO-06-428T, Statement of Joseph A. Christoff, Director, International Affairs and Trade, February 8, 2006, www.gao.gov/new.items/d06428t.pdf.

42. Ibid.

43. Seth G. Jones, Jeremy M. Wilson, Andrew Rathmell, and K. Jack Riley, *Establishing Law and Order After Conflict* (Arlington, VA: RAND, 2005), 105–106, www.rand.org/pubs/monographs/2005/RAND_MG374.pdf.

44. Resolution 1637 (2005) adopted by the Security Council at its 5,300th meeting on November 8, 2005, www.iamb.info/pdf/unsc1637.pdf.

45. Evans and Sahnoun, "The Responsibility to Protect."

46. Jones et al., *Establishing Law and Order After Conflict,* xiii.

17

Dilemmas of Donor Assistance

Michael Bell

DONOR ASSISTANCE can and must play an important role in Iraqi reconstruction. Iraqis today, and for the foreseeable future, lack the structures, institutions, and best practices required for nation building. They have emerged from sanctions and the Saddam era to find themselves confronted by a vigorous insurgency, unbottled ethnic tensions, and an economy in shambles. Without an enhanced security environment, economic growth, personal well-being, and democratization will remain distant goals. Reconstruction assistance will dry up, as it is already doing. Whatever the odds, however, Iraq cannot be abandoned without horrendous global consequences. Donors therefore have every interest in an Iraqi success story. The United States and Britain, who led the intervention, must remain involved and committed. The rest of us, including Iraqi decisionmakers, must reenergize ourselves, work better together, and use fewer resources to greater effect. We need to be better organized. We need vigorously remodeled, if not new, institutions, based on sustainable goals.

■ Donor Fatigue

Donor fatigue has set in. After more than four years' effort, the Iraq enterprise seems to many to have become a bottomless pit into which money goes, but from which few results emerge. An unfortunate but popular perception is that donors are fighting a battle where failure is foreordained. Reassurances from the Bush administration are greeted with an increasing weariness, reinforced by what many perceive as a US ideological imperative, great power unilateralism, and a bias toward opaqueness. Much of today's debate on "Whither Iraq?" is sustained by argument about the past, over whether the administration took courageous right-minded decisions or made tragic mistakes. These are valid questions and they may be emotionally satisfying for some, but they get us no place on the ground, which is where success or failure will be determined.

The Consequences of Failure

We are today, more than ever, faced with tough decisions, which will profoundly affect not only the future of Iraq, the Iraqi people, and their neighbors, but the entire international community. Failure in Iraq will redefine power relationships in the region and affect the geo-strategic equation worldwide. It is in no one's interest that Iraq fragment, that the Middle East be transformed into a Sunni-Shia battlefield or that Salafist influence become pervasive, with Iraq's Sunni triangle its breeding ground. To avoid the worst, tough decisions are necessary now, and not only respecting reconstruction. We must learn from the past and then shift the paradigm. We must be brutally realistic in defining what the situation is and what it is not. The international community and its Iraqi partners must establish the limits of the possible, then reenergize and recommit themselves.

The Security Imperative

Time is running out for Iraq's new government to demonstrate its effectiveness. Security must improve dramatically. Reconstruction can only be successful if the streets are safe. One is not a substitute for the other; rather, economic and social progress is utterly dependent on the rule of law prevailing. Iraqis must begin to feel better about themselves. Daily life must be seen to improve for there to be a commitment to the kind of entrepreneurial activity the US government has said it so badly wants and which Iraq almost certainly needs.

This is notwithstanding the contention that in parts of the country, particularly in Kurdistan, progress is evident, or the argument that, excepting Baghdad, the economic situation is better than it was prior to the coalition's intervention. Progress in specific regions and statistical data in isolation do not, however, mean success, especially when the government's writ does not run within the country and when sectarian militias, whose loyalty to the state is minimal, become the guarantors of security. Basra is now largely controlled by insurgents, gangs, and tribal factions. Nor can the importance of Baghdad, Iraq's anchor, be dismissed. Baghdad is the largest Sunni city in Iraq, the largest Shia city, and the largest Kurdish city. It is the pulse of the Iraqi "nation," essential to its existence.

The Consequences of Lawlessness

Terror and intimidation have become a tragic part of the landscape, but the absence of security is more than just wear and tear. It not only has a direct psychological and physical effect, it impacts seriously on the entire economic life of the country. From this reality there is no escape. A June 2006 *New York Times* article provides a vivid demonstration of the impact of lawlessness on the oil industry.[1] Sabotage attacks have been a long-standing feature of that industry since the US intervention in 2003, reducing exports dramatically.

According to the *New York Times*, these attacks have turned into a profitable enterprise for insurgents and criminal gangs because pipeline sabotage forces the government to import as much fuel as possible by truck, with as much as 30 percent of those imports ending up in the hands of smugglers. The latter then sell the gasoline on the black market. This forces ordinary Iraqis onto the black market where they pay more than US$2.50 a US gallon. In total, 40 percent of the gasoline consumed in Iraq is purchased on the black market, while an even greater percentage of diesel, kerosene, and liquid gas, used for cooking and heating, is purchased illicitly. Truckers are forced by these insurgents and criminal gangs to pay protection money to use public roads. The *New York Times* also reports that senior officials are implicated.

■ The Consequences of Disengagement

The alternative to a conscious shared effort by Iraqis and the international community to ensure meaningful change is the risk that coalition members and other third-party players will write off the transformation exercise. By mid-2006, the only significant new financial commitment to the International Reconstruction Fund Facility for Iraq (IRFFI), the sole multilateral mechanism for reconstruction assistance, came from the European Union. This falloff needs correction but if the US administration's overriding priority becomes disengagement, others will quickly follow. Collapse and civil war will then become a self-fulfilling prophecy. The prospects of such a descent have until recently been taboo in the administration's discourse but the potential is too real, and the consequences too great, for us to ignore this possibility any longer.

Can the rebuilding enterprise survive without renewed external involvement? Without strong external commitment, the already fragile institutions of state, further weakened by sweeping de-Baathification, will be incapable of withstanding further disaggregation. Iraqi citizens, emerging from Saddam's culture of oppression, will be forced to make their peace with whatever authorities remain, be they legitimate or not. They will look to the militias, insurgents, and warlords who exercise real power and can therefore provide basic security, a citizen's most sought-after goal. Only with security can political, social, and economic needs be met. This is an all-important assertion, of which donors are acutely aware.

For those who doubt that legitimate, fair-minded, and effective security mechanisms are the essential prerequisite for economic and social growth, they will be challenged to find a single example where safety in daily life has not been primordial. Among those who loathe Saddam, many volunteer that his regime did offer one essential element: predictability respecting security on the streets. If Iraqi transformation is to be successful, the security imperative has to be faced squarely.

■ **The Need for New Thinking**

Thankfully, some are doing just that. Among others, the Saban Center, the RAND Corporation, and the International Crisis Group argue that with renewed will and fresh thinking security can still be achieved, but only if the United States and Britain are capable of both maintaining their will and demonstrating flexibility.[2] While those at public policy institutions are not decisionmakers, they do understand that if Iraqis are afraid to leave home or, if they do, to travel any distance; if commodities do not reach their intended recipients, if power systems fail due to sabotage, and if there is no external investment, any effort will come to naught. One sobering example of how pervasive security questions remain, beyond the widely publicized reports of suicide bombings, is contained in a 2006 UN Iraq Trust Fund newsletter, which addresses the rehabilitation of schools. The newsletter reports that figures released by the Ministry of Education show that sixty-four children were killed and fifty-seven injured in 417 attacks against schools over the six-month period from October 2005 to March 2006.[3]

Many officials on the ground in Iraq continue to believe that single events—the referendum on the constitution or the formation of a new government, for instance—might be enough to turn the tide, to create a new reality and a self-realizing path to success.[4] This, however, is to view the world through rose-colored glasses, because one wants so badly to see a turnaround. One-off events have seldom successfully reversed the tide of socioeconomic and security challenges. One example has been the new constitution that so many had waited for with much anticipation: although approved by referendum, there remained many questions over it. The necessary social and political consensus to make it work is not in place, nor are prospects auspicious.

Similarly, there is a tendency among some involved in reconstruction on the ground in Iraq to believe that the commitment of those Iraqis they work with directly, and the many other Iraqis like them, will carry the day. I was struck, some months ago, speaking in Baghdad to the head of a major NGO, whose entire operation is located outside the Green Zone, as to how impossible the situation had become.[5] He was convinced that the overwhelming number of Iraqis wanted transformation to succeed, and in this I believe him to be correct. He volunteered, however, that his local staff did much work from their homes because their association with an outside NGO meant their lives were directly at risk. There is only one solution here: to improve security to the extent that those who work to reconstruct civil society can do so without risking their lives.

How Donors Act

We all learn from the errors of the past. Not only has the US administration misjudged the situation but donor governments as a whole assumed too much going in, expecting that the structures of state would somehow survive the transition or that they could be reinvented within months under US leadership. The United States decided, however, not to bring in security personnel and resources in the numbers needed to assure normality throughout Iraq. Those who knew the country and felt its pulse were deemed suspect by US decisionmakers. On the military front, the administration favored a near-single focus on the search for insurgents who, despite a litany of coalition claims to the contrary, never diminished in number or capacity and are unlikely to do so in the foreseeable future, despite the demise of their most notorious combatant, Abu Musab al-Zarqawi.

Lack of security has been a constraint on the morale and the ability of Iraqis to contribute to reconstruction, but a hostile environment similarly affects the flexibility with which donors are able to operate. Poor security has meant far fewer third-country nationals on the ground. Most outsiders who reside in country are confined to the Green Zone. Entirely legitimate fears have meant that many reconstruction agencies have based themselves not in Iraq but in Amman, in the Gulf, in Cyprus, or even in North America. In short, these agencies are based anywhere but in the country to whose welfare they are meant to contribute. They say, and are correct, that Iraqis are willing to travel out of their own country to work with them in safety and in fact find the respite from uncertainties at home welcome. However, this alone is not an adequate response. In fact, the deputy prime minister responsible for economic affairs and reconstruction issues, Barham Saleh, told the author in mid-2006 that training outside Iraq would no longer be accepted because it undermines the nation-building effort.[6] Building countries is an incredible challenge even in the most benign of circumstances. Success in Iraq demands a constant security presence, until Iraq's new leaders truly believe they are ready to shoulder the burden alone.

The established pattern, however, is a different one. The bulk of advisers stay well out of Iraq. A compelling example comes from a discussion I had in October 2005 with a senior foreign oil executive based offshore.[7] His job was to guide the rebuilding of essential infrastructure. He had never been in Iraq and had no thought of going there. As understandable as this might be in terms of personal safety, the cost in human dynamics is hard to calculate. After a good session in Kuwait, guided by an expert who had never seen their working environment or felt their reality, Iraqi engineers returned home, with e-mails and mobile phones their communication tools. Any ongoing human contact with mentors had been foresworn pending the next trip out.

That donors want involvement, although not at any price, has logic on its side. The costs of risk avoidance, however, posit serious limitations. Lack of human contact on the ground cannot be explained away as inconsequential. Nevertheless, there may be at least some light at the end of the tunnel. After long and serious consideration, the World Bank decided to act to establish a permanent office with a country director in Iraq to play a more effective role in coordinating donor assistance.[8] This requires replication. Even though situated in the Green Zone and thereby living an artificial reality, with all the drawbacks this entails, donors make a very visible commitment.

There are solutions, but only the United States and Britain have the essential ingredients in their hands: inter alia, vigorous pursuit of dialogue with insurgents; significant strengthening of Iraqi security forces; the abandonment of rhetoric about success where there has been none; the constitution of clean and effective paramilitary forces; deployment throughout the country; the harnessing of the tribal patronage system; the inauguration of an amnesty program; and the creation of ethnically integrated security formations.[9] The full list seems endless but effective new strategies constitute a sine qua non for reconstruction.

If this still appears too daunting after months of discouragement and failure, existing doubts about the Iraq enterprise will become firm conclusions. At that point, US political pressure on its best friends will be incapable of ensuring even the feeblest commitment to reconstruction. On the security front, Spanish and Italian troops have left Iraq. Remaining contributors are edgy.

■ The Rule of Law

Reconstruction of the economy is mainly but not only constrained by security factors. Political and institutional barriers also play their role. The question of corruption is particularly sensitive, yet if not addressed, success cannot be expected. Corruption undermines hope for political and economic reform. It undermines institutions, destroys the proper functioning of the market, and ensures authorities will not primarily respond to citizens' needs. Some on the scene in Baghdad believe that intermittent electrical supply in some areas is often as much the result of corruption as of the insurgency.[10] Saddam's draconian regime did limit corruption and its collapse released unanticipated forces that neither Iraqis nor the United States yet have the ability to cope with. This is not to diminish, however, the role of many Iraqis in positions of responsibility. The physical risks they take daily in their commitment to see their country succeed is more than noteworthy.

Fortunately, Saddam's methods of fighting corruption are not the only ones. Ensuring that laws are enforced, increasing penalties for those who fall prey to the temptations of corruption, and making certain that rewards and incentives are there for those who resist, would constitute a good start. The February 2006 study of the Saban Center for Middle East Policy suggests privatization as an important means of reducing risks and rewarding integrity.[11] One could debate this, but what is certain is that pervasive corruption delegitmizes those in authority and leads a frustrated citizenry to consider radical solutions. This makes the failure of our common efforts even more likely.

■ Bureaucratic Impasse

Not all issues postdate Saddam. That is part of the irony. The energy infrastructure was already close to collapse, not only because of sanctions and the war economy but also through decades-long neglect of normal maintenance requirements. Cheap oil has historically distorted the economy and created a dependency that is difficult to break. Infrastructure, human costs, and physical and institutional degradation date well back, as far as the war with Iran in the 1980s.

Available evidence suggests that enormous amounts of capital are moving out of Iraq. Domestic investment is minimal, it being a simpler matter to rely on reconstruction assistance.[12] Even then, complications multiply. Billions in donor funds have been expended on long-term infrastructure, much of it now sitting idle. Mega-project generators sit unconnected. In areas with little violence, approved projects are aborted because of bureaucratic bottlenecks. There is often a simple unwillingness even at the most senior level to take responsibility for making decisions. Some major long-term projects cannot disburse because no one knows what Iraqi law requires.[13] Some projects become special preserves that attract opportunists. This will not change until there is carefully honed decentralization and both regional and central governments are able to make their writ felt in a fair-minded way. As an example, movement toward the elimination of subsidies, one key economic reform, remains untouched. This is likely to continue given the fragility of the Iraqi polity, although the government did propose to reduce subsidies by 25 percent during the 2006 budget year.[14]

Line ministries run many projects out of Baghdad that are more properly the domain of regional governments. In the past and still today, certain bilateral donors and UN agencies wander freely "project shopping" with little coordination or planning, at whatever level and with whatever ministry will take their money. Serious efforts are being made by Iraqi officials to deal with this dysfunction and there is some success, but the situation begs for still better coordination. Undoubtedly, many of those dealing with donor coordination will contest this view. Perhaps a looser model is appropriate elsewhere. However, the prevailing extraordinary situation requires extraordinary measures in order to yield success.

Successful efforts are in fact being made, but to date they have only met with tentative results. The Iraqi government has created mechanisms to promote coordination and accountability. Yet officials involved in planning at the center say that bilateral donors too often make their own deals with line ministries without consultation. It has sometimes proven difficult for the Iraqi center to articulate overall priorities for fear of offending line ministers or regional governors. Aid inflows have still not been integrated into the budget process. Issues such as this arise in many situations, including in the most sophisticated economies, but Iraq cannot afford such luxuries. There is no way forward without effective economic management, and Iraqis can no longer afford the wishful thinking that donors can somehow pull it off without the total commitment of the government of Iraq.

■ The Imperative Today

There has been much debate over the appropriate balance between long-term (mainly infrastructure) assistance and short-range projects, which have nearly immediate impact but are unlikely to be sustainable into the future. Many have favored the long-term approach in the hope of avoiding the dependency that more immediately focused undertakings can create. I recognize this risk but worry that without short-term relief, there will simply be no long term. What Iraqis need, however, is a mixture of both: quick-impact involvement on humanitarian issues, as well as in basic services such as health and education, and long-term institution building, without which there will be insufficient capacity to manage the essential institutions of the state.

A too-often discouraged and frightened Iraqi citizenry must feel beneficial results now if they are to face successfully the many challenges and risks they confront daily, despite the risk of economic distortions over the longer term. The question is less whether electrical power delivery has, for example, improved beyond that existing in the last days of Saddam than whether Iraqis see their situation improving. If the short term is not won, there simply will be no future left to worry about. The UN and World Bank trust funds, much to their credit, recognize this human requirement and deserve more credit than they sometimes receive. In my view, all donors must direct their attention to meeting the expectations of Iraq's citizens. Per capita GDP is less than 50 percent of what it was fifteen years ago and unemployment is desperately high, with some estimates suggesting it stands at 40 percent; others assess it even higher still.[15] The employment gap was of course seriously exacerbated by the wholesale disbanding of Saddam's military and security services, which pushed over half a million young men into the streets in one fell swoop.

■ **Donor Response**

It is time for donors to weigh the costs of tying their contributions to specific undertakings when these do not meet Iraq's most essential needs. Development commitments that benefit donors' export industries might be the norm globally, but Iraq is not a "normal" case. "White elephant" projects cannot and should not be sustained. New priorities have to be set with those funds that still may be made available, through clear and frank discussions between donors and, most of all, between donors and Iraqis. While there may be many on the ground in Iraq and among donor agencies who believe this is happening, my own experience suggests a more somber conclusion.

Nor is unilateralism an answer. Certainly, the reservations of many actual and prospective donors regarding the US intervention have meant that a coordinated multilateral role in reconstruction was not feasible from the very beginning. Nor would it have been welcomed, with the US administration seemingly determined to remake Iraq without the flexibility others saw as a sine qua non for their own participation in reconstruction. The United States, to its credit, implemented a massive development program, even if with mixed results. As in any complex situation, some of its failures were probably inevitable.

Nevertheless, the administration still shows reluctance to work with other donors or to pool resources for the common good. It actively participates in the meetings of the International Reconstruction Fund Facility for Iraq, but declines to consider funneling any of its own monies through the multilateral UN and World Bank trust funds that the IRFFI mechanism is designed to sustain. It encourages third countries to donate to this multinational vehicle but declines to do so itself, except at the modest level necessary to ensure membership. This should be changed.

■ **Multilateral Options**

The IRFFI has considerable underutilized potential through the UN and World Bank trust funds, which have administered the US$1.5 billion the IRFFI received in contributions over the first three years of its existence. Heavily underwritten by Japan and the European Union, in particular, its potential remains great. That potential may be a significant tool in facilitating an Iraqi turnaround. The record to date, despite earlier doubts by some, is solid, since the UN and World Bank funds have in-depth ability to ensure a coordinated strategy, a meaningful ongoing dialogue with the Iraqi authorities, and the means to deliver on their agreements, which few, if any other donors, share. The UN trust fund, for instance, operating under IRFFI auspices, has meant that for the first time UN agencies have adopted common planning, funding, coordinated implementation, and reporting arrangements for a large-scale operation. They relate to Iraqi ministries as a single external entity in facilitating coordinated planning.

Yet many donors are reluctant to use these multilateral mechanisms as their vehicle for reconstruction, preferring bilateral options or simply tiring of the process and retreating from the field. Still more disheartening is that certain UN specialized agencies choose to work outside the trust funds, soliciting funding from other donors to assure their greater independence and profile. As the US government completes its major bilateral programs, this shotgun approach is a luxury neither Iraqis nor the international community, in its own interest, can afford.

The United Nations, in particular, can play a vital role in institutional, social, and economic development beyond the trust funds as it can react quickly and in a coordinated way, with privileged access to top Iraqi decisionmakers. If given the necessary support and tools, the world body could become the focal point of international involvement, barring security, for which there is no viable alternative to the United States and Britain. The United States' responsibility is more than ever to fight the natural tendency of a superpower to assert full control. It should truly share in the reconstruction effort; listen as well as cajole others into involving themselves; work with the UN and sympathetic partners; encourage the Iraqis to take the initiative; and at the same time, ensure that security becomes a reality.

■ The Cost of Loose Thinking

Iraqis themselves must focus single-mindedly on a successful transition. This may seem obvious but reality shows sectarianism that is increasingly dominant, personal rivalries that are more intense, and a deeply divided, although newly elected, government and parliament. The central government and regional ministries are too often immobile and without necessary leadership, but sometimes with a capacity for severe self-delusion. Certain key Iraqi decisionmakers still speak of a Marshall Plan, while no donor has the stomach for it. On the other hand, some outsiders continue to profess the belief that Iraq can finance its reconstruction because of the country's oil wealth. This mantra seems resilient, unencumbered by reference to any particular time or circumstance, despite the fact that oil output was expected to rise marginally in 2006. Sabotage and accidents have, for instance, almost totally shut down exports from Kirkuk.[16]

■ The Way Ahead

Reconstruction under these circumstances is difficult but not impossible, provided there is flexibility, a willingness to take risks, a determination to involve others, and, most dramatically, a realistic view of the tragic consequences of failure. New models can, and are, being considered that envision the UN holding a more prominent role in economic, social, civil, and institutional reconstruction. In fact, that organization's record to date has been as good as anyone's and better than most. However, the more the situation in Iraq deteriorates, assuming that present disaggregation continues, the less likely the international community will be to buy into what could be seen as a US effort to offload a failing enterprise. This very concern weighed heavily in the debate concerning the Iraqi "Compact Summit" proposal to rejuvenate the reconstruction process in the summer and fall of 2006. The United States is a strong supporter, but whatever pathways are ultimately pursued, such engagement must be sustainable.

It is not only the United States and the new Iraqi government that will have to reconsider their direction. Despite much goodwill, there is a sense of disengagement among third parties generally, as Iraq becomes an ongoing media staple. Neighboring states seem content too often to watch from the sidelines, immobilized and fearing either Shia dominance or Sunni radicalism. The Arab states of the Gulf pledged massive assistance in the form of soft loans at the Madrid conference in the wake of the intervention by the United States and Britain. Since then, however, they have been unwilling to provide funding to what they perceive as a Shia-Kurd-controlled government. This is so despite the consequences a failed Iraq will have for their region. Meanwhile, many, including the RAND Corporation, call for a regional strategy, changing the rhetorical language of "democratization" to "stabilization," a concept Iraq's neighbors would accept more easily.[17] Efforts continue to pull the Gulf states into the rebuilding process, but there remains a long way to go.

The donor community, as it stands now, is tired and frankly too disorganized, to have the maximum effect. The tendency of even the most effective bureaucracies, despite the best intentions of those involved, to avoid risk is a severe impediment to new thinking and clear decisions. A committed and collective effort to reenergize and reorganize the entire process is indispensable.

At the political level, some seem more content to hold essentially public-relations events, which are at best symbolic, as was the donor meeting of foreign ministers held in Brussels in June 2005. Flamboyant speeches were given and much goodwill expressed, but the Baghdad "street" felt little. Such meetings hold potential, but only if they provide new direction and respond in material ways to real needs. The organizers of the Brussels conference, knowingly, did not do that. A true international alliance, with assertive leadership and a powerful steering group of those most involved, Iraqis and outsiders, is essential. This is why any "Compact" exercise must entail a clear balance between commitments, benchmarks, timelines, and realistic funding levels. Strong support and a determination to succeed can still be the keys, but organization, multilateral cooperation, and continuous dialogue must underpin any effort. Such an outcome requires a truly meaningful lessons-learned exercise, based on a real appreciation of the situation today, as it is, not as we wish it might be. Responsible members of the international community share an obligation in making this happen. It remains, however, an open question whether they are up to the task or not.

▉ Notes

1. James Glanz and Robert F. Worth, "Attacks on Iraqi Oil Industry Aid Vast Smuggling Scheme," *New York Times,* 4 June 2006 [online newspaper], www.nytimes.com/2006/06/04/world/middleeast/04smuggle.html?_r=1&oref=slogin&pagewanted=all (accessed June 9, 2006).

2. International Crisis Group (ICG), "The Next Iraqi War? Sectarianism and Civil Conflict," *Middle East Report* 52 (February 27, 2006), www.crisisgroup.org/home/index.cfm?id=3980&l=1 (accessed June 9, 2006); Kenneth M. Pollack et al., "Switch in Time: A New Strategy for America in Iraq," *Saban Center Analysis* (Saban Center for Middle East Policy at the Brookings Institution), no. 7 (February 15, 2006), www.brookings.edu/fp/saban/analysis/20060215_iraqreport.pdf (accessed June 10, 2006); see also the chapters by James Dobbins and Nora Bensahel in this volume.

3. *UNDG Iraq Trust Fund Newsletter* 3, no. 4 (April 2006) [online], siteresources.worldbank.org/IRFFI/64168382-092419001661/20924208/UNDGITFApril2006Newsletter.pdf (accessed June 9, 2006).

4. Discussion with the author, Ditchley Park, October 15–16, 2005.

5. Discussion with the author, Baghdad, May 20, 2005.

6. Discussion with the author, Baghdad, June 16, 2006.

7. Discussion with the author, Ditchley Park, October 16, 2005.

8. "World Bank to Strengthen Existing Presence in Iraq," *[The World Bank] News Release* No. 2006/412/MNA (May 16, 2006) [online], web.worldbank.org/WBSITE/EXTERNAL/COUNTRIES/MENAEXT/IRAQEXTN/0,,contentMDK:20924512~menuPK:313111~pagePK:141137~piPK:141127~theSitePK:313105,00.html n (accessed June 9, 2006).

9. The Saban Center study is replete with ideas respecting how security and military operations can be improved; see Pollack et al., "Switch in Time," 9–15.

10. Discussion with the author, Baghdad, June 17–19, 2006.

11. Pollack et al., "Switch in Time," 77.

12. Ibid., 103.

13. World Bank officials in discussions with the author, Washington, March 15, 2006.

14. Economist Intelligence Unit, "Iraq Country Report" (March 2006), available at portal.eiu.com/index.asp?layout=displayIssue&publication_id=1220000922 (accessed June 9, 2006).

15. Ibid.

16. Ibid., 30.

17. See James Dobbins's chapter in this volume.

18

Strategic Coordination of International Engagement

Bruce D. Jones

THIS VOLUME EXPLORES the prospects for a stable transition in Iraq and the factors that may contribute to it. This chapter explores a specific aspect of that question, namely, the nature of international engagement and the options for organizing and orchestrating it under conditions of gradual stabilization (Nora Bensahel's chapter in this volume explores the cognate question of international military engagement).

Should the conflict in Iraq generate ongoing instability at the regional and global levels, the demand for deeper international engagement in the political and economic reconstruction process will grow. Although in many contemporary cases it is the United Nations that leads reconstruction efforts, recent history suggests that the UN is not the right locus of international engagement. Not only does the UN not have the capacities necessary for performing the lead function in coordinating international assistance to post-transition Iraq, it does not have the requisite legitimacy to do so either.

Rather, more complicated arrangements that reflect the complex regional and international politics of Iraq must be envisioned. Ideas for the organization of such an engagement can be informed by recapping the salient aspects of the role of the UN and other international actors in previous transitional operations, especially those shaped by comparable geo-politics as those that shape the situation in Iraq. Critical features of any arrangements will include: strong and visible Iraqi leadership, a multilayer mechanism that can accommodate international and regional actors, and strong coordination mechanisms to ensure that international assistance to Iraq is actually supportive of state and social reconstruction and not—as is sometimes the case—of prolonged dependency on outsiders.

■ **International Engagement in Small and Big Wars**

In the more than two dozen wars that have ended since 1990, direct international engagement—in the form of military support for war termination, economic assistance, humanitarian assistance, and much else besides—has been a critical part of the process for building peace. That is, it is a critical part of the process through which once-warring parties forge new or revive old mechanisms for political debate, resolve grievances, and reconstruct the social and economic basis of (more or less) sustainable and (more or less) peaceful development.

Organizing the International Presence

The roles played by international actors in the postconflict reconstruction process are as varied as the list of actors is long. Because this is so, and because in the early days of postwar reconstruction domestic state capacity is often limited, spread thin, and less than wholly trusted by the citizenry, transitional and early national governments' ability to control or coordinate the international presence is often constricted. Thus, other international actors are often called upon to coordinate or help the government coordinate the overall international response. At the extreme, international actors displace government authority and serve not merely to coordinate the broader international presence but to function in lieu of governments—the so-called transitional authority operations.[1]

Successful operations ultimately hinge upon the relationship between international actors—which includes the major industry surrounding "peace building"—and domestic state authority. Where international engagement fails to strengthen that authority or, worse, actually erodes or undermines it, peacebuilding objectives will tend not to be met. Indeed, this is the subject of growing concern, both among the builders and the built, about the efficiency and effect of such operations.

The high-water marks of direct international involvement were in Kosovo and East Timor, where the United Nations (in the former case supported by NATO, in the latter by an Australian-led multinational force) took on full-blown executive authority under Chapter VII of the UN Charter. Though often counted as at least partial successes, these two episodes raised concerns—not least within the United Nations—about the impact of international authority on the process of building legitimate and capable domestic state institutions, as well as about the accountability of international actors in such settings. Since these episodes, spurred by the Brahimi report,[2] the United Nations has hewn, at least in principle if not always in practice, to a "lighter footprint" approach—an approach reflected not necessarily in the size of the UN's presence but in its degree of authority. Several critics question whether even such presences actually displace more national capacities than they build.[3]

Despite the ongoing debates on the merits of varied levels of international involvement, the mythic yet powerful creature "the international community" continues to turn to the United Nations, regional organizations, and others to perform a set of postwar functions. The transitional authorities in postwar settings seek extensive international aid, and deepening international norms demand that both international and domestic authorities engage in practices designed to meet now well-developed standards for human rights, transitional justice, and the rule of law. All of this keeps demand for postconflict engagement high.

This engagement is more than technical; it is constitutive. The deployment of a postwar operation, mandated by the United Nations, and of significant donor resources, has become a part of how nascent postwar authorities are legitimated, consolidated, and "certified."

The "Vital Role" of the United Nations

The importance of this process was highlighted by the sharp debate in the UN Security Council in the summer of 2003, in the immediate aftermath of the US invasion of Iraq, over the question of the United Nations having a "vital role" in the postinvasion transition. Having the United States, by then installed as occupying authorities in Baghdad, accept a "vital role" for the United Nations in the reconstruction process was a precondition (ultimately, not met) of the Security Council members' support for Security Council Resolution 1483, which designated on-the-ground US forces as a multinational force and authorized their presence there. The "vital role" was not an argument about the scale of UN involvement, or the degree of its authority vis-à-vis emergent Iraqi authorities, but an argument that important international actors—European states, states within the region, some of the permanent members of the Security Council—were more willing to recognize the constituting authority of the United Nations than that of a single member state acting under contested authority.[4]

The phrase "a vital role" would later be adopted by the UN General Assembly when at the UN World Summit in September 2005 it decided to create a Peacebuilding Commission, among whose core functions would be to coordinate international responses to postconflict operations—doing so, primarily, through the mechanism of providing advice in the first instance to the Security Council, but also by the mere fact of bringing around a single table the joint capacities of the major bilateral donors, the international financial institutions, troop contributors, regional actors, and the United Nations itself.[5]

The creation of the Peacebuilding Commission highlights the fact that the United Nations has often been at the heart of postconflict coordination arrangements, as well as providing a range of direct support and operational roles ranging from electoral assistance to the panoply of humanitarian services.

The Limited Role of the United Nations

But the UN's role in postconflict operations, including its coordination function, has varied considerably from case to case, region to region, and, most importantly, by the scale of the war—a scale measured not in geographic and military terms but in geo-strategic ones.

Indeed, in wars that rise to the level of strategic significance—that is to say, where one or more of the great powers has a substantial interest in the outcomes of the conflict—the United Nations has rarely had a leading role in postconflict operations or even in their coordination. In such cases, the UN has been joined by regional actors, major states, neutral states, international financial institutions, and others, not only in operations but also in coordination.

If—as this volume takes as its premise—the medium-term future in Iraq is one that requires significant international support, we can reasonably expect two things: that the United Nations will be involved, as it is now on a limited basis, in providing direct assistance to the Iraqi authorities and people; and secondly, that it will not be doing so alone or even in a leading role. Not only does the United Nations not have the capacities necessary for performing the lead function in coordinating international assistance to post-transition Iraq, it does not have the requisite legitimacy to do so either.

■ Past International Engagement in Iraq

The constraints on UN legitimacy in Iraq are a direct function of its past involvement in that country's troubled recent past—a past to whose troubles the United Nations has contributed, or at least in which it has participated.

The UN in Iraq: A Troubled Past

The basic outline of UN operational engagement in Iraq is well known and needs only to be recapped briefly here. In the aftermath of the Gulf War, the United Nations in the spring of 1991 launched what was one of the first of the large and complex cross-border humanitarian operations that would then characterize the 1990s. The UN's effort was initially concentrated on Kurdish areas in northern Iraq. The humanitarian operation was supported by a multinational military one, Operation Provide Comfort.[6] In parallel, an interagency mission assessing the humanitarian needs in Iraq and Kuwait found that Iraq had been "relegated to a preindustrial age, but with all the disabilities of post-industrial dependency on an intensive use of energy and technology" and warned that "the Iraqi people may soon face a further imminent catastrophe, which could include epidemic and famine, if massive life-supporting needs are not rapidly met."[7]

Following this report, the United Nations proposed measures to enable Iraq to sell limited quantities of oil to avert a humanitarian crisis.[8] However, the government of Iraq initially declined the UN's original offer in 1991. This changed in April 1995, when the Security Council established the now infamous oil-for-food program with the adoption of Resolution 986, which enabled Iraq to sell oil to finance the purchase of humanitarian goods.[9]

In 2002, the Security Council expanded the program beyond its initial emphasis on food and medicines to include a more comprehensive agenda, including infrastructure rehabilitation, health and nutrition, electricity, agriculture and irrigation, education, transport and telecommunications, water and sanitation, housing, settlement rehabilitation for internally displaced persons and programming for especially vulnerable groups, mine action, and oil industry spare parts and equipment. The program was implemented in large part by UN specialized agencies, notably the World Food Programme (WFP).

Oil-for-food of course took place against the backdrop of sanctions. In August 1990, the Security Council adopted Resolution 661, imposing comprehensive sanctions on Iraq, following that country's invasion of Kuwait. The humanitarian effects of sanctions were serious at best, severe at worst.

There has been much discussion and debate concerning the hardships that ensued for the Iraqi people—in particular, children—in the intervening years. In 1995, members of a UN Food and Agricultural Organization (FAO) study team that had examined health and nutritional conditions in Iraq asserted that sanctions were responsible for the deaths of 567,000 Iraqi children.[10] Two years later, this estimate would be revised downward when a follow-up study yielded mortality rates that were "several-fold lower than the estimate for 1995" for "unknown reasons." In an independent study evaluating surveys conducted on Iraq by the United Nations Children's Fund (UNICEF), the WFP, the FAO, the Harvard Study Team, and the Center for Economic and Social Rights, public health specialist Richard Garfield estimated total excess deaths (that is, as a result of the imposition of sanctions) among those under five years of age at more than two hundred thousand.[11] Based on this and subsequent studies, UNICEF executive director Carol Bellamy declared the situation an "ongoing humanitarian emergency" that had arisen at least in part as a result of prolonged sanctions imposed by the Security Council.

While they differ on its exact dimensions, what most accounts agree upon is the fact that the sanctions regime imposed by the UN Security Council created a humanitarian crisis of major proportions.[12] The political consequences of this crisis—in terms of Iraqi perceptions of the UN—were very much a reality as the UN reentered Iraq after the Iraq War began in 2003.

Sanctions were still in place and the oil-for-food program was still operational in the spring of 2003 in the lead-up to war. The UN international staff was evacuated on March 18, 2003, following an announcement by Secretary-General Kofi Annan that the United Nations was no longer in a position to guarantee their safety and security. UN staff returned to Baghdad in summer 2003. On August 19, a suicide bomber attacked the UN compound in Baghdad, killing over twenty UN staff, including the Secretary-General's Special Representative Sergio Vieira de Mello. Despite this—the largest single attack against UN personnel in the organization's history—the United Nations remained operational in Iraq, though most international staff were initially relocated to Amman, Jordan.

In the aftermath of war, of course, US and Iraqi accusations about misuse of the oil-for-food program generated one of the largest scandals in UN history. The Secretary-General called for an independent commission to investigate allegations of corruption, which was headed by Paul Volcker. Though in its conclusions the Volcker commission found only limited evidence of corruption within the UN Secretariat, both the report itself and more importantly the press and the political scandal that surrounded it badly dented the UN's reputation, in Iraq and beyond.[13]

The combination of the humanitarian consequences of sanctions and of Iraqi perceptions of the UN's behavior in the context of oil-for-food mean' that the UN's legitimacy to act, in Iraqi eyes, is badly scarred. Innumerable statements from Iraqi leaders and civil-society actors confirm that the UN's legitimacy in the Iraqi context has been seriously eroded by the role it was assigned and by the way in which it executed that role. The cloud of sanctions and oil-for-food hung over the UN as it established its postwar presence as the United Nations Assistance Mission for Iraq (UNAMI)—mandated by Security Council Resolution 1546 to facilitate the political process in Iraq.[14]

UNAMI plays an important role in helping to coordinate international assistance. But it operates in a context of the far larger role played by the United States and the coalition. And if recent history is any guide, when it comes to orchestration of large-scale reconstruction in a later transitional phase, the United Nations is unlikely to be given the main role in orchestrating that effort.

■ Learning from Past Coordination Models

In past cases that share with Iraq the features of complexity and high strategic import, the international community has adopted a series of coordination models to orchestrate international assistance. Three major instances of such arrangements, and their significant features, can be briefly recapped.

Post-Oslo Support to the Palestinian Authority

In the post–Cold War era, the first major instance of large-scale, coordinated international support for the implementation of a peace agreement came in the form of the widespread and multifaceted international engagement in supporting the Oslo Peace Accords of 1993—a more-than-cease-fire, less-than-peace deal, which brought an end to the 1989 intifada and with it, for the first time, international and Israeli recognition of a Palestinian authority over designated parts of otherwise Israeli-occupied territory. The Palestine Liberation Organization (PLO), recognized by the Israelis and by the international community (if not by all Palestinians) as the sole representative of the Palestinian people through the Oslo process, returned from long exile, the latest in Tunis, to establish the Palestinian National Authority (PNA, later simply PA) initially in Gaza and in Jericho.

International engagement post-Oslo was unusual in comparison to most peace-implementation processes in the post–Cold War era in that it came with no troops and vast sums of money. While many, perhaps the majority of, postconflict international engagements have taken the form of peacekeeping operations and have routinely been short of funding, international support in the Palestinian territory was shaped by that region's unusual international political configuration. Widespread Israeli distrust of international, and especially UN, peacekeeping engagement has kept international peacekeeping forces out of the Palestinian territory, despite frequent Palestinian and Arab calls for their deployment. The enormous international political significance of the Middle East context has also meant that the peace process has never been short of political attention, media attention, or funds—all usually in short supply in peacebuilding contexts.

Coordinating international assistance in a context of nascent authorities, no international peacekeeping presence, and deep pools of money required creative implementation arrangements. These were created by the Norwegian government, which had sponsored the Oslo process and was subsequently tasked with orchestrating part of the accords' implementation. The complex set of arrangements put in place by the Norwegians in 1994 reflected the complex requirements of the implementation environment. These included (1) the need to bolster both the legitimacy and the capacity of the PA, in a context of sharply limited administrative capacity and acute political and military competition among Palestinian factions; (2) the fact that Israel still controlled the borders and all entry points into Palestinian self-governing territories; (3) the flow of large quantities of donor money into the territory and the need for tight monitoring thereof; and (4) the importance for political and legitimating purposes of keeping the Arab neighbors and regional geographic powers engaged in a process of supporting the establishment of the PA. All of this had to be achieved while support had to be built for authorities whose final configuration, territorial or legal, had yet to be negotiated.[15]

The overlapping mechanisms set up to establish these functions were overseen by the Ad Hoc Liaison Committee for Assistance to the Palestinian People—a donor coordination body composed of all of the major international donors, several regional contributors (including Egypt and Saudi Arabia), and the cochairs of the by-then-surpassed Madrid multilateral mechanism (the United States and Russia). The AHLC, as it was known, was chaired by Norway as the leading donor and neutral state; the World Bank served as secretariat. The AHLC oversaw the work of an in-territory mechanism, the Local Aid Coordination Committee (LACC). The United Nations and the World Bank served as cosecretariat to the LACC, to ensure coordination, while the Norwegians chaired, along with, critically, the Palestinian Authority. PA cochairmanship of the LACC ensured domestic ownership and appropriate targeting of resources.[16]

Supporting both of these mechanisms was the Holst Fund, a World Bank–managed trust fund through which the main donors channeled their funds. The Holst Fund disbursed against PA-specified priorities, but worked in tandem with Bank and International Monetary Fund monitoring mechanisms that provided to-the-penny accounting to donors and insurance against misdirection and corruption. The United Nations also established the Office of the Special Coordinator for the Occupied Territories (UNSCO) to facilitate these coordination mechanisms on the ground and to provide political support to the Palestinian Authority in its role vis-à-vis the international community.

Through the first years of the Oslo process, these coordination arrangements served two vital purposes. First, they created the necessary arrangements for donors to provide large-scale financial support to the Palestinian Authority, helping it thus to build up its institutions, while it also represented a major source of economic activity for the Palestinian people. Second, they created an informal political mechanism in which Israel, the Palestinian Authority, and all the major international actors participated, providing opportunities to solve economic, institutional, and even political problems associated with implementation of the Oslo Accords and additional subsequent agreements (notably the 1994 Paris Protocol, which governed border-control and trade-related arrangements).

These coordination arrangements would remain in place through 2001 and during that time did much to ensure continued donor support to the process of building PA "state" and administrative capacity. After the dramatic events of 9/11 and changes in PA-US relations (and against the backdrop of the second intifada), this mechanism was over time displaced by the establishment of the Quartet, a UN-conceived, US-chaired mechanism that brought together the United States, the United Nations, the European Union, and Russia. It is worth noting that in the period, in which the Quartet was most active in facilitating political dialogue and overseeing evolving aid-support arrangements, it often did so in informal coordination with the so-called Quartet Plus Three mechanism—the "plus three" being Saudi Arabia, Jordan, and Egypt, selected nominally for their positions as cosponsors of the follow-up process to the Arab League resolution that endorsed a Saudi peace initiative in March 2003. The establishment of a quasi-formal mechanism for international consultation with the United States, and through it international consultation with these Arab states on the peace process, served to contain international disagreement and fallout during the tense period of 2001–2003.

Unlike the AHLC, the Quartet was designed primarily as a political mechanism, which incidentally backed into aid coordination and aid-support arrangements. It provided a means to orchestrate political negotiations between these principal international actors and in turn between them and Israel and the Palestinian Authority in a period in which those parties engaged only in sporadic talks. Its main formal output has been the "roadmap," which has been accepted by both Israel and the Palestinian Authority—in word, if not in deed—as the basis for current action and future negotiations. In 2004, the Quartet also appointed its own Special Envoy, former World Bank president James Wolfensohn, to coordinate international policy and activity in the context of Israel's 2005 withdrawal from Gaza.

The most salient points about this example include:

1. its establishment in a context of no troops and lots of money;
2. its bridging of international and regional actors, political and financial;
3. its cochairing and cosecretariat arrangements designed to enhance coordination among the international actors; and
4. critically, the Palestinian chairmanship of the in-territory coordination arrangements.

Bosnia: Post-Dayton Implementation

A second major post–Cold War instance of coordination of a complex set of international actors is found in the post-Dayton arrangements in Bosnia. The Dayton Accords had been negotiated in part through an international Contact Group, comprising the main political actors involved in shepherding the parties toward the eventual conclusion of those agreements. Useful in the political negotiation process, the Contact Group had a major weakness in terms of its potential role in implementation, namely, the fact that major financial donors such as Japan were not included. As the process moved from the negotiation of the Dayton Accords to their implementation, the coordination arrangements had to evolve to incorporate a wider set of significant actors.[17]

What was established in the place of the Contact Group was a much wider mechanism known as the Peace Implementation Council (PIC). At its most expansive, the PIC incorporated fifty-eight governments, donors, and other kinds of contributors to the implementation process in Bosnia—the number being testimony to the scale of international attention given to this case. Its original purpose was to bring these actors into a common framework of support to implementation processes, but it went considerably beyond this purpose in practice, taking decisions about issues such as the timing of elections, the process of refugee returns, the adoption of common standards across the Bosnian entities, and other matters. The PIC had the *power* to decide these issues, though a questionable source of *authority*— simply, it arrogated power to itself.

This relationship between power and authority was reflected in the primary operational instrument through which the PIC functioned, namely the Office of the High Representative (OHR). The OHR was a unique arrangement; it embodied the deployment of a high-level international envoy with executive powers, similar to those of the UN's transitional authority operations in Kosovo and East Timor, but with powers conferred not by the UN Security Council but again simply arrogated to the OHR by the parties to the peace process.

The powers of the OHR, in particular the ability to dismiss from office even elected Bosnian officials, have been the subject of much assessment and evaluation, plenty of it critical.[18] Similarly, the fact that the Bosnian parties did not—and do not—participate in the deliberations of the Peace Implementation Council, or in the decisions of the Office of the High Representative, has been widely viewed as illegitimate and capacity diminishing, not capacity building. Defenders of the institutions argue that the PIC and OHR have served to make tough decisions that domestic Bosnian politicians could not have taken on in the early years of reconstruction, creating better policy outcomes in the short and medium term. Critics counter that while there is merit in this argument, the cost has been significant in terms of diminished expectation of and support for accountable, democratic governance in the long term among Bosnians.[19] History will be the judge.

The salient features of this model are:

1. the orchestration of a large number of contributing states into a single coordination mechanism;
2. the creation of a highly empowered, single executive envoy working on behalf of the broader international community (a model, minus

the powers, partially copied by the Quartet in 2005 in that mec... nism's appointment of its Special Envoy for Gaza Disengagement);
3. the arrogation of executive powers to the PIC and the OHR;
4. the nonparticipation of Bosnian parties in the decisionmaking and coordination processes; and
5. operation in a context of high strategic attention, significant international military presence, and substantial economic resources, not least in the form of the powerful carrot of ultimate entry into the European market.

Afghanistan

Most recent in time (among cases with strategic importance), and perhaps most similar in terms of the basic configuration of the international response, is Afghanistan—where the United States and NATO maintain military operations, as well as strong political influence, and the United Nations maintains an important civilian and humanitarian presence.

Afghanistan has in fact been a laboratory of coordination arrangements, notably for the "strategic framework" mechanism, a precursor to the now-standard integrated mission mechanisms used by the UN in contexts where it is in the lead.[20]

In the most recent iteration, the UN's Special Envoy Lakhdar Brahimi carefully used the Bonn process to ensure that the interim Afghan authority was established before international civilian mechanisms were set up, and thus, that the external presence could be formally invited in by the nascent regime, an important dimension of its legitimacy. On the basis of the Bonn agreements, Brahimi led in Afghanistan the establishment of a mission with a "light footprint"—a reference not to the size or scale of the mission but to its supportive rather than authoritative role vis-à-vis the Afghan authorities (although some of Brahimi's staff have also acknowledged that operating with a light political footprint is easier when US Strategic Air Command is an operational ally).

Second, Brahimi established an "integrated mission." The United Nations Assistance Mission in Afghanistan (UNAMA) had a "two-pillar" structure. One branch of the mission was devoted to providing the interim Afghan authorities with political advice and support, and a second was devoted to development coordination functions, including donor mobilization and interagency coordination. Each pillar was led by a Deputy Special Envoy of the Secretary-General.

It is notable that this integrated mission structure did not in its first instance succeed in deterring the UN's operational agencies from establishing large international presences, some of which detracted from, rather than supported, government authority. However, UNAMA subsequently worked closely with the Afghan government to bolster its own attempt to establish its authority and control over the international presence. Working closely with the internationally savvy finance minister, former World Bank vice president Ashraf Ghani, Brahimi supported a mechanism whereby the government established key sectors and insisted that donors stick to clear priorities. Donors were in effect given a choice: stick to government priorities or feel free not to spend money here. Such a device, of course, is one that is available only to governments in contexts of high strategic value, where money is available in plentiful quantities.

In Afghanistan, as in Palestine, local ownership was the key to the international coordinating presence. In both cases, international mechanisms for coordination—elaborate ones at that—were established, but unlike in Bosnia, these reinforced, rather than displaced, local and national government authority. This will surely be the key to any effort in Iraq.

▇ Options for Organizing International Engagement

There is no medium-term scenario for Iraq that is not highly complex in terms of the likely needs of the Iraqi state and its people, the regional political configuration, and the degree and nature of international contestation about the case and about post-transition arrangements.

In her chapter on a potential international military presence, Nora Bensahel outlines three potential scenarios: status quo (political and security instability, but at moderate levels); separation of the territory into separate spheres (Kurdish, Shia, Sunni); and civil war. Under conditions of civil war, it is likely that international aid and political actors would largely withdraw from operational involvement in Iraq, retreating to a humanitarian posture, probably largely based on cross-border operations from Jordan and Turkey. In either of the other two scenarios, however, significant international engagement in a reconstruction process is likely.

Under a separation scenario, international assistance to the separate elements of a former Iraqi state would be similar to those we can envisage for the current Iraqi state, just fractured out to each of the then separate territories. The primary determinant of international support to separate territorial elements of the current Iraqi state would be the perception of whether separation had been a necessary process to avoid civil war, or was a process of "ethnic cleansing" by other means.

Under the most benign of these scenarios—a continuing gradual drawdown of US forces and its political presence, reasonable levels of domestic, cross-sectarian support for the constitutional government, broad regional support for the government, and most importantly, widespread stability throughout most Iraqi provinces—it is possible to imagine a form of orchestrated international support to Iraq that could help to consolidate (as this volume's introduction puts it) a "strong and successful" Iraqi state. In this context, the definition of "successful" presumably includes the notion of an Iraqi state that provides at least minimum physical protection to all sectarian groups and to all minorities in the country and provides at least a basic framework of constitutional order through which political and economic relationships between different facets of Iraqi society are organized.

In that scenario, international assistance could be orchestrated by a set of arrangements that draw on relevant experiences, in particular in Palestine and Afghanistan. These could include: a "contact group" that would bring together the major actors; chairmanship and management of that contact group along with a secretariat function to it; and potentially, a senior international in-country representative. The dimensions and options for each of these elements can be briefly elucidated.

Membership of the Contact Group

The active participation of the United States in any follow-on mechanism in Iraq is a given and a necessity. Indeed, the nature of the US relationship to post-transition Iraqi authorities will be heavily determinant of the shape of broader international engagement, for good or ill. And in turn, the US-Iraqi relationship will of course be heavily shaped by the nature of the eventual US drawdown, by Iraqi perceptions of that process, by US domestic political support for sustained engagement, by the international political standing of the United States, and by the nature of US relationships with Iraq's neighbors. So, too, will this relationship be shaped by the unpredictable question of whether post-transition Iraqi authorities seek a continued US military presence in Iraq or at least along its borders—hard to imagine given current political conditions, but far from inconceivable over the medium term.

Although high levels of European (and Japanese, as well as some other Asian countries') financial and political support for a post-transition Iraqi state is a near certainty, the precise shape of that support and the extent of their willingness to engage directly in the reconstruction effort will depend in part on the precise tenor of contemporary European governments and their relationships with the US administration.

The context for broader international involvement will be heavily influenced by the contemporary domestic situation among Iraq's neighbors, particularly Syria and Iran. In Syria, the ultimate impact on the Syrian state and government of the process of implementing Security Council Resolution 1559 cannot yet be determined, but is likely to be significant, both in terms of shaping the internal politics of Damascus and Syria's relationship with Western and other Arab states. This will decide the options for organizing regional support to the Iraqi state.

A positive, or at least a passive, role for Iran is critical to stabilization. Should international tensions over the Iran nuclear question deepen, its willingness to contribute to positive developments in Iraq will likely be diminished. More specifically, the state of relations between the United States and the European Union 3 (EU-3), on the one hand, and Iran on the other (with the rest of the permanent five members of the Security Council perhaps somewhere in between, or perhaps tilting in one direction or the other) will greatly determine the post-transition environment Iraq faces.

A critical factor is whether or not the issue of Iran is handled *within* the Security Council. The issue cuts in two directions. First, if the issue is not handled within the UNSC, this will reflect an inability to maintain unity among the permanent five (P5), and this will both express and contribute to deepening international tensions that will heavily complicate any international engagement in Iraq. Second, conversely, if it is handled within the Security Council, this may result in relations between Iran and the permanent members of the Security Council per se becoming worse than if the issue moves beyond the Council's chambers.

This underlines that the participation of the other permanent members of the Security Council in the reconstruction of Iraq is not a given, but is important and likely. Ensuring a constructive relationship among the permanent members is important to ensuring an effective transition, just as tensions among them were a negative influence in the years leading up to the last war. These relations are likely to be shaped, in the near to medium term, most profoundly by the aforementioned question of Iran. If the case of Iran plays out in the international arena as a repeat of the Iraqi case in 2003, the role of the Security Council and of the United Nations as a whole will be thrown into doubt.

Chairmanship

In both the Palestinian and Afghan cases, we saw that national chairmanship of the "contact group" or donor coordination process was vital. Similarly, there are both substantive and political reasons to insist on Iraqi chairmanship of any set of arrangements to orchestrate international assistance.

The substantive reason emerges from lessons learned from past operations, namely, that only a sovereign government has the real authority to exert control and thus ensure coordination over international bodies. While international actors, when badly behaved, can easily ignore one another and engage in ritualistic, Potemkin coordination, none of them can maintain an in-country presence or operate its programs without national governmental consent. So long as the government has the capacity to coordinate, it is by far and away the most likely to succeed.

But the substantive, or functional, rationale is less important than the political: that only through Iraqi chairmanship can it be ensured that there is domestic ownership of the process, and that international assistance is actually targeted on real Iraqi priorities.

One option is that the United States could cochair or serve as vice chair of the contact group. This approach is suggested by two facts: that Iraqi administrative capacity to take on a real coordination function may be seriously limited, and that the United States will inevitably be by far and away the largest and most important donor, even in a post-drawdown context.

Secretariat Arrangements

Three organizations could reasonably be asked to play the secretariat role to a contact group of this type. First, there is the League of Arab States, which has twice convened meetings of international actors, and which has facilitated local political and second-track contacts in efforts to enhance stability. The participation of the Arab League would give the mechanisms a regional legitimacy it would otherwise lack. Second, there is the United Nations, which has considerable experience in the coordination of postconflict reconstruction and reservoirs of civilian talent on which to draw. And third, there is the World Bank, with its long experience in the coordination and implementation of economic reconstruction.

Past experience suggests that an alternative is to have these organizations serve as a cosecretariat. This would accomplish two things: it would ensure coordination between these entities, and it would ensure that the contact group could draw at any point on the political, financial, and other inputs of all three regional or international bodies.

Senior International Representative

Most speculative is the idea of deploying a senior representative of the contact group as a lead in-country figure, tasked with supporting government-led coordination mechanisms.

The case for doing so stems from the fact that Iraqi government figures are unlikely to have the kind of international relationships and experience that do much to translate formal coordination authority into effective practice. Appointment of a figure with seniority, international respect, and real depth of experience of international mechanisms could add depth to the government's capacity. To be clear, what is being proposed here is something in the mold of the role played by James Wolfensohn as the Quartet's Special Envoy; this is in *contrast* to the role of the High Representative in Bosnia.

In short, the most viable (and most likely) set of arrangements is:

1. An international contact group, building on the participants at the Arab League–hosted Sharm el-Shaikh meeting of 2004–2005, and comprised of the permanent five members of the UN Security Council, the major contributors to the International Reconstruction Fund Facility for Iraq, and other principal donors, northern and regional. Further options include participation by all or some of Iraq's neighbors, either as part of the contact group or as a contact group–plus mechanism; and the nonpermanent members of the UN Security Council from the Arab grouping, if any.

2. Chairmanship of the contact group by the Iraqi state authorities. An option is for the United States to play the role of cochair or vice chair.

3. Secretariat arrangements involving specific roles for the League of Arab States, the World Bank, and the United Nations. An option is a cosecretariat arrangement involving all three organizations.

4. Potentially, appointment of a senior representative of the international contact group. An option is for such a figure to be cross-appointed to the United Nations, as lead in-country coordinator of international assistance.

■ Conclusion: International Appetite for Ambitious Roles in Iraq

Although the external actors and their aims are almost a fixed quantity, the core purpose of international assistance will differ substantially according to Iraqi political developments. In other words, the extent to which Iraqi authority evolves along the lines of a centralized, decentralized, federal, confederal, or other set of relations between central, provincial, and local authorities will substantially determine the nature of international engagement. But even more than this, international engagement will be shaped by the international political climate as well—not just vis-à-vis Iraq.

In the immediate aftermath of the US invasion, there was moderately high international political support for seeing the US-led reconstruction process succeed; no one stood to gain from a wholesale Iraqi collapse. However, the combination of the erosion of the security situation in Iraq, the postwar revelations about the absence of nuclear, biological, or chemical weapons materials in Iraq, and the sharp debate inside the United States about whether the administration or actors within the administration misled the press and Congress in the lead-up to war has seriously eroded international willingness to support the US-led effort in Iraq.

The international political climate vis-à-vis Iraq is likely to be shaped primarily by the relationship between two sets of actors and the United States: regional actors and European governments. Moreover, it will be heavily shaped—under drawdown scenarios—by the nature and degree of US consultations with the major international actors and the United Nations during the withdrawal process. Should the United States withdraw without extensive consultations with international and regional actors, states' willingness to shoulder significant burdens in the post-transition phase will be constrained. Reconstruction would likely founder, to everyone's loss, as a result.

◼ Notes

1. See Simon Chesterman, *You, the People: The United Nations, Transitional Administration, and State-Building* (Oxford: Oxford Univ. Press, 2005).

2. Formally, the "Report of the Independent Panel on Peacekeeping Operations."

3. For a reflection on this critique, and a partial defense, see David Harland, "Legitimacy and Effectiveness in International Administration," *Global Governance* 10, no. 1 (January–March 2004).

4. Author's notes. During the period in question, the author assisted the UN Department of Political Affairs in identifying options for UN engagement in Iraq.

5. UN Resolution A/Res/60/1.

6. For a brief review of Operation Provide Comfort, see www.globalsecurity .org/military/ops/provide_comfort.htm.

7. "Report on Humanitarian Needs in Iraq in the Immediate Post-Crisis Environment by a Mission to the Area Led by the Undersecretary-General for Administration and Management, March 10–17, 1991," S/22366, March 20, 1991; available at www.un.org/Depts/oip/background/reports/s22366.pdf.

8. Office of the Iraq Programme: Oil-for-Food, *About the Programme: Oil-for-Food*, available at www.un.org/Depts/oip/background/index.html, updated November 4, 2003 (accessed May 12, 2006).

9. Ibid.

10. Sarah Zaidi and Mary C. Smith-Fawzi, "Health of Baghdad's Children," *Lancet* 346, no. 8988 (December 2, 1995): 1485.

11. Richard Garfield, "Changes in Mortality in Iraq in the 1990s: Assessing the Impact of Sanctions" (unpublished manuscript, Columbia University, April 9, 1998), 30. Referenced in Frances Stewart and Jo Boyden, "Harnessing Globalisation for Children: A Report to UNICEF"; available at www.unicef-icdc.org/research/ESP/ globalization/chapter14.pdf.

12. David Cortright, "Are Sanctions Just? The Problematic Case of Iraq," *Journal of International Affairs* 52, no. 2 (spring 1999), www.fourthfreedom. org/Applications/cms.php?page_id=35.

13. "Report on the Management of the Oil-for-Food Programme," issued by the Independent Inquiry Committee into the United Nations Oil-for-Food Programme on September 7, 2005; available at www.iic-offp.org/documents.htm.

14. UN Security Council Resolution 1546; available at daccessdds.un.org/doc/ UNDOC/GEN/N04/381/16.

15. Rex Brynen, *A Very Political Economy: Peacebuilding and Foreign Aid in the West Bank and Gaza* (Washington, DC: USIP Press, 2000).

16. Jon Pedersen and Rick Hooper, eds., *Developing Palestinian Society: Socio-Economic Trends and Their Implications for Development Strategies* (Oslo: FAFO, 1998).

17. A theme repeated in several similar processes, as recounted in Teresa Whitfield's pathbreaking analysis of these mechanisms *Friends Indeed: The Role of "Friends" Groups* (Washington, DC: US Institute for Peace Press, 2006).

18. Including Elizabeth Cousens and David Harland, "Post-Dayton Bosnia and Herzegovina," in *Twenty-First Century Peace Operations*, ed. William Durch (Washington, DC: US Institute for Peace Press, forthcoming).

19. Chesterman, *You, the People*.

20. Bruce Jones, "Conclusion: Aid, Peace and Justice in a Re-Ordered World," in *Nation-Building Unraveled? Aid, Peace, and Justice in Afghanistan*, ed. Antonio Donini, Norah Niland, and Karen Wermester (London: Kumarian Press, 2004).

PART 3

Conclusion

19

Looking Ahead: Preventing a New Generation of Conflict

Markus E. Bouillon, Ben Rowswell, and David M. Malone

THE CENTRAL PREMISE of this volume is that state fragility lies at the heart of Iraq's instability. Iraq was a fragile state before Saddam Hussein rose to power, passing from one military junta to another for decades. Saddam turned the state into a powerful weapon, but his highly personalized rule undermined its institutions and left little more than a shell. When external military intervention shattered that shell in 2003, the country collapsed into chaos. As Iraq's former defense minister Ali Allawi wrote in early 2007, the Iraqi state

> had held for nearly one-hundred years by a mixture of foreign occupation, outside meddling, brutal dictatorships and minority rule. At the same time, it signally failed in providing a permanent sense of legitimacy to its power, engaged its citizens in their governance, or provided a modicum of well-being and a decent standard of existence for its people.[1]

Whether Iraq remains a fragile state or is now a failed state, as the journal *Foreign Policy* has suggested,[2] this volume has argued that the consequences of either fragility or failure are too grave for the international community to sit back and wring its hands in despair. Clear, dispassionate analysis suggests measures that can be taken to influence the situation: if state fragility—or failure—is the problem, then state building provides the answer. Such an undertaking will, of course, be an extraordinarily difficult and complex task, with challenges at the domestic, regional, and international levels. It is to those challenges that we turn in this concluding chapter.

■ The Domestic Foundations of State Building

Rebuilding Iraq will be, first and foremost, a critical test for Iraqis themselves. It will require imagining and then bringing into being a common future for the twenty-four million people living within Iraq's current borders, in whichever arrangement can achieve the widest endorsement by all Iraqi communities. Against the background of the proliferation of armed militias, increasing corruption, enduring socioeconomic crisis, and growing sectarian strife that threatens to spiral out of control, Iraqis urgently need to begin laying the foundations for lasting peaceful coexistence through national dialogue and consensus building.

In his chapter in this volume, Nicholas Haysom identifies a core objective for the state-building process, arguing that "an inclusive social contract agreed across the fault lines that divide Iraq is a necessary condition for a long-term peace." His argument is of critical importance to the broader peacebuilding effort in Iraq:

> There are many ways of imagining the constitutional formulations and institutions that could secure these conditions. However, for any of the possible formulations to be successful it must meet one difficult but necessary condition: the three main Iraqi communities must be willing to accept it. Whatever degree of autonomy the constitution allows for regions, and for Kurdistan in particular, whatever the form of state, the critical question is how to facilitate the necessary consensus, how to agree on formulations that the different Iraqi groups can live with, whatever their aspirations may be.

Haysom argues for an inclusive—though not necessarily integrationist—social contract among Iraqis, with four constitutive elements: first, "a substantial measure of autonomy for Kurdistan (that is, without a significant deviation from current arrangements)"; second, "a decentralized or federal arrangement for the rest of Iraq, provided there is the equitable sharing of natural resources"; third, "the development of rule of law and parliamentary institutions, which guarantee constitutional promises, particularly with respect to the human rights provisions contained in the constitution"; and finally, "an appropriate framework for subordinating the military and militias to civilian control and authority and the establishment of institutions to entrench accountability."

Larry Diamond has echoed the call for an inclusive social contract elsewhere:

> The overriding initial task must be to fashion a political bargain in which all major Iraqi groups feel they have a stake in the country's political future. In the months and years ahead, the answer to the question of whether Iraq can become a democracy will depend, most of all, on Iraqi political leaders, and the decisions they make to widen the political arena or not, to share power and resources or not, to build a system of mutual security or, instead, try to dominate and even crush their opponents.[3]

A national dialogue or an Afghan-style *loya jirga* with political, clerical, and tribal leaders may be a necessary mechanism and first step toward building an inclusive polity.[4]

In this volume, Toby Dodge, Phebe Marr, Roel Meijer, Juan Cole, and others have argued that all Iraqi communities have a stake in the successful consolidation of an Iraqi state—as long as it manages to satisfy their diverse aspirations. Indeed, the violence in Iraq, evolving from a broad-based insurgency against a military occupation into sectarian conflict, has persistently been a fight for control of the state itself, not over its dismantlement.

The lines of conflict between Sunnis and Shia, Arabs and Kurds, are closely tied to the nature, scope, and role of the state in Iraq. As a result, conflict can be seen not necessarily as an inevitable expression of irreconcilable sectarian and communitarian interests, but as a struggle to define the parameters of the state. The political struggle among Arab Iraqis, in particular, is better described in terms of competition for control of the Iraqi state than as a conflict between two distinct regions that can only be resolved by separating them.

As Dodge argues in this volume, the sustainability of the state is conditioned by the extent to which it is considered legitimate in the eyes of its citizens. In consequence, the peacebuilding effort must first and foremost concentrate on building the institutions and parameters of a state that is acceptable to all Iraqis. As Dodge writes, "the growth of stable state institutions, with a meaningful presence in people's lives, forms the framework within which the longer-term goal of successful state building, the reconstruction of an Iraqi nation, can be achieved."

Much depends on Iraqi political leaders. In this context, the chapter by Phebe Marr in this volume provides invaluable insight into the current mindset of those leaders. Dozens of interviews with leaders of all communities lead her to conclude that "Iraq is currently undergoing two revolutions." The first revolution is a "fundamental change in domestic political leadership and the direction it is taking the country." The second revolution is a radical decentralization of power from Baghdad to the regions.

In view of these two revolutions, the new Iraqi political leaders have to work to create a "new vision around which most Iraqis can willingly coalesce and cooperate," grounded in and based on a single Iraqi state and a common Iraqi identity. The present process of erosion of a unified Iraqi identity can only be reversed if new or revitalized institutions regain the trust of ordinary Iraqi citizens, at this stage a vast and uncertain project. Violence and conflict caused by the erosion of the state, its authority and its institutions, have led Iraqis to seek refuge in communitarian, sectarian, tribal, and other parochial identities and interests. And this process will only be reversed if Iraqi political leaders rise above the fold and begin building the foundations for a common polity responding to all communities' basic interests.

Abdel Salam Sidahmed's analysis in this volume explores elements that could be used in the reinforcement of a unified—and unifying—Iraqi identity and that could form the backdrop to a national dialogue. Careful to point out that both Islamism and Iraqi nationalism have only limited potential and indeed are associated with many pitfalls, Sidahmed shows that the two could nevertheless serve as important building blocks for a united Iraq. In order to circumvent some of the obstacles, Sidahmed advocates "a vision of Islam devoid of sectarianism and an Iraqi identity based on national consensus rather than a narrative of domestic oppression and external antagonism." Such a vision would need time to evolve. Should continued military stalemate convince the rival communities that there is no realistic alternative to an eventual accommodation, and should their leaders demonstrate sufficient leadership, such a broad vision could help forge an inclusive and accommodating political system over time.

■ Key Challenges: Security and the Economy

The foundations of a unified Iraqi state, of which a new political leadership will need to be the public face, must be based on a number of elements, as the contributions in this volume make clear. Marr identifies the two most fundamental ingredients: security and economic development, which, as she writes, are "the missing links" whose return will "ease, if not solve, the identity problem" currently beleaguering Iraq. This sentiment has been mirrored in other studies reflecting on how best to prevent another generation of conflict.[5]

Other chapters in this volume confirm these foundations for a successful peacebuilding strategy for Iraq. Security challenges will involve more than security sector reform, along with the reconstruction and training of the Iraqi army and the police. Most centrally, the struggle to confront, disarm, and bring the myriad armed groups and militias in Iraq under the control of the government is a key challenge. As *New York Times* correspondent Dexter Filkins wrote in late May 2006,

> the outcome of the struggle has far-reaching implications for Iraq's future, as Iraqi and American officials try to curb the abuses that threaten to push the country closer to a sectarian war without impeding the government's ability to fight the Sunni-led guerilla insurgency.[6]

In this volume, the chapters by Roel Meijer and Juan Cole paint a clear picture of the difficulties associated with the task, but also provide some avenues for further exploration.

Juan Cole's chapter outlines the danger to Iraq of the growing power of armed militias. While ethnic and sectarian paramilitaries can "provide local security at a time of guerrilla war and criminality on a vast scale," they also "form death squads and engage in their own excesses." Most fundamentally, militias "deny the new state its monopoly on the use of force, a key definition of state success." Building on this argument, it emerges clearly that governmental measures to tame the myriad militias will be a key ingredient to building a successful and sustainable state in Iraq. At the same time, as Cole also points out, the reliance of Shia political leaders on paramilitaries, as well as the strength of the Kurdish community derived from the existence and control of the *peshmerga* in the areas of the Kurdish Regional Government, will continue to make it difficult to confront the militias. Doing so, however, is not only a central requirement for the establishment of an exclusive and unified sovereign authority for all Iraqis; it will also be a precondition for an integration of the alienated Sunni community, as Roel Meijer's chapter illuminates.

The challenge has been further exacerbated by the growing infiltration of the army and the police by individuals and units loyal to militia forces. Split loyalties within national forces can fracture unity of command at key junctures and represents one of the most worrying trends (along with basic lack of professionalism, due to inadequate training) undermining these critical national-security institutions.

A positive aspect is that among at least parts of the Sunni community there has been a significant shift in favor of political participation, as Roel Meijer's chapter demonstrates. However, such participation will only find support among the wider Sunni community if the political process is inclusive and addresses the fundamental fear prevailing amongst Iraqi Sunnis: that of exclusion, revenge, and "reverse oppression." If the political process can provide a real stake for Sunnis, security will likely be improved, as groups engaged in the insurgency will increasingly be drawn into participation in the process of shaping a new Iraqi polity.

Resources are also crucial, as security must be underpinned by economic recovery and development. The success of an inclusive political process in Iraq will depend critically on an improvement of living conditions and a fair sharing of the country's natural resources. In contrast to most other cases of state failure or postconflict state building, Iraq does have the good fortune of possessing sizable oil reserves. This wealth could eventually contribute to the improvement in conditions necessary to inspire trust in the new Iraqi state among all its citizens. Economic development is not only impeded by ongoing sectarian strife and the insurgency but also by the effects of decades-long mismanagement and politicization, as well as a sanctions regime that brought the economy to its knees during the 1990s.

Jon Pedersen's chapter in this volume shows that in order "to create a viable economy and social structure major restructuring is needed, a restructuring that is likely to generate new conflicts." Such change is both necessary and potentially risky for efforts to construct an inclusive political arena. The economy will be central to the success of any effort to reconstruct coherent state structures and satisfy the basic demands of the population. As such, Iraqi political leaders will have to shoulder the burden of seeking to overcome the legacies of the devastating Iran-Iraq War, domestic unrest and repression, and international sanctions.

In this context, the formulae devised to share the revenues from Iraq's natural resources will become either a cornerstone or a stumbling block for a collective future of the Iraqi people. The constitution adopted by Iraqis in October 2005 has reserved most powers related to the allocation and management of natural resources to the regions, according them primacy over the federal government.

The federal government also lacks an independent power to tax. Since every other federation in the world provides the central government with this power, it is difficult to imagine how the federal government in Baghdad will be able to develop meaningful capacity without it. Many students of Iraq question whether the largely decentralized, loosely federal arrangements of the 2005 constitution can truly provide the basis for an inclusive social, economic, and political system. Further doubts were fueled by the early escalation of a dispute between the Kurdish Regional Government and Baghdad in September 2006, culminating in a public invocation by Kurdish prime minister Nechirvan Barzani of the threat of secession from Iraq.[7]

■ Forging a New Social Contract: Building on the Constitutional Framework

The social contract that Iraqis need should not be limited to the constitution, but it does need to begin there. As the foremost expression of the relationship between individual citizens and between communities, the constitution is the linchpin of the political order. The 2005 constitution, adopted in spite of its overwhelming rejection by Sunni Arabs, does not yet enjoy the credibility and legitimacy it requires if it is to serve as the bedrock of a new political order. Like many constitutions, however, Iraq's is not set in stone. David Cameron's chapter in this volume describes the 2005 constitution as "a gigantic work site," requiring much work to be done to flesh out the Iraqi federation that was envisaged to come into being.

To establish a framework in which all Iraqis find themselves adequately reflected, the most fundamental document setting out a new political order for Iraq must seek to reconcile the concerns of all communities. In doing so, the constitution would truly represent, in principle, spirit, and on paper, the compromise that would make coexistence amongst Iraq's diverse communities a lasting and sustainable possibility.

For all the concern about the marginalization of Sunni Arabs in the new constitutional order, it was in fact the question of Kurdistan that elicited the most heated debate in the May 2006 conference that generated this volume. Viciously oppressed by Saddam Hussein for much of his reign, the Kurds have had every reason to yearn for autonomy. Their governorates are the best administered in the country. Kurdish reluctance to settle for less than they have and to renounce claims to more is perfectly understandable. Many Kurds have a national project, that of creating a state of their own in northern Iraq. While this project is risky in terms of its regional implications, it is not difficult to understand why it commands a high degree of support within the Kurdish community.

The strength of support for secession in Kurdish public opinion demonstrates that this outcome is a real possibility. The absence of Sunni engagement and Shia compromise could create momentum for the establishment of an independent Kurdish state. Others have made a strong case for greater Kurdish autonomy or eventual statehood cogently and rationally.[8]

Regardless of one's views for or against, the question will not go away, and threatens to generate new conflict if not managed carefully. Even if secession did not threaten to trigger a new Kurdish-Arab front in an Iraqi civil war, it might provoke further atomization of the original state, provoking new violence as overlapping populations seek to create—or retreat to—coherent territories where their community will rule unchallenged. The prospects for further violence are terrifying should an attempt emerge to partition formally the Kurdish, Shia, and Sunni inhabitants of Baghdad and much of Iraq's central region. If the movement for a separate Kurdish state gains momentum, the more useful question for Iraq's political leaders and constitutional negotiators might be not so much whether Iraq should remain united, but what sort of relationship the various political communities of present-day Iraq should have with one another in the future.

One of the advantages of the 2005 constitution is that it provides a defensible answer to that question, one which for the time being has kept Kurdistan within Iraq. In his chapter in this volume, John McGarry identifies the basis of the constitution as democratic pluralism, or liberal consociationalism. He holds this form of decentralization up as a source of success since it satisfies at the very least the basic aspirations of Iraqi Kurds, while also enjoying the support of the Shia community. This defense of the original draft of the constitution is an important one, highlighting as it does the concerns of the Kurdish community and pointing, rightly so, to the fact that the constitution was "endorsed by 78 out of every 100 Iraqi voters on a very high turnout." In this light, Brendan O'Leary argues in his chapter in this volume that a major recalibration to accommodate Sunni Arabs might be both unfair and unfeasible.

Cameron's chapter provides a different assessment of Iraq's constitution. He argues that the level of decentralization manifest in the 2005 constitution could set in motion centrifugal pressures that would break Iraq apart. To counter these, he proposes a number of useful recommendations to create a more durable political framework. These include efforts to delay the creation of regions, while giving the central government time to gather political and financial strength. Supported by a cadre of national politicians, Iraq's federal authorities could still exploit whatever areas of exclusive jurisdiction they may retain, entrenching the central government's revenue-raising capacity. They could thus lay the basis for an ultimately effective and sustainable unified federal government. Within ten years, this could produce a balanced and stable federation, in which the central government would be "reasonably well-equipped with the power and resources to manage Iraq's multiple diversities and to hold the country together," and in which "conflict is dispersed and institutionalized within a complex pattern of intergovernmental relations."[9]

Forging the social contract will, however, require efforts well beyond the constitutional realm. With political leadership and the determination to turn lofty pronouncements of a commitment to the maintenance of a unified Iraqi polity into a reality in the streets of Iraq, a revision of the Iraqi constitution to better reflect the concerns of the alienated Sunni Arab community will be an important step toward the establishment of lasting and sustainable peace in the country. This is easier said than done; Iraq's transitional government proved a deep disappointment and there is no guarantee that Prime Minister al-Maliki's national reconciliation program will fare better. A number of parties can be counted upon to combat it at every step.

Events may also continue to conspire to poison efforts at national reconciliation. There will be many cases in which the commitment of Iraq's communities to find compromises and creative solutions to their diverging aspirations will be tested. One such case is that of Kirkuk, which Joost Hiltermann explores in detail in this volume. Kirkuk is in many ways a microcosm of the larger challenges Iraq confronts in the process of reestablishing a political framework. A predominantly, but not exclusively, Kurdish city, Kirkuk is claimed by the Kurds, who would like to see it become the capital of their region. This assertion of Kurdish rights is contested by the city's Arabs, Turkomans, and Christians. Under the 2005 constitution, the city's status has to be determined by December 2007 at the latest. This will either force compromise and accommodation or accelerate and exacerbate the process of a forced separation of Iraq's communities.

As Hiltermann's contribution makes clear, Kirkuk could conversely provide a test case for building an inclusive and pacified Iraq. Hiltermann's proposal for the resolution of the Kirkuk question suggests parameters that might be useful for consideration of a broader peacebuilding strategy for Iraq: a solution that might be "preferred by no one but [that] may address the core concerns of all without overstepping existential red lines . . . a solution in other words that perhaps all could accept once they individually reach the understanding that they cannot achieve their maximalist demands."

■ Regional Contributions to State Building

Four years after the US-led invasion of Iraq, the Middle East is a fundamentally different region than it was in 2003. In the first few years of the new millennium, the Middle East has undergone upheavals and shifts on a scale unseen since the end of the mandate period in the region. The erstwhile defining crucible of international tension, the Arab-Israeli conflict, has undergone major changes and has increasingly been complemented by the emergence of additional yet separate epicenters of instability and conflict in the broader region. With conflict, or potential conflict, surfacing in each of Iraq, Iran, the Israeli-Palestinian arena, Lebanon, and, last but not least, *within* a number of key Arab regimes such as Egypt, Jordan, or Saudi Arabia, the Middle East is perhaps more fragile and more dangerous than ever before.

The new fragility flows to a degree from Iraq, but is also manifest within it. With tension, both within Iraq and in the wider region, also increasingly focusing on blocs—radicals and moderates, Sunnis and Shiites, Arabs and "Persians," as some would describe the dichotomies—it is becoming increasingly clear that domestic and regional stabilization depend on and mutually reinforce each other. As a result, Iraq's stabilization should be considered a major interest of all in the region. In addition, success or failure in Iraq will influence how external actors are interpreted within the region and consequently will contribute to determining how much further external engagement is likely to prove possible and rewarding. As Toby Dodge has written elsewhere:

> If the present domestic situation does not stabilize, then violence and political unrest can be expected to spread across Iraq's long and porous borders. A violently unstable Iraq, bridging the *mashreq,* the most populous area of the Middle East and the oil-rich Gulf, would further weaken the fragile stability of surrounding states. Iraq's role as a magnet for radical Islamists eager to fight US troops on Middle Eastern soil would only increase. In addition, there is a strong possibility that neighboring states will be drawn into [the] country, competing for influence and using proxies to further their own interests.[10]

In consequence, persistent failure in Iraq will have implications for governments throughout the region, will influence the regional policies of individual players and overhang inter-Arab as well as Arab-Iranian ties, and will shape relations between the international community and the Middle East.

In his chapter, postconflict reconstruction expert James Dobbins argues that the primary sources of outside support for rebuilding Iraq must henceforth come from within the region. He goes further to argue that securing the active participation of Iraq's neighbors must now become the top priority for the United States. He adds that the Arab League and the Organization of the Islamic Conference should play important roles in supporting the state-building process in Iraq alongside the United Nations, the European Union, NATO, and others.

Regional players are important for two reasons. Many of Iraq's neighbors, in particular bordering Arab states, have an inherent interest in seeing the stabilization effort succeed. Others, such as Turkey and Iran, have to be integrated proactively and positively into the broader international engagement, lest they jeopardize this effort. Jon Alterman's chapter on Iraq's Arab neighbors states: "As terrifying a prospect as Saddam Hussein was to many of them, the prospect of growing chaos in Iraq is more terrifying still." The lessons of peacebuilding efforts elsewhere, most notably in Afghanistan and the Balkans, also show that regional players are critical to the success of the international engagement.

Alterman's contribution shows that there are many things that Arab states could do collectively to help improve conditions. Iraq's Arab neighbors could undertake "symbolic gestures that could help reassure those who feel left out of the current political process that they have not been abandoned," most notably the Sunni population of Iraq. Arab League engagement for this purpose should be complemented by efforts to stem the tide of transnational support for the insurgency. In the longer term, Iraq's wealthy Arab neighbors, in particular Saudi Arabia and Kuwait, will be called upon to forgive Iraqi debt. And finally, as he writes, the engagement of the Arab states bordering Iraq will be critical in creating a contact group integrating others into the broader international effort in support of Iraq.

The authors in this volume argue consistently that inclusion and constructive engagement will be important to attain success. This also goes for Turkey, which has extended its economic engagement in recent years, particularly in Iraq's Kurdistan region. As Robert Olson pointed out in a presentation to the Ottawa conference, this evolution in Turkey's position has taken place against the background of Turkey's possible accession to the European Union and its integration into broader efforts to build regional alliances, such as the Broader Middle East and North Africa Initiative (BMENAI).[11]

Iran has thus far benefited most from the situation prevailing in Iraq and will be critical to efforts to bring lasting stability to the Gulf region and the new Iraqi polity. The Islamic Republic has also increasingly become the focus of targeted criticism for playing a particularly unhelpful role in Iraq. Yet, as its approach to Afghanistan since 2001 suggests, it may see stability in neighboring countries as a preferable outcome to the maximization of its own influence within the state involved. Iran may also have more than one view on the outcome it would prefer to Iraq's current travails. Its regional interests extend far beyond Iraq, radiating through Central Asia, the Caucasus, and, of course, the Gulf where it copes with many ancient rivalries. A degree of stability and mutual accommodation exists in its relationships with Pakistan and Turkey. Given the tense situation to which its nuclear energy program and its alleged aspirations in the region have given rise with the great powers and with some in the region, the temptation may exist in Tehran to view Iraq as a useful pawn in that game. However, Tehran may equally prefer to hold Iraq in reserve for now: destabilization might not gain it the yields it may be seeking, and constructive engagement, if afforded the possibility, may well prove beneficial to Iranian interests. In sum, a simplistic view of Iran's strategies in Iraq is unhelpful: it backs a number of horses in Iraq, who favor a variety of outcomes.

■ International Support for Iraqi State Building

Engaging regional actors is but one challenge in building broader international support for rebuilding Iraq. The main extraregional actor in Iraq since 2003 has been the one country that forced a change of regime on Iraq: the United States. The United States' controversial role in Iraq polarized the international community, with the result that it has had little effective support from other countries in its efforts to foster a new political order there. What allies it had in the 2003 coalition have been dropping off since then. Spain and Ukraine withdrew their troops in 2005; both Japan and Italy followed in 2006. While the United Kingdom remains steadfast in its commitment to the US-led effort, Washington is clearly feeling the burden of its increasing isolation in Iraq, as John Kornblum has written:

> All burdens have fallen on the Americans, but our credibility is too tarnished to handle them. Neither world public opinion nor American political dynamics will allow us to stay there long enough to stabilize Iraqi society, even if we could. No one country has either the resources or the credibility to do the job alone. We need direct and long-term engagement by other major countries, including a credible multilateral military force, and we need it fast.[12]

The increasing loneliness of the United States in Iraq is more than a problem for the United States, however. It deprives Iraq of crucial international support as it goes through an extremely difficult period in its reconstruction phase, just as a broad civil war threatens to engulf any progress made to date. Even if Iraqis bear the primary responsibility of rebuilding their state, they cannot do so without international assistance: they need all the help they can get.

There are three major roles the international community can play in helping to stabilize Iraq. These reflect the three major tasks Iraqis must address in rebuilding their state: political support to help Iraqis forge a common identity and an inclusive social contract; security forces to help the Iraqi state reassert its monopoly on violence; and international assistance to reform the Iraqi economy.

The prospects for enhanced international efforts for two of these three roles look remote indeed. The United States is likely to remain virtually alone in assisting Iraqi security forces to reestablish law and order until Iraqis can do so for themselves. In this volume, Nora Bensahel's chapter outlines both the myriad tasks international security forces already oversee and the challenges they confront in the future. She argues that the role of international security forces will increasingly not only be dictated by the demands of a difficult security situation but also by the available supply of troops, and she concludes that that supply will continue to diminish.

At a time when the Iraqi state-building enterprise will continue to depend on international support in the realm of security, the calls for a drawdown and withdrawal of US troops from Iraq will only grow and are likely to be answered sooner rather than later. Bensahel concludes that the withdrawal of international troops below the minimum number necessary to fulfill the vital missions they now help carry out "would put the future of Iraq's national government at great risk and would increase the centrifugal forces that threaten to tear the country apart."[13]

Constraints on the availability of additional international security forces for Iraq are, of course, not simply a question of numbers. The robust counterinsurgency mandate of the US-led Multinational Force–Iraq (MNF-I) raises concerns in some quarters that these forces may actually undermine security in Iraq as well as reinforce it. Incidents such as the killing of civilians at Haditha in November 2005 only reinforce such concerns. In his chapter in this volume, Pierre Gassmann argues that if the mandate of international security forces in Iraq were reoriented around the protection of civilians, it would enjoy broader international legitimacy.

At the same time, the scale of the crisis in Iraq, as of early 2007, also makes clear that it cannot simply now be dumped into the lap of the United Nations, as a recent report underscores.[14] Resort to the UN needs to be more than an "exit strategy." The UN could convey a broader degree of international legitimacy if it provided an umbrella under which neighboring countries and other interested parties could be pulled together, and a high-level team offering the Secretary-General's "good offices" might assist in launching a productive discussion. And the UN's political instruments and skills may also be useful for a number of other contingencies ahead. But Iraq has clearly moved beyond the UN's capacity to help through such instruments as peacekeeping, under whichever mandate.

Our sense is that there would be little appetite among noncoalition member states of the UN to volunteer for a peacekeeping or "protection" force, just as there was little appetite to volunteer for a force the Security Council authorized in 2004 to protect UN personnel in Iraq under the umbrella of the coalition.[15] However, more international civilian personnel, helping to launch a constructive dialogue and fulfilling a mediating function, would doubtless help build momentum for greater confidence that normalcy might one day return to the country.

Prospects are also dim for stronger international efforts in the realm of donor assistance. Iraq cannot hope for significant bilateral assistance beyond, perhaps, that of the coalition countries and some of its Gulf Arab neighbors. Iraq's oil wealth and the poor returns on assistance provided since 2003 make it an unattractive target for massive financial aid from the perspective of the conventional Western donor group, which already suffers aid fatigue with respect to Iraq, as Michael Bell points out in his chapter.

Bell outlines some of the shortcomings of donor assistance to date and makes clear that the sole alternative to a "conscious shared effort by Iraqis and the international community to ensure meaningful change" would be "writing off the transformation exercise." Given this, the International Reconstruction Fund Facility for Iraq (IRFFI), the shared UN and World Bank mechanism for reconstruction assistance, will need to be strengthened. Coordination will have to be enhanced, transparency and accountability improved. International engagement will have to enable Iraqi leaders to work toward early results, while emphasizing and prioritizing in parallel the development of institutional capacity, infrastructure, and long-term economic growth. It is the latter that donors ultimately will be looking for, and it is by the latter that success will be measured.

Since the international community is unlikely to take up a more active role in reestablishing security or increased donor assistance, international engagement should focus on the task of enhancing its political support for Iraq. This is no small task. Efforts to forge a broad and inclusive social contract are central to rebuilding the Iraqi state and thus restoring stability. This undertaking cannot succeed if the international community acts at cross-purposes, with outside countries supporting the claims of one community or another at the expense of the state-building effort. It may even require a concerted push from the international community.

The Iraq Compact proposed by the al-Maliki government in June 2006 could prove a useful basis for forging new consensus across Iraq's divergent communities. Alternatively, it could prove to be a half-hearted attempt by Iraqi leaders founded on the unlikely hope that the US-led coalition will continue to retain major responsibility for both the security and the finances of post-Baath Iraq. Only coordinated and coherent communication from international actors inside and outside the coalition can convince the Iraqi political class that it has no real alternative but to work together to pull the country out of its downward spiral.

■ Coordinating Regional and International Efforts

In the absence of additional security forces or donor assistance, the most significant contribution the international community can make would be unified political support for domestic efforts to forge a broad and inclusive political order. Moving from the US-led coalition to a more broadly based international engagement will require a degree of diplomatic engineering. A credible outreach effort yielding genuine international engagement would facilitate gradual US military withdrawal, while building greater international legitimacy into the equation—for Iraq, in the region, and internationally. But, as the UN's former Special Envoy in Iraq, Lakhdar Brahimi, made clear in remarks during the Ottawa conference, this simply will not happen as long as Washington seeks to determine what roles international actors should play and how. Active engagement with Iraq will only become attractive to noncoalition countries and multilateral organizations if they can chart their own path freely, alongside Iraqis and the coalition.

There is little sign yet that the United States is prepared to promote such an overtly freewheeling process. The publication in December 2006 of the Iraq Study Group, led by former secretary of state James A. Baker and former congressman Lee H. Hamilton, revealed considerable interest in US political circles outside the administration to draw regional (perhaps even Syria and Iran) and allied partners into a more equal dialogue on Iraq's future.[16] Nevertheless, President Bush's decision the following month to "surge" military efforts with an additional 20,000 troops confirmed that the United States continues to prefer to set its own strategy for Iraq, even if this requires continued reliance on its own resources.[17]

Who would pick up the leadership role for the international community in Iraq should the United States agree to share real decisionmaking? Michael Bell argues that the United Nations should come to play a much more prominent role than it currently does in this effort. Given the expertise of UN staff, the ability and experience of the UN with coordinating broad international reconstruction efforts, the international organization's role should be significantly strengthened with a view to "economic, social, civil, and institutional reconstruction."

In many respects, its encounter with Iraq has been traumatic for the United Nations, culminating in the bombing of its headquarters in Baghdad in August 2003, which claimed twenty-two lives.[18] Further, since the Security Council's painful deadlock over Iraq in March 2003, the divisions in the Council have not yet fully healed. Of course, Iraq has shown the limits of US power—and by extension, the power of the UN Security Council.

Thus, new approaches may yet emerge, and efforts by the five permanent members to work together may yet reassert themselves, of which there was some actual evidence on North Korea in October 2006 and Iran toward the end of the year. This might eventually, again, extend to Iraq itself. However, the Council's brief attention span and tendency to improvise in response to immediate stimuli—its tendency, in the words of the former UN undersecretary-general for political affairs Sir Kieran Prendergast, to "expediency"— do not inspire confidence.[19]

As Bruce Jones notes in his chapter, the legacy of the Security Council in Iraq is a mixed one. The costs borne in Iraq of a sanctions regime decreed in New York have doubtless contributed to nascent militancy in Iraq. Many Iraqis—whether Sunni or Shia—felt disempowered, disenfranchised, and disillusioned by the Security Council's strategy in the 1990s. It is not clear that the UN holds out much prospect of serving as a circuit breaker in Iraq's violence. That said, it has an excellent track record as an umbrella for a wide variety of diplomatic activities, not least Bonn Conference–type activities, as argued above.

The United Nations can also continue to provide the legal framework for the evolving international assistance to Iraq. While the initial invasion and occupation were opposed by many, the Security Council has since endorsed the presence of coalition troops in Iraq.[20] In the months ahead, thought might be given to a restructuring of the presence of international security forces on the principle of a responsibility to protect Iraqi civilians or, more realistically, to an empowered "good offices" role played by the Secretary-General and his staff. At the same time, the UN should be wary of being instrumentalized to the extent that it often was in the years 2004–2005 when it was assigned a place that stood in sharp variance with the Security Council's repeated endorsement of its "vital role" in Iraq.[21]

A growing international, nonmilitary presence would also help reassure Iraqis that they have not been written off by the United Nations and other world bodies, in reprisal, so to speak, for the earlier collective failure of international and regional actors to take meaningful steps to support Iraqi civilians and improve governance in their country. Models and precedents to guide the outlook of multilateral mechanisms for coordination and engagement abound. Jones's chapter in this volume advances lessons that can be learned from them, as well as some of their basic premises, though he also emphasizes that the UN's role will remain limited. The UN's credibility *within* Iraq will continue to be burdened heavily by the experience of the past generation of conflict and of collective international failure vis-à-vis Iraq and the Iraqi people. And yet, as Jones equally underscores, if international engagement, endorsed by the United Nations and involving a significant UN presence on the ground, builds on Iraqi ownership and leadership in the effort to construct an inclusive political arena and a sustainable economy and society, then the collaboration between Iraqi leaders and the international community may yet meet with success.

Jones suggests that an international contact group involving members of the Arab League and other regional players, the permanent five members of the Security Council, as well as major contributors to the IRFFI and other principal donors, might offer a suitable forum to underpin an enhanced international engagement. Such a contact group would be chaired, or cochaired, by Iraqi leaders, with a cosecretariat supporting and coordinating international assistance specifically involving the Arab League, the World Bank, and the United Nations. A meeting on the model of the Bonn Conference on Afghanistan of 2001 might provide a useful starting point for a more meaningful UN engagement with Iraq in the years ahead. Such a meeting would draw in not only major domestic stakeholders but also key international actors in a place and under a form of conference management that in the case of the Bonn process demonstrated that various perspectives could be accommodated in a workable consensus.

■ **The Path Forward for Iraq**

As we write, insurgency and increasing sectarian strife torment central Iraq and the Iraqi government. There is no end in sight to this violence yet. But the news is not all bad. Wide swathes of Iraq have reconnected with a degree of normalcy. Iraq's north seems, for now, sheltered from depredations by an irredentist central government. Mutual accommodation among Iraq's factious communities remains a possibility, even if it is unclear whether these will achieve it, given that they cannot be forced from the outside, and whether they will be able—and willing—to maintain it once coalition troops depart.

The levels of violence in Iraq since the 2003 invasion, intended to turn Iraq into a democratic state that could serve as a model to the region, have made a mockery of this objective. Yet this may remain a short-term impression. After all, the experts have often been wrong about what to expect next in Iraq. If Iraqis can step back from the abyss and if their international partners can examine a dire situation without succumbing to despair, then all can join hands to devise a path out of the conflict. Such cooperation among Iraqis and their international friends could point the way toward saving Iraq, the region, and the world from a new generation of devastating conflict.

■ **Notes**

1. Ali Allawi, "For the First Time, a Real Blueprint for Peace in Iraq," *The Independent*, January 5, 2007.

2. The 2006 "Failed States Index," produced by the Carnegie Endowment's journal *Foreign Policy*, ranked Iraq fourth-highest among failed states in the world, trailing only Sudan, the Democratic Republic of Congo, and Côte d'Ivoire. See Foreign Policy and the Fund for Peace, "The Failed States Index," *Foreign Policy* (May/June 2006).

3. Larry Diamond, *Squandered Victory: The American Occupation and the Bungled Effort to Bring Democracy to Iraq* (New York: Times Books, 2005), 331–335.

4. In fairness to the coalition, a number of such consultations, on constitutional and other matters, did occur after April 2003 under the watch of the Coalition Provisional Authority, but the weight of the United States and its instinct to guide outcomes undermined the usefulness (and perhaps, in Iraqi eyes, the legitimacy) of these processes.

5. See, for example, Kenneth M. Pollack and the Iraq Policy Working Group of the Saban Center for Middle East Policy at the Brookings Institution, "Switch in Time: A New Strategy for America in Iraq," *Saban Center Analysis* (Saban Center for Middle East Policy at the Brookings Institution) no. 7 (February 15, 2006).

6. Dexter Filkins, "Armed Groups Propel Iraq Toward Chaos," *New York Times,* 24 May 2006.

7. In a September 27 press statement, Barzani accused the Iraqi government of sabotaging foreign investment in the oil sector in the Kurdish region. He went on to say that "the people of Kurdistan chose to be in a voluntary union with Iraq on the basis of the constitution. If Baghdad ministers refuse to abide by that constitution, the people of Kurdish reserve the right to reconsider our choice." See "Statement by Prime Minister Nechirvan Barzani on Non-implementation of the Iraqi Consititution," press release of the Kurdish Regional Government at www.krg.org.

8. See Peter W. Galbraith, *The End of Iraq: How American Incompetence Created a War Without End* (New York: Simon & Schuster, 2006).

9. The September 2006 effort by the Shia-dominated United Iraqi Alliance to pass legislation to create a single, powerful Shia region suggests that many in the current government prefer to force the pace of decentralization instead. See "Lawmakers Debate Breaking Iraq Up into Rival Regions," Agence France-Presse, 6 September 2006.

10. Toby Dodge, *Iraq's Future: The Aftermath of Regime Change* (London: Routledge, 2005), 8.

11. Robert Olson, "Possibilities for Peacebuilding Principles and Cooperative Political and Economic Relations Among Turkey, Iraq, Kurdistan-Iraq, the Wider Middle East, and Iran," presentation given at the conference Iraq: Preventing Another Generation of Conflict, held in Ottawa, May 11–12, 2006.

12. John Kornblum, "Help Wanted in Iraq," *Washington Post*, 27 June 2006.

13. One element not much discussed at the conference but that clearly has a bearing on suspicions of US intentions within Iraq and that may be fueling anticoalition sentiment is the opaque nature of Washington's planning for continuing military bases in Iraq after the coalition's formal withdrawal. A US base in Kurdish Iraq might prove a stabilizing factor, but elsewhere in the country the idea of a continuing US presence could provoke allergic reactions.

14. Daniel L. Byman and Kenneth M. Pollack, *Things Fall Apart: Containing the Spillover from an Iraqi Civil War*, Analysis Paper 11, Saban Center for Middle East Policy at the Brookings Institution, January 2007.

15. See David M. Malone, *The International Struggle over Iraq: Politics in the UN Security Council 1980–2005* (Oxford: Oxford Univ. Press, 2006), 232–233.

16. James A. Baker III, and Lee H. Hamilton, Co-Chairs, with Lawrence S. Eagleburger, Vernon E. Jordan Jr., Edwin Meese III, Sandra Day O'Connor, Leon E. Panetta, William J. Perry, Charles S. Robb, and Alan K. Simpson, *The Iraq Study Group Report* (New York: Vintage, 2006). A similar yet further-reaching proposal was put forward by the International Crisis Group (ICG), which suggested a "New Iraqi National Compact" in late December 2006. See ICG, "After Baker-Hamilton: What to Do in Iraq," *Middle East Report* 60 (December 19, 2006), www.crisisgroup.org.

17. See Marc Tran, "Top US Inquiry to Call for Iraq Policy Change," *Guardian,* October 16, 2006; and David E. Sanger, "G.O.P.'s Baker Hints Iraq Plan Needs Change," *New York Times,* October 9, 2006.

18. Iraq has also proved damaging to the reputation of the United Nations. The October 27, 2005, report of the Independent Inquiry Committee into the United Nations oil-for-food program, which can be found at www.iic-offp.org/documents.htm, exposed a degree of mismanagement and even corruption in the UN administration of this controversial program in the late 1990s and early 2000s.

19. See Malone, *International Struggle over Iraq,* 285.

20. In Security Council Resolution 1483 of May 22, 2004.

21. See, for example, Security Council Resolution 1546 of June 8, 2004.

Bibliography

ABC News. *ABC News Poll: Iraq—Where Things Stand* (2005). abcnews.com/poll-vault.html.

Abdul-Jabar, Falah, ed. *Ayatollahs, Sufis, and Ideologues*. London: Saqi Books, 2002.

Abedin, Mahan. "Dossier: Hezb al-Daawa al-Islamiyya: Islamic Call Party." *Middle East Intelligence Bulletin* 5, no. 6 (June 2003). www.meib.org/articles/0306_iraqd.html.

———. "Dossier: The Supreme Council for the Islamic Revolution in Iraq (SCIRI)." *Middle East Intelligence Bulletin* 5, no. 10 (October 2003). www.meib.org/articles/0310_iraqd.htm.

Alterman, Jon B. "Not in My Backyard: Iraq's Neighbors' Interests." *Washington Quarterly* 26, no. 3 (summer 2003): 149–160.

Amnesty International. *Iraq: Amnesty International's Concerns with Regard to "Operation Swarmer."* AI Index: MDE 14/011/2006 (Public) News Service No. 067, March 17, 2006.

Anderson, Liam, and Gareth Stansfield. *The Future of Iraq: Dictatorship, Democracy, or Division*. Updated ed. New York: Palgrave Macmillan, 2005.

al-'Asqalani, Mahmoud A. *Al-Da'wa al-Salafiyya* [The Salafist Call]. Alexandria: Dar al-Iman, 2004.

Ayubi, Nazih. *Over-Stating the Arab State: Politics and Society in the Middle East*. London: I. B. Tauris, 1995.

Baker, James A., III, and Lee H. Hamilton, Co-Chairs, with Lawrence S. Eagleburger, Vernon E. Jordan Jr., Edwin Meese III, Sandra Day O'Connor, Leon E. Panetta, William J. Perry, Charles S. Robb, and Alan K. Simpson. *The Iraq Study Group Report*. New York: Vintage, 2006.

Baram, Amatzia. "Who Are the Insurgents? Sunni Rebels in Iraq." *USIP Special Report* 134 (April 2005).

———. "Two Roads to Revolutionary Shi'ite Fundamentalism in Iraq." In *Accounting for Fundamentalisms: The Dynamic Character of Movements*. Vol. 4 of the Fundamentalism Project, edited by Martin E. Marty and R. Scott Appleby. Chicago: Univ. of Chicago Press, 2004.

Batatu, Hanna. "Shi'ite Organizations in Iraq: Al-Da'wah al-Islamiyah and al-Mujahidin." In *Shi'ism and Social Protest*, edited by Juan Cole and Nikki R. Keddie. New Haven: Yale Univ. Press, 1986.

———. *The Old Social Classes and the Revolutionary Movements of Iraq: A Study of Iraq's Old Landed and Commercial Classes and of its Communists, Baathists, and Free Officers.* Princeton, NJ: Princeton Univ. Press, 1978.

Bensahel, Nora. "Mission Not Accomplished: What Went Wrong with Iraqi Reconstruction." *Journal of Strategic Studies* 29, no. 3 (2006).

Biddle, Stephen. "Seeing Baghdad, Thinking Saigon." *Foreign Affairs* 85, no. 2 (March/April 2006).

Brancati, Dawn. "Is Federalism a Panacea for Post-Saddam Iraq?" *Washington Quarterly* 25, no. 2 (2004).

Bremer, L. Paul, III, with Malcolm McConnell. *My Year in Iraq: The Struggle to Build a Future of Hope.* New York: Simon & Schuster, 2006.

Brown, Nathan. "The Final Draft of the Iraqi Constitution: Analysis and Commentary." *Carnegie Endowment for International Peace* (September 16, 2005). www.carnegieendowment.org/files/FinalDraftSept16.pdf.

Brubaker, Rogers. *Ethnicity Without Groups.* Cambridge, MA: Harvard Univ. Press, 2006.

———. *Nationalism Reframed.* Cambridge, MA: Cambridge Univ. Press, 1995.

———. "Aftermaths of Empire and the Unmixing of Peoples." *Ethnicity and Racial Studies* 18, no. 2 (April 1995).

Brynen, Rex. *A Very Political Economy: Peacebuilding and Foreign Aid in the West Bank and Gaza.* Washington, DC: US Institute for Peace Press, 2000.

Buci-Glucksmann, Christine. *Gramsci and the State.* London: Lawrence and Wishart, 1980.

Burnham, Gilbert, Riyadh Lafta, Shannon Doocy, and Les Roberts, "Mortality After the 2003 Invasion of Iraq: A Cross-sectional Cluster Sample Survey." *Lancet On-line,* October 11, 2006. DOI: 10.1016/S0140-6736(06)69491-9. www.thelancet.com.

Bush, George W. Address to the American Enterprise Institute. February 26, 2003. www.whitehouse.gov/news/releases/2003/02/20030226-11.html.

———. "Strategy for Victory in Iraq." Speech given at the US Naval Academy, Annapolis, MD, November 30, 2005. www.whitehouse.gov/news/releases/2005/11/20051130-2.html.

Byman, Daniel L. "Building the New Iraq: The Role of Intervening Forces." *Survival* 45, no. 2 (summer 2003).

Byman, Daniel L., and Kenneth M. Pollack. *Things Fall Apart: Containing the Spillover from an Iraqi Civil War,* Saban Center Analysis No. 11, January 2007. Saban Center for Middle East Policy at the Brookings Institution.

Caverzasio Sylvie Giossi, ed. *Strengthening Protection in War: A Search for Professional Standards.* Geneva: International Committee of the Red Cross, 2001.

Chesterman, Simon. *You, the People: The United Nations, Transitional Administration, and State-Building.* Oxford: Oxford Univ. Press, 2005.

Christoff, Joseph A. *Rebuilding Iraq: Stabilization, Reconstruction, and Financing Challenges.* GAO-06-428T. Washington, DC: General Accounting Office (GAO), February 8, 2006. www.gao.gov/new.items/d06428t.pdf.

Cockayne, James, with Cyrus Samii. *The Iraq Crisis and World Order: Structural and Normative Changes.* International Peace Academy (IPA) Conference Report, Bangkok, Thailand, August 16–18, 2004.

Cole, Juan. "Civil War? What Civil War? Desperate to Convince Voters We're Winning, Bush Is Denying That Iraq Is Having a Civil War. But the Facts Contradict Him." *Salon,* March 23, 2006. www.salon.com/opinion/feature/2006/03/23/civil_war/print.html.

————. "The United States and Shi'ite Religious Factions in Post-Ba'thist Iraq." *Middle East Journal* 57, no. 4, (autumn 2003): 543–566.

————. "The Iraqi Shiites: On the History of America's Would-Be Allies." *Boston Review* (fall 2003). bostonreview.net/BR28.5/colr/html.

————. *Sacred Space and Holy War: The Politics, Culture, and History of Shi'ite Islam.* London: I. B. Tauris, 2002.

Cordesman, Anthony. "Iraq's Evolving Insurgency and the Risk of Civil War." Washington, DC: Center for Strategic and International Studies, April 26, 2006 (revised working draft). www.reliefweb.int/library/documents/2006/csis-irq-26apr.pdf.

Cortright, David. "Are Sanctions Just? The Problematic Case of Iraq." *Journal of International Affairs* 52, no. 2 (spring 1999). www.fourthfreedom.org/Applications/cms.php?page_id=35.

Cousens, Elizabeth, and David Harland. "Post-Dayton Bosnia and Herzegovina." In *Twenty-First Century Peace Operations,* edited by William Durch. Washington, DC: US Institute for Peace Press, forthcoming.

CPA. "Reform of Salaries and Employment Conditions of State Employees." Coalition Provisional Authority Order No. 30, September 2003. www.cpa-iraq.org/regulations.

Davis, Mike. *Late Victorian Holocausts: El Niño Famines and the Making of the Third World.* London: Verso, 2000.

Dawde, Soran. "Kirkuk Council Split on Roles." *Iraqi Crisis Report* 121 (April 18, 2005). iwpr.net/?p=icrf&o=244854&apc_state=heniicr2005.

Dawisha, Adeed, and Karen Dawisha. "How to Build a Democratic Iraq." *Foreign Affairs* 82, no. 3 (2003).

Dawisha, Adeed, and Larry Diamond. "Iraq's Year of Voting Dangerously." *Journal of Democracy* 17, no. 2 (2006).

Day, Graham, and Christopher Freeman. "Policekeeping Is the Key: Rebuilding the Internal Security Architecture of Postwar Iraq." *International Affairs* 79, no. 2 (2003).

Diamond, Larry. *Squandered Victory: The American Occupation and the Bungled Effort to Bring Democracy to Iraq.* New York: Times Books, 2005.

Dobbins, J. J. G., K. McGinn, S. G. Crane, R. Lal Jones, A. Rathmell, R. Swanger, and A. Timilsina. *America's Role in Nation-Building from Germany to Iraq.* Santa Monica, CA: RAND, 2003.

Dobbins, James, et al. *The RAND History of Nation-Building.* 2 vols. Santa Monica, CA: RAND, 2005.

Dodge, Toby. "Negotiating with the Iraqi Insurgency: Dilemmas and Doubts." *IISS Strategic Comments* 12, no. 1 (February 2006). www.iiss.org/stratcom.

————. *Iraq's Future: The Aftermath of Regime Change.* London: Routledge, 2005.

————. *Inventing Iraq: The Failure of Nation Building and a History Denied.* New York: Columbia Univ. Press, 2003.

Doran, Michael Scott. "Palestine, Iraq, and American Strategy." *Foreign Affairs* 81, no. 1 (January/February 2002).

Economist Intelligence Unit. "Iraq Country Report." March 2006. Available at portal.eiu.com/index.asp?layout=displayIssue&publication_id=1220000922 (accessed June 9, 2006).

Eisenstadt, Michael, and Jeffery White. "Assessing Iraq's Sunni Arab Insurgency." *PolicyFocus* (Washington Institute for Near East Policy) 50 (December 2005).

Etherington, Mark. *Revolt on the Tigris: The Al-Sadr Uprising and the Governing of Iraq.* Ithaca, NY: Cornell Univ. Press, 2005.

Etzioni, Amitai. "A Self-Restrained Approach to Nation-Building by Foreign Powers." *International Affairs* 80, no. 1 (2004): 1–17.

Evans, Gareth, and Mohamed Sahnoun. "The Responsibility to Protect." *Foreign Affairs* 81, no. 6 (November 2002).

Fawcett, John, and Victor Tanner. *The Internally Displaced People of Iraq.* Washington, DC: Brookings Institution, October 2002.

Foreign Policy and the Fund for Peace. "The Failed States Index." *Foreign Policy* (May/June 2006).

Galbraith, Peter W. *The End of Iraq: How American Incompetence Created a War Without End.* New York: Simon & Schuster, 2006.

Gerges, Fawaz. *The Far Enemy: Why Jihad Went Global.* Cambridge, MA: Cambridge Univ. Press, 2005.

Ghai, Yash, and Jill Cottrell. "A Review of the Constitution of Iraq." www.law.wisc.edu/ils/glsi/arotcoi.pdf.

Giossi Caverzasio, Sylvie, ed. *Strengthening Protection in War: A Search for Professional Standards.* Geneva: International Committee of the Red Cross, 2001.

Gordon, Michael R., and Bernard E. Trainor. *Cobra II: The Inside Story of the Invasion and Occupation of Iraq.* New York: Pantheon, 2006.

Harland, David. "Legitimacy and Effectiveness in International Administration." *Global Governance* 10, no. 1 (January/March 2004).

Hashim, Ahmed S. *Insurgency and Counter-Insurgency in Iraq.* London: Hurst, 2006.

———. "The Sunni Insurgency." *Middle East Institute Perspective* (August 15, 2003). www.mideasi.org/articles/doc89.html.

Heckman, J. "The Common Structure of Statistical Models of Truncation, Sample Selection, and Limited Dependent Variables and a Simple Estimator for Such Models." *Annals of Economic and Social Measurement* 5 (1976): 475–492.

Henderson, Errol A., and J. David Singer. "Civil War in the Post-Colonial World, 1946–1992." *Journal of Peace Research* 37, no. 3 (May 2000).

Henderson, Simon. *Instant Empire: Saddam Hussein's Ambition for Iraq.* San Francisco, CA: Mercury House, 1991.

Henriot, Christian, and Wen-hsin Yeh, eds. *Shadow of the Rising Sun: Shanghai Under Japanese Occupation.* Cambridge, MA: Cambridge Univ. Press, 2004.

al-Hirmizi, Arshad. *The Turkmen Reality in Iraq.* Istanbul: Kirkuk Foundation, 2005.

Holt, Victoria. "The Responsibility to Protect: Considering the Operational Capacity for Civilian Protection." Washington, DC: Henry L. Stimson Center Working Paper, January 2005.

Hopkins, A. G. "The 'Victory' Strategy: Grand Bargain or Grand Illusion?" *Current History* 105, no. 687 (January 2006).

Horowitz, Donald. *A Democratic South Africa: Constitutional Engineering in a Divided Society.* Berkeley, CA: Univ. of California Press, 1991.

Human Rights Watch. *Iraq: Forcible Expulsion of Ethnic Minorities.* New York: Human Rights Watch, March 2003. www.hrw.org.

———. *Iraq's Crime of Genocide: The Anfal Campaign Against the Kurds.* New Haven: Yale Univ. Press, 1995. Original report available at www.hrw.org/reports/1993/iraqanfal.

———. "US Minimizes Civilian Casualties in Iraq." Press release. New York: Human Rights Watch, March 17, 2006. hrw.org/english/docs/2006/03/16/iraq13022.htm.

Hume, Cameron R. *The United Nations, Iran and Iraq: How Peacemaking Changed.* Bloomington: Indiana Univ. Press, 1994.

International Crisis Group. "After Baker-Hamilton: What to Do in Iraq." *Middle East Report* 60 (December 19, 2006).

———. *Governing Iraq.* Baghdad, Washington, DC, Brussels: International Crisis Group, 2003.

———. *In Their Own Words: Reading the Iraqi Insurgency.* Baghdad, Washington, DC, Brussels: International Crisis Group, 2006.

———. "Iraq: Allaying Turkey's Fears over Kurdish Ambitions." *Middle East Report* 35 (January 26, 2005).

———. "Iraq's Kurds: Toward an Historic Compromise?" *Middle East Report* 26 (April 8, 2004).

———. *Iraq's Shiites Under Occupation.* Baghdad, Brussels: International Crisis Group, 2003.

———. *Shi'ism: Varied Social Settings, Rival Center of Power and Conflicting Visions.* Baghdad, Washington, DC, Brussels: International Crisis Group, 2003.

———. "The Next Iraqi War? Sectarianism and Civil Conflict." *Middle East Report* 52 (February 27, 2006).

———. *Unmaking Iraq: A Constitutional Process Gone Awry.* Baghdad, Washington, DC, Brussels: International Crisis Group, 2005.

———. "War in Iraq: What's Next for the Kurds?" *Middle East Report* 10 (March 19, 2003).

Jabar, Faleh A. *Formative Forces in the Development of the Modern Iraqi State.* Washington, DC: United States Institute of Peace, April 15, 2004. www.usip.org/fellows/reports/2004/0415_jabar.html.

———. "Post-conflict Iraq: A Race for Stability, Reconstruction and Legitimacy." *USIP Special Report* 120 (May 2004).

———. "Sheikhs and Ideologues: Deconstruction and Reconstruction of Tribes Under Patrimonial Totalitarianism in Iraq, 1968–1998." In *Tribes and Power: Nationalism and Ethnicity in the Middle East,* edited by Faleh A. Jabar and Hosham Dawod. London: Saqi, 2003.

———. *The Shi'ite Movement in Iraq.* London: Saqi, 2003.

Jones, Bruce. "Conclusion: Aid, Peace, and Justice in a Re-Ordered World." In *Nation-Building Unraveled? Aid, Peace, and Justice in Afghanistan.* London: Kumarian Press, 2004.

Jones, Seth G., Jeremy Wilson, Andrew Rathmell, and K. Jack Riley. *Establishing Law and Order After Conflict.* Arlington, VA: RAND, 2005. www.rand.org/pubs/monographs/2005/RAND_MG374.pdf.

Kaplan, Robert. "The Coming Normalcy." *Atlantic Monthly,* April 2006.

Karadaghi, Kamran. "Minimizing Ethnic Tensions in a Post-Saddam Iraq." In *How to Build a New Iraq After Saddam,* edited by Patrick Clawson. Washington, DC: Washington Institute for Near East Policy, 2002.

Karsh, Efraim, and Inari Rautsi. *Saddam Hussein: A Political Biography.* London: Futura, 1991.

Kasfir, Nelson. "Domestic Anarchy, Security Dilemmas, and Violent Predation." In *When States Fail: Causes and Consequences,* edited by Robert I. Rotberg. Princeton, NJ: Princeton Univ. Press, 2004.

———. "Explaining Ethnic Political Participation." In *The State and Development in the Third World,* edited by Atol Kholi. Princeton, NJ: Princeton Univ. Press, 1986.

Kaviraj, Sudipta. "On the Construction of Colonial Power: Structure, Discourse,

Hegemony." In *Contesting Colonial Hegemony: State and Society in Africa and India*, edited by Dagmar Engles and Shula Marks. London: British Academic Press, 1994.

Kedward, H. R. *Occupied France: Collaboration and Resistance: 1940-1944.* Oxford: Blackwell, 1985.

Khadduri, Majid. *Republican Iraq: A Study in Iraqi Politics Since the Revolution of 1958.* London: Oxford Univ. Press, 1969.

al-Khafaji, Isam. "State Terror and the Degradation of Politics in Iraq." *Middle East Report* (May–June 1992): 15–21.

al-Khalil, Samir (Kanan Makiya). *Republic of Fear: The Inside Story of Saddam's Iraq.* New York: Pantheon, 1989.

———. *Republic of Fear: The Politics of Modern Iraq.* London: Hutchinson Radius, 1989.

Khomeini, Ruhollah. *Islamic Government.* New York: Manor Books, 1979.

Khosrokhavar, Farhad. *Suicide Bombers: Allah's New Martyrs.* London: Pluto Press, 2005.

al-Khursan, Saleh. *Hizb al-Da'wa al-Islamiyya: Haqa'iq wa watha'iq* [The Islamic Da'wa Party: Facts and Documents]. Damascus: Al-Mu'assassa al-'Arabiyya li'l -Dirasat wa'l-Buhuth al-Istratijiyya, 1999.

Kratoska, P. H. *The Japanese Occupation of Malaya: A Socio-Economic History.* Honolulu: Univ. of Hawaii Press, 1997.

al-Kubaysi, Muhammad Ayyash. *Min Fiqh al-Muqawama.* Amman: al-Sabil, 2006.

Laitin, David D. *The Russian-Speaking Populations in the Near Abroad.* Ithaca, NY: Cornell Univ. Press, 1998.

Legrain, Jean-Francois. "Palestinian Islamism: Patriotism as a Condition of Their Expansion." In *Accounting for Fundamentalisms: The Dynamic Character of Movements.* Vol. 4 of the Fundamentalism Project, edited by Martin E. Marty and R. Scott Appleby. Chicago: Univ. of Chicago Press, 2004.

Lijphart, Arend. "Self-Determination Versus Pre-Determination of Ethnic Minorities in Power-Sharing Systems." In *The Rights of Minority Cultures*, edited by Will Kymlicka. Oxford: Oxford Univ. Press, 1995.

Litvak, Meir. *Shi'ite Scholars of Nineteenth Century Iraq.* Cambridge, MA: Cambridge Univ. Press, 1998.

Long, Jerry. *Saddam's War of Words: Politics, Religion, and the Iraqi Invasion of Kuwait.* Austin: Univ. of Texas Press, 2004.

Luizard, Pierre-Jean. *La formation de l'Irak contemporain* [The Formation of Contemporary Iraq]. Paris: Editions du Centre National de la Recherche Scientifique, 1991.

Makiya, Kanaan (aka Samir al-Khalil). *Republic of Fear: The Inside Story of Saddam's Iraq.* New York: Pantheon Books, 1989.

Malone, David M. *The International Struggle over Iraq: Politics in the UN Security Council 1980–2005.* New York: Oxford Univ. Press, 2006.

Mann, Michael. "The Autonomous Power of the State: Its Origins, Mechanisms and Results." In *States, War, and Capitalism: Studies in Political Sociology*, edited by Michael Mann. Oxford: Blackwell, 1988.

al-Marashi, Ibrahim. "Iraq's Security and Intelligence Network: A Guide and Analysis." *Middle East Review of International Affairs* 6, no. 3 (September 2002).

Marr, Phebe. "Comments." *Middle East Policy* 7, no. 4 (October 2000).

———. "Iraq 'the Day After.'" In *Naval War College Review* 61, no. 1 (winter 2003).

————. *The Modern History of Iraq*. 2d ed. Boulder, CO: Westview, 2004.

————. "Who Are Iraq's New Leaders? What Do They Want?" *USIP Special Report* 160 (March 2006).

Matar, Fuad. *Saddam Hussein: The Man, the Cause, and the Future*. London: Third World Centre, 1981.

Mayer, Jane. "Outsourcing Torture: The Secret History of America's 'Extraordinary Rendition' Program." *New Yorker*, February 14, 2006.

Meierhenrich, Jens. "Forming States After Failure." In *When States Fail: Causes and Consequences*, edited by Robert I. Rotberg. Princeton, NJ: Princeton Univ. Press, 2004.

Meijer, Roel. "Muslim Politics Under Occupation: The Association of Muslim Scholars and the Politics of Resistance." *Arab Studies Journal* 13, no. 2 (fall 2005) and 14, no. 1 (spring 2006).

————. "'Defending Our Honor': Authenticity and the Framing of Resistance in the Iraqi Town of Falluja." *Etnofoor* 17, nos. 1–2 (2005).

————. "The Association of Muslim Scholars in Iraq." *Middle East Report* 237 (winter 2005).

Migdal, Joel S. *Strong Societies and Weak States: State-Society Relations and State Capabilities in the Third World*. Princeton, NJ: Princeton Univ. Press, 1988.

Milton-Edwards, Beverley. *Islamic Politics in Palestine*. London: I. B. Tauris, 1996.

Mohammdeou, Mahmoud A. Ould. *Report on a Roundtable on the Transformation of Warfare, International Law, and the Role of Transnational Armed Groups*. Cambridge, MA: Humanitarian Policy and Conflict Research Occasional Paper, Harvard University, April 2006. www.hpcr.org/pdfs/OccasionalPaper6.pdf.

Morrow, Jonathan. "Weak Viability: The Iraqi Federal State and the Constitutional Amendment Process." *USIP Special Report* 186 (July 2006).

————. "Iraq's Constitutional Process II: An Opportunity Lost." *USIP Special Report* 155 (November 2005).

Nakash, Yitzhak. *The Shi'is of Iraq*. Princeton, NJ: Princeton Univ. Press, 1994.

Napoleoni, Loretta. *Insurgent Iraq: Al-Zarqawi and the New Generation*. London: Constable & Robinson, 2005.

National Security Council. "National Strategy for Victory in Iraq." Washington, DC: White House, 2005. www.whitehouse.gov/infocus/iraq/iraq_strategy_nov2005. html#part1 (accessed April 2006).

North Atlantic Treaty Organization (NATO). "Revised Operational Plan for NATO's Expanding Mission in Afghanistan." www.nato.int/issues/afghanistan_stage3/index.html (accessed April 2006).

Obaid, Nawaf. "Meeting the Challenge of a Fragmented Iraq: A Saudi Perspective." Washington, DC: Center for Strategic and International Studies, April 2006. www.comw.org/warreport/fulltext/0604obaid.pdf.

Odom, Lieutenant-General (ret.) William. "Withdraw Now." *Current History* 105, no. 687 (January 2006).

O'Flynn, Ian, and David Russell. *Power-Sharing: New Challenges for Divided Societies*. London: Pluto Press, 2005.

O'Hanlon, Michael E., and Nina Kamp. *Iraq Index*. Washington, DC: Brookings Institution, April 27, 2006. www.brookings.edu/iraqindex.

O'Leary, Brendan. "Debating Consociation: Normative and Explanatory Arguments." In *From Power-Sharing to Democracy: Post-Conflict Institutions in Ethnically Divided Societies*, edited by Sid Noel. Toronto: McGill-Queen's Univ. Press, 2005.

O'Leary, Brendan, Bernard Grofman, and Jorgen Elklit. "Divisor Methods for

Sequential Portfolio Allocation in Multi-Party Executive Bodies: Evidence from Northern Ireland and Denmark." *American Journal of Political Science* 49, no. 1 (2005).

O'Leary, Brendan, John McGarry, and Khaled Salih, eds. *The Future of Kurdistan in Iraq.* Philadelphia: Univ. of Pennsylvania Press, 2005.

Olson, Robert W. "Possibilities for Peacebuilding Principles and Cooperative Political and Economic Relations Among Turkey, Iraq, Kurdistan-Iraq, the Wider Middle East, and Iran." Presentation given at the conference Iraq: Preventing Another Generation of Conflict, held in Ottawa, May 11–12, 2006.

Owen, Roger. *State, Power, and Politics in the Making of the Modern Middle East.* London: Routledge, 1992.

Packer, George. *Assassin's Gate: America in Iraq.* New York: Farrar, Straus and Giroux, 2005.

Patriotic Union of Kurdistan. *Ethnic Cleansing Documents in Kurdistan.* Kirkuk: Patriotic Union of Kurdistan, 2004.

Pedersen, Jon, and Rick Hooper, eds. *Developing Palestinian Society: Socio-Economic Trends and Their Implications for Development Strategies.* Oslo: FAFO, 1998.

Phillips, David L. *Losing Iraq: Inside the Post-War Reconstruction Fiasco.* Boulder, CO: Westview, 2005.

Piscatori, James, ed. *Islamic Fundamentalisms and the Gulf Crisis.* A Fundamentalism Project Report. Chicago: Univ. of Chicago Press, 1991.

Pollack, Kenneth M., and the Iraq Policy Working Group of the Saban Center. "Switch in Time: A New Strategy for America in Iraq." *Saban Center Analysis* (Saban Center for Middle East Policy at the Brookings Institution) no. 7 (February 15, 2006).

Posner, Daniel N. "Civil Society and the Reconstruction of Failed States." In *When States Fail: Causes and Consequences*, edited by Robert I. Rotberg. Princeton, NJ: Princeton Univ. Press, 2004.

Powell, Colin L. "Remarks to the National Foreign Policy Conference for Leaders of Nongovernmental Organizations," October 26, 2001. 66.249.93.104/search?q=cache:LXjRsgox564J:www.yale.edu/lawweb/avalon/s ept_11/powell_brief31.htm+ngo+colin+powell+force+multipliers&hl=en&ct=c lnk&cd=4&client=safari.

Prados, Alfred B. "Syria: US Relations and Bilateral Issues." *CRS Issue Brief for Congress*, Order Code IB92075 (March 13, 2006).

Rathmell, Andrew, Olga Oliker, Terrence K. Kelly, David Brannan, and Keith Crane. *Developing Iraq's Security Sector.* Santa Monica, CA: RAND, MG-365-OSD, 2005.

Rotberg, Robert I. "Failed States in a World of Terror." *Foreign Affairs* 81, no. 4 (July–August 2002).

———. "The Failure and Collapse of Nation-States: Breakdown, Prevention, and Repair." In *When States Fail: Causes and Consequences*, edited by Robert I. Rotberg. Princeton, NJ: Princeton Univ. Press, 2004.

———. "The New Nature of Nation-State Failure." *Washington Quarterly* 25, no. 3 (summer 2002).

———, ed. *State Failure and State Weakness in a Time of Terror.* Washington, DC: Brookings Institution, January 2003.

Rothchild, Donald. "Reassuring Weaker Parties After Civil Wars: The Benefits and Costs of Executive Power-Sharing Systems in Africa." *Ethnopolitics* 4, no. 3 (2005).

Rothchild, Joseph. *Ethnopoltics: A Conceptual Framework.* New York: Columbia Univ. Press, 1981.

Sabina, Alkire. "Conceptual Framework for Human Security." Working Paper prepared for the Human Security Commission, February 16, 2002. www.humansecurity-chs.org/activities/outreach/frame.pdf.

Sakai, Keiko. "Modernity and Tradition in the Islamic Movements in Iraq." *Arab Studies Quarterly* 23, no. 1 (winter 2001): 37–52.

Salamey, Imad, and Frederic Pearson. "The Crisis of Federalism and Electoral Strategies in Iraq." *International Studies Perspectives* 6, no. 2 (2005).

Slim, Hugo. "Why Protect Civilians? Innocence, Immunity and Enmity in War." *International Affairs* 79, no. 3 (2003): 481–501.

Snyder, Jack. *From Voting to Violence: Democratization and Nationalist Conflict.* New York: W. W. Norton, 2000.

Special Inspector-General for Iraqi Reconstruction. "Memorandum for Deputy Secretary of Defense: Management of Commanders' Emergency Response Program for Fiscal Year 2004." Report No. SIGIR 05-014. October 12, 2005. www.sigir.mil/reports/pdf/audits/SIGIR_Audit_05-014-Memo-CERP-2005-Letter.pdf#search='CERP%20funds%20Iraq (accessed April 2006).

Stansfield, Gareth. "Breaking Up Iraq: A Radical Plan to Save the Country." *Prospect*, May 2006.

———. "The Transition to Democracy in Iraq: Historical Legacies, Resurgent Identities, and Reactionary Tendencies." In *The Iraq War and Democratic Politics*, edited by Alex Danchev and John Macmillan. London: Routledge, 2005.

Sweets, John. *Choices in Vichy France: The French Under Nazi Occupation.* Oxford: Oxford Univ. Press, 1986.

Talabany, Nouri. *Arabization of the Kirkuk Region.* Uppsala: Kurdistan Studies Press, 2001.

Talentino, Andrea Kathryn. "The Two Faces of Nation-Building: Developing Function and Identity." *Cambridge Review of International Affairs* 17, no. 3 (October 2004).

Tripp, Charles. *A History of Iraq.* 2nd ed. London: Cambridge Univ. Press, 2002.

———. "Regional Organizations in the Arab Middle East." In *Regionalism in World Politics: Regional Organizations and International Order,* edited by Louise Fawcett and Andrew Hurrell. Oxford: Oxford Univ. Press, 1995.

United Nations Assistance Mission for Iraq (UNAMI). *Human Rights Report 1 November–31 December 2006.* Baghdad: UNAMI, December 2006.

United Nations Assistance Mission for Iraq (UNAMI) Office of the Constitutional Support Unit. "Executive Summary of the Oil and Gas Resource in Iraq Multiparty Dialogues." Unpublished report, April 4–6, 2006.

———. "Issues for Consideration by the Proposed Constitutional Review." Unpublished report, February 2006.

———. "The Making of the Iraqi Constitution and Evaluation of the Process." Unpublished report, December 2005.

———. "Critical Review and Analysis of the Iraqi Constitution." Unpublished report, December 2005.

United Nations Children's Fund (UNICEF). *The State of the World's Children 2004.* New York: UNICEF, 2004.

United Nations Development Programme (UNDP). *Human Development Report 2004.* New York: UNDP, 2004.

————. *The Millennium Development Goals in Arab Countries, Toward 2015: Achievements and Aspiration.* New York: UNDP, 2003.

————. *Human Development Report 2001.* New York: UNDP, 2001.

————. *Human Development Report 1995.* New York: UNDP, 1995.

————. *Human Development Report 1990.* New York: UNDP, 1990.

United Nations High Commissioner for Refugees (UNHCR). *UNHCR Briefing Notes: Iraqi Displacement.* www.unhcr.org/news/NEWS/454b1f8f2.html.

United States Department of Defense. "Measuring Stability and Security in Iraq." May 2006. Report to Congress. www.defenselink.mil/home/features/Iraq_Reports/Index.html.

United States Embassy in Iraq. "Fact Sheet on Provincial Reconstruction Teams (PRTs)." February 23, 2006. baghdad.usembassy.gov/iraq/20060223prtfactsheet.html.

United States National Intelligence Council (NIC). *Prospects for Iraq's Stability: A Challenging Road Ahead.* United States National Intelligence Estimate (NIE), January 2007.

van Creveld, Martin. *The Transformation of War.* New York: New Press, 1991.

Visser, Reidar. "Centralism and Unitary State Logic in Iraq from Midhat Pasha to Jawad al-Maliki: A Continuous Trend?" www.historiae.org/maliki.asp.

————. "Iraq's Partition Fantasy." *Open Democracy,* May 19, 2006. www.openDemocracy.net.

————. "The Maliki Government—What It Could Mean to Southern Iraq." May 23, 2006. www.historiae.org/Maliki-Government.

Walt, Stephen M. *The Origins of Alliances.* Ithaca and London: Cornell Univ. Press, 1987.

Watts, Ronald L. *Comparing Federal Systems.* Montreal: McGill-Queen's Univ. Press, 1999.

Weber, Max. *Economy and Society.* Vol. 1. Berkeley: Univ. of California Press, 1978.

————. "Politik als Beruf." *Gesammelte Politische Schriften.* Muenchen: Duncker and Humboldt, 1921.

Weiss, Martin A. "Iraq's Debt Relief: Procedure and Potential Implications for International Debt Relief." *CRS Report for Congress,* Order Code RL33376, April 21, 2006.

Wheeler, Victoria, and Adele Harmer. "Resetting the Rules of Engagement: Trends and Issues in Military-Humanitarian Relations." HPG Research Briefing 23, March 2006. www.odi.org.uk/hpg/papers/HPGbrief21.PDF.

White House Office of the Press Secretary. "Fact Sheet: Strategy for Victory: Clear, Hold, and Build." March 20, 2006. www.whitehouse.gov/news/releases/2006/03/20060320-6.html.

Whitfield, Teresa. *Friends Indeed: The Role of "Friends" Groups.* Washington, DC: US Institute for Peace Press, 2006.

Wiley, Joyce. *The Islamic Movement of Iraqi Shi'as.* Boulder, CO: Lynne Rienner, 1992.

Wimmer, Andreas. "Democracy and Ethno-Religious Conflict in Iraq." *Survival* 45, no. 4 (2003).

Woodward, Bob. *Plan of Attack.* New York: Simon & Schuster, 2004.

Woolsey, R. James. Address to UCLA Conference of Americans for Victory over Terrorism, April 2, 2003.

World Bank. *Rebuilding Iraq: Economic Reform and Transition.* Washington, DC: World Bank, 2006.

World Food Programme. *Baseline Food Security Analysis in Iraq.* Rome: World Food Programme, 2004.

Zaidi, Sarah, and Mary C. Smith-Fawzi. "Health of Baghdad's Children." *Lancet* 346, no. 8988 (December 2, 1995).

Zartman, I. William. "Posing the Problem of State Collapse." In *Collapsed States: The Disintegration and Restoration of Legitimate Authority,* edited by I. William Zartman. Boulder, CO: Lynne Rienner, 1995.

The Contributors

Jon B. Alterman is senior fellow and director of the Middle East Program at the Center for Strategic and International Studies (CSIS). Prior to joining the CSIS, he served as a member of the Policy Planning Staff at the US Department of State and as a special assistant to the assistant secretary of state for Near Eastern affairs. Before entering the government, he was a scholar at the United States Institute of Peace and at the Washington Institute for Near East Policy. From 1993 to 1997, Alterman was an award-winning teacher at Harvard University. He is a former international affairs fellow at the Council on Foreign Relations and also has worked as a legislative aide on foreign policy and defense issues for Senator Daniel P. Moynihan (D-NY). He is the author of *Egypt and American Foreign Assistance, 1952–1956: Hopes Dashed*; *New Media, New Politics? From Satellite Television to the Internet in the Arab World*; and the editor of *Sadat and His Legacy: Egypt and the World, 1977–1997*.

Michael Bell was appointed chair of the International Reconstruction Fund Facility for Iraq in March 2005. In his role as chair he has worked with the Iraqi government, particularly the Ministry of Planning, and acted as an interlocutor between the Iraqis, the UN, the World Bank, and donors. He has spent thirty-six years in the Canadian Department of Foreign Affairs, focusing largely on the Middle East. He has served as Canada's ambassador to Jordan (1987–1990), Egypt (1994–1998), and Israel (1990–1992 and 1999–2003). He is currently the Paul Martin (Sr.) Senior Scholar in Diplomacy at the University of Windsor, as well as codirector of the Jerusalem Old City Initiative.

Nora Bensahel is a senior political scientist at RAND Corporation, specializing in military strategy and doctrine. Her recent work has examined post-conflict reconstruction in Afghanistan and Iraq, military coalitions, and multilateral intervention. Her recent publications include *The Counterterror Coalitions: Cooperation with Europe, NATO, and the European Union* and *The Future Security Environment in the Middle East.* She has held fellowships at the Center for International Security and Cooperation at Stanford University and at the John M. Olin Institute for Strategic Studies at Harvard University. She also serves as an adjunct professor in the Security Studies Program at the Edmund A. Walsh School of Foreign Service at Georgetown University and serves on the Executive Board of Women in International Security.

Markus E. Bouillon is senior associate for Middle East and Special Programs at the International Peace Academy. He previously served as a political affairs officer and special assistant under Terje Rød-Larsen and Alvaro de Soto in the Office of the United Nations Special Coordinator for the Middle East Peace Process and as political adviser to Rød-Larsen in his capacity as the Secretary-General's special envoy for the implementation of Security Council Resolution 1559 (2004). He has also worked with the Secretary-General's special adviser on the Middle East, Michael C. Williams, and has extensive field experience throughout the region. He is author of *The Peace Business: Money and Power in the Palestine-Israel Conflict.*

David Cameron is chair and professor in the Department of Political Science at the University of Toronto and a member of the Board of the Forum of Federations. He was an adviser to the drafting committee of the Iraqi Constitution. Cameron has served as a public servant, holding the post of assistant secretary to the federal cabinet for strategic and constitutional planning; assistant undersecretary of state for education support; and deputy minister of intergovernmental affairs in the Province of Ontario. His research centers on questions of federalism, nationalism, and constitutional reform, and he has provided advice on related issues at the provincial, national, and international levels. He is the author or coauthor of numerous publications, including *Nationalism, Self-Determination and the Quebec Question*; *The Referendum Papers: Essays on Secession and National Unity*; and *Street Protests and Fantasy Parks: Globalization, Culture and Society*, with Janice Stein.

Juan Cole is professor of modern Middle East and South Asian history in the History Department at the University of Michigan. He has written extensively about modern Islamic movements in Egypt, the Persian Gulf, and South Asia, and his current research focuses on Shiite Islam in Iraq and Iran and the jihadi strain of Muslim radicalism. He is the author of *Sacred*

Space and Holy War; *Roots of North Indian Shi'ism in Iran and Iraq*; *Colonialism and Revolution in the Middle East: Social and Cultural Origins of Egypt's 'Urabi Movement*; and *Modernity of the Millennium.* He coedited *Shi'ism and Social Protest* and edited *Comparing Muslim Societies.* He has written and commented widely on contemporary political developments in the Middle East and US involvement in the region.

James Dobbins directs RAND Corporation's International Security and Defense Policy Center. He has held State Department and White House posts including assistant secretary of state for Europe, special assistant to the president for the Western Hemisphere, special adviser to the president and secretary of state for the Balkans, and ambassador to the European Community. He also handled a variety of crisis management assignments as the Clinton administration's special envoy for Somalia, Haiti, Bosnia, and Kosovo, and the Bush administration's first special envoy for Afghanistan. He is the principal author of RAND's two-volume *History of Nation Building.* In the wake of September 11, 2001, Dobbins was designated as the Bush administration's representative to the Afghan opposition. He helped organize and then represented the United States at the Bonn Conference where a new Afghan government was formed.

Toby Dodge is a reader in international politics in the Department of Politics at Queen Mary, University of London, and a consulting senior fellow for the Middle East at the International Institute for Strategic Studies. He has published *Inventing Iraq: The Failure of Nation Building and a History Denied* and *Iraq's Future: The Aftermath of Regime Change.* He is coeditor of *Iraq at the Crossroads: State and Society in the Shadow of Regime Change* and *Globalisation and the Middle East: Islam, Economics, Culture and Politics.* He has written numerous journal articles and commented widely on Iraqi history and politics, particulary as it relates to the post–Saddam Hussein reconstruction process.

Pierre Gassmann is currently an adviser to the Program on Humanitarian Policy and Conflict Research at Harvard University. He worked for twenty-four years with the International Committee of the Red Cross (ICRC), finishing his service as the head of delegation in Baghdad from July 2003 to June 2004. He has also been the head of delegation for the ICRC in Colombia, the former Yugoslavia, El Salvador, Uganda, Mozambique, and Angola. His high-level operations management assignments at the ICRC Geneva included head of operations for Eastern Europe (2000–2003) and Africa (1988–1991). He has also held the position of chair of the UN Inter-Agency Standing Committee Working Group on the Millennium (1999–2000).

Nicholas "Fink" Haysom is the chief constitutional adviser for the United Nations Assistance Mission to Iraq (UNAMI). A constitutional expert, Haysom was designated by the UN to lead its team working with Iraqis to draft a new constitution. He served as chief legal adviser throughout Nelson Mandela's presidency in South Africa and continues to work with him on his private initiatives. Since leaving the office of the president upon Mandela's retirement in 1999, Haysom has been involved in the Burundi peace talks as chairman of the committee negotiating constitutional issues. He has vast experience having worked as a consultant on constitutional reform, conflict resolution, and good governance in Lebanon, Nigeria, Burundi, Indonesia, Philippines, East Timor, Sudan, Somalia, Sri Lanka, Burma, Lesotho, Colombia, Congo, Tanzania, Zimbabwe, Kenya, and Nepal.

Joost R. Hiltermann is deputy program director of the Middle East and North Africa for the International Crisis Group. He manages a team of analysts based in Amman, Beirut, Dubai, Jerusalem, Tehran, and Damascus, conducting research in the countries of the Middle East and writing policy-focused reports on the factors that increase the risk of and drive armed conflict. His areas of expertise include Iraq and its political transition and constitutional process, as well as the Kurds, Jordan, Israel-Palestine, and thematic issues in the Middle East more broadly. He previously worked as the executive director of the Arms Division and as the director of the Iraq Documents Project of Human Rights Watch. He has also worked as both a research director and analyst with the Palestinian NGO Al-Haq in Ramallah. He is the author of *A Poisonous Affair: America, Iraq, and the Gassing of Halabja* and B*ehind the Intifada: Labor and Women's Movements in the Occupied Territories.*

Bruce D. Jones is codirector of the Center for International Cooperation (CIC) at New York University. Jones has served as deputy research director for the High-level Panel on Threats, Challenges, and Change; deputy to the special adviser to the UN Secretary-General; and supported the assistant-secretary-general for strategic planning on negotiations on security issues during the "In Larger Freedom" reform effort. He also has worked as the chief of staff to the UN's special coordinator for the Middle East Peace Process, as a member of the UN's Advance Mission in Kosovo, and on the planning team for the UN Transitional Administration in East Timor. He is the author of several monographs and articles on UN postconflict, transitional authority, and humanitarian operations. He has served as a consultant to the UK Department for International Development, the Canadian Foreign Ministry, and the United Nations.

David M. Malone currently serves as Canada's high commissioner to India and ambassador to Bhutan and Nepal. From 2004 to 2006, he oversaw multilateral and economic diplomacy within Canada's Foreign Ministry. From 1998 to 2004, he was president of the International Peace Academy, a research and policy development institution in New York. A former Canadian ambassador to the UN in New York, he has written extensively on issues related to the UN and security and has taught at Columbia University, the University of Toronto, the Norman Paterson School of International Affairs at Carleton University, New York University School of Law, and l'Institut d'Études Politiques in Paris. His most recent book is *The International Struggle over Iraq: Politics in the UN Security Council, 1980–2005.*

Phebe Marr was until recently a senior fellow at the United States Institute of Peace (USIP). A prominent historian of modern Iraq, she was research professor at the National Defense University and associate professor in the history departments at the University of Tennessee and Stanislaus State University in California. Marr was a senior scholar at the Wilson Center in 1999–2000. She has authored numerous articles and books on Iraq and the Middle East, including "Who Are Iraq's New Leaders? What Do They Want?" a USIP Special Report; "Democracy in the Rough" in *Current History*; *The Modern History of Iraq*; *Egypt at the Crossroads: Domestic Stability and Regional Rule* (editor and contributor); and *Riding the Tiger: The Middle East After the Cold War* (editor and contributor). She is a frequent contributor to media discussions about Iraq and has testified before many congressional committees on these issues in recent years.

John McGarry is professor of political studies and Canada research chair in nationalism and democracy at Queen's University in Kingston, Ontario. His areas of research interest include national and ethnic conflict regulation, the politics of Northern Ireland, and the policing of ethnically divided societies. He is a regular contributor to public media and has coauthored, coedited, and edited twelve books on ethnic conflict and the politics of Northern Ireland. His latest book, coauthored with Brendan O'Leary, is *The Northern Ireland Conflict: Consociational Engagements*. He has also written numerous articles on conflict regulation via consociationalism, secession, territorial autonomy, federalism, and state-directed population movements in a variety of edited collections and in prominent journals.

Roel Meijer is lecturer at Radboud University in Nijmegen, the Netherlands, where he teaches modern history of the Middle East, and a fellow of the International Institute for the Study of Islam in the Modern

World (ISIM) in Leiden. He is the author of a monograph on Egypt entitled *The Quest for Modernity: Secular, Liberal, and Left-wing Political Thought in Egypt, 1945–1958* and has published numerous articles and chapters on Iraq and Saudi Arabia, including "The Association of Muslim Scholars in Iraq" in *Middle East Report*; "Muslim Politics Under Occupation: The Association of Muslim Scholars and the Politics of Resistance in Iraq" in *Arabic Studies Journal*; and "The 'Cycle of Contention' and the Limits of Terrorism in Saudi Arabia" in *Saudi Arabia in the Balance: Political Economy, Society, Foreign Affairs*. He is also the editor of several volumes including *Alienation or Integration of Arab Youth—Between the Family, the State and the Street* and *Cosmopolitanism, Identity and Authenticity in the Middle East*. He is currently doing comparative research on the debate within Islamist movements in Egypt, Saudi Arabia, and Iraq on violence.

Brendan O'Leary, an Irish citizen, is Lauder Professor of Political Science at the University of Pennsylvania, where he directs the Solomon Asch Center. He was previously professor of political science and chair of the Department of Government at the London School of Economics and Political Science before moving to the United States in 2002. He specializes in national and ethnic conflict, self-determination disputes, electoral systems, theories of the democratic state, and conflict-regulation and power-sharing systems—including federations. He served as one of the international constitutional advisers to the Kurdish National Assembly and the Kurdish Regional Government during the making of the Transitional Administrative Law in 2004 and the making of the constitution of Iraq in 2005. He is the author, coauthor, or coeditor of fifteen books and numerous articles and chapters. He is the lead editor of *The Future of Kurdistan in Iraq* and coeditor of *Terror, Insurgency and the State*. O'Leary has been a constitutional adviser in Northern Ireland, Somalia, and South Africa.

Jon Pedersen is deputy managing director of the Fafo Institute for Applied International Studies in Norway, which conducts policy-related research at the international level, concentrating primarily on countries undergoing substantial structural changes and nation building. He has written numerous reports on the social effects of conflict in the West Bank and Gaza as well as the wider Palestinian diaspora. Pedersen led a major UN Development Programme–sponsored survey on living conditions in Iraq. He is visiting professor at Lanzhou University and Nankai University, People's Republic of China.

Ben Rowswell is manager of the Democracy Unit in the Department of Foreign Affairs and International Trade Canada and senior associate at the Center for Strategic and International Studies (CSIS) in Washington, DC.

Previously, he was Canada's diplomatic representative in Baghdad (2003, 2004–2005). Since joining the Department of Foreign Affairs and International Trade in 1993, he has also served at Canada's mission to the United Nations and the Canadian Embassy in Egypt. Outside the Foreign Service, he has served on the Borders Task Force for the deputy prime minister of Canada, was diplomate invité at the Université du Québec à Montréal, and senior program manager with the National Democratic Institute in Erbil and Baghdad, Iraq (2004).

Abdel Salam Sidahmed is professor in the Department of Political Science at the University of Windsor, Canada. Prior to joining the university, he was director of Amnesty International's Middle East and North Africa program in London. He has published volumes on Islamic fundamentalism (with Anoushiravan Ehteshami) and modern Sudanese history. His research interests include international human rights, diaspora studies, Islamic politics, and Islamic political thought.

Index

Al-Bait Sa'idah tribe, 118
Abdul-Rahman, Sami, 23
Al-Adalah (newspaper), 114
Afghanistan: counterterrorism air operations over, 218; international community in, 287–288; International Security Assistance Force in, 233, 257; Northern Alliance in, 110; six-plus-two forum in, 207; Taliban in, 207; United States goals in, 207, 208
Aflaq, Michel, 7
African Union: regional security consultations by, 209
Allawi, Ali, 297
Allawi, Ayad, 24, 31, 42, 92, 93, 99, 101, 102, 118, 128, 175
Alterman, Jon, 213–225, 306
al-Amiri, Hadi, 54n9, 117
Anfal campaign, 125, 136n2
Annan, Kofi, 5, 282
Arab countries: effect of bilateral relations with United States on assistance from, 16, 215; fear motivating relations with United States, 213; lack of enthusiasm for democratic governance in Iraq, 215; negative feelings over occupation of Iraq by foreigners, 4; opposition to Kurdish takeover of Kirkuk, 132, 215; population discontent over cooperation with United States, 213; public distancing from United States by, 215; resistance to "normalization" in

Kurdish territory, 128; sectarian rivalries among, 213; tensions between, 213
Arabization, 125, 127–129, 136, 140n45
Arab League, 19n57, 211, 224, 285, 291–292, 306, 312
Aref, Abdul Salem, 7
Army of the Mujahidin, 102
Al-'Ashur, 118
Ashura, 23
al-Askariya Mosque, destruction of, 23, 117, 148
Assassinations, 118, 119, 120, 139n28, 223
Association of Muslim Scholars (AMS), 249; accusations against Badr Organization, 116; anti-US stance, 90, 92, 95; ascendancy of, 91–93; assassinations of members, 97; attempts to split Shia into rival factions, 95; boycott of political process, 90, 95–97; ethnic inclusion in, 91; founding, 91; hegemony of, 95–97; ideology of resistance, 93–95; as Islamo-nationalist movement, 92; political program of, 92, 93; rejection of cooperation by, 92; *sharia* role in governance and, 50; support for armed struggle, 90; use of media for propaganda purposes, 91–92
Association of Southeast Asian Nations (ASEAN): regional security consultations by, 209

About the Book

AN ENDURING EPICENTER of conflict and instability in the Middle East, Iraq has not only experienced domestic upheavals, but also generated threats to international peace and security for more than 25 years. Is an end to the violence, and the establishment of an enduring peace within a unified state, a realistic goal? How can it be achieved, and what may stand in its way?

Addressing these questions—and arguing that a downward spiral of violence and possible state collapse can be avoided—the authors of *Iraq: Preventing a New Generation of Conflict* consider the sources of conflict in the country and outline the requirements for a successful peacebuilding enterprise.

Markus E. Bouillon is head of the International Peace Academy's (IPA) Middle East Program. Previously political adviser on the Middle East peace process at the UN, he is author of *The Peace Business: Money and Power in the Palestine-Israel Conflict.* **David M. Malone** returned to the Canadian Foreign Service after serving for six years as president of the IPA and is now Canada's high commissioner to India and nonresident ambassador to Nepal and Bhutan. His recent publications include *The UN Security Council: From the Cold War to the 21st Century* and *The International Struggle over Iraq.* **Ben Rowswell**, Canada's diplomatic representative in Iraq in 2003–2005, continues to serve in the Canadian Foreign Service and is also senior associate at the Center for Strategic and International Studies in Washington, DC.